Social Indicators Research Series

Volume 64

This series provides a public forum for authored and edited volumes on social indicators research. It is a companion series to the journal Social Indicators Research. The book series deals with problems associated with the quality of life from a broad perspective. It welcomes research on a wide range of substantive areas, including health, crime, housing, education, family life, leisure activities, transportation, mobility, economics, work, religion and environmental issues. The topics represented in this series cover and involve a variety of segmentations, such as social groups, spatial and temporal coordinates, population composition, and life domains. The series presents empirical, philosophical and methodological studies that cover the entire spectrum of society and are devoted to giving evidence through indicators. It considers indicators in their different typologies, and gives special attention to indicators that are able to meet the need of understanding social realities and phenomena that are increasingly more complex, interrelated, interacted and dynamic. In addition, it presents studies aimed at defining new approaches in constructing indicators. An international review board for this series ensures the high quality of the series as a whole.

Available at 25% discount for International Society for Quality-of-Life Studies (ISQOLS).

Dong-Jin Lee • M. Joseph Sirgy

Happiness in the Marketplace

A Study of Consumption, Consumers and Wellbeing

Springer

Dong-Jin Lee
School of Business
Yonsei University
Seoul, Korea (Republic of)

M. Joseph Sirgy
Dept. of Marketing
Virginia Tech
Dublin, VA, USA

ISSN 1387-6570 ISSN 2215-0099 (electronic)
Social Indicators Research Series
ISBN 978-3-032-04442-6 ISBN 978-3-032-04443-3 (eBook)
https://doi.org/10.1007/978-3-032-04443-3

This Springer imprint is published by the registered company Springer Nature Switzerland AG
The registered company address is: Gewerbestrasse 11, 6330 Cham, Switzerland

This book is dedicated to:

- *Academics and scholars who have committed to doing research and writing on this very important topic of quality of life and disseminating the knowledge created to their students*
- *Business and marketing executives who care about the well-being of their customers*
- *Management consultants who are in the business of helping their clients develop and implement effective customer loyalty and well-being programs*
- *Public policy officials who have devoted their professional careers to protect consumers and enhance their well-being*

Preface

This book provides a systematic review of research literature related to the effectiveness of organizational policies and programs on human wellbeing in the marketplace. The book describes policies, programs, and practices related to wellbeing in several contexts, namely shopping, ownership, and marketplace experiences.

This volume provides guidance for business and marketing executives who care about the wellbeing of their customers. The book is also designed to help public policy officials dealing with consumer issues develop more effective policies that can benefit consumers across many industries and globally. Management consultants who are in the business of helping their clients develop and implement effective customer loyalty and wellbeing programs should benefit significantly from reading this book. Finally, some academics and scholars have committed to researching and writing on this important topic of quality of life and disseminating this knowledge to their students; this book could be used as reference material.

Seoul, Republic of Korea — Dong-Jin Lee
Dublin, VA, USA — M. Joseph Sirgy

Contents

About the Authors

Dong-Jin Lee is Professor Emeritus at the School of Business, Yonsei University, Seoul, Korea. He received his Ph.D. in marketing from Virginia Tech and has published extensively in quality-of-life studies. Before joining Yonsei University (2003–present), he was on the faculty of the University of Western Australia (1996–1999) and the State University of New York at Binghamton (2000–2002). He served as Vice President for Academic Affairs and Vice President for Publication for the International Society for Quality-of-Life Studies (ISQOLS) in 1997–1999 and 2002–2008, respectively; he was Director of Academic Affairs for the Academy of Marketing Science in 2002–2004; he was Section Editor of *Applied Research in Quality of Life* (ARQOL) from 2009 to 2011; he was Associate Dean at Yonsei University from 2007 to 2010 and Dean of Sangnam Management Institute at Yonsei University from 2017 to 2019. He won the W. Bradford Wiley Memorial Research Award in 2001 and the Best Paper Award from *Applied Research in Quality of Life* in 2021 and in 2025. He is currently a member of the Board of Directors of the Management Institute for Quality-of-Life Studies.

M. Joseph Sirgy is a management psychologist (Ph.D., U/Massachusetts, 1979) and the Virginia Tech Real Estate Professor Emeritus of Marketing at Virginia Polytechnic Institute and State University (USA) and Extraordinary Professor at the Work-Well Research Unit at North-West University, Potchefstroom Campus (South Africa). He has published extensively in marketing, management, business ethics, and quality of life (QOL). He co-founded the International Society for Quality-of-Life Studies (ISQOLS) in 1995 and served as its Executive Director/Treasurer from 1995 to 2011 and as Development Co-Director (2011–present). In 1998, he received the Distinguished Fellow Award from ISQOLS. In 2003, ISQOLS honored him as the Distinguished QOL Researcher for research excellence and a record of lifetime achievement in QOL research. He also served as President of the Academy of Marketing Science (2002–2004) from which he received the Distinguished Fellow Award in the early 1990s and the Harold Berkman Service Award in 2007 (lifetime achievement award for serving the marketing professoriate). In the early 2000s, he helped co-found the Macromarketing Society and the

Community Indicators Consortium and served as a board member of these two professional associations. He co-founded the journal, *Applied Research in Quality of Life*, the official journal of the International Society for Quality-of-Life Studies, in 2005, and he has served as co-founding editor (1995–present). He has also served as editor of the QOL section in the *Journal of Macromarketing* (1995–2016). He received the Virginia Tech's Pamplin Teaching Excellence Award/Holtzman Outstanding Educator Award and University Certificate of Teaching Excellence in 2008. In 2010, ISQOLS honored him for excellence and lifetime service to the society. In 2010, he won the Best Paper Award in the *Journal of Happiness Studies* for his theory of the balanced life; in 2011, he won the Best Paper Award in the *Journal of Travel Research* for his goal theory of leisure travel satisfaction. In 2012, he was awarded the EuroMed Management Research Award for outstanding achievements and groundbreaking contributions to wellbeing and quality-of-life research. In 2019, the Macromarketing Society honored him with the Robert W. Nason Award for extraordinary and sustained contributions to the field of macromarketing. He was recognized by the Program in Real Estate at Virginia Tech with the 2021 Blackwood Award for Exemplary Faculty Service and with the Founding Faculty Award. In 2022, he won the Best Paper Award in *Applied Research in Quality of Life* for his (and colleagues') theory on shopping well-being. In 2025, he was recognized by the American Phygital Association with the Lifetime Achievement and Academic Impact Award. He was the editor of ISQOLS/Springer book series including *International Handbooks in QOL* (2008–2015), *Community QOL Indicators: Best Cases* (2004–2015), and *Applied Research in QOL: Best Practices* (2008–2012). He is currently serving as co-editor in chief of the *Journal of Macromarketing* (2020–present). Also, he is currently the co-editor of Springer book series *Human Well-Being and Policy Making* (2015–present). To know more about Joe Sirgy, please visit his personal website at https://sites.google.com/a/vt.edu/joe-sirgy-personal-website/.

Part I
Introduction

In Part I of the book, we try to accomplish the following:

- Introduce the reader to a theoretical framework that would serve to unify and integrate many of the concepts and research related to consumer wellbeing.
- Describe common and well-established views of wellbeing and happiness.
- Briefly review the research on the antecedents and consequences of wellbeing and happiness.
- Zero in on the concept and research dealing with material wellbeing, a concept highly integral to consumer wellbeing.

Chapter 1
Theoretical Framework

We see our customers as invited guests to a party, and we are the hosts. It's our job every day to make every important aspect of the customer experience a little bit better.

—Jeff Bezos (https://www.forbes.com/sites/blakemorgan/2019/04/03/101-of-the-best-customer-experience-quotes/#:~:text=%E2%80%9CAlways%20remember%20that%20everyone%20with%20whom%20you%20have,friends%20do%20business%20with%20you.%E2%80%9D%20%E2%80%93%20Chip%20Bell)

Theoretical Framework

As Fig. 1.1 shows, the theoretical framework of this book shows that feelings related to engagement in consumption activities (engagement in consumption activities) influence feelings about consumption at large (consumption happiness), which in turn influence feelings in the consumer life domain (consumer happiness). Feelings in the consumer life domain (i.e., consumer happiness), in turn, play a significant role in influencing subjective wellbeing (positive and negative affect, and life satisfaction).

The theory of *bottom-up spillover of subjective wellbeing* (e.g., Brief et al., 1993; Diener, 1984) makes the case that positive and negative emotions spill over from concrete events (i.e., life events) to domain satisfaction (e.g., satisfaction with consumer life), which in turn plays a role in influencing feelings related to overall life—life satisfaction and positive and negative affect (e.g., Rahtz et al., 2004). Thus, the happiness hierarchy as shown in Fig. 1.1. is based on the notion that individual's satisfaction with life domains (e.g., satisfaction with consumer life or consumption happiness) mediates the relationship between satisfaction with specific consumption activities and satisfaction with consumer life (or what we're calling consumer happiness) (e.g., Zhong & Mitchell, 2010). Similarly. an individual's satisfaction with consumer life mediates the relationship between satisfaction with consumption happiness and overall happiness (e.g., Brief et al., 1993).

D.-J. Lee, M. J. Sirgy, *Happiness in the Marketplace*, Social Indicators Research Series 64, https://doi.org/10.1007/978-3-032-04443-3_1

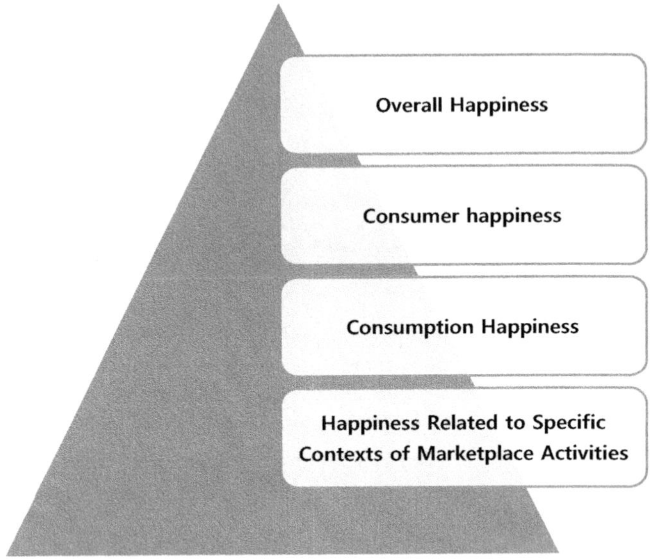

Fig. 1.1 Happiness related to specific contexts of marketplace activities

Overall happiness is a combination of frequent experience of positive emotions (e.g., elation, pleasure, sense of mastery and accomplishment) along with a cognitive evaluation of one's life (e.g., satisfaction judgment with life overall) (e.g., Diener et al., 1985; Lyubomirsky et al., 2005). Thus, experiencing short-term consumption happiness can potentially contribute to consumers' subjective wellbeing (Diener et al., 1999; Fredrickson, 2001; Lyubomirsky, 2001). We will elaborate on the major dimensions of the hierarchy of happiness (as shown in Fig. 1.1) in the sections below.

Overall Happiness (or Subjective Wellbeing)

Subjective wellbeing (or overall happiness) is an overall sense that life is good involving many positive situations and emotions (e.g., Ahuvia, 2008; Lyubomirsky, 2008; Lyubomirsky et al., 2005; Myers, 1992). Specifically, Professor Ed Diener and his colleagues) defined subjective wellbeing in terms of three major dimensions: (1) life satisfaction, (2) a preponderance of positive over negative emotions, and (3) absence of depression (Diener, 1984; Diener et al., 1999). Life satisfaction reflects people's evaluations of their lives; it involves both cognitive judgments of satisfaction with life overall, capturing affective appraisals of moods and emotions at large (Kesebir & Diener, 2008; Veenhoven, 1991). Life satisfaction is a sense that one's life is good, meaningful, and worthwhile. Preponderance of positive over negative emotions involves the experience of more positive emotions (e.g., joy, contentment, elation, and harmony) relative to negative emotions (e.g., anger, fear, hate, disgust, jealousy, envy, and anxiety). Absence of depression is self-explanatory. Much research has demonstrated that subjective wellbeing is measurable, predictable, and comparable across contexts (see literature reviews of Diener, 1984; Diener et al., 1999; Layard, 2005; Lyubomirsky, 2001).

More recently, the concept of "overall happiness" has been treated as involving two major dimensions: hedonic happiness and eudaimonic happiness (e.g., Diener et al., 1985; Lyubomirsky & Lepper, 1999; Ryff, 1989; Waterman et al., 2008; Seligman, 2011; Sheldon & Hilpert, 2012). *Hedonic happiness* can be viewed as subjective wellbeing in the traditional sense. It involves the three dimensions as described above: life satisfaction, a preponderance of positive over negative emotions, and absence of depression. In contrast, *eudaimonic happiness* is much more encompassing of positive traits and emotions such as positive emotions, avowed satisfaction with life, contributing to society, social integration, social growth and potential, acceptance of others, social interest and coherence, self-acceptance, environmental control or mastery, positive relations with others, personal growth, autonomy, and having a purpose in life (Keyes, 2002).

As such, throughout the book, we will be using the term "happiness" in the broad sense, capturing both hedonic and eudaimonic aspects of wellbeing. Also, it should be noted that the terms "subjective wellbeing" and "happiness" are used interchangeably in the literature (e.g., Costa & McCrae, 1980; Dolan et al., 2008; Hsee et al., 2009; Veenhoven, 2003).

Consumer Happiness

Consumer happiness focuses on happiness in the individual's life domain relegated to marketplace experiences (i.e., consumer life domain). Consumer happiness (or consumer wellbeing) involves two major dimensions, one that ties into hedonic wellbeing, the other to eudaimonic wellbeing: Let's describe these two dimensions in some detail.

Concerning the hedonic dimension, consumer happiness reflects global perceptions of satisfaction in the consumer life domain (e.g., Sirgy, 2021; Lee et al., 2002; Bosnjak et al., 2016). This is a relatively stable state of wellbeing in a life domain, which we coin as "consumer life" (e.g., general feeling about one's experiences in the marketplace). Specifically, it is an enduring judgment that captures overall satisfaction with marketplace experiences.

Consumer happiness can be viewed as the sum of momentary consumption experiences over a period. Yet, consumer happiness is more than a simple summation of consumption happiness because consumer happiness is also influenced by overall happiness. This influence is referred to in the subjective wellbeing literature as "top-down theory of subjective wellbeing" (e.g., Diener et al., 2000; Oishi & Diener,

2001). That is, in evaluating their marketplace experiences (i.e., consumer life), the consumer may be influenced by their current feelings of overall happiness (cf. Schwarz & Strack, 1999).

Consumer happiness is customarily measured in terms of global feelings of satisfaction with marketplace experiences (e.g., Lee et al., 2002; Sirgy, 2021), satisfaction with consumption needs (e.g., El Hedhli et al., 2013), satisfaction with standard of living (e.g., Nakano et al., 1995), satisfaction with cost of living (e.g., Samli, 2003), and consumer sentiment towards marketing activities (e.g., Gaski & Etzel, 2005), among others.

Concerning the eudaimonic dimension, research has demonstrated that consumer wellbeing is high when consumers experience eudaimonic happiness as well as hedonic happiness (Bosnjak et al., 2016). Some consumption experiences do not only produce pleasure (i.e., hedonic wellbeing) but also contribute to feelings related to contributing to society, social integration, social growth and potential, acceptance of others, social interest and coherence, self-acceptance, environmental control or mastery, positive relations with others, personal growth, autonomy, and/or having a purpose in life.

Consumption Happiness

Consumption happiness refers to an overall satisfaction rating and positive/negative emotional reflection of their consumption activities (Desmeules, 2002). Specifically, this construct is defined as a state of happiness in consumer life related to a specific consumption activity (Mogilner et al., 2012; van Boven & Gilovich, 2003). As such, consumption happiness is different from consumer happiness in that consumption happiness is momentary happiness resulting from consumption activities related to a particular good or service. Frequent consumption experiences with that good or service spillover to consumer happiness, which is the stable and enduring happiness construct associated with the consumer life domain.

Consumption happiness is treated as a positive emotion experienced by the consumer in relation to a particular good or service, a positive emotion such as joy or elation (e.g., Richins, 1997; Laros & Steenkamp, 2005). Consumption happiness has been measured by asking how happy one feels or how happy a product or a situation makes one feel (e.g., Nicolao et al., 2009; Thomas & Millar, 2013; Van Boven & Gilovich, 2003). For example, consumption happiness related to a brand is a judgment made by consumers regarding the extent to which the focal brand makes a significant contribution to his or her quality of life (Merunka & Sirgy, 2011).

The Hierarchy of Happiness

The theoretical framework shown in Fig. 1.1 makes the case that consumption behaviors influence consumption happiness which in turn influences consumer happiness.

The bottom-up spillover perspective argues that overall happiness is psychologically constructed from domain satisfaction; that is, overall happiness is derived from a sense of whether different life domains are satisfactory (Kahneman, 1999), with each domain weighted by its importance to life goals (Oishi & Diener, 2001). As such, we also argue that consumption happiness has an influence on consumer happiness, which in turn influences overall happiness. Consumption happiness is momentary happiness, and it is influenced more by marketplace activities and events related to the purchase experience of a specific consumer good or service, experience related to the preparation of the product for consumption, experiences related to the actual consumption of the product, experiences related to the maintenance and repair of the product, and experiences related to the disposal of the product (e.g., Van Boven & Gilovich, 2003; Thomas & Millar, 2013). In contrast, consumer happiness is cumulative, long-term happiness in the consumer life domain.

Consumer happiness is significantly influenced by a host of cumulative short-term consumption happiness—positive experiences related to shopping, material possession, and other marketplace experiences over time. Consumption happiness from a particular purchase is momentary, and cumulative positive experiences tend to prompt consumers to evaluate their consumer life more favorably. For example, research has shown that adding a material component to an experience serves to foster long-term consumer happiness (Sääksjärvi et al., 2016).

There is another way to view these concepts. Specifically, our hierarchy of happiness framework posits that consumer happiness is influenced by shopping happiness, happiness related to material possessions, and experiential happiness in the marketplace. These three sets of experiences will be discussed in Part IV of the book. And, of course, the argument is that consumer happiness, along with satisfaction in other life domains, spills over to overall life.

Table 1.1 captures the main concepts discussed so far. The table highlights the scope of evaluation, dimensions, and characteristics of overall happiness, consumer happiness, and consumption happiness. Focusing on overall happiness, the scope of evaluation is overall life. That is, the individual evaluates his or her own life overall. The dimensions of overall happiness involve hedonic and eudaimonic wellbeing. The outcome can be described as comparable and enduring. That is, the evaluations made by the individuals can be compared across time and with other individuals.

Focusing on consumer happiness, the scope of the evaluations is restricted to consumer life (i.e., a life domain capturing affective experiences in the marketplace). The consumer makes evaluations related to two dimensions: hedonic and eudaimonic consumer happiness. These evaluations can be characterized as

Table 1.1 Overall happiness, consumer happiness, and consumption happiness

	Overall happiness	Consumer happiness	Consumption happiness
Scope of evaluation	Overall life	Consumer life domain	Specific consumption experience
Dimensions	Hedonic wellbeing Eudaimonic wellbeing	Hedonic consumer happiness Eudaimonic consumer happiness	Shopping (acquisition) happiness Ownership (possession) Happiness Experiential (consumption) happiness
Characteristics	Comparable and enduring	Cumulative and enduring	Transient and momentary happiness

cumulative and enduring. That is, the evaluations tend to be global, capturing cumulative marketplace experiences, and they are enduring in the sense that they are stable over time.

Finally, concerning consumption happiness, the scope of evaluations tends to be much restricted to specific consumption experiences (e.g., consumption experiences related to specific contexts). We will discuss consumption happiness, consumer happiness, and overall happiness in three major contexts, namely shopping (i.e., affective experiences related to shopping in retail stores or acquisition experiences), material possessions (i.e., affective experiences related to the possession of a consumer good), and marketplace experiences (i.e., affective experiences related to consumption of a service).

Goals of this Book

Consumers seek to buy goods and services not only for what they are but also for the emotional experiences they have. Today's consumers seek marketplace experiences that can be emotionally rewarding in four ways: (1) emotionally rewarding in the immediate marketplace situation, (2) in the way this marketplace activity contributes to consumption satisfaction concerning a brand, (3) in the way that the consumption satisfaction with that brand contributes significantly to satisfaction with consumer life overall, and (4) in the way that satisfaction with consumer life contributes significantly to overall happiness.

As such, the goal of this book is to present a comprehensive review of the research on these linkages, namely links between engagement in specific forms of consumption activities and consumption happiness, links between consumption happiness and consumer happiness, and links between consumer happiness and overall happiness. In this book, we will also examine questions related to whom, why, and under what conditions can marketers and policy makers enhance happiness in the marketplace.

References

Ahuvia, A. C. (2008). Wealth, consumption and happiness. In A. Lewis (Ed.), *The Cambridge handbook of psychology and economic behavior* (pp. 199–226). Cambridge University Press.

Bosnjak, M., Brown, C. A., Lee, D. J., Yu, G. B., & Sirgy, M. J. (2016). Self-expressiveness in sport tourism: Determinants and consequences. *Journal of Travel Research, 55*(1), 125–134.

Brief, A. P., Butcher, A. H., George, J. M., & Link, K. E. (1993). Integrating bottom-up and top-down theories of subjective well-being: The case of health. *Journal of Personality and Social Psychology, 64*(4), 646–653.

Costa, P. T., & McCrae, R. R. (1980). Influence of extraversion and neuroticism on subjective well-being: Happy and unhappy people. *Journal of Personality and Social Psychology, 38*(4), 668–678.

Desmeules, R. (2002). The impact of variety on consumer happiness: Marketing and the tyranny of freedom. *Academy of Marketing Science Review, 12*(1), 1–18.

Diener, E. (1984). Subjective well-being. *Psychological Bulletin, 95*(3), 542–575.

Diener, E. D., Emmons, R. A., Larsen, R. J., & Griffin, S. (1985). The satisfaction with life scale. *Journal of Personality Assessment, 49*(1), 71–75.

Diener, E., Suh, E. M., Lucas, R. E., & Smith, H. L. (1999). Subjective well-being: Three decades of progress. *Psychological Bulletin, 125*(2), 276–302.

Diener, E., Napa-Scollon, C. K., Oishi, S., Dzokoto, V., & Suh, E. M. (2000). Positivity and the construction of life satisfaction judgments: Global happiness is not the sum of its parts. *Journal of Happiness Studies, 1*(2), 159–176.

Dolan, P., Peasgood, T., & White, M. (2008). Do we really know what makes us happy? A review of the economic literature on the factors associated with subjective well-being. *Journal of Economic Psychology, 29*(1), 94–122.

El Hedhli, K., Chebat, J. C., & Sirgy, M. J. (2013). Shopping well-being at the mall: Construct, antecedents, and consequences. *Journal of Business Research, 66*(7), 856–863.

Fredrickson, B. L. (2001). The role of positive emotions in positive psychology: The broaden-and-build theory of positive emotions. *American Psychologist, 56*(3), 218–226.

Gaski, J. F., & Etzel, M. J. (2005). National aggregate consumer sentiment toward marketing: A thirty-year retrospective and analysis. *Journal of Consumer Research, 31*(4), 859–867.

Hsee, C. K., Yang, Y., Li, N., & Shen, L. (2009). Wealth, warmth, and well-being: Whether happiness is relative or absolute depends on whether it is about money, acquisition, or consumption. *Journal of Marketing Research, 46*(3), 396–409.

Kahneman, D. (1999). Objective happiness. In D. Kahneman, E. Diener, & N. Schwarz (Eds.), *Well-being: The foundations of hedonic psychology* (pp. 3–25). Russell Sage.

Kesebir, P., & Diener, E. (2008). In pursuit of happiness: Empirical answers to philosophical questions. *Perspectives on Psychological Science, 3*(2), 117–125.

Keyes, C. L. M. (2002). The mental health continuum: From languishing to flourishing in life. *Journal of Health and Social Behavior, 43*(2), 207–222.

Laros, F. J., & Steenkamp, J. B. E. (2005). Emotions in consumer behavior: A hierarchical approach. *Journal of Business Research, 58*(10), 1437–1445.

Layard, R. (2005). *Happiness: Lessons from a new science*. Penguin.

Lee, D. J., Sirgy, M. J., Larsen, V., & Wright, N. D. (2002). Developing a subjective measure of consumer well-being. *Journal of Macromarketing, 22*(2), 158–169.

Lyubomirsky, S. (2001). Why are some people happier than others? The role of cognitive and motivational processes in well-being. *American Psychologist, 56*(3), 239–249.

Lyubomirsky, S. (2008). *The how of happiness: A scientific approach to getting the life you want*. The Penguin Press.

Lyubomirsky, S., & Lepper, H. S. (1999). A measure of subjective happiness: Preliminary reliability and construct validation. *Social Indicators Research, 46*(2), 137–155.

Lyubomirsky, S., King, L., & Diener, E. (2005). The benefits of frequent positive affect: Does happiness lead to success? *Psychological Bulletin, 131*(6), 803–855.

Merunka, D. R., & Sirgy, M. J. (2011). Distinguishing consumer satisfaction from consumer well-being in brand post-purchase behavior: A positive psychology perspective. In *Proceedings for the Inaugural Conference on Positive Marketing, Center for Positive Marketing* (pp. 21–22).

Mogilner, C., Aaker, J., & Kamvar, S. D. (2012). How happiness affects choice. *Journal of Consumer Research, 39*(2), 429–443.

Myers, D. G. (1992). *The Pursuit of happiness: Who is happy and why*. William Morrow and Company.

Nakano, N., MacDonald, M., & Douthitt, R. (1995). Toward consumer well-being: Consumer socialization effects of work experience. In M. J. Sirgy & A. C. Samli (Eds.), *New dimensions of marketing/quality-of life research* (pp. 151–175). Quorum Books.

Nicolao, L., Irwin, J. R., & Goodman, J. K. (2009). Happiness for sale: Do experiential purchases make consumers happier than material purchases? *Journal of Consumer Research, 36*(2), 188–198.

Oishi, S., & Diener, E. (2001). Re-examining the general positivity model of subjective well-being: The discrepancy between specific and global domain satisfaction. *Journal of Personality, 69*(4), 641–666.

Rahtz, D. R., Sirgy, M. J., & Lee, D. J. (2004). Further validation and extension of the quality-of-life/community-healthcare model and measures. *Social Indicators Research, 69*(2), 167–198.

Richins, M. L. (1997). Measuring emotions in the consumption experience. *Journal of Consumer Research, 24*(2), 127–146.

Ryff, C. D. (1989). Happiness is everything, or is it? Explorations on the meaning of psychological well-being. *Journal of Personality and Social Psychology, 57*(6), 1069–1081.

Sääksjärvi, M., Hellén, K., & Desmet, P. (2016). The effects of the experience recommendation on short-and long-term happiness. *Marketing Letters, 27*(4), 675–686.

Samli, A. C. (2003). The consumer price index and consumer well-being: Developing a fair measure. *Journal of Macromarketing, 23*(2), 105–111.

Schwarz, N., & Strack, F. (1999). Reports of subjective well-being: Judgmental processes and their methodological implications. In D. Kahneman, E. Diener, & N. Schwarz (Eds.), *Well-being: The foundations of hedonic psychology* (pp. 61–84). Russell Sage.

Seligman, M. E. (2011). *Flourish*. Free Press.

Sheldon, K. M., & Hilpert, J. C. (2012). The balanced measure of psychological needs (BMPN) scale: An alternative domain general measure of need satisfaction. *Motivation and Emotion, 36*(4), 439–451.

Sirgy, M. J. (2021). Macromarketing metrics of consumer well-being: An update. *Journal of Macromarketing, 41*(1), 124–131.

Thomas, R., & Millar, M. (2013). The effects of material and experiential discretionary purchases on consumer happiness: Moderators and mediators. *The Journal of Psychology, 147*(4), 345–356.

Van Boven, L., & Gilovich, T. (2003). To do or to have? That is the question. *Journal of Personality and Social Psychology, 85*(6), 1193–1202.

Veenhoven, R. (1991). Is happiness relative? *Social Indicators Research, 24*(1), 1–34.

Veenhoven, R. (2003). Hedonism and happiness. *Journal of Happiness Studies, 4*(4), 437–457.

Waterman, A. S., Schwartz, S. J., & Conti, R. (2008). The implications of two conceptions of happiness (hedonic enjoyment and eudaimonia) for the understanding of intrinsic motivation. *Journal of Happiness Studies, 9*(1), 41–79.

Zhong, J. Y., & Mitchell, V. W. (2010). A mechanism model of the effect of hedonic product consumption on well-being. *Journal of Consumer Psychology, 20*(2), 152–162.

Chapter 2
Views of Happiness

Beauty is everywhere. You only have to look to see it.

—Bob Ross (https://www.goodhousekeeping.com/life/g22521771/happy-quotes/?utm_source=google&utm_medium=cpc&utm_campaign=mgu_ga_ghk_md_dsa_prog_org_us_g22521771&gad_source=1&gclid=EAIaIQobChMI_p_kkpGJiAMV8U9HAR3EySucEAAYAiAAEgLyJfD_BwE)

Three Philosophical Views of Happiness

In general terms, happiness means an overall sense that life is good reflecting many positive situations, traits, and emotions (e.g., Ahuvia, 2008; Lyubomirsky et al., 2005; Myers, 1992; Veenhoven, 1991). In technical terms, happiness is formally treated as the experience of joy, contentment, or positive wellbeing, combined with a sense that one's life is good, meaningful, and worthwhile (Lyubomirsky, 2008). Read this definition closely. It is loaded with meaning. To appreciate this definition of happiness, we must first refer to how philosophers regard this concept.

There are three different philosophical views on happiness: hedonic, prudential, and perfectionist happiness (Haybron, 2000). This classification is in line with Seligman's (2002) theory of *authentic happiness* (*pleasant life*, *engaged life*, and *meaningful life*). According to the authentic theory of happiness, there are three different routes to happiness, and all routes contribute positively to happiness: *happiness as pleasure*, *happiness as engagement*, and *happiness as meaning*. The three routes to happiness include *hedonic happiness* (life of pleasure devoted to hedonic happiness), *engagement happiness* (life satisfaction and experiences of flow), and *meaningful happiness* (meaning aimed at a connection to something broader than the self) (Sirgy, 2002, Chap. 1).

Some scholars treat happiness as an overarching evaluation of life events and life overall. Specifically, happiness encompasses both cognitive judgments of life satisfaction and affective appraisals of moods and emotions (e.g., Kesebir, 2018).

D.-J. Lee, M. J. Sirgy, *Happiness in the Marketplace*, Social Indicators Research Series 64, https://doi.org/10.1007/978-3-032-04443-3_2

Research demonstrates that happiness is measurable, predictable, and comparable across contexts (Diener, 1984; Diener et al., 1999; Layard, 2005).

Based on this classification of happiness, three types of wellbeing measures have been developed (Peterson et al., 2005; OECD, 2013). These measures are: (1) those related to *emotional wellbeing* that capture an individual's feelings or psychological state during a certain point or period in time, (2) those related to life evaluation in which an individual evaluates his or her fulfilment and engagement in life, and (3) those related to the concept of eudaimonia which captures an individual's goal orientation and life purpose.

Psychological Happiness (Life of Pleasure)

Psychological happiness is a state of mind involving feelings of joy, serenity, and affection. It is an affective evaluation of life—focus is on the experience of positive emotions over time or hedonic wellbeing (Haybron, 2000).

Psychological (or hedonic) happiness can be conceptualized in terms of positive and negative affect. It is a state akin to emotional wellbeing. Using this approach, one can measure the two types of affect, positive and negative, and then sum up the scores to derive an index of subjective wellbeing (in conjunction with judgment of life satisfaction) (Simsek, 2009). Additionally, hedonic happiness can be conceptualized as hedonic sensations of momentary pleasures and pains. As such, one can sum up the scores of separate momentary pleasures and pains (Parducci, 1995).

This conception of hedonic happiness is akin to Seligman's (2002) concept of "the pleasant life." The pleasant life focuses on basic pleasures, such as body needs, and the motivation to gain more positive feelings and thrills. The key motive is to minimize pain and maximize pleasure regularly. Here are examples of measurement items capturing hedonic wellbeing (pleasant life). Survey respondents are asked to agree or disagree with the following statements: "Life is too short to postpone the pleasures it can provide," "I go out of my way to feel euphoric," and "In choosing what I do, I always take into account whether it will be pleasurable" (Peterson et al., 2005). In contrast, Kahneman (1999) uses the *Experience Sampling Method* (ESM) to measure momentary perceptions of positive and negative affect and assess hedonic happiness. This method involves being contacted periodically, prompting the subject to report how they feel at the moment along a set of positive and negative emotions.

Prudential Happiness (Life of Engagement)

Prudential happiness refers to the cognitive evaluation of one's life engagement. Thus, happiness is achieved when the individual achieves desire fulfilment through engagement (Seligman, 2002). In other words, prudential happiness comes from experiencing a high level of engagement in worthwhile and satisfying activities and is consistent with the engaged life (Seligman, 2002). Prudential happiness can also be construed as cognitive judgments of fulfilment of one's needs, goals, and desires (Diener et al., 1985).

Moreover, prudential happiness may be viewed as flow and engagement in events and activities. In this conceptualization, an excellent life is to engage in activities that help us grow and fulfill our potential (Csikszentmihalyi, 1975, 1990, 1997). The engaged life is more connected to our desires and the extent to which these desires are fulfilled using our strengths and experiences of *flow* (Csikszentmihalyi, 1990). Flow refers to the extent to which we become absorbed in activities involving special skills. Additionally, research has shown that life satisfaction is significantly enhanced when people engage in activities that are most congruent with their deeply held values and personal identity (Waterman, 1993).

Example items capturing life of engagement as a major source of happiness include "Regardless of what I am doing, time passes very quickly," "I seek out situations that challenge my skills and abilities," and "I am always absorbed in what I do." (Peterson et al., 2005).

Perfectionist Happiness (Life of Meaning)

Perfectionist happiness refers to a life that is good in all respects, including a moral life. It is about achieving virtue and is constituted from experiences that relate to a sense of connectedness to a greater whole—a meaningful life (Seligman, 2002). The concept reflects purpose and meaning in life. Individuals considered high on perfectionist happiness are aware of what aspects of life are most vital to themselves and others (i.e., personal and social values) and conduct their lives consistently with those values (Diener et al., 2010; Schulenberg & Melton, 2010).

Transcending the self and connecting to something larger than the self (e.g., society, nature, God or Gods, etc.) acts as a powerful source of meaning and purpose. Meaningful behaviors include volunteering time, spending money with a person in need, working hard toward achieving their goals, and preserving valued goals even in the face of obstacles (Steger et al., 2008). Example of survey items capturing eudaimonia happiness (the meaningful life) include: "My life serves a higher purpose," "In choosing what I do, I always consider whether it will benefit other people," and "I have a responsibility to make the world a better place" (Peterson et al., 2005).

In summary, happiness can be different, and our actions toward a happier life depend highly on what one desires to achieve. We have discussed three different approaches to happiness: psychological happiness (positive emotions, pleasure, the pleasant life; hedonic wellbeing), prudential happiness (flow, achievement, the engaged life; life satisfaction, cognitive wellbeing), and perfectionist happiness (purpose, fulfillment, meaningful life, eudaimonic wellbeing) (see Table 2.1).

Table 2.1 Three philosophical views on general happiness

	Psychological happiness	Prudential happiness	Perfectionist happiness
Definition	Affective evaluation of life and focus on the experience of positive emotions over time	Cognitive evaluation of life is achieved when individuals achieve desire fulfilment through engagement	Achieving virtue comes from experiencing a sense of connectedness to a greater whole and is consistent with a meaningful life
Key dimensions	Positive and negative affect	Flow, achievement, and fulfillment through engagement	Purpose and meaning in life
Life orientation	Life of pleasure	Life of engagement	Life of meaning

These various conceptualizations of happiness are interrelated. Research has uncovered that perfectionist happiness (eudaimonic wellbeing) influences psychological happiness (hedonic wellbeing), which in turn influences prudential happiness (cognitive wellbeing) (Sanjuan, 2011). In essence, happiness can be viewed as the experience of joy and contentment, combined with a sense of satisfaction with life and beliefs that one's life is meaningful and worthwhile (Lyubomirsky, 2008).

Two Conceptions of Wellbeing (Hedonic Versus Eudaimonic Wellbeing)

Historically, wellbeing (happiness) research has reflected two major perspectives: (1) the hedonic perspective, emphasizing positive affect and satisfaction with life, and (2) the eudaimonic perspective, emphasizing positive psychological functioning and human flourishing. Thus, wellbeing is best conceived as consisting of hedonic (i.e., subjective wellbeing) and eudaimonic (i.e., psychological wellbeing) dimensions (e.g., Compton et al., 1996; King & Napa, 1998; McGregor & Little, 1998; Ryan & Deci, 2001). In other words, hedonic wellbeing and eudaimonic wellbeing together constitute overall wellbeing (e.g., Dodge et al., 2012; Huta & Ryan, 2010).

Let us be a little more formal in defining these concepts and show the reader how wellbeing researchers measure them. *Hedonic wellbeing* (or subjective wellbeing) refers to the state of pleasantness characterized by positive emotions, lack of negative emotions, and satisfaction with life (Huta & Waterman, 2014). As such, a happy person from the hedonic perspective is someone who feels generally satisfied with life, experiences a preponderance of positive emotions over negative emotions. A happy person not only has a large repertoire of positive feelings (and harbors low amounts of negative feelings) but also is satisfied with life overall (Diener, 2009). In sum, the hedonic view of wellbeing is based on the notion that the goal of life is to experience as much pleasure as possible and the avoidance of pain (e.g., Carlisle et al., 2009; Smith & Diekmann, 2017).

In contrast, *eudaimonic wellbeing* refers to the state of "being good." This translates into high levels of self-actualization, self-expressiveness, and meaning in life (Huta & Waterman, 2014; Waterman et al., 2008). The eudaimonic view is connected to the ancient Greek philosopher Aristotle. This view emphasizes positive psychological functioning that goes beyond positive emotions and evaluations (Jayawickreme et al., 2012; Ryff, 1989). As such, a happy person from the eudaimonic perspective is a person who has a sense of competency, balances autonomy with high-quality relationships, experiences opportunities for personal growth, accepts oneself, and enjoys a sense of being engaged in meaningful goals (Ryff, 1989). Much research has shown that eudaimonic wellbeing is positively associated with realization of human potential through meaningful activities (e.g., Cloninger, 2004; Smith & Diekmann, 2017; Waterman, 1993), good functioning (e.g., Keyes & Annas, 2009) and living a life with intrinsically worthwhile goals (e.g., Deci & Ryan, 2008; Ryan & Deci, 2001; Ryan et al., 2008).

In the next two sections, we'll try to be more specific in defining these two concepts of wellbeing and help the reader better appreciate these concepts by showing how wellbeing researchers go about measuring them.

Hedonic Wellbeing

To reiterate, hedonic wellbeing is characterized by pleasure and achieved through maximizing pleasure and satisfaction of desires (Waterman, 1993). Examples of consumer behaviors that may induce hedonic wellbeing include going to a big party, drinking alcohol, shopping for non-essentials, and watching a movie that is pure entertainment (Huta, 2016). Through these hedonic behaviors, consumers experience a range of positive affective states that include positive affect, satisfaction of wants and needs, carefreeness and light-heartedness, and comfort, low negative affect, low strain, and relief (Huta, 2016).

Hedonic wellbeing is closely aligned with the commonly known concept known as "subjective wellbeing." Subjective wellbeing is defined as the presence of positive feelings, the absence of negative feelings, and overall satisfaction with life (Diener et al., 1999). Subjective wellbeing consists of an affective component (preponderance of positive affect over negative affect) and a cognitive component (high levels of life satisfaction).

Here are some important correlates of hedonic wellbeing that may help the reader better appreciate the concept:

- The affective component of hedonic wellbeing involves positive emotions experienced in reaction to specific events.
- Positive affect fluctuates with recent events (Eid & Diener, 2004) and tends to be induced by satisfaction of social needs (Tay & Diener, 2011).

- Positive affect and negative affect are not on opposite ends of the same continuum, but rather, operate relatively independently of one another (Bradburn, 1969; Carver, 2001; Tellegen et al., 1999).
- The affective component of hedonic wellbeing is influenced by specific events and activities (Luhmann et al., 2012). That is, the affective component reflects a shorter time frame and involves self-reported emotions during an interval or activity episode (Diener, 2009).

In contrast, the cognitive component of hedonic wellbeing is commonly characterized as follows:

- Evaluation of life as a whole and evaluations of life domains (Kim-Prieto et al., 2005).
- A cognitive evaluation that is long-term—stable over time (Diener, 2009).
- Strongly correlated with fulfilment of basic needs and factors affecting living conditions (e.g., income, unemployment). (Howell & Howell, 2008; Tay & Diener, 2011).
- It is better predicted by frequency of happiness rather than intensity of happiness (Diener et al., 1991; Kesebir, 2018).

The Affective Component of Hedonic Wellbeing

The affective component of hedonic wellbeing is supported by several theories of wellbeing. Popular examples include theories of affect balance (Watson et al., 1988; Västfjäll et al., 2002; Simsek, 2009) and the theory of objective happiness (Kahneman, 1999).

Theories of affect balance focus on the difference between positive and negative affect experiences (Watson et al., 1988; Västfjäll et al., 2002; Simsek, 2009). That is, a person who is happy experiences more positive than negative affect. Measures of affective balance include The Positive and Negative Affect Scale (Watson et al., 1988), The Swedish Core Affect Scale (Västfjäll et al., 2002), The Scale of Positive and Negative Experience (Diener et al., 2010), and the Measure of Hedonic Sensations of Momentary Pleasure. Details of these measures are as follows.

The Positive and Negative Affect Scale (PANAS) captures experiences of positive and negative affect (Watson et al., 1988). The PANAS scale is comprised of 20 items, with 10 items measuring positive affect (e.g., attentive, interested, alert, excited, enthusiastic, inspired, proud, determined, strong, active) and 10 items measuring negative affect (e.g., irritable, ashamed, nervous, jittery, afraid, upset, distressed, guilty, hostile).

Each item is rated on a five-point intensity rating scale, ranging from 1 = *very slightly or not at all* to 5 = *extremely* (capturing the extent to which the affect has been experienced in a specified time frame). An individual's PA score was computed by adding up the ratings across the ten PA items. Similarly, an individual's NA score was computed by adding up the responses across the ten NA items. For example, the mean score for PANAS PA at the moment was 29.7 with standard deviation of 7.9 while the mean score for the PANAS NA score was 14.8 with standard deviation of 5.4 (Watson et al., 1988). The measure is designed to capture affect in various time frames: at the present moment, the past day, week, or year, or in general (on average). When used with short-term instructions (e.g., at the moment or today), they are sensitive to fluctuations in mood, whereas they exhibit trait-like stability when longer-term instructions are used (e.g., past year or general). The Positive and Negative Affect Scale was found to be a reliable and valid means for measuring these two important dimensions of mood (Watson et al., 1988). See the measure in Table 2.2.

Table 2.2 The PANAS scale

This scale consists of several words that describe different feelings and emotions. Read each item and then mark the appropriate answer in the space next to that word. Indicate to what extent [INSERT APPROPRIATE TIME INSTRUCTIONS HERE]
Use the following scale to record your answers:
1 = very slightly or not at all; 2 = a little; 3 = moderately; 4 = quite a bit; 5 = extremely
The Positive Affect (PA) Scale • attentive • interested • alert • excited • enthusiastic • inspired • proud • determined • strong • active
The Negative Affect (NA) Scale • scared • afraid • upset • distressed • jittery • nervous • ashamed • guilty • irritable • hostile Possible time instructions: • Moment (you feel this way right now, that is, at the present moment) • Today (you have felt this way today) • Past few days (you have felt this way during the past few days) • Week (you have felt this way during the past week) • Past few weeks (you have felt this way during the past few weeks) • Year (you have felt this way during the past year) • General (you generally feel this way, that is, how you feel on the average)

Source: Adapted from Watson et al. (1988)

The Swedish Core Affect Scale captures both valence and activation of affect (Västfjäll et al., 2002). There are six self-report rating scales characterizing the two orthogonal dimensions of core affect, namely valence and activation. See Table 2.3.

The Scale of Positive and Negative Experience (SPANE) Affect Balance captures differences between frequency of positive affect and negative affect (Diener et al., 2010). Difference between positive and negative affect is then computed to generate an Affect Balance score. Specifically, SPANE produces a frequency score for positive feelings (1 = rarely, 5 = always) for six positive feelings items (positive, good, pleasant, happy, joyful, and contented, 1 = rarely, 5 = always), a frequency score for negative feelings items (negative, bad, unpleasant, sad, afraid, and angry, 1 = rarely, 5 = always), and the two can be combined to create a balance score (difference between the scores of positive feelings and negative feelings scores). See the measure in Table 2.4.

The *theory of objective happiness* focuses on capturing real time individual's experiences (Kahneman, 1999). The experiential sampling method (Kahneman, 1999) captures real time hedonic experiences. In this method, subjects are contacted at set time intervals during the day and are asked to report their positive and negative feelings they have experienced now. See Table 2.5.

Table 2.3 The Swedish core affect scale

Participants are asked to indicate the degree to which the adjectives described how they felt at the particular moment. A scale is printed with endpoints and a middle point defined by the numbers 10 (not at all), 50 (average), and 90 (extremely much) written in boxes from left to right
Valence:
• Displeased-Pleased • Sad-Glad • Depressed-Happy
Activation
• Sleepy-Awake • Dull-Peppy • Passive-Active
Pleasant activation-unpleasant deactivation (PAUD)
• Bored-interested • Indifferent-engaged • Pessimistic-optimistic
Unpleasant activation–pleasant deactivation (UAPD)
• Tense-serene • Anxious-calm • Nervous-relaxed

Source: Adapted from Västfjäll et al. (2002)

Table 2.4 The SPANE scale

Please think about what you have been doing and experiencing during the past 4 weeks. Then report how much you experienced each of the following feelings, using the scale below. For each item, select a number from 1 to 5, and indicate that number on your response sheet (1 = very rarely or never, 2 = rarely, 3 = sometimes, 4 = often, 5 = very often or always)
• Positive • Negative • Good • Bad • Pleasant • Unpleasant • Happy • Sad • Afraid • Joyful • Angry • Contented
Scoring: The measure can be used to derive an overall affect balance score but can also be divided into positive and negative feeling scales Positive feelings (SPANE-P): Add the scores varying from 1 to 5, for the six items: Positive, good, pleasant, happy, joyful, and contented. The score can vary from 6 (lowest possible) to 30 (highest possible)
Negative feelings (SPANE-N): Add the scores varying from 1 to 5, for the six items: Negative, bad, unpleasant, sad, afraid, and angry. The score can vary from 6 (lowest possible) to 30 (highest possible)
Affect balance (SPANE-B): The negative feelings score is subtracted from the positive feelings score, and the resultant difference score can vary from −24 (unhappiness possible) to +24 (happiest possible)

Source: Adapted from Diener et al. (2010)

Table 2.5 Measuring hedonic sensations of momentary pleasure

Method	Details
Ecological momentary assessment	Participants are given a sampling diary and are instructed to rate their current feelings on a series of affect adjectives (happy, tired, stressed, frustrated, and angry) on 5-point scales (1 = not at all, and 5 =very much) at 6 time points: At the office, at bedtime, 30 min after waking the next morning, noon, and at 3 pm
Day reconstruction method	A diary is completed online at the end of each 24 h period. Participants are asked to recall the monitoring period as a continuous series of episodes (e.g., similar to episodes of a television show). Each episode is defined in terms of time of onset and duration, location, social situation, and activity. After the complete 24 h are reconstructed, participants rate their feelings related to each episode on a series of affective states (happy, tired, worry, feeling hassled, angry, and frustrated) on 7-point scales (0 = not at all and 6 = very much)

Source: Adapted from Dockray et al. (2010)

The Cognitive Component of Hedonic Wellbeing

The cognitive component of hedonic wellbeing is supported by different theories and metrics. Here is a synopsis of this research. Many wellbeing researchers treat *life satisfaction* as the cognitive component of hedonic wellbeing (see Diener, 1984; and Veenhoven, 2000, 2003 for literature reviews). It may involve judgments of fulfilment of one's needs, goals, and wishes. This view is essentially based on seminal studies of the founding fathers of the life satisfaction research movement: Andrews and Withey (1976), Campbell et al. (1976), Cantril (1965), Diener (1984), and Michalos (1985).

Diener et al. (1985) articulated this concept well by asserting that life satisfaction is "a cognitive judgmental process dependent upon a comparison of one's circumstances with what is thought to be an appropriate standard" (p. 71); thus, the lower the discrepancy between the perception of life achievements and some standard the higher the life satisfaction.

Typical studies of life satisfaction use surveys in which respondents are asked to assess how their lives have been going over a designated period, such as the last few weeks, months, or years. A typical way of measuring life satisfaction is a single item with a three-point scale: "Taken all together, how would you say things are these days—would you say that you are very happy (1), pretty happy (2), or not happy (3)?" (Andrews & Robinson, 1991).

A very popular measure of life satisfaction is Satisfaction with Life Scale (SWLS). Diener et al. (1985) developed this measure that involves five questions, rated on a 7-point Likert scale. The items are shown in Table 2.6. The SWLS has been validated in many contexts (e.g., Bai et al., 2011; Gouveia et al., 2009; Swami et al., 2009; Wu & Wu, 2008).

The Cantril Ladder (Cantril, 1965), yet another popular measure of life satisfaction. It employs a visual graph of a ladder to capture the respondent's feelings about his or her life overall. The instructions related to this measure are shown in Table 2.7.

Sometimes, wellbeing researchers use the term *emotional wellbeing* to mean a cognitive evaluation of their emotional state. To appreciate this view of hedonic wellbeing, consider the measure developed by Simsek (2009) that captures positive and negative affect with references to life at large. See Table 2.8 for examples of specific items.

Table 2.6 The satisfaction with life scale

• In most ways my life is close to ideal.
• The conditions of my life are excellent.
• I am satisfied with my life.
• So far, I have gotten the important things I want in life.
• If I could live my life over, I would change almost nothing.
Response scale: Responses are captured on 7-point Likert-type scales varying from 1 = strongly disagree to 7 = strongly agree

Source: Adapted from Diener et al. (1985)

Table 2.7 Instructions related to the Cantril Ladder

The respondent is first asked to describe wishes and hopes for his or her future and then describe what would be the most unhappy life for him or her. The respondent is then presented with a picture of a ladder numbered from zero on the bottom rung to nine on the top rung. The respondent is then asked to suppose that the top of the ladder represents the best possible life for him or her, and the bottom represents the worst possible life. The respondent is then asked: "Where on the ladder do you feel you stand at the present time? Here is a picture of a ladder. Suppose the top of the ladder represents the best possible life for you and the bottom of the ladder the worst possible life. Where on the ladder do you feel you personally stand at the present time? (0–10 rating scale using a picture of a ladder)

Source: Adapted from Cantril (1965)

Table 2.8 An emotional wellbeing scale

Positive emotional wellbeing: • Life gives me pleasure. • Life excites me. • I feel at peace with life. • I am content with life. • I appreciate the life I lead. • I completely accept life as it is.
Negative emotional wellbeing: • I feel pain about my life. • I feel upset about my life. • The life I lead gets me down. • The life I lead frightens me. • I worry about the life I lead. • The life I lead saddens me. • I feel I'm wasting my life.
Response scale: 5-point Likert scale varying from "1 = strong disagree" to 5 = strongly agree."

Source: Adapted from Simsek (2009)

Another treatment of the cognitive component of hedonic wellbeing involves the concept and metrics of *domain satisfaction*. That is, high wellbeing is defined as satisfaction in salient life domains. The basic theoretical premise underlying the concept of domain satisfaction is the notion of bottom-up spillover (e.g., Andrews & Withey, 1976; Campbell et al., 1976). Bottom-up spillover is the spillover of affect from subordinate life domains to superordinate ones, specifically from life domains such as leisure, family, job, and health to overall life. That is, feelings within a given life space within the overall hierarchy of life experiences (captured subjectively as cognitions) spill vertically from bottom (most concrete cognitions) to top (most abstract cognitions).

Things happen to people, both positive and negative. They get divorced; they experience death in the family; they find themselves in financial debt, etc. These are examples of negative life events. For positive life events, they may fall in love, they get promoted at work and get a raise; their grown-up children fall in love and get married. And so on! Positive life events, of course, produce positive affect; and conversely, negative life events produce negative affect. Positive and negative affect related to these life events influence subjective wellbeing.

Table 2.9 The personal wellbeing index

Part 1: Life Satisfaction Overall:
Thinking about your own life and personal circumstances, how satisfied are you with your life as a whole?
Part 2: Domain Life Satisfaction:
1. How satisfied are you with your standard of living? 2. How satisfied are you with your health? 3. How satisfied are you with what you are achieving in life? 4. How satisfied are you with your personal relationships? 5. How satisfied are you with how safe you feel? 6. How satisfied are you with feeling part of your community? 7. How satisfied are you with your future security? 8. How satisfied are you with your religion or spirituality?
Response scale: Responses are recorded on an 11-point scale varying from 0 (extremely dissatisfied) to 10 (extremely satisfied)

Source: Adapted from Yiengprugsawan et al. (2010)

Based on a review of the literature, Diener (2009) concluded that studies have shown that life events do influence subjective wellbeing. Good events are related to positive affect, and bad events are related to negative affect. There is also evidence that one's ability to control life events may amplify or reduce the influence of these events on subjective wellbeing. In other words, if people feel responsible for the good events that happen to them, they may experience higher levels of subjective wellbeing than if they feel they have little control over these events.

The work of Robert Cummins, a renowned wellbeing researcher, is worth noting. Cummins and his colleagues developed a measure of domain satisfaction called the ComQuality of Life-A5 (Cummins, 1993, 1996, 1997a, b; Cummins et al., 1994; Jovanovic et al., 2019). The concept involves seven life domains: (1) material well-being, (2) health, (3) productivity, (4) intimacy, (5) safety, (6) place in community, and (7) emotional wellbeing. The measurement of wellbeing in each domain is carried out through a composite satisfaction score of that domain weighted by the perceived importance of that domain. Thus, a total subjective score is derived by summing the product of domain satisfaction scores weighted by perceived importance. The ComQuality of Life-A5 is now replaced by the Personal Wellbeing Index (PWI) developed by Cummins and his colleagues (Cummins et al., 2003; Nielsen et al., 2010a, b; Renn et al., 2009; Smyth et al., 2010; Tiliouine et al., 2006). See Table 2.9 for the survey items of the PWI.

Eudaimonic Wellbeing

To reiterate, eudaimonic wellbeing is achieved when individuals engage in personally expressive activities that facilitate self-realization through personal growth and development (Waterman, 1993). Daimon (potentialities of a person) represents the ideal sense of being. Efforts to live per the daimon, to realize those potentials (self-realization), give rise to a condition termed eudaimonia (Waterman, 1993). That is, eudaimonia is a higher state of flourishing that is shaped through self-realization (Ryff & Singer, 2008).

Behaviors reflective of eudaimonic wellbeing include planning personal goals, volunteering, expressing gratitude, listening to another person's point of view, and persevering at a specific valued goal despite obstacles (Huta, 2016). For example, personal expressive activities that offer opportunities for balanced skill and challenge, self-realization of values, effort, and importance are more closely aligned with eudaimonia (Waterman et al., 2008) than hedonic wellbeing. Through eudaimonic experiences, the individual experiences (Huta, 2016):

- feelings of meaning, value, and purpose.
- elevation, inspiration, awe, and transcendence.
- feelings of self-connectedness and authenticity.
- feelings of accomplishment, progress, and non-hubristic pride.
- engagement, immersion, interest, and flow.
- personal expressiveness and deep fit with one's activities.
- life satisfaction and happiness.
- vitality and feeling alive.

Whereas hedonic wellbeing is consistently defined as the experience of pleasant affect and life satisfaction, eudaimonic wellbeing consists of a range of constructs unified around the major theme of growth, meaning, authenticity, and mastery (Huta & Waterman, 2014; Kashdan et al., 2008).

A more formal treatment of eudaimonia involves the following behavioral states:

- flow (i.e., being immersed and absorbed in what they are doing) (Csikszentmihalyi, 1990).
- environmental mastery/competence (i.e., choosing and controlling of one's environment or finding one that suits one's personal needs and capacities) (Ryff & Singer, 2008).
- excellence (i.e., attainment of a high standard, utilizing what is the best in oneself and developing signature strengths) (Huta & Waterman, 2014).
- self-actualization (i.e., personal growth, reaching one's potential and full-functioning, self-actualization, and maturity) (Huta & Waterman, 2014).
- relatedness (i.e., feeling understood, respected, and supported, social enjoyment and community, friendship, and love) (Hayborn, 2016; Ryff & Singer, 2008).
- authenticity/personal expressiveness (i.e., existential notions such as identity, autonomy, integrity, and personal expressiveness, where the individual becomes more like or discovers their true self) (Huta & Waterman, 2014; Ryff & Singer, 2008).
- meaning/purpose in life (i.e., seeing a purpose in what one is doing, taking a long-term perspective, or a concern for and a desire to contribute to the broader context, thus serving something that you believe is bigger than the self) (Huta & Waterman, 2014; Seligman, 2011).

Well-established theories and metrics of eudaimonic wellbeing include Ryff's theory of psychological wellbeing, Seligman's PERMA theory of human flourishing, Waterman's theory of personal expressiveness, Csikszentmihalyi's theory of flow, Diener's theory of flourishing, the Schulenberg/Melton's theory of purpose and meaning of life, and Ryan/Deci's theory of self-determination, Sheldon's theory of intrinsic goals, and Keyes' theory of positive mental health.

Ryff's Theory of Psychological Wellbeing

Concerning Ryff's theory of psychological wellbeing, eudaimonic wellbeing is conceptualized in terms of six dimensions: (1) self-acceptance, (2) positive relations with others, (3) personal growth, (4) purpose in life, (5) environmental mastery, and (6) autonomy (Ryff, 1989). That is, an individual is regarded as high on eudaimonia if and when s/he is accepting of his/her actual self; has established positive relationships with others, especially significant others; has experience personal growth over time (i.e., matured emotionally and socially), carries on with a sense of life purpose; feels much in control over his/her immediate environment as experienced in various life domains (e.g., family life, work life, social life, financial life); and feels autonomous in making important life decision. .

The Scale of Psychological Wellbeing (SPWB) is a structured, self-report instrument and is based on six dimensions that point to different aspects of positive functioning (Ryff, 1989; Ryff & Singer, 2008). To reiterate, individuals with high psychological wellbeing has the following characteristics (1) self-acceptance (e.g., possesses a positive attitude toward the self; acknowledges and accepts multiple aspects of self including good and bad qualities; feels positive about past life), (2) positive relations with others (e.g., has warm, satisfying, trusting relationships with others; is concerned about the welfare of other others; is capable of strong empathy, affection, and intimacy; understands give and take of human relationships), (3) personal growth (e.g., has a feeling of continued development; sees self as growing and developing; is open to new experiences; has sense of realizing his or her potential; sees improvement in self and behavior over time; is changing in ways that reflect more self-knowledge and effectiveness), (4) purpose in life (e.g., has goals in life and a sense of directedness; feels there is meaning to present and past life; holds beliefs that give life purpose; has aims and objectives for living), (5) environmental mastery (e.g., has a sense of mastery and competence in managing the environment; controls complex array of external activities; makes effective use of surrounding opportunities; able to choose or create contexts suitable to personal needs and values), and (6) autonomy (e.g., is self-determining and independent; able to resist social pressures to think and act in certain ways; regulates social pressures to think and act in certain ways; regulates behavior from within; evaluates self by personal standards) (Ryff & Singer, 2008). See Table 2.10 showing the various items involved in the six dimensions.

Table 2.10 Ryff's psychological wellbeing measure

Autonomy: • I am not afraid to voice my opinions even when they are in opposition to the opinions of most people. • My decisions are not usually influenced by what everyone else is doing. • I have confidence in my opinions even if they are contrary to the consensus. • Being happy with myself is more important than having others approve of me. • I tend to worry about what other people think of me. (reverse coded) • I often change my mind about decisions if my friends and family disagree. (reverse coded) • It is difficult for me to voice my own opinions on controversial matters. (reverse coded)
Positive Relations with Others: • Most people see me as loving and affectionate. • I enjoy personal and mutual conversations with family members or friends. • People would describe me as a giving person, willing to share my time with others. • I know that I can trust my friends and they know that they can trust me. • I often feel lonely because I have few close friends with whom to share my concerns. (reverse coded) • I don't have many people who want to listen when I need to talk. (reverse coded) • It seems to me that most other people have more friends than I do. (reverse coded)
Environmental Mastery: • I am quite good at managing the many responsibilities of my daily life. • I generally do a good job of taking care of my personal finances and affairs. • I am good at juggling my time so that I can fit everything that needs to be done. • I have been able to build a home and a lifestyle for myself that is to my liking. • I do not fit very well with the people and the community around me. (reverse coded) • I often feel overwhelmed by my responsibilities. (reverse coded) • I have difficulty arranging my life in a way that is satisfying to me. (reverse coded)
Personal Growth: • I think it is important to have new experiences that challenge how you think about the world. • I have the sense that I have developed a lot as a person over time. • I am not interested in activities that expand my horizons. (reverse coded) • I don't want to try new ways of doing things; my life is fine the way it is. (reverse coded) • When I think about it, I haven't really improved much as a person over the years. (reverse coded) • I do not enjoy being in new situations that require me to change my old familiar ways to doing things. (reverse coded)
• There is a truth in the saying that you can't teach an old dog new tricks. (reverse coded) **Purpose in Life:** • I am an active person in carrying out the plans I set for myself. • I enjoy making plans for the future and working to make them a reality. • I tend to focus on the present because the future nearly always brings me problems. (reverse coded) • My daily activities often seem trivial and unimportant to me. (reverse coded) • I don't have a good sense of what it is I am trying to accomplish in life. (reverse coded) • I used to set goals for myself, but that now seems a waste of time. (reverse coded)
Response scale: Responses are captured on 6-point Likert-type scales varying from 1 (strongly disagree) to 6 (strongly agree)

Source: Adapted Ryff (1989)

Seligman's PERMA Theory of Human Flourishing

In Seligman's (2011) multidimensional PERMA theory of flourishing, wellbeing is defined in terms of five domains: positive emotions (P), engagement (E), relationships (R), meaning (M), and accomplishment (A). Each of these five components is intrinsically rewarding, representing worthwhile ends for doing anything. Together, the combination of these five dimensions of wellbeing purportedly gives rise to human flourishing (Seligman, 2011).

According to the theory, *positive emotions* (P) refer to hedonic feelings of happiness (e.g., feeling joyful, content, and cheerful), understood as the affective component or feeling good, in combination with a positive appraisal. It is a general tendency to feel contentment and joy. *Engagement* (E) refers to a psychological connection to activities or organizations (e.g., feeling absorbed, interested, and engaged in life). Engagement is the state of flow, or being one with an activity, experiencing a sense of time stopping, and the loss of self-consciousness during an activity. *Relationships* (R) indicate a feeling of belongingness, support from, and connection with others; it implies the belief that one is cared for, loved, and valued. Positive relationships include feeling socially integrated, cared about, and supported by others, and satisfied with one's social connections. *Meaning* (M) refers to the belief that one's life is valuable and feeling connected to something greater than oneself. *Accomplishment* (A) involves making progress toward goals, feeling capable of doing daily activities, and having a sense of achievement. The PERMA theory integrates wellbeing concepts from both hedonic (e.g., positive emotions) and eudaimonic (e.g., meaning) traditions (Seligman, 2011; Goodman et al., 2018). PERMA constitutes different elements that contribute to an individual's wellbeing (Seligman, 2018).

The measure of PERMA-profiler (Butler & Kern, 2016) is frequently used for PERMA, and this measure includes a set of 15 questions (three items per PERMA dimension).Using the measure of PERMA-Profiler, Goodman et al. (2018) found each of the elements of PERMA correlated moderately highly (range .37 to .79, mean = .61) with each other and also found that a composite index of the five dimensions is highly correlated with SWB (a latent correlation = .98). See Table 2.11.

Waterman's Theory of Personal Expressiveness

The Questionnaire for Eudaimonic Wellbeing (QEWB) may provide the reader with an understanding of Waterman's theory of personal expressiveness. The QEWB consists of 21 items covering the six interrelated elements associated with eudaimonic wellbeing theorized by Waterman (Waterman et al., 2008, 2010). These are (1) self-discovery, (2) perceived development of one's best potentials, (3) a sense of purpose and meaning in life, (4) investment of significant effort in pursuit of excellence, (5) intense involvement in activities, and (6) enjoyment of activities as personally expressive. Examples of items of QEWB include "I believe I have discovered

Table 2.11 The measure of PERMA

Positive Emotion
• How often do you feel joyful? (0 = never; 10 = always)
• How often do you feel positive? (0 = never; 10 = always)
• To what extent do you feel contented? (0 = not at all; 10 = completely)
Engagement
• How often do you become absorbed in what you are doing? (0 = never; 10 = always)
• To what extent do you feel excited and interested in things? (0 = not at all; 10 = completely)
• How often do you lose track of time while doing something you enjoy? (0 = never; 10 = always)
Relationship
• To what extent do you receive help and support from others when you need it? (0 = not at all; 10 = completely)
• To what extent have you been feeling loved? (0 = not at all; 10 = completely)
• How satisfied are you with your personal relationships? (0 = not at all; 10 = completely)
Meaning
• To what extent do you lead a purposeful and meaningful life? (0 = not at all; 10 = completely)
• To what extent do you feel that what you do in your life is valuable and worthwhile? (0 = not at all; 10 = completely)
• To what extent do you generally feel you have a sense of direction in your life? (0 = not at all; 10 = completely)
Accomplishment
• How much of the time do you feel you are making progress towards accomplishing your goals? (0 = never; 10 = always)
• How often do you achieve the important goals you have set for yourself? (0 = never; 10 = always)
• How often are you able to handle your responsibilities? (0 = never; 10 = always)

Source: Adapted from Butler and Kern (2016)'s PERMA-Profiler

who I really am" (self-discovery), "I believe I know what my best potentials are and I try to develop them whenever possible" (perceived development one's best potentials), "I can say that I have found my purpose in life" (a sense of purpose and meaning in life), "I feel best when I am doing something worth investing a great deal of effort in" (investment of significant effort in pursuit of excellence), "I find I get intensely involved in many of the things I do each day" (intense involvement in activities), and "It is more important that I really enjoy what I do than that others are impressed by it" (enjoyment of activities as personally expressive).

The QEWB measure contains 14 positively worded items and 7 negatively worded items. The results of confirmatory factor analysis indicate that the 21-item measure loaded onto a common factor for the two large-sized US samples (Waterman et al., 2010) as well as for the non-Western adolescent sample (Areepattamannil & Hashim, 2017). The 21-item statements in QEWB are responded to on a 5-point Likert-type scale, with possible choices ranging from 0 (Strongly Disagree) to 4 (Strongly Agree). The single-factor QWEB score for an individual is computed by summing the 21 items. Thus, the possible range of scores on the QEWB was from 0 to 84 (85 points) (Waterman et al., 2010). See Table 2.12.

Table 2.12 Questionnaire for Eudaimonic Wellbeing (QEWB)

This questionnaire contains a series of statements that refer to how you may feel things have been going in your life. Read each statement and decide the extent to which you agree or disagree with it. Try to respond to each statement according to your own feelings about how things are actually going, rather than how you might wish them to be.
Please use the following scale when responding to each statement. • I find I get intensely involved in many of the things I do each day. • I believe I have discovered who I really am. • I think it would be ideal if things came easily to me in my life. (R) • My life is centered around a set of core beliefs that give meaning to my life. • It is more important that I really enjoy what I do than that other people are impressed by it. • I believe I know what my best potentials are, and I try to develop them whenever possible. • Other people usually know better what would be good for me to do than I know myself. (R) • I feel best when I'm doing something worth investing a great deal of effort in. • I can say that I have found my purpose in life. • If I did not find what I was doing rewarding me, I do not think I could continue doing it. • Yet, I've not figured out what to do with my life. (R) • I can't understand why some people want to work so hard on the things that they do. (R) • I believe it is important to know how what I'm doing fits with purposes worth pursuing. • I usually know what I should do because some actions just feel right to me. • When I engage in activities that involve my best potential, I have this sense of really being alive. • I am confused about what my talents really are. (R) • I find a lot of the things I do are personally expressive for me. • It is important to me that I feel fulfilled by the activities that I engage in. • If something is really difficult, it probably isn't worth doing. (R) • I find it hard to get really invested in the things that I do. (R) • I believe I know what I was meant to do in life.
Notes: (R) = reverse coded
Response scale = Strongly Disagree 0 1 2 3 4 Strongly Agree

Source: Waterman et al. (2010)

The Personally Expressive Activity Questionnaire (PEAQ) measure is another popular survey instrument capturing self-expressiveness, a major element of eudaimonia (Waterman, 1990, 1993). Self-expressiveness refers to the subjective experiences associated with intrinsically motivated, personally salient, and identity-related activities. In contrast to flow experiences in which the focus is on the experiences immediately present when engaged in an activity, feelings of personal expressiveness involve reflections on the role of the activity in a person's life, including contrasting an activity with other types of activities in which the person engages. See the measure in Table 2.13. The measure contains items designed to capture both hedonic and eudaimonic wellbeing.

Table 2.13 The Personally Expressive Activity Questionnaire (PEAQ)

To what extent do you agree with each of the following statements:

Eudaimonic wellbeing associated with an activity

- This activity gives me my greatest feeling of really being alive.
- This activity gives me my strongest feelings that this is who I really am.
- When I engage in this activity, I feel more intensely involved than I do in most other activities.
- When I engage in this activity, I feel that this is what I was meant to do.
- I feel more complete or fulfilled when engaging in this activity than I do when engaged in most other activities.
- I feel a special fit or meshing when engaging in this activity.

Hedonic wellbeing associated with an activity

- This activity gives me my strongest sense of enjoyment.
- This activity gives me my greatest pleasure.
- When I engage in this activity, I feel more satisfied than I do when engaged in most other activities.
- When I engage in this activity, I feel good.
- When I engage in this activity, I feel a warm glow.
- When I engage in this activity, I feel happier than I do when engaged in most other activities.

Response scale: a seven-point Likert scale ranging from 1 = strongly disagree to 7 = strongly agree

Source: Waterman (1993)

Csikszentmihalyi's Theory of Flow

Flow experiences refer to an intrinsically rewarding or optimal state that results from intense engagement with daily activities (Csikszentmihalyi, 1990). Flow experiences result from matching a high level of challenges with a high level of skills. Mismatching of challenges and skills results in lower wellbeing, such as boredom or anxiety (Csikszentmihalyi, 1990). During flow experiences, individuals experience intense involvement, deep concentration, lack of self-consciousness, and loss of a sense of time. That is, flow is a state of consciousness that yields both a deep feeling of enjoyment and concentration.

The scale of flow experience pertains to the subjective experiences immediately present when a person is fully engaged in an activity (Csikszentmihalyi, 1990). The subjective experiences assessed include (1) having clear goals, (2) not feeling self-conscious, (3) feeling in control, (4) losing track of time, (5) knowing how well one is doing, (6) maintaining a high level of concentration, (7) forgetting personal problems, and (8) feeling fully involved with the activity. The items measuring state of flow include "I feel I have clear goals," "I feel self-conscious (reverse-scored)," "I feel in control," "I lose track of time," "I feel I know how well I am doing," "I have a high level of concentration," "I forget personal problems," and "I feel fully involved" (not at all characteristics of me/ very characteristic of me).

Flow experiences result in satisfaction with experiences and enhanced self-esteem through personal development (Csikszentmihalyi, 1990, 2002; Wells, 1988). Flow state results in both feeling of hedonic enjoyment and eudemonic self-growth (Csikszentmihalyi, 1990; Peterson et al., 2005). That is, flow experiences produce enjoyable optimal experiences that are associated with meaning and self-actualization.

Diener's Theory of Flourishing

Ed Diener and his colleagues (Diener et al., 2010) made a case that a person who is "flourishing in life" can be characterized as having positive relationships, high self-esteem, purpose in life, optimism, and competence. The Flourishing Scale is a brief 8-item summary measure capturing these conceptual dimensions of flourishing.

Each item of the Flourishing scale is answered on a 7-point scale that ranges from strong disagreement to strong agreement. All items are phrased in a positive direction. Scores can range from 8 (Strong Disagreement with all items) to 56 (Strong Agreement with all items). High scores signify that respondents view themselves in positive terms in important areas of functioning. This brief measure of flourishing provides information on overall psychological wellbeing. See Table 2.14.

Schulenberg/Melton's Theory of Purpose and Meaning of Life

Regarding the *theory of purpose and meaning in life*, eudaimonic wellbeing is achieved when the individual is said to live his/her life with purpose and meaning (Diener et al., 2010; Schulenberg & Melton, 2010). Purpose and meaning refer to a concern for and a desire to contribute to the broader context (e.g., something bigger than the self). Individuals who live their lives consistently with worthwhile values are likely to experience high levels of eudaimonia.

Table 2.14 The flourishing scale

Below are eight statements with which you may agree or disagree. Using the 1–7 scale below, indicate your agreement with each item by indicating that response for each statement.
• I lead a purposeful and meaningful life. • My social relationships are supportive and rewarding. • I am engaged and interested in my daily activities. • I actively contribute to the happiness and wellbeing of others. • I am competent and capable in the activities that are important to me. • I am a good person and live a good life. • I am optimistic about my future. • People respect me.
Response scale is a 7-point Likert-type scale [1 = Strongly disagree, 2 = Disagree, 3 = Slightly disagree, 4 = Mixed or neither agree nor disagree, 5 = Slightly agree, 6 = Agree, 7 = Strongly agree]

Source: Adapted from Diener et al. (2010)

Table 2.15 Meaning in Life Questionnaire-Presence (MLQ-P) subscale

Please take a moment to think about what makes your life feel important to you. Please respond to the following statements as truthfully and accurately as you can, and please remember that these are very subjective questions and that there are no right or wrong answers.
• I understand my life's meaning. • I am looking for something that makes my life feel meaningful. • I am always looking to find my life's purpose. • My life has a clear sense of purpose. • I have a good sense of what makes my life meaningful. • I have discovered a satisfying purpose in life. • I am always searching for something that makes my life feel significant. • I am seeking a purpose or mission for my life. • My life has no clear purpose. (reverse coded). • I am searching for meaning in my life.
Response scale: 1 = Absolutely Untrue, 2 = Mostly Untrue, 3 = Somewhat Untrue, 4 = Can't Say True or False, 5= Somewhat True, 6 = Mostly True, 7 = Absolutely True

Source: Steger et al. (2006)

Examples of wellbeing measures based on the concept of purpose and meaning in life include the Meaning in Life Questionnaire-Presence Subscale (MLQ-P; Steger et al., 2006). An example of a measurement item is "I understand my life's meaning." See Table 2.15.

Ryan/Deci's Theory of Self-Determination

Concerning *self-determination theory*, eudaimonic wellbeing is construed in terms of meeting a set of universal basic needs (Ryan & Deci, 2000). The theory is that an individual is likely to experience eudaimonia when three basic needs are met: (1) the need for competence, (2) the need for relatedness, and (3) the need for autonomy. Meeting these basic needs constitutes human flourishing. Research has demonstrated that those who successfully pursue autonomy, competence, and relatedness goals experience lasting gains happiness (Sheldon et al., 2010).

The Balanced Measure of Psychological Needs (BMPN) assesses the three basic needs of the self-determination theory: relatedness, competence, and autonomy (Sheldon & Hilpert, 2012). The measure is composed of 18 items, six for each dimension, three negatively worded. See Table 2.16.

Sheldon's Theory of Intrinsic Goals

Concerning *intrinsic goals theory*, people experience eudaimonia when their goals are self-concordant (i.e., pursued for autonomous, not controlled reasons) or intrinsic in content (i.e., concerning growth and connection, not money and status) (Sheldon & Kasser, 1998). Research has shown that *self-concordant goal* pursuit promotes sustained effort over time, which leads to greater progress in goals, which

Table 2.16 The Balanced Measure of Psychological Needs (BMPN)

Please read each of the following statements carefully, thinking about how true it is for you.
Autonomy
• I was free to do things my own way. • I had a lot of pressures I could do without (R). • My choices expressed my "true self." • There were people telling me what I had to do (R). • I was really doing what interests me. • I had to do things against my will (R).
Competence • I was successfully completing difficult tasks and projects. • I experienced some kind of failure or was unable to do well at something (R). • I took on and mastered hard challenges. • I did something stupid that made me feel incompetent (R). • I did well even at the hard things. • I struggled doing something I should be good at (R).
Relatedness • I felt a sense of contact with people who care for me, and whom I care for. • I was lonely(R).
• I felt close and connected with other people who are important to me. • I felt unappreciated by one or more important people (R). • I felt a strong sense of intimacy with the people I spent time with. • I had disagreements or conflicts with people I usually get along with (R).
Response scale: The rating scale is from 1 (totally disagree) to 5 (totally agree).

Source: Sheldon and Hilpert (2012)

leads to more satisfying daily experiences, which finally lead to changes in global wellbeing (Sheldon & Elliot, 1999).

Self concordance of goals are measured by summing the intrinsic reason score (e.g., "you pursue this striving because of the fun and enjoyment it provides you") with the identified reason score (e.g., "you pursue this striving because you believe it is an important goal to have") and then subtracting the introjected reason score (e.g., "you pursue this striving because you would feel ashamed, guilty or anxious if you didn't") and then subtracting external reason score (e.g., "you pursue this striving because somebody else want you to do or because the situation demands it"). In other words, the self-concordance of goals score is computed using the following formula:

Self-concordance of goals score = [(intrinsic reason score + identified reason score) – (introjected reason score + external reason score)].

Responses to each item are captured on a 9-point rating scale varying from "1 = not at all for the reason" to "9 = completely for this reason" (Sheldon & Elliot, 1999).

Keyes' Theory of Positive Mental Health

Regarding the *theory of positive mental health*, eudaimonic wellbeing is achieved when positive mental health is maintained (Keyes, 1998, 2002). In other words, eudaimonic wellbeing is conceptualized as positive mental health. The presence of positive mental health is flourishing in life, and the absence of positive mental health is languishing in life.

Marsh et al. (2020) developed a measure of positive mental health. The items include:

- *competence* (e.g., "Most things I do, I do well"),
- *clear thinking* (e.g., "I am able to think clearly"),
- *emotional stability* (e.g., "I am emotionally balanced and even-tempered"),
- *engagement* (e.g., "I feel excited by many of the things I do"),
- *meaning* (e.g., I feel I have a sense of direction in my life"),
- *optimism* (e.g., "I am always optimistic about my future"),
- *positive emotions* (e.g., "I am happy most of the time"),
- *positive relations* (e.g., "I have close and secure relationships"),
- *resilience* (e.g., "It does not take me long to recover from a stressful event"),
- *self-esteem* (e.g., "A lot of things about me are good."),
- *vitality* (e.g., "I feel full of energy most of the time."),
- *self-acceptance* (e.g., "I can admit my shortcomings without shame or embarrassment"),
- *autonomy* (e.g., "I feel free to do whatever I decide to do."),
- *empathy* (e.g., "I easily get caught up in other people's feelings"), and
- *prosocial* (e.g., "I frequently offer to help others").

Summary and Conclusion

Based on the preceding discussion of hedonic and eudaimonic wellbeing, we note significant differences. First, about hedonic wellbeing, happiness is understood as pleasure, enjoyment, and the absence of discomfort. Common dimensions of hedonic wellbeing include the presence of positive mood, absence of negative mood, satisfaction with various domains of life (e.g., work, leisure), and global life satisfaction. Concerning eudaimonic wellbeing, happiness is understood in terms of higher virtues, meaning, and self-actualization, as opposed to mere pleasure. Common dimensions of eudaimonic wellbeing include a sense of control or autonomy, competence, personal expressiveness, personal growth, feelings of belongingness, self-acceptance, social contribution, and feelings of meaning and purpose.

Second, the main concern related to hedonic wellbeing is the life of pleasure. Individuals with hedonic wellbeing focus on need satisfaction that is mostly sensory and seek pleasure in the present. In contrast, the main concern related to eudaimonic wellbeing is a life of engagement and meaning. Individuals high on eudaimonic wellbeing focus on social engagement, personal identity, personal growth, self-fulfillment, self-development, engagement in multiple roles, and optimal performance of meaningful behavior. Their behavior is enduring and meaningful.

Despite these differences, evidence has shown a high level of statistical covariance between the experience of hedonia and eudaimonia, suggesting substantial overlap between the two types of wellbeing. Evidence suggests that experiencing eudaimonia necessarily results in experiencing hedonic enjoyment, but hedonic enjoyment does not necessarily lead to eudaimonia.

In summary, the hedonic approach to wellbeing treats wellbeing in terms of pleasure attainment and pain avoidance, and happiness is understood as a subjective affective state. In contrast, the eudaimonic approach to wellbeing defines wellbeing in terms of the degree to which a person is fully functioning and happiness is understood in terms of higher virtues, meaning and self-actualization, as opposed to mere pleasure.

While the experience of hedonic happiness is transient (i.e., feelings that exist in the present), the experience of eudaimonic happiness is enduring and involves life purpose and meaning beyond the present and integrating future and past.

While measures of hedonic wellbeing and eudaimonic wellbeing are conceptually related, they are distinguishable from one another. Measures of hedonic wellbeing are associated with the pursuit of projects that are fun and likely to be successful, and they are present-focused activities. In contrast, measures of eudaimonic wellbeing are associated with projects that are closely aligned with one's values and identity, challenging activities, and moral behavior. Table 2.17 sums up the distinctions between hedonic and eudaimonic wellbeing.

Figure 2.1 captures the preceding discussion in graphic form.

Table 2.17 Comparing hedonic vs. eudaimonic wellbeing

	Hedonic wellbeing (subjective wellbeing)	Eudaimonic wellbeing (psychological wellbeing)
Definition	Happiness is understood as an affective state Here, happiness is conceived as pleasure, enjoyment, and the absence of discomfort	Happiness is understood in terms of higher virtues, meaning, and self-actualization, as opposed to mere pleasure Here, happiness is conceived as an activity reflecting virtue, excellence, the best within us, and the full development of our potential
Dimensions	– Presence of positive mood – Absence of negative mood – Satisfaction with various domains of life – Global life satisfaction	– Sense of control or autonomy – Competence – Personal expressiveness – Personal growth – Feelings of belongingness – Self-acceptance – Social contribution – Feeling of meaning and purpose
Orientation to happiness	Life of pleasure	– Life of engagement – Life of meaning
Main concerns	– Pleasure – Personal need satisfaction	– Social engagement – Personal identity – Personal growth, – Self-fulfillment, – Self-development, – Full engagement, and – Optimal performance of meaningful behavior
Time perspective	Present-focused	Integration of past, present, and future
Experience of positive affect	Transient	Enduring

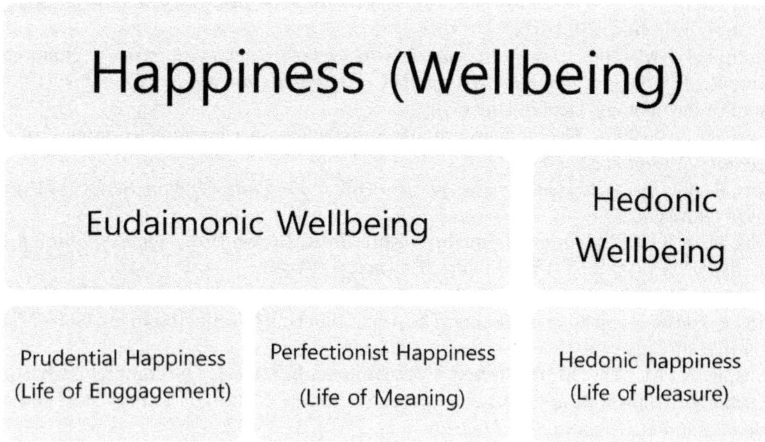

Fig. 2.1 Perspective on happiness (wellbeing)

References

Ahuvia, A. C. (2008). Wealth, consumption and happiness. In A. Lewis (Ed.), *The Cambridge handbook of psychology and economic behavior* (pp. 199–226). Cambridge University Press.
Andrews, F. M., & Robinson, J. P. (1991). Measures of subjective well-being. In J. P. Robinson, P. R. Shaver, & L. S. Wrightsman (Eds.), *Measures of personality and social psychological attitudes* (Vol. 1, pp. 61–76). Academic.
Andrews, F. M., & Withey, S. B. (1976). *Social indicators of well-being: America's perception of life quality*. Plenum Press.
Areepattamannil, S., & Hashim, J. (2017). The questionnaire for Eudaimonic well-being (QEWB): Psychometric properties in a non-western adolescent sample. *Personality and Individual Differences, 117*, 236–241.
Bai, X., Wu, C., Zheng, R., & Ren, X. (2011). The psychometric evaluation of the Satisfaction with Life Scale using a nationally representative sample of China. *Journal of Happiness Studies, 12*(2), 183–197.
Bradburn, N. M. (1969). *The structure of psychological well-being*. Aldine.
Butler, J., & Kern, M. L. (2016). The PERMA-Profiler: A brief multidimensional measure of flourishing. *International Journal of Wellbeing, 6*(3), 1–48.
Campbell, A., Converse, P. E., & Rodgers, W. L. (1976). *The quality of American life: Perceptions, evaluations, and satisfactions*. Russell Sage.
Cantril, H. (1965). *The pattern of human concerns*. Rutgers University Press.
Carlisle, S., Henderson, G., & Hanlon, P. W. (2009). 'Wellbeing': A collateral casualty of modernity. *Social Science & Medicine, 69*(10), 1556–1560.
Carver, C. S. (2001). Affect and the functional bases of behavior: On the dimensional structure of affective experience. *Personality and Social Psychology Review, 5*(4), 345–356.
Cloninger, C. R. (2004). *Feeling good: The science of well-being*. Oxford University Press.
Compton, W. C., Smith, M. L., Cornish, K. A., & Qualls, D. L. (1996). Factor structure of mental health measures. *Journal of Personality and Social Psychology, 71*(2), 406–413.
Csikszentmihalyi, M. (1975). *Beyond boredom and anxiety*. Jossey-Bass.
Csikszentmihalyi, M. (1990). *Flow. The psychology of optimal experience*. Harper Perennial.

Csikszentmihalyi, M. (1997). Flow and the psychology of discovery and invention. *Harper Perennial, New York, 39*, 1–16.
Csikszentmihalyi, M. (2002). *Flow: The classic work on how to achieve happiness*. Random House.
Cummins, R. A. (1993). *Comprehensive quality of life scale for adults (ComQol-A4)* (4th ed.). School of Psychology, Deakin University.
Cummins, R. A. (1996). The domains of life satisfaction: An attempt to order chaos. *Social Indicators Research, 38*, 303–332.
Cummins, R. A. (1997a). *Comprehensive quality of life scale-adult: Manual*. School of Psychology, Deakin University.
Cummins, R. A. (1997b). Assessing quality of life. In R. Brown (Ed.), *Quality of life for people with disabilities* (pp. 116–150). Stanley Thornes.
Cummins, R. A., Eckersley, R., Pallant, J., van Vugt, J., & Misajon, R. (2003). Developing a national index of subjective wellbeing: The Australian Unity Wellbeing Index. *Social Indicators Research, 64*(2), 159–190.
Cummins, R. A., McCabe, M. P., Romeo, Y., & Gullone, E. (1994). The comprehensive quality of life scale: Instrument development and psychometric evaluation on tertiary staff and students. *Educational and Psychological Measurement, 54*(2), 372–382.
Deci, E. L., & Ryan, R. M. (2008). Self-determination theory: A macro theory of human motivation, development, and health. *Canadian Psychology/Psychologie Canadienne, 49*(3), 182–185.
Diener, E. (1984). Subjective well-being. *Psychological Bulletin, 95*(3), 542–575.
Diener, E. (2009). Subjective well-being. In E. Diener (Ed.), *The science of well-being: The collected works of Ed Diener* (pp. 11–58). Springer.
Diener, E. D., Emmons, R. A., Larsen, R. J., & Griffin, S. (1985). The satisfaction with life scale. *Journal of Personality Assessment, 49*(1), 71–75.
Diener, E., Sandvik, E., & Pavot, W. (1991). Happiness is the frequency, not the intensity, of positive versus negative affect. In F. Strack, M. Argyle, & N. Schwarz (Eds.), *Subjective well-being: An interdisciplinary perspective* (pp. 119–139). Pergamon Press.
Diener, E., Suh, E. M., Lucas, R. E., & Smith, H. L. (1999). Subjective well-being: Three decades of progress. *Psychological Bulletin, 125*(2), 276–302.
Diener, E., Wirtz, D., Tov, W., Kim-Prieto, C., Choi, D. W., Oishi, S., & Biswas-Diener, R. (2010). New well-being measures: Short scales to assess flourishing and positive and negative feelings. *Social Indicators Research, 97*(2), 143–156.
Dockray, S., Grant, N., Stone, A., Kahneman, D., Wardle, J., & Steptoe, A. (2010). A comparison of affect ratings obtained with ecological momentary assessment and the say reconstruction method. *Social Indicators Research, 99*(2), 269–283.
Dodge, R., Daly, A. P., Huyton, J., & Sanders, L. D. (2012). The challenge of defining wellbeing. *International Journal of Wellbeing, 2*(3), 222–235.
Eid, M., & Diener, E. (2004). Global judgments of subjective well-being: Situational variability and long-term stability. *Social Indicators Research, 65*(3), 245–277.
Goodman, F. R., Disabato, D. J., Kashdan, T. B., & Kauffman, S. B. (2018). Measuring well-being: A comparison of subjective well-being and PERMA. *The Journal of Positive Psychology, 13*(4), 321–332.
Gouveia, V. V., Milfont, T. L., Nunes da Fonesca, P., de Miranda, P., & Coelho, J. A. (2009). Life satisfaction in Brazil: Testing the psychometric properties of the Satisfaction with Life Scale (SWLS) in five Brazilian Samples. *Social Indicators Research, 90*(2), 267–277.
Haybron, D. M. (2000). Two philosophical problems in the study of happiness. *Journal of Happiness Studies, 1*(2), 207–225.
Haybron, D. M. (2016). The philosophical basis of eudaimonic psychology. In *Handbook of eudaimonic well-being* (pp. 27–53). Springer.
Howell, R. T., & Howell, C. J. (2008). The relation of economic status to subjective well-being in developing countries: A meta-analysis. *Psychological Bulletin, 134*(4), 536–560.

Huta, V. (2016). Eudaimonic and hedonic orientations: Theoretical considerations and research findings. In J. Vitterso (Ed.), *Handbook of eudaimonic well-being* (pp. 215–232). Springer.

Huta, V., & Ryan, R. M. (2010). Pursuing pleasure or virtue: The differential and overlapping well-being benefits of hedonic and eudaimonic motives. *Journal of Happiness Studies, 11*(6), 735–762.

Huta, V., & Waterman, A. S. (2014). Eudaimonia and its distinction from hedonia: Developing a classification and terminology for understanding conceptual and operational definitions. *Journal of Happiness Studies, 15*(6), 1425–1456.

Jayawickreme, E., Forgeard, M. J., & Seligman, M. E. (2012). The engine of well-being. *Review of General Psychology, 16*(4), 327–342.

Jovanovic, V., Cummins, R. A., Weinberg, M., Kaliterna, L., & Prizmic-Larsen, Z. (2019). Personal Wellbeing Index: A cross-cultural measurement invariance study across four countries. *Journal of Happiness Studies, 20*(3), 759–775.

Kahneman, D. (1999). Objective happiness. In D. Kahneman, E. Diener, & N. Schwarz (Eds.), *Well-being: The foundations of hedonic psychology* (pp. 3–25). Russell Sage.

Kashdan, T. B., Biswas-Diener, R., & King, L. A. (2008). Reconsidering happiness: The costs of distinguishing between hedonics and eudaimonia. *The Journal of Positive Psychology, 3*(4), 219–233.

Keyes, C. L. (1998). Social well-being. *Social Psychology Quarterly, 61*(2), 121–140.

Keyes, C. L. (2002). The mental health continuum: From languishing to flourishing in life. *Journal of Health and Social Behavior, 43*(2), 207–222.

Keyes, C. L., & Annas, J. (2009). Feeling good and functioning well: Distinctive concepts in ancient philosophy and contemporary science. *The Journal of Positive Psychology, 4*(3), 197–201.

Kesebir, P. (2018). Scientific answers to the timeless philosophical question of happiness. In E. Diener, S. Oishi, & L. Tay (Eds.), *Handbook of well-being* (pp. 8–20). DEF Publishers.

Kim-Prieto, C., Diener, E., Tamir, M., Scollon, C., & Diener, M. (2005). Integrating the diverse definitions of happiness: A time-sequential framework of subjective well-being. *Journal of Happiness Studies, 6*(3), 261–300.

King, L. A., & Napa, C. K. (1998). What makes a life good? *Journal of Personality and Social Psychology, 75*(1), 156–165.

Layard, R. (2005). *Happiness: Lessons from a new science*. Penguin.

Luhmann, M., Hawkley, L. C., Eid, M., & Cacioppo, J. T. (2012). Time frames and the distinction between affective and cognitive well-being. *Journal of Research in Personality, 46*(4), 431–441.

Lyubomirsky, S. (2008). *The how of happiness: A scientific approach to getting the life you want*. Penguin.

Lyubomirsky, S., King, L., & Diener, E. (2005). The benefits of frequent positive affect: Does happiness lead to success? *Psychological Bulletin, 131*(6), 803–855.

Marsh, H. W., Huppert, F. A., Donald, J. N., Horwood, M. S., & Sahdra, B. K. (2020). The well-being profile (WB-Pro): Creating a theoretically based multidimensional measure of well-being to advance theory, research, policy, and practice. *Psychological Assessment, 32*(3), 294–313.

McGregor, I., & Little, B. R. (1998). Personal projects, happiness, and meaning: On doing well and being yourself. *Journal of Personality and Social Psychology, 74*(2), 494–512.

Michalos, A. C. (1985). Multiple discrepancies theory (MDT). *Social Indicators Research, 16*(4), 347–413.

Myers, D. G. (1992). *The pursuit of happiness: Who is happy and why*. William Morrow and Company.

Nielsen, I., Paritski, O., & Smyth, R. (2010a). Subjective well-being of Beijing taxi drivers. *Journal of Happiness Studies, 11*(6), 721–733.

Nielsen, I., Smyth, R., & Zhai, Q. (2010b). Subjective well-being of China's off-farm migrants. *Journal of Happiness Studies, 11*(3), 315–333.

OECD. (2013). *OECD guidelines on measuring subjective well-being. OECD Publishing*. https://doi.org/10.1787/9789264191655-en

Parducci, A. (1995). *Happiness, pleasure, and judgment: The contextual theory and its applications.* : Lawrence Erlbaum Associates, Inc.

Peterson, C., Park, N., & Seligman, M. E. (2005). Orientations to happiness and life satisfaction: The full life versus the empty life. *Journal of Happiness Studies, 6*(1), 25–41.

Renn, D., Pfaffenberger, N., Platter, M., Mitmansgruber, H., Cummins, R. A., & Hofer, S. (2009). International well-being index: The Austrian version. *Social Indicators Research, 90*(2), 243–256.

Ryan, R. M., & Deci, E. L. (2000). Self-determination theory and the facilitation of intrinsic motivation, social development, and well-being. *American Psychologist, 55*(1), 68–78.

Ryan, R. M., & Deci, E. L. (2001). On happiness and human potentials: A review of research on hedonic and eudaimonic wellbeing. *Annual Review of Psychology, 52*(1), 141–166.

Ryan, R. M., Huta, V., & Deci, E. L. (2008). Living well: A self-determination theory perspective on eudaimonia. *Journal of Happiness Studies, 9*(1), 139–170.

Ryff, C. D. (1989). Happiness is everything, or is it? Explorations on the meaning of psychological well-being. *Journal of Personality and Social Psychology, 57*(6), 1069–1081.

Ryff, C. D., & Singer, B. H. (2008). Know thyself and become what you are: A eudaimonic approach to psychological wellbeing. *Journal of Happiness Studies, 9*(1), 13–39.

Sanjuán, P. (2011). Affect balance as mediating variable between effective psychological functioning and satisfaction with life. *Journal of Happiness Studies, 12*(3), 373–384.

Schulenberg, S. E., & Melton, A. M. (2010). A confirmatory factor-analytic evaluation of the purpose in life test: Preliminary psychometric support for a replicable two-factor model. *Journal of Happiness Studies, 11*(1), 95–111.

Seligman, M. E. P. (2002). *Authentic happiness: Using the new positive psychology to realize your potential for lasting fulfillment*. The Free Press.

Seligman, M. E. (2011). *Flourish: A visionary new understanding of happiness and well-being*. Simon and Schuster.

Seligman, M. (2018). PERMA and the building blocks of well-being. *The Journal of Positive Psychology, 13*(4), 333–335.

Sheldon, K. M., Abad, N., Ferguson, Y., Gunz, A., Houser-Marko, L., Nichols, C. P., & Lyubomirsky, S. (2010). Persistent pursuit of need-satisfying goals leads to increased happiness: A 6-month experimental longitudinal study. *Motivation and Emotion, 34*(1), 39–48.

Sheldon, K. M., & Hilpert, J. C. (2012). The balanced measure of psychological needs (BMPN) scale: An alternative domain general measure of need satisfaction. *Motivation and Emotion, 36*(4), 439–451.

Sheldon, K. M., & Kasser, T. (1998). Pursuing personal goals: Skills enable progress, but not all progress is beneficial. *Personality and Social Psychology Bulletin, 24*(12), 1319–1331.

Sheldon, K. M., & Elliot, A. J. (1999). Goal striving, need satisfaction, and longitudinal well-being: The self-concordance model. *Journal of Personality and Social Psychology, 76*(3), 482–497.

Simsek, O. F. (2009). Happiness revisited: Ontological well-being as a theory-based construct of subjective well-being. *Journal of Happiness Studies, 10*(5), 505–522.

Sirgy, M. J. (2002). *The psychology of quality of life*. Kluwer Academic Publishers.

Sirgy, M. J. (2021). *The Psychology of quality of life: Wellbeing and positive mental health* (3rd ed.). Springer Nature Switzerland AG.

Smith, M. K., & Diekmann, A. (2017). Tourism and wellbeing. *Annals of Tourism Research, 66*, 1–13.

Smyth, R., Nielsen, I., & Zhai, Q. (2010). Personal well-being in urban China. *Social Indicators Research, 95*(2), 231–251.

Steger, M. F., Frazier, P., Oishi, S., & Kaler, M. (2006). The meaning in life questionnaire: Assessing the presence of and search for meaning in life. *Journal of Counseling Psychology, 53*(1), 80–93.

Steger, M. F., Kashdan, T. B., & Oishi, S. (2008). Being good by doing good: Daily eudaimonic activity and well-being. *Journal of Research in Personality, 42*(1), 22–42.
Swami, V., & Chamorro-Premuzic, T. (2009). Psychometric evaluation of the Malay Satisfaction with Life Scale. *Social Indicators Research, 92*(1), 25–33.
Tay, L., & Diener, E. (2011). Needs and subjective well-being around the world. *Journal of Personality and Social Psychology, 101*(2), 354–365.
Tellegen, A., Watson, D., & Clark, L. A. (1999). On the dimensional and hierarchical structure of affect. *Psychological Science, 10*(4), 297–303.
Tiliouine, H., Cummins, R. A., & Davern, M. (2006). Measuring wellbeing in developing countries: The case of Algeria. *Social Indicators Research, 75*(1), 1–30.
Västfjäll, D., Friman, M., Gärling, T., & Kleiner, M. (2002). The measurement of core affect: A Swedish self-report measure derived from the affect circumplex. *Scandinavian Journal of Psychology, 43*(1), 19–31.
Veenhoven, R. (1991). Is happiness relative? *Social Indicators Research, 24*, 1–34.
Veenhoven, R. (2000). The four qualities of life. *Journal of Happiness Studies, 1*, 1–39.
Veenhoven, R. (2003). Hedonism and happiness. *Journal of Happiness Studies, 4*, 437–457.
Waterman, A. S. (1990). Personal expressiveness: Philosophical and psychological foundations. *Journal of Mind and Behavior, 11*(1), 47–74.
Waterman, A. S. (1993). Two conceptions of happiness: Contrasts of personal expressiveness (eudaimonia) and hedonic enjoyment. *Journal of Personality and Social Psychology, 64*(4), 678–691.
Waterman, A. S., Schwartz, S. J., & Conti, R. (2008). The implications of two conceptions of happiness (hedonic enjoyment and eudaimonia) for the understanding of intrinsic motivation. *Journal of Happiness Studies, 9*(1), 41–79.
Waterman, A. S., Schwartz, S. J., Zamboanga, B. L., Ravert, R. D., Williams, M. K., Bede Agocha, V., et al. (2010). The questionnaire for eudaimonic well-being: Psychometric properties, demographic comparisons, and evidence of validity. *The Journal of Positive Psychology, 5*(1), 41–61.
Watson, D., Clark, L. A., & Tellegen, A. (1988). Development and validation of brief measures of positive and negative affect: The PANAS scales. *Journal of Personality and Social Psychology, 54*(6), 1063–1070.
Wells, A. (1988). Self-esteem and optimal experience. In M. Csikszentmihalyi & I. Csikszentmihalyi (Eds.), *Optimal experience* (pp. 327–341). Cambridge University Press.
Wu, C.-H., & Wu, C.-Y. (2008). Life satisfaction in persons with schizophrenia living in the community. *Social Indicators Research, 85*(3), 447–460.
Yiengprugsawan, V., Seubsman, S., Khamman, S., Lim, L. L.-Y., Sleigh, A. C., & The Thai Cohort Study Team. (2010). Personal Wellbeing Index in a national cohort of 87,134 Thai adults. *Social Indicators Research, 98*(2), 201–215.

Chapter 3
Consequences of General Happiness

Folks are usually about as happy as they make their minds up to be.

—Abraham Lincoln (https://www.xavier.edu/jesuitresource/online-resources/quote-archive1/happiness-quotes)

Behavioral Outcomes Produced by General Happiness

Happiness in life overall has many positive consequences. Research suggests that general happiness fosters better health, better work performance, better social relationships, and more positive consumption behavior (e.g., Lyubomirsky et al., 2005).

Better Health

Happy people maintain better physical health and live longer than those who are less happy (e.g., Diener & Chan, 2011; Diener et al., 2017). Happiness fosters better health because it leads to healthy behaviors, buffers against the harmful effects of stress, and positively impacts our physiology (e.g., cardiovascular and immune system) (e.g., Boehm & Kubzansky, 2012; Ong, 2010).

Consider Boehm/Kubzansky's (2012) literature review linking positive psychological wellbeing (e.g., eudaimonic wellbeing, hedonic wellbeing, optimism, and other measures of wellbeing) with cardiovascular health. The review also factored in health behaviors most relevant to cardiovascular disease (e.g., smoking, alcohol consumption, physical activity, sleep quality and quantity, and food consumption) and biological functions (e.g., cardiovascular, inflammatory, and metabolic processes). The review suggested that positive psychological wellbeing plays a significant role in protecting against cardiovascular disease, independently of traditional risk factors and ill-being. Specifically, optimism was found to reduce the risk of

D.-J. Lee, M. J. Sirgy, *Happiness in the Marketplace*, Social Indicators Research Series 64, https://doi.org/10.1007/978-3-032-04443-3_3

cardiovascular events. In general, positive psychological wellbeing was found to be positively associated with restorative health behaviors and biological function. Conversely, wellbeing seems to be inversely associated with deteriorative health behaviors and biological function.

Empirical evidence suggests that happy people engage in healthy behaviors (e.g., better diet, regular exercise, and better sleep) (e.g., Blanchflower & Oswald, 2008; Garg et al., 2007), have lower levels of stress and a stronger immune system (e.g., Cohen & Pressman, 2006; Cohen et al., 2003; Diener et al., 2017).

Better Work Performance

Happy individuals report high job performance at work (e.g., Matthews et al., 2014; Suldo et al., 2014). Happy employees are more likely to report higher levels of career satisfaction, lower turnover intentions, and higher organizational commitment (e.g., Erdogan et al., 2012). Moreover, they are likely to earn significantly higher levels of income later in life (e.g., De Neve et al., 2012).

In other words, happiness fosters better work performance. Why? First, happy employees are likely to cooperate and collaborate with others, and customers also prefer to interact with them—more so than unhappy employees. Consider the study conducted by Söderlund and Rosengren (2010). These researchers designed an experimental study to assess the impact of the service worker's display of emotions on customer satisfaction under the conditions of different levels of technical service quality. Specifically, they manipulated the display of emotions (unhappiness vs. happiness) and technical service quality (poor vs. good) in the experiment. The study findings indicate that customer satisfaction is highest when service employees express positive emotions conjoined with good service quality.

Second, happy individuals are more likely to feel energetic and interested in doing things and tend to be more curious, creative, and versatile in cognitive processing and flexible thinking (e.g., Amabile et al., 2005; Fredrickson, 2001; Hinton, 2008). Consider the following study. Amabile et al. (2005) conducted a study that explored how positive emotions relate to creativity at work. The researchers used both quantitative and qualitative longitudinal data from the daily diaries of 222 employees in seven companies to examine the positive affect-creativity relationship. The study findings indicate that positive emotions relate positively to creativity in organizations. Time-lagged analyses were able to demonstrate that positive emotions are indeed an antecedent of creative thought. Furthermore, qualitative analyses showed that positive emotions were a consequence of creative thought events, too.

Consider the literature review linking negative emotions (e.g., anxiety and depression) with poor memory and learning (Valiente et al., 2012). Specifically, the authors reviewed research findings linking situational and dispositional negative/positive emotions to academic achievement. Based on this review, the authors suggest that negative emotions play a significant role in dampening student achievement, whereas positive emotions elevate achievement.

Good Social Relationships

Research has shown that happy individuals have satisfying social relationships (e.g., Diener & Seligman, 2002; Lyubomirsky et al., 2005). In other words, happiness may lead to good social relationships. This can be explained as follows. First, positive emotions reinforce social activities and facilitate affiliation and close social interactions. Happy people tend to be more sociable (e.g., Diener & Seligman, 2002). As such, they engage in approach-oriented behaviors like meeting new people (e.g., Lucas et al., 2000), which in turn leads to good social relationships.

Second, interacting with happy individuals is rewarding. Happy individuals tend to show greater compassion, perspective taking, and sympathy for a person experiencing distress (e.g., Nelson, 2009). Thus, spending time with happy individuals is likely to make a person more positive, too. That is, interacting with happy people is likely to result in supportive and rewarding relationships. Consider the experiment conducted by Nelson (2009). Two experiments were conducted with US college students to demonstrate that affective states (positive, neutral, and negative affect) influence cross-cultural empathy. Subjects read about a person who experienced distress and evaluated the person under two conditions: taking on a perspective consistent versus inconsistent with US norms. Subjects in the positive affect condition exhibited greater perspective taking and feelings of compassion and sympathy for the dissimilar target (compared to subjects in the neutral and negative affect conditions).

Third, happy individuals tend to be cooperative and engage in pro-social behaviors (e.g., Carnevale, 2008; Carlson et al., 1988). Also, evidence suggests that interacting with happy people tends to reduce relationship conflict (e.g., Kansky et al., 2016), making the relationship last longer.

Positive Consumption Behavior

Happiness is associated with high levels of self-control and long-term perspective in consumption. Why? First, happy individuals are likely to exert more self-control in their spending (e.g., Ifcher & Zarghamee, 2011). That is, they tend to exercise self-control regarding their spending in the present and save more for the future. Initial empirical evidence of this phenomenon comes from the General Social Survey, which in three waves measured happiness ("Taken all together, how would you say things are these days - would you say that you are very happy, pretty happy, or not too happy?") and time preference (agreement or disagreement with the statement, "Nowadays, a person has to live pretty much for today and let tomorrow take care of itself"). The survey data indicate that happier respondents were less likely to agree with the "live for today" statement than were less happy respondents.

In other words, happy individuals tend to embrace a long-term perspective in consumption. Specifically, they seem to be willing to consider the long-term implications of decisions taken in the present, leading to better decisions for themselves and society at large (cf. Guven, 2012). In other words, happy consumers are less likely to engage in frequent impulsive purchases. They tend to forego smaller short-term benefits to receive larger benefits in the future.

Furthermore, happy consumers are more likely to engage in pro-social activities. They are likely to donate their money to charity, help strangers, and engage in volunteer activities (e.g., Aknin et al., 2012, 2013; Oishi et al., 2007). When people are in a positive mood, they tend to help others, and helping others in turn fosters future happiness.

Summary and Conclusion

We described selected research showing how general happiness leads to certain positive outcomes: better health, better work performance, good social relationships, and positive consumption behavior. First, happiness fosters better health because it leads to healthy behaviors, buffers against the harmful effects of stress, and positively impacts our physiology (e.g., cardiovascular and immune system).

Second, happiness plays a major role in increased job satisfaction and work performance. Specifically, research indicates that happy employees are more likely to report higher levels of work performance, job (and career) satisfaction, organizational commitment, and lower levels of turnover intentions. Research also shows that happy individuals report high academic performance, cognitive flexibility, and critical thinking.

Third, much evidence suggests that happiness facilitates good social relationships. Happiness facilitates approach-oriented behaviors and social interactions, leading to cooperative and prosocial behaviors, while reducing relationship conflict. The result is facilitating long-lasting relationships. Research also found that happy people tend to be more sociable, engage in approach-oriented behaviors, and show greater compassion, perspective taking, and sympathy for others experiencing distress. Moreover, research also found that interacting with happy people tends to reduce relationship conflict.

Fourth, many studies demonstrate that happiness fosters positive consumption behaviors. Happy individuals are likely to exert more self-control in their spending, employ a long-term perspective in their marketplace decision-making, and are less likely to engage in impulsive purchases. They also engage in pro-social activities (e.g., donation, helping). See Table 3.1 for a summary of this research.

As such, the reader should conclude that general happiness is indeed an important area of study because it leads to many positive behavioral outcomes.

Table 3.1 Consequences of general happiness

Dimension	Description
Better health	Happiness protects individuals from the harmful effects of stress. Happiness leads to healthy behavior. Happiness positively impacts physiology (e.g., cardiovascular and immune system).
Better work performance	Happiness leads to high job satisfaction and high performance. Happy employees are more likely to report lower turnover intentions, higher organizational commitment, and higher income. Happiness leads to high academic performance. Happiness leads to energetic academic curiosity, cognitive flexibility, and critical thinking, which contribute to high academic performance.
Good social relationship	Happiness facilitates approach-oriented behaviors and social interactions. Happiness leads to cooperative and prosocial behaviors. Happiness reduces relationship conflict and makes the relationship lasting.
Positive consumption behaviors	Happiness results in a high level of self-control in spending (e.g., increase in planned purchases). Happiness leads to long-term perspective in consumption (e.g., reduced impulsive buying). Happiness facilitates pro-social spending.

References

Aknin, L. B., Dunn, E. W., & Norton, M. I. (2012). Happiness runs in a circular motion: Evidence for a positive feedback loop between prosocial spending and happiness. *Journal of Happiness Studies, 13*(2), 347–355.

Aknin, L. B., Barrington-Leigh, C. P., Dunn, E. W., Helliwell, J. F., Burns, J., Biswas-Diener, R., et al. (2013). Prosocial spending and well-being: Cross-cultural evidence for a psychological universal. *Journal of Personality and Social Psychology, 104*(4), 635–652.

Amabile, T. M., Barsade, S. G., Mueller, J. S., & Staw, B. M. (2005). Affect and creativity at work. *Administrative Science Quarterly, 50*(3), 367–403.

Blanchflower, D. G., & Oswald, A. J. (2008). Hypertension and happiness across nations. *Journal of Health Economics, 27*(2), 218–233.

Boehm, J. K., & Kubzansky, L. D. (2012). The heart's content: The association between positive psychological well-being and cardiovascular health. *Psychological Bulletin, 138*(4), 655–691.

Carlson, M., Charlin, V., & Miller, N. (1988). Positive mood and helping behavior: A test of six hypotheses. *Journal of Personality and Social Psychology, 55*(2), 211–229.

Carnevale, P. J. (2008). Positive affect and decision frame in negotiation. *Group Decision and Negotiation, 17*(1), 51–63.

Cohen, S., & Pressman, S. D. (2006). Positive affect and health. *Current Directions in Psychological Science, 15*(3), 122–125.

Cohen, S., Doyle, W. J., Turner, R. B., Alper, C. M., & Skoner, D. P. (2003). Emotional style and susceptibility to the common cold. *Psychosomatic Medicine, 65*(4), 652–657.

De Neve, J. E., Christakis, N. A., Fowler, J. H., & Frey, B. S. (2012). Genes, economics, and happiness. *Journal of Neuroscience, Psychology, and Economics, 5*(4), 193–211.

Diener, E., & Chan, M. Y. (2011). Happy people live longer: Subjective well-being contributes to health and longevity. *Applied Psychology: Health and Wellbeing, 3*(1), 1–43.

Diener, E., & Seligman, M. E. P. (2002). Very happy people. *Psychological Science, 13*(1), 81–84.

Diener, E., Pressman, S. D., Hunter, J., & Delgadillo-Chase, D. (2017). If, why, and when subjective well-being influences health, and future needed research. *Applied Psychology: Health and Wellbeing, 9*(2), 133–167.

Erdogan, B., Bauer, T. N., Truxillo, D. M., & Mansfield, L. R. (2012). Whistle while you work: A review of the life satisfaction literature. *Journal of Management, 38*(4), 1038–1083.

Fredrickson, B. L. (2001). The role of positive emotions in positive psychology: The broaden-and-build theory of positive emotions. *American Psychologist, 56*(3), 218–226.

Garg, N., Wansink, B., & Inman, J. J. (2007). The influence of incidental affect on consumers' food intake. *Journal of Marketing, 71*(1), 194–206.

Guven, C. (2012). Reversing the question: Does happiness affect consumption and savings behavior? *Journal of Economic Psychology, 33*(4), 701–717.

Hinton, C., Miyamoto, K., & Della-Chiesa, B. (2008). Brain research, learning and emotions: Implications for education research, policy and practice 1. *European Journal of Education, 43*(1), 87–103.

Ifcher, J., & Zarghamee, H. (2011). Happiness and time preference: The effect of positive affect in a random-assignment experiment. *American Economic Review, 101*(7), 3109–3129.

Kansky, J., Allen, J. P., & Diener, E. (2016). Early adolescent affect predicts later life outcomes. *Applied Psychology: Health and Well-being, 8*(2), 192–212.

Lucas, R. E., Diener, E., Grob, A., Suh, E. M., & Shao, L. (2000). Cross-cultural evidence for the fundamental features of extraversion. *Journal of Personality and Social Psychology, 79*(3), 452–468.

Lyubomirsky, S., King, L., & Diener, E. (2005). The benefits of frequent positive affect: Does happiness lead to success? *Psychological Bulletin, 131*(6), 803–855.

Matthews, R. A., Wayne, J. H., & Ford, M. T. (2014). A work–family conflict/subjective well-being process model: A test of competing theories of longitudinal effects. *Journal of Applied Psychology, 99*(6), 1173–1187.

Nelson, D. W. (2009). Feeling good and open-minded: The impact of positive affect on cross cultural empathic responding. *The Journal of Positive Psychology, 4*(1), 53–63.

Oishi, S., Diener, E., & Lucas, R. E. (2007). The optimum level of well-being: Can people be too happy? *Perspectives on Psychological Science, 2*(4), 346–360.

Ong, A. D. (2010). Pathways linking positive emotion and health in later life. *Current Directions in Psychological Science, 19*(6), 358–362.

Söderlund, M., & Rosengren, S. (2010). The happy versus unhappy service worker in the service encounter: Assessing the impact on customer satisfaction. *Journal of Retailing and Consumer Services, 17*(2), 161–169.

Suldo, S. M., Gormley, M. J., DuPaul, G. J., & Anderson-Butcher, D. (2014). The impact of school mental health on student and school-level academic outcomes: Current status of the research and future directions. *School Mental Health, 6*(2), 84–98.

Valiente, C., Swanson, J., & Eisenberg, N. (2012). Linking students' emotions and academic achievement: When and why emotions matter. *Child Development Perspectives, 6*(2), 129–135.

Chapter 4
Material Wellbeing

The very nature of materiality is entanglement. Matter itself is always already open to, or rather entangled with, the Other. The intra-actively emergent parts of phenomena are constituted.

—Karen Barad (https://www.goodreads.com/quotes/7443810-the-very-nature-of-materiality-is-an-entanglement-matter-itself#:~:text=The%20very%20nature%20of%20materiality%20is%20an%20entanglement.,parts%22%20of%20phenomena%20are%20coconstituted)

Definitions and Metrics of Material Wellbeing

Material wellbeing refers to satisfaction with various aspects of material life. The material life domain houses emotional reactions related to household income, savings, investment, material possessions, and other material resources related to personal wealth (Sirgy, 2019). Specifically, it can be viewed in terms of satisfaction with the economic situations, satisfaction with one's own and family financial situation, satisfaction with income adequacy, feelings of financial security, aggregate feelings about major goods and services, satisfaction with standard of living, aspirations and attainment of material goods, and aggregate satisfaction with marketplace activities (Sirgy, 2018, 2021a, b). We will discuss these definitions and corresponding metrics in the sections below.

Satisfaction with the Economic Situation

Material wellbeing is defined in terms of satisfaction with a range of economic concerns such as government's handling of the economy, taxes, the cost of necessities, household income, pay and fringe benefits from one's job, financial security,

D.-J. Lee, M. J. Sirgy, *Happiness in the Marketplace*, Social Indicators Research Series 64, https://doi.org/10.1007/978-3-032-04443-3_4

standard of living, and agreement within the family regarding how money should be spent (Andrews & Withey, 1976).

Andrews and Withey (1976) were the first to develop metrics related to this definition of material wellbeing. This construct reflects consumer feelings about economic concerns such as satisfaction with the economic situation, financial satisfaction, income adequacy, and feelings of financial security. Respondents are prompted to answer a few questions about the country's economic situation and their own financial situation. "How do you feel about the following?"

- What is the government doing about the economy—jobs, prices, profits.
- The taxes you pay—mean the local, state, and national taxes all together.
- What you have to pay for necessities such as food, housing, and clothing.
- The income you (and your family) have.
- The pay and fringe benefits you get, and the security of your job.
- How secure you are financially.
- Your standard of living—the things you have like housing, car, furniture, recreation, and the like.
- How well your family agrees on how the family income should be spent.

Response scale: Responses were captured on 7-point affect rating scales (1 = Terrible, 2 = Unhappy, 3 = Mostly Dissatisfied, 4 = Mixed, 5 = Mostly Satisfied, 6 = Pleased, and 7 = Delighted).

Financial Situation

Material wellbeing is conceptualized as satisfaction of one's financial situation (e.g., Diener et al., 1993; Lane, 1991; Plagnol & Easterlin, 2008; Veenhoven, 1991; Vera-Toscano et al., 2006; Xiao et al., 2009).

An example of a metric is a simple single survey item such as "Indicate how satisfied or dissatisfied you are with your financial situation: from 1 = Very dissatisfied to 5 = Very satisfied" (Xiao et al., 2009).

Income Adequacy

Material wellbeing is also conceptualized as *income adequacy* or the extent to which one's income is adequate for one's needs.

The perceived adequacy of income is typically measured by asking respondents whether their current level of income is sufficient to cover their expenses, allowing them to indicate whether it is enough with money left over, just enough, no difficulty, some difficulty, and much difficulty (Chan et al., 2002).

A variation of this measure is: "Thinking of your household's total monthly income, is your household able to make ends meet? 1 = With great difficulty, 2 =

With difficulty, 3 = With some difficulty, 4 = Fairly easily; 5 = Easily; and 6 = Very easily" (Popova & Pishniak, 2017).

The perceived adequacy of income has also been measured by asking about material hardship. For example, Lewin and Stier (2017) used a material hardship measure using three sets of questions capturing hardship in providing necessities for oneself and one's family. Respondents are asked whether during the previous 12 months financial difficulties had forced them to forgo things such as a hot meal every day, inviting family members or friends home for meals, buying clothes or shoes, heating or cooling of their dwelling, house repairs, paying household bills, and whether any utilities were disconnected.

It should be noted that it is the *perceived* income adequacy that is likely to influence the sense of material wellbeing rather than the *actual* amount of income (Cracolici et al., 2014; Grable et al., 2013). Using data from an economically and racially diverse sample, Grable et al. (2013) found that perceived income adequacy is associated with financial satisfaction.

Perceived Financial Security

Furthermore, material wellbeing is conceptualized as perceived financial security. Perceived financial security is measured using the Money Index (Andrews & Withey, 1976), the In-Charge Financial Distress/Financial Wellbeing Scale (Prawitz et al., 2006), and financial wellbeing (Bruggen et al., 2017; Netemeyer et al., 2018).

Andrews and Withey (1976) measured individual feelings of financial security using their *Money Index*. This index involves survey items related to three categories: (1) feelings about how secure they are financially, (2) feelings about how secure they are with their family incomes, and (3) feelings of security regarding how well-off they think they are financially. Responses were captured on 7-point affect rating scales (1 = Terrible, 2 = Unhappy, 3 = Mostly Dissatisfied, 4 = Mixed, 5 = Mostly Satisfied, 6 = Pleased, and 7 = Delighted).

The *In-Charge Financial Distress/Financial Wellbeing Scale* (Prawitz et al., 2006) involves eight items in which responses are recorded on a 10-point scale (1 = no confidence, 10 = high confidence) capturing respondents perceived level of financial security (e.g., How confident are you that you could find the money to pay for a financial emergency that costs about $1,000?). The average of the eight items is treated as each respondent's financial security score, and the higher the score, means greater the financial security.

Additionally, Bruggen et al. (2017) defined *financial wellbeing* as the perception of being able to sustain current and anticipated desired living standard and financial freedom (p. 229). Netemeyer et al. (2018) defined perceived financial wellbeing in terms of expected future financial security and current money management stress.

Aggregate Satisfaction with Marketplace Activities

Material wellbeing is defined as an aggregation of evaluations of related marketplace activities. Specifically, Meadow and Sirgy (2008) conceptualized the material life domain in terms of: (1) obtained goods and services, (2) interactions with retail personnel, and (3) interactions with goods and service institutions. Specifically, 11 consumer subdomains were identified, and within each, the retail institutions that consumers interface with were also identified. These are:

1. Food (retail institutions, such as eating and drinking establishments, take-home food outlets).
2. Housing (retail institutions, such as real estate agencies, people/firms who rent, hotel/motel establishments).
3. Household operations (retail institutions, such as utilities, household repair facilities, clothes care facilities).
4. Household furnishing (retail institutions, such as appliance outlets, department stores/furniture outlets, hardware outlets, gift shops).
5. Clothing and accessories (retail institutions, such as clothing stores, shoe stores, jewelry stores).
6. Personal care (retail institutions, such as hair styling facilities, health spas).
7. Medical care (retail institutions, such as hospitals, doctors/dentists, drug stores, counseling services).
8. Recreation (retail institutions, such as travel agencies, sporting goods outlets, establishments selling reading materials, spectator admission facilities, hobby shops).
9. Transportation (retail institutions, such as automobile service outlets, auto dealers, airlines, bus services, train services, taxi services).
10. Education (retail institutions, such as colleges and trade schools).
11. Other (retail institutions, such as insurance services, legal services, banking services).

Satisfaction with the Standard of Living

Material wellbeing is conceptualized as *satisfaction with standard of living*. Yu et al. (2020) measured satisfaction with standard of living in terms of individual's feelings about the things they own, their standard of living, and their financial situation overall on 5-point semantic differential scales (unhappy/happy, bad/good, miserable/enthusiastic, frustrated/satisfied, disappointed/realized, and very poor/wealthy). An average composite score was then computed.

Nakano et al. (1995) defined standard of living in terms of material possessions and the extent to which physical needs are met. Their instrument involved two questions: (1) How do you feel about your standard of living—the things you have like housing, car, furniture, recreation, and the like? and (2) How do you feel about the extent to which your physical needs are met? Responses were captured on 5- point satisfaction rating scales varying from 1 = very dissatisfied to 5 = very satisfied.

Bohnke (2008) conceptualized standard of living as involving four dimensions: problems with accommodation, affordability of basic goods, making ends meet, and solvency problems.[1] Here is more information about these dimensions and their metrics.

1. Problems with accommodation (e.g., Do you have any of the following problems with your accommodation? Shortage of space, rot in windows/doors/flats, damp/leaks, lack of indoor flushing toilet? [Yes]).
2. Affordability of basic goods (There are some things that many people cannot afford, even if they would like them: keep home adequately warm, holiday, furniture, meal with meat, clothes, having friends or family for a drink, car, home computer, washing machine? [Cannot afford it]).
3. Making ends meet (A household may have different sources of income and more than one household member may contribute to it. Thinking of your household's total monthly income, is your household able to make ends meet? [With great difficulty/with difficulty]).
4. Solvency problems (Has your household been in arrears at any time during the past 12 months, that is, unable to pay as scheduled any of the following? Rent or mortgage payment for accommodation, utility bills such as electricity, water, gas, etc. [Yes]).

Aggregate Feelings About Major Goods and Services

Material wellbeing is conceptualized as *aggregate feelings about major goods and services* consumers use. Andrews and Withey (1976) measured this construct through their *Consumer Index.* This index involves a set of survey items capturing respondents' feelings about transportation and access to work and shopping, the medical services in their area, and the goods and services they can get when they buy in their area (e.g., food, appliances and clothes).

Similarly, Smits and Steendijk (2015) developed the *International Wealth Index* (IWI) related to a set of products consumers own. Households with an IWI value of 100 have a TV, fridge, phone, car, a house with piped drinking water, electricity, a flush toilet, good quality floor material, and 3+ rooms. Households with a value of 0, on the other extreme, own none of the above items or have poor quality items.

[1] The standard of living index is calculated by summing up individual items of problem areas. Individuals with few problems are considered to have high standard of living.

Aspirations and Attainment of Material Goods

Material wellbeing involves the gap between aspirations and actual attainment of material goods. The greater the gap the lower the material wellbeing (Plagnol & Easterlin, 2008). The measurement items of the aspirations-attainments measure are as follows.

(1) We often hear people talk about what they want out of life. Here are several different things. (HAND RESPONDENT CARD). When you think of the good life—the life you'd like to have, which of the things on this list, if any, are part of that good life as far as you personally are concerned?
(2) Now, would you go down that list and call off all the things you now have?

- A home you own
- A yard and lawn
- A car
- A second car
- A vacation home
- A swimming pool
- Travel abroad
- A color TV set
- A second color TV set
- Really nice clothes
- A lot of money

Answers to Question 1 highlight the individual's aspirations; those to Question 2, their attainments. The excess of aspirations over attainments (the gap) is the extent to which aspirations are unfulfilled (Plagnol & Easterlin, 2008).

Material Wellbeing and Overall Happiness

Figure 4.1 should help the reader see the big picture of the links between overall happiness, the most salient constructs of material wellbeing, and the factors influencing material wellbeing.

Money Resources and Overall Happiness

In discussing the influence of money resources on overall happiness, we highlight two tracks of research, namely (1) income and overall happiness, and (2) the nature of the positive association between income and subjective wellbeing.

For the first track (*income and overall happiness*), research has demonstrated that satisfaction with material life contributes to life satisfaction, and dissatisfaction

Fig. 4.1 Conceptual boundaries of material wellbeing

with money is associated with dissatisfaction with life. Andrews and Withey (1976) found the Money Index (a measure of material wellbeing) to be a significant and strong predictor of life satisfaction. Studies found that overall life satisfaction is positively and significantly influenced by the amount of income (e.g., Veenhoven, 1991), perceived income adequacy (e.g., Walker et al., 1990), changes in income (e.g., Schyns, 2001), and positive financial behaviors as saving and planned spending (e.g., Xiao et al., 2009). Using consumer financial narratives, several large-scale surveys, and two experiments, Netemeyer et al. (2018) were able to demonstrate that perceived financial wellbeing (conceptualized in terms of current money management stress and expected future financial security) plays a significant role in subjective wellbeing. That is, studies found that income is positively correlated with subjective wellbeing (e.g., Frank, 2012; Hagerty & Veenhoven, 2003; Veenhoven, 1991).

We believe that income positively contributes to overall happiness for two reasons. First, income is a material resource that provides consumers with numerous beneficial outcomes, including good physical health, good mental health, and low stress (e.g., Furnée et al., 2011; Lynch et al., 2000; Brady & Matthews, 2002). Second, income is a resource that buffers against negative life events or life hassles and works to obtain goods and services for consumer need fulfilment (e.g., Diener et al., 2013; Tay & Diener, 2011).

Concerning the second track (*positive association between income and subjective wellbeing*), we highlight two major points. First, studies found that the strength of the association between income and subjective wellbeing depends on the type of wellbeing measure. Research has shown that income has a stronger association with life satisfaction than with affective wellbeing measures (e.g., Diener et al., 2010a, b). This is because income softens life adversities by providing physiological protection, while positive feeling is strongly associated with fulfillment of psychological needs (Diener et al., 2010a, b). That is, although increased income can soften life adversities, it often does not buy affective wellbeing (e.g., Kahneman & Deaton, 2010; Diener & Biswas-Diener, 2002). Consumers often evaluate their life satisfaction based on the amount of income and financial situation, but they evaluate their affective wellbeing based on what the person is doing and who the person was with (e.g., Diener et al., 2010a, b; Tay & Diener 2011; Lyubomirsky et al., 2005). Thus, income has a stronger association with life satisfaction than with affective wellbeing.

Second, evidence suggests that income has a declining marginal effect on subjective wellbeing. Income is positively correlated with life satisfaction and happiness by providing necessities and physiological protection. Yet, the strength of the relationship wanes as income rises beyond a certain point (Diener & Biswas-Diener, 2002; Deaton, 2008; Diener et al., 2010a, b; Howell & Howell, 2008). For example, Kahneman and Deaton (2010) managed to demonstrate that in the United States, there might be an income threshold for emotional wellbeing around US$75,000, after which emotional wellbeing does not increase. In a worldwide sample of over 1.7 million respondents, Jebb et al. (2018) were able to demonstrate that despite substantial variation across regions, higher incomes stopped contributing to more positive life evaluations at $95,000, and to higher emotional wellbeing at $60,000 to $75,000.

In summary, the non-comparative income has a positive association with life satisfaction with a certain saturation point. Yet, it should be noted that income and happiness have only a weak association under certain conditions. First, income and happiness have only a weak association because consumers evaluate their income *relatively* (i.e., the *upward social comparison* effect). Specifically, consumers evaluate their income through upward social comparisons (Ferrer-i-Carbonell, 2005), and this relative income has a stronger effect on happiness than absolute income (Clark et al., 2008). Social comparison weakens the association between income and happiness.

Second, income and happiness have only a weak association because consumers have unequal income and engage in comparative evaluations (referred to as the *income distribution inequity* effect). Even when income or national GDP does increase, consumers are less happy because the national income may not be distributed to individual consumers (Diener et al., 2010a, b), or engage in social comparisons (Boyce et al., 2010). Income of the reference group plays an important role in material wellbeing (Ferrer-i-Carbonell, 2005). In other words, the perception of inequity in income distribution weakens the association between income and happiness over time.

Time Resources and Overall Happiness

Time is also an important resource for overall happiness. Having more spare time is associated with greater happiness and life satisfaction, even after controlling for income (Kasser and Sheldon, 2009). Studies found that those who value time over money report greater happiness (Hershfield et al., 2016; Whillans et al., 2016).

Time is a valuable resource that is closely related to the self in that individuals view their time spending as more reflective of who they are as a person than they do their monetary spending (Gino & Mogilner, 2014; Mogilner & Aaker, 2009). For example, individuals view donations of time as more moral and self-expressive than donations of money (Reed et al., 2007). Time is a valuable and limited resource important for happiness (Carstensen et al., 1999). When time is perceived as limited, it is important to use time resources efficiently and effectively for happiness.

Consumers experience increased happiness by spending their limited time on connecting with others (Carstensen et al., 1999; Mogilner, 2010), helping others (Whillans et al., 2016), and engaging in active leisure activities (Lathia et al., 2017). In contrast, lack of time in everyday life is associated with increased stress, loss of control, and reduced mental health (Strazdins et al., 2016).

To sum up, both income and time are valuable material resources for happiness. Consumers can use their consumption activities (spending, possession, and experiences) to enhance material happiness. It is not ownership of these resources that enhances material happiness but their effective use in consumption activities, which in turn contributes to material happiness.

Material Consumption and Overall Happiness

Material consumption can contribute to happiness. Consumption is a better measure than income in measuring material living standards (Headey et al., 2008). Shifting the focus from income to consumption, many studies have examined the relationship between consumption and happiness (Dumludag, 2015; Gokdemir, 2015; Headey et al., 2008; Noll & Weick, 2015; Zhang & Xiong, 2015). The study findings are illuminating. First, the total consumption amount is significantly associated with subjective wellbeing. The degree of association depends on the measure of subjective wellbeing (Tsurumi et al., 2021). Specifically, total consumption contributes to life satisfaction (prudential happiness) and eudaimonia (perfectionist happiness) but no more than a certain threshold for hedonic wellbeing. Increased consumption contributes to meeting their basic needs (e.g., food, safety, health, and comfortable housing) up to a point and thus is more likely to lead to enhanced subjective wellbeing regardless of social comparisons. In an empirical analysis on the relationship between consumption expenditures and subjective wellbeing, Noll and Weick (2015) found that larger consumption expenditures positively correlated with increasing levels of life satisfaction, and that voluntary consumption abstinence does not significantly reduce life satisfaction.

Second, relative consumption is significantly associated with subjective wellbeing. Relative consumption refers to the perceived level and quality of one's consumption relative to that of significant others. Those who can consume at, or above, the same level as their peers tend to feel more satisfied than those who cannot. In other words, relative deprivation is negatively associated with subjective wellbeing, especially for conspicuous products and experiences (MacDonald & Douthitt, 1992; Fafchamps & Shilpi, 2008; Guillen-Royo, 2011). Evidence suggests that consumers' expenditure on conspicuous products relative to those of other households significantly influences life satisfaction (Wu, 2020).

Third, the strength of the association between total consumption amount and subjective wellbeing is high for experiential consumption. Experiential consumption contributes to consumer happiness through the mediating effects of positive self-concept and social satisfaction (De Leire & Kalil, 2010; Nicolao et al., 2009; Noll & Weick, 2015; Thomas & Millar, 2013; Van Boven & Gilovich, 2003). Increased consumption of basic material goods (e.g., food and housing) does enhance individual happiness by alleviating material hardship or making life easier. The effect of material product consumption on subjective wellbeing diminishes with higher levels of material wellbeing. In other words, material product consumption has a diminishing marginal utility for consumer happiness (Dolan et al., 2008). Thus, the marginal effect of material consumption tends to be lower than that of experiential consumption on all subjective wellbeing measures (Tsurumi et al., 2021).

Fourth, the strength of positive association between material product consumption and subjective wellbeing is high for conspicuous products. This is because the use of conspicuous products can enhance a positive self-concept that contributes to individual happiness and life satisfaction (Perez-Truglia, 2013; Wu, 2020). For example, Hudders and Pandelaere (2012) demonstrated that luxury consumption leads to an enhanced positive mood, a reduced negative mood, and an increased level of satisfaction with life.

Yet, it should be noted that consumer's high materialism is associated with lower life satisfaction (Richins & Dawson, 1992), reduced happiness (Belk, 1985; Dittmar & Kapur, 2011), decreased psychological need satisfaction (Kashdan & Breen, 2007), and increased levels of depression and anxiety (Kasser & Ryan, 1993). When consumers are highly materialistic, consumers are less likely to experience intrinsic benefits and positive affect with the products they own and use (Kasser & Ahuvia, 2002). They tend to be more concerned about their financial constraints (Dittmar et al., 2014) and engage in frequent unrealistic social comparisons (Sirgy, 1998). Yet, materialism may not be detrimental for consumer wellbeing if materialism involves self-signaling (e.g., purchase of material products for their true self-expression, which reflects intrinsic motivation) instead of other signaling (i.e., purchase of material products to make a good impression on others which reflects extrinsic motivation) (Shrum et al., 2013).

Fifth, the strength of the association between consumption and subjective wellbeing is high for consumption that is involved with others (e.g., relational products consumed along with other people, experiences with social interactions, pro-social spending). This is because increased use of relational products and pro-social spending facilitates social sharing and provides consumers with a feeling of relatedness that contributes to consumer happiness. In addition, social sharing about the owned products allows consumers to savor their positive experiences (Lyubomirsky et al., 2006) and facilitates positive social interactions and social satisfactions (Schnebelen & Bruhn, 2018). Prosocial spending is also more likely to lead to consumer happiness when acts of generosity facilitate social connection with others (e.g., taking a friend out for dinner instead of giving a gift coupon) (Aknin et al., 2013). In other words, the positive effect of pro-social spending on consumer happiness is higher when their pro-social spending provides them with opportunities to connect with other people and their pro-social spending provides them with satisfaction of relatedness need (Aknin et al., 2013).

Factors Influencing Material Wellbeing

Based on extant research in material wellbeing we will describe evidence related to factors influencing this construct: personal factors, psychological factors, and environmental factors.

Demographic Factors

Research has shown that demographic factors such as age, family structure, education, employment, and financial resources play a significant role in determining material wellbeing.

Age

For *age*, evidence suggests a curvilinear relationship. Specifically, younger and older individuals seem to be more satisfied with their material life than those in the middle-aged group. The effect of age on material wellbeing is U-shaped in that material wellbeing bottoms out at mid-age (e.g., Blanchflower & Oswald, 2000; Hayo & Seifert, 2003). For example, a study conducted by Carcolici et al. (2014) shows that financial wellbeing was low for middle-aged people because of their low income in their early-stage career and the high cost of raising children.

Financial wellbeing increases after the mid-ages, which is consistent with financial development as financial capital improves and savings accrues (Collins & Urban, 2021). Older adults, despite their low income, tend to report higher levels of financial satisfaction than younger adults because of greater assets and low debt compared to their younger counterparts (Hansen et al., 2008).

Family Structure

Research has demonstrated that *family structure* exerts influence on financial wellbeing (of the family) (Cracolici et al., 2014). Financial wellbeing is high for couples with no children because of the high cost of raising children. Conversely, financial wellbeing is low for couples with many children and those who are divorced and widowed (cf. Hayo & Seifert, 2003). Similarly, Malone et al. (2010) found that women in non-traditional families (single mothers, cohabitors, and stepfamilies) expressed worries about their financial future than women in first marriages.

Education

Evidence also suggests a positive association between *education* and material wellbeing (Hayo & Seifert, 2003; Malone et al., 2010). Education is an important skill that helps the individual succeed in the workforce, thus providing the individual with financial resources. As such, higher education contributes to material wellbeing.

Unemployment

Research also suggests a strong association between *unemployment* and material wellbeing (Hayo & Seifert, 2003). Unemployment deprives the individual of an income that plays an important role in satisfaction with material life. Good employment provides consumers with financial resources for material wellbeing.

Financial Resources

Finally, we have *financial resources* (income and wealth) also playing a significant role in determining material wellbeing. That is, evidence suggests that financial resources are positively associated with material wellbeing. Let's delve a little into this relationship. First, research shows that income is positively associated with financial satisfaction (Hsieh, 2004; Seghieri et al., 2006), economic wellbeing (Hayo & Seifert, 2003), and subjective wellbeing (Zuzanek, 2013). In addition to income, wealth and consumption are also strongly associated with material wellbeing. Using data from a national survey of women, Malone et al. (2010) provided evidence that women with higher incomes had more positive perceptions of their financial situation.

Second, research has demonstrated that accumulated wealth (e.g., high financial assets and low debt) is positively associated with financial satisfaction (Hsieh, 2004), satisfaction with financial life (Nickerson et al., 2003, 2007), and life satisfaction (Nickerson et al., 2003, 2007). Specifically, a broad measure of wealth and consumption (i.e., housing, business assets, equity and cash investments, bank accounts, accumulated pension holdings, vehicles and collectibles, housing debt, credit cards, student debt, and personal debt, as well as food expenditure) is a stronger predictor of life satisfaction than income alone (Headey et al., 2008). These results support the notion that income, wealth, and consumption have a considerable influence on both satisfaction with the standard of living and life satisfaction.

Third, the effect of income on subjective wellbeing seems to be moderated by materialism (captured through financial aspirations). The positive effect of income on subjective wellbeing seems to hold mostly for individuals who are less materialistic and without too high financial aspirations (Nickerson et al., 2003, 2007; Kasser & Ryan, 1993).

Behavioral Factors

Research has demonstrated that several behavioral factors are associated with material wellbeing, namely extraversion, neuroticism, materialism, financial aspirations, financial literacy, positive financial behavior, and compulsive buying behavior.

Extraversion and Neuroticism

Extraversion (*neuroticism*) has a positive (negative) influence on perception of material wellbeing, which in turn influences subjective wellbeing. This suggests that personality can influence subjective wellbeing through the mediating effects of material wellbeing. Using data from the World Values Survey, Ng (2015) was able to demonstrate that personality traits such as extraversion and neuroticism influence subjective wellbeing through the mediation effects of material concerns (e.g., satisfaction with financial situation, satisfaction with standard of living). Individuals rated high on extraversion are satisfied with their financial situation and standard of living because they socialize with others, and such sociability can play an important role in job performance and financial security (Roberts et al., 2003). In contrast, individuals high on neuroticism are less likely to be satisfied with their jobs and less likely to feel financially secure. That is, neurotics are likely to be less satisfied with their financial situation than non-neurotics (Ng, 2015; Sirgy, 2018).

Materialism

Materialism has been defined in various ways: as a focus on socioeconomic and physical security (Inglehart, 1977); as the combined personality traits of envy, non-generosity, and possessiveness (Belk, 1985); and as the belief that the consumption of tangible objects is an important life goal, signals success, and leads to happiness (Richins, 2004; Richins & Dawson, 1992). Most simply, materialism is the "importance ascribed to the ownership and acquisition of material goods in achieving major life goals or desired states" (Richins, 2004, p. 210).

A popular measure of materialism is the Materialism Value Scale (MVS; Richins & Dawson, 1992; Richins, 2004). The MVS is composed of subscales reflecting three components. First, *acquisition centrality* refers to a consumer's belief that having material items is important (e.g., "I put less emphasis on material things than most people I know." reverse-scored). Second, the *pursuit of happiness through acquisition* reflects a belief that possessions can increase life satisfaction and welbeing (e.g., "My life would be better if I owned certain things I don't have."). Third, *possession-defined success* gauges a person's tendency to judge accomplishments (the self's and others') by the number and prestige of accumulated possessions (e.g., "I admire people who own expensive homes, cars, and clothes.").

What are some key patterns of materialistic people's behavior? Many of the patterns of materialistic people's behavior can be explained by *escape theory* that posits that individuals seek to free themselves from aversive states of self-awareness through acquisition and possessions of materials goods (Donnelly et al., 2016). That is, materialistic individuals who feel dissatisfied with their standard of living cope with failure and life stressors by immersing themselves in shopping, buying, and other marketplace experiences.

Based on escape theory, materialistic consumers cope with life stressors and strains in different ways. First, materialistic people set expectations for their standard of living based on ideals (Sirgy, 1998; Sirgy et al., 2013) and frequently engage in upward social comparisons. These upward social comparisons result in feelings of deprivation (Kim et al., 2017). As such, materialists become disappointed with their income and standard of living (e.g., Ahuvia & Wong, 1995; Richins & Dawson, 1992; Sirgy et al., 2013).

Second, materialists tend to see themselves as inadequate and blame themselves for personal shortcomings. Materialism is linked to low self-esteem (e.g., Richins & Dawson, 1992; Ruvio et al., 2014). They are prone to feeling insecure and may seek to compensate for such insecurity through material goods (e.g., "I want to buy things that make me feel more like the person I want to be.") (e.g., Dittmar et al., 2007; Richins, 2011; Rindfleisch et al., 2009).

Third, materialists tend to be highly concerned with how others perceive them (e.g., Christopher et al., 2007) and purchase things that are highly visible to others to symbolize their high status. Materialism is negatively correlated with a desire to feel unique (e.g., Fitzmaurice & Comegys, 2006; Schroeder & Dugal, 1995). Yet, the values of materialistic consumers tend to focus on promoting the self and less so on bolstering the welfare of other people or society at large (Donnelly et al., 2016).

Fourth, materialism is associated with indicators of negative emotions such as depression (e.g., Burroughs & Rindfleisch, 2002; Claes et al., 2010; Kashdan & Breen, 2007), as well as lack of self-worth (e.g., Frost et al., 2007). Evidence also suggests that materialists feel less positive (and more negative) about their social relationships (e.g., Donnelly et al., 2016).

Fifth, materialists lack creativity and flexible thinking; they focus on immediate thoughts and sensations (instead of abstract concepts); and pursue proximal (instead of distal) goals (e.g., Baumeister, 1990). Because materialists have a narrow mental focus on the present (without adequate consideration of future consequences), they become more predisposed to lack restraint and act impulsively in the marketplace (e.g., Donnelly et al., 2016).

As such, it can be said that consumer *materialism* has a negative influence on material wellbeing. Consumers with high materialism are likely to experience more dissatisfaction with material life than satisfaction. This accounts for the negative relationship between materialism and subjective wellbeing (e.g., Ahuvia, 2002; Dittmar et al., 2014; Fournier & Richins, 1991; Furnham, 1983; Furnham & Lewis,

1986; Inglehart, 1971, 1977, 1979, 1990; Kasser, 1997; Kasser & Ryan, 1993; Richins & Dawson, 1992; Rubenstein, 1981; Sirgy, 1998, 2019; Sirgy et al., 1998, 2013).

Financial Aspirations

With respect to *financial aspirations*, research suggests that increased income is often not associated with increased material wellbeing. Higher income and increased consumption do not have an impact on material happiness when increased consumption is neutralized by changes in consumer expectations and needs (e.g., Diener & Oishi, 2000; Kapteyn & Wansbeek, 1982). As income rises, consumer aspirations about consumption needs and expectations about adequate income also change. This adaptive change of needs and expectations weakens the association between income and material happiness over time. Supporting this, Plagnol and Easterlin (2008) have empirically demonstrated that financial satisfaction is a direct function of the gap between material aspirations (i.e., goals) and attainments.

Financial Literacy

Financial literacy was found to enhance material wellbeing (e.g., financial satisfaction). Financial literacy protects consumers from risky financial decisions and helps consumers increase personal control over the finances, thus helping them make financial decisions that are beneficial to financial wellbeing. Vlaev and Elliott (2014) were able to empirically demonstrate that personal control over finances is a strong predictor of satisfaction in financial life. Netemeyer et al. (2018) was able to also demonstrate that perceived financial self-efficacy plays a significant role in perceived financial wellbeing. Financial education influences financial wellbeing through positive financial behaviors (e.g., Lyons, 2008).

Positive Financial Behaviors

The construct of *positive financial behaviors* plays a significant and positive role in financial satisfaction and material wellbeing. Conversely, risky financial behaviors decrease financial satisfaction (e.g., Xiao et al., 2014). Positive financial behaviors refer to positive or desirable behaviors endorsed by consumer economists designed to improve financial satisfaction and material wellbeing. Examples of positive financial behaviors designed to improve financial and material wellbeing include expense management practices (e.g., tacking monthly expenses, spending within the budget, review bills each month for accuracy), balance control (e.g., maintaining sufficient balances in the bank account, paying bills on time each month, paying off credit card balance in full each month), and saving (e.g., saving money regularly, setting aside money for emergencies, contributing to an investment or retirement account, willing to take investment risks, and planning for money long-term) (e.g., Sirgy, 2021a, b). Thus, the evidence suggests that positive financial behaviors increase financial satisfaction and reduce financial risk (e.g., Gutter & Copur, 2011; Xiao et al., 2006). Similarly, research has documented the positive link between positive financial behavior and perceived financial wellbeing (e.g., Gutter & Copur, 2011; Joo & Grable, 2004; Netemeyer et al., 2018; O'Neill et al., 2005; Shim et al., 2009; Vosloo et al., 2014; Xiao et al., 2006, 2009).

Compulsive Buying

Compulsive buying has a negative effect on material wellbeing. Consumers with a compulsive buying tendency experience irresistible buying urges, lose control over buying decision-making, and suffer harmful consequences (e.g., Dittmar, 2004). Compulsive buying is influenced by several sources of motivation. First, compulsive buying is motivated by strong inner urges to alleviate emotional discomfort. Compulsive buying is chronic, repetitive purchasing that becomes a primary response to negative events or feelings (e.g., O'Guinn & Faber, 1989).

Second, compulsive buying behaviors are motivated by self-discrepancy (i.e., gap between actual and ideal self) (e.g., Dittmar, 2005). In other words, compulsive buying behaviors serve to reduce the gap between actual self and ideal self, and in doing so, the individual gains satisfaction of self-enhancement needs.

Third, compulsive buying is partly motivated by materialism (e.g., Dittmar, 2005; Pham et al., 2012). Consumers engage in compulsive buying behaviors because they believe the acquisition of material goods is a key to self-definition and happiness, a central life goal, and a prime indicator of success (e.g., Richins & Dawson, 1992). The relief of negative affect and satisfaction of self-enhancement needs as a direct result of compulsive buying is usually brief. However, unfortunately, these behaviors are often followed by feelings of guilt, shame, and anxiety (e.g., Williams & Grisham, 2012). Also, unfortunately, compulsive consumption behaviors are addictive or tend to be beyond the control of the consumer (e.g., Faber & O'Guinn, 1992). That is, consumers with compulsive buying tendencies do not have control over their spending and usually do not have enough financial knowledge to manage their spending e.g. (Pham et al., 2012). As such, compulsive buyers frequently overspend due to their strong, irrepressible urges to buy, with detrimental effects on their financial wellbeing (e.g., McElroy et al., 1994; O'Guinn & Faber, 1989).

Environmental Factors

Research has provided evidence suggesting that environmental factors such as national income and a positive economic environment play a role in determining material wellbeing.

National Income

Evidence suggests that material wellbeing is influenced by *national income*. There is a substantial positive correlation between national income and material wellbeing and happiness at the national level (e.g., Deaton, 2008; Dolan et al., 2008; Lawless & Lucas, 2011). Furthermore, the relationship between national income and national-level subjective wellbeing is much more evident in lower than higher income countries (e.g., Levin et al., 2011; Schyns, 1998; Veenhoven, 1991). This is because increased national income shields consumers from life adversities (e.g., Diener & Seligman, 2004). Thus, we can say that increases in national income is positively associated with material wellbeing.

Positive Economic Environment

Material wellbeing is also influenced by a *positive economic environment* of a country, which can be characterized in terms of several dimensions: good handling of economy, lower taxation, lower economic fluctuations, low cost of living, trust in society, and others (e.g., Andrews & Withey, 1976). Why?

First, material wellbeing is influenced by economic fluctuations in the country. Economic booms play a positive role in enhancing material wellbeing (e.g., financial wellbeing), while economic busts do undermine people's material wellbeing (e.g., Madden, 2011).

Second, material wellbeing is high when the cost of living in the community is low (e.g., Sirgy, 2021a, b; Lee et al., 2002). Increases in prices of goods and services (i.e., inflation) decrease consumers' purchasing power of goods and services needed to maintain a certain level of overall wellbeing (e.g., Samli, 2003). Research indicates that the cost of living in a large community (e.g., urban city) is higher than the cost of living in a small rural community (e.g., Hayo & Seifert, 2003). High cost of living tends to decrease economic satisfaction and material wellbeing.

Third, material wellbeing is high when consumers trust the marketing practices in the country at large. Consumers' overall experience with consumer goods and services reflects consumers' general sentiment towards the marketing institution. Consumers' positive experiences tend to increase consumers' trust in these institutions, which in turn contribute positively to material wellbeing (e.g., Ekici & Peterson, 2009). In other words, material wellbeing is high when marketing practices in society is positive and can be trusted (e.g., Peterson & Ekici, 2007).

Summary and Conclusion

Material wellbeing is a very important concept in quality-of-life studies, economics, social psychology, consumer studies, sociology, finance, marketing, policy sciences, environmental sciences, among other disciplines and fields of study. It is an umbrella concept that cuts across these disciplines and fields of study. Material wellbeing conjoined with satisfaction in other life domains (work life, social life, family life, leisure life, spiritual life, cultural life, …) plays a very important role in subjective wellbeing. Tables 4.1, 4.2, and 4.3 summarize much of what was discussed in this chapter. In conclusion, the research on material wellbeing is rich. Specifically, Table 4.1 summarizes the research on definitions and metrics of

Table 4.1 Definitions and metrics of material wellbeing

Definitions	Key dimensions	Metrics
Satisfaction with material life domain (Sirgy, 2019)	Satisfaction with the economic situation	Measures capturing the degree of satisfaction with the government's handling of the economy, taxes, the cost of necessities, household income, pay and fringe benefits from one's job, financial security, standard of living, and agreement within the family regarding how money should be spent
	Satisfaction with financial situation	Measures capturing the degree of satisfaction with the financial situation
	Satisfaction with income adequacy	The degree to which the current level of income is sufficient to cover their expenses, allowing them to indicate whether it is enough with money left over, just enough, no difficulty, some difficulty, and much difficulty
	Satisfaction with financial security	Money Index In-Charge Financial Distress/Financial wellbeing Scale Measures of financial wellbeing
	Aggregate satisfaction with marketplace activities	Measures capturing satisfaction with (1) obtained goods and services, (2) interactions with retail personnel, and (3) interactions with goods and service institutions
	Satisfaction with the standard of living	Measures capturing individuals' feelings about the things they own, their standard of living, and their financial situation overall Measures of satisfaction with material possessions and the extent to which physical needs are met Measures capturing the degree of problems with accommodation, affordability of basic goods, making ends meet, and solvency problems
	Aggregate feelings about major goods and services	The Consumer index (feelings about transportation and access to work and shopping, the medical services in their area, and the goods and services they can get when they buy in their area The International Wealth Index (degree of ownership of quality products including TV, fridge, phone, car, a house with piped drinking water, electricity, a flush toilet, good quality floor material, and 3+ rooms)
	Aspiration and attainment of material goods	Measures of the gap between aspirations and actual attainment of material goods

Table 4.2 Material wellbeing and overall happiness

Material wellbeing dimensions	Relationship with overall happiness	Mechanisms
Money resources	Overall life satisfaction is positively and significantly influenced by the amount of income, perceived income adequacy, changes in income, and positive financial behaviors (e.g., saving and planned spending).	Income is a material resource providing consumers with numerous benefits such as good physical health, good mental health, and low stress. Income is a resource that buffers against negative life events/ life hassles and works to obtain goods and services for consumer need fulfilment.
	Income has a stronger association with life satisfaction than with affective wellbeing measures.	Income softens life adversities by providing physiological protection, while positive feeling is strongly associated with fulfillment of psychological needs. Consumers often evaluate their life satisfaction based on the amount of income and financial situation, but they evaluate their affective wellbeing based on what the person is doing and whom the person was with. Yet, the strength of the relationship wanes as income rises beyond a certain point.
Time resources (spare time)	Time as a resource is positively associated with overall happiness.	Having more spare time is associated with greater happiness and life satisfaction, even after controlling for income. Consumers experience increased happiness by spending their limited time connecting with others, helping others, and engaging in active leisure activities. In contrast, lack of time in everyday life is associated with increased stress, loss of control, and reduced mental health.

(continued)

Table 4.2 (continued)

Material wellbeing dimensions	Relationship with overall happiness	Mechanisms
Material consumption	Total consumption is positively associated with overall happiness.	Larger consumption expenditures are positively correlated with increasing levels of life satisfaction because of greater need satisfaction.
	Relative consumption is significantly associated with overall happiness.	Those who can consume at, or above, the same level as their peers tend to feel more satisfied than those who cannot, especially for conspicuous products and experiences. .
	The strength of the association between total consumption amount and overall happiness is high for experiential consumption compared to material consumption.	This is because experiential consumption increases positive self-concept and social satisfaction.
	The strength of the positive association between material consumption and subjective wellbeing is higher for conspicuous (than inconspicuous) products.	This is because the use of conspicuous products can enhance a positive self-concept that contributes to individual happiness and life satisfaction.
	The strength of the positive association between material consumption and subjective wellbeing is lower for materialistic (than nonmaterialistic) consumers.	This is because materialistic consumers tend to experience lower life satisfaction, reduced happiness, decreased psychological need satisfaction, and increased levels of depression and anxiety.
	The strength of the association between consumption and overall happiness is high for consumption that is involved with others (compared to self-centered consumption).	This is because sharing of products allows consumers to savor their positive experiences and facilitate positive social interactions, which in turn contribute to life satisfaction.

Table 4.3 Factors influencing material wellbeing

Factors affecting material wellbeing	Relationship to material wellbeing	Why?
Demographic factors	Age (younger and older individuals are more satisfied with their material life than those in the middle-aged group)	Financial wellbeing is low for middle-aged consumers because of their low income and the high cost of raising children
	Family structure (low for couples with many children and those who are divorced or widowed)	Financial wellbeing is low for couples with many children and those who are divorced or widowed because of the greater financial demand
	Education (there is a positive association between education and material wellbeing)	Education is an important skill facilitating career development, which translates into greater financial resources
	Unemployment (there is a negative association between unemployment and material wellbeing)	Unemployment deprives consumers of income that is imperative in satisfying consumption needs
Behavioral factors	Extraversion (extroverts tend to experience higher material wellbeing than introverts)	Extraverts tend to socialize with others more than introverts, and such sociability plays an important and positive role in job performance and financial security
	Neuroticism has a negative influence on material wellbeing	Consumers high on neuroticism are less likely to be satisfied with their jobs, less likely to perform well at work, which may lead to financial insecurity
	Materialism has a negative influence on material wellbeing	Materialism prompts consumers to make frequent evaluations of standard of living based on ideal expectations, which in turn induces dissatisfaction with standard of living
	Financial aspirations are negatively associated with material wellbeing	Increases in financial aspirations widen the gap between desired and actual income, causing dissatisfaction
	Financial literacy (consumers with higher levels of financial literacy tend to experience higher levels of material wellbeing)	Financial literacy serves to increase personal control over finances (e.g., expense management, balance control, saving), which in turn increases satisfaction with one's finances and reduces financial risk
	Positive financial behavior (this construct plays a positive role in material wellbeing)	Positive financial behavior (e.g., expense management, balance control, saving) serve to reduce financial risk and increase satisfaction with one's finances
	Compulsive buying decreases material wellbeing	Compulsive buying behaviors are motivated by negative emotions, the widening gap between actual and ideal self, and materialism

(continued)

Table 4.3 (continued)

Factors affecting material wellbeing	Relationship to material wellbeing	Why?
Environmental factors	National income (national income is positively associated with material wellbeing)	Increased national income shields consumers from life adversities
	A positive economic environment in the country is positively associated with material wellbeing	Material wellbeing is enhanced by economic boom in the country, low cost of living, and trust in business practices

material wellbeing. As such, it is important to understand the various conceptualizations of this concept and select the right metric to measure the concept with specific population segments, especially vulnerable groups such as the poor, the disabled, minority groups, women, among others. The same can be said in relation to geographic segments such as countries and smaller geographic regions, such as counties and provinces, as well as cities, towns, and other urban areas.

Table 4.2 summarizes much of the research showing how material wellbeing contributes to overall happiness. The research clearly shows that material wellbeing plays a significant role in overall happiness. It does so by allowing consumers to use money and time resources to satisfy their needs. The research also points to several factors moderating the effect of material wellbeing on overall happiness. These include total consumption (the larger consumption expenditures the greater the happiness because larger consumption signals greater need satisfaction), relative consumption (levels of consumption that compares to the peer group because consumers tend to compare their marketplace experiences with their peers), experiential consumption (experiential consumption produces greater happiness than material consumption because experiential consumption is more affect-laden), conspicuous consumption (conspicuous consumption produces greater happiness than inconspicuous consumption because of signaling effects of status and prestige), materialism (the happiness effect is dampened for materialistic consumers because these consumers tend to evaluate their marketplace experiences with inflated and unrealistic standards causing dissatisfaction), and sharing with others (the happiness effect is greater when marketplace experiences are shared with others because sharing allows consumers to savor the positive marketplace experiences). As such, to produce greater happiness in marketplace experiences, marketers are advised to

- Target consumers whose material wellbeing is best served with products.
- Encourage and help consumers spend their money effectively to meet their consumption needs.
- Help consumers focus more on the intrinsic qualities of products rather than extrinsic social comparisons.
- Encourage consumers to spend more on experiential consumption than material consumption.
- Encourage consumers to use their material possessions in conspicuous ways.

- Avoid targeting highly materialistic consumers.
- Encourage consumers to share their marketplace experiences with others.

Table 4.3 summarizes much of the research showing what determines material wellbeing – demographic, behavioral, and environmental factors. Demographic factors influencing material wellbeing include age, family structure, education, unemployment, and financial resources. Concerning age, the research shows that younger and older consumers tend to be more satisfied with their material life than those in the middle-aged group. This may be due to the middle-aged consumers experiencing greater financial strain. Regarding family structure, research shows that financial wellbeing is low for couples with many children and those who are divorced or widowed. Again, this may be due to this group experiencing greater financial strain. Focusing on education, evidence suggests there is a positive association between education and material wellbeing. Educated consumers are likely to have greater financial resources. Research also shows that unemployment is negatively associated with material wellbeing, obviously because the unemployed experience financial strain.

Behavioral factors affecting material wellbeing include extraversion, neuroticism, materialism, financial aspirations, financial literacy, positive financial behavior, and compulsive buying. For extraversion, research shows that extraverts tend to experience higher levels of material wellbeing than introverts. This may be due to their sociability, which plays a positive role in job performance and financial security. Research also shows that neurotics experience lower levels of material wellbeing. Perhaps this is because they don't do well at work, which may adversely affect their income. Evidence also suggests that materialism is negatively associated with material wellbeing. Materialistic consumers tend to make frequent evaluations of their standard of living based on inflated and unrealistic expectations, which in turn causes dissatisfaction. Research on financial aspirations shows a negative relationship with material wellbeing. Increased financial aspirations cause consumers to feel dissatisfied with their income. Study findings also suggest that financial literacy plays a positive role in material wellbeing. Financial literacy increases consumers' control over their finances, thus reducing financial risk and enhancing financial satisfaction. Compulsive buying affects material wellbeing in adverse ways. It is caused by negative emotions conjoined with a widening gap between the actual and ideal self, and high levels of materialism.

The research literature reveals two important environmental factors influencing material wellbeing, namely national income and a positive economic environment. For national income, evidence suggests that national income is positively associated with material wellbeing. This may be due to national income serving as a buffer, protecting consumers from life adversities. Moreover, material wellbeing is positively influenced by a positive economic environment in the country at large. A positive economic environment means that the country is experiencing economic growth, the cost of living is acceptable, and there is trust in business practices in general.

As such, to produce greater happiness in marketplace experiences, marketers are advised to reduce consumers' financial difficulties and preserve/enhance their wellbeing. Examples include:

- Marketers can provide affordably priced, small-packaged products to vulnerable consumers (those with financial difficulties), such as making prices more affordable for the unemployed, illiterate, materialistic, compulsive, and neurotic consumers.
- Marketers can provide financial information to vulnerable consumers and help them make good financial decisions to preserve/enhance their material wellbeing such as providing incentives for future consumption and saving for the future.
- Marketers can enhance experiential quality (instead of the quality of material possessions) in their offerings such as providing products involving social interactions and sharing of experiences about the product with others.

References

Ahuvia, A. C. (2002). Individualism/collectivism and cultures of happiness: A theoretical conjecture on the relationship between consumption, culture and subjective wellbeing at the national level. *Journal of Happiness Studies, 3*(1), 23–36.

Ahuvia, A. C., & Wong, N. (1995). Materialism: Origins and implications for personal wellbeing. In F. Hansen (Ed.), *European advances in consumer research* (Vol. 2, pp. 172–178). Association for Consumer Research.

Aknin, L. B., Dunn, E. W., Sandstrom, G. M., & Norton, M. I. (2013). Does social connection turn good deeds into good feelings? On the value of putting the 'social' in prosocial spending. *International Journal of Happiness and Development, 1*(2), 155–171.

Andrews, F. M., & Withey, S. B. (1976). *Social indicators of wellbeing: America's perception of life quality*. Plenum Press.

Baumeister, R. F. (1990). Suicide as escape from self. *Psychological Review, 97*(1), 90–113.

Belk, R. W. (1985). Materialism: Trait aspects of living in the material world. *Journal of Consumer Research, 12*(3), 265–280.

Blanchflower, D. G., & Oswald, A. (2000). *Wellbeing overtime in Britain and the USA*. NBER Working Paper 7487.

Bohnke, P. (2008). Does society matter? Life satisfaction in the enlarged Europe. *Social Indicators Research, 87*(2), 189–210.

Boyce, C. J., Brown, G. D., & Moore, S. C. (2010). Money and happiness: Rank of income, not income, affects life satisfaction. *Psychological Science, 21*(4), 471–475.

Brady, S. S., & Matthews, K. A. (2002). The influence of socioeconomic status and ethnicity on adolescents' exposure to stressful life events. *Journal of Pediatric Psychology, 27*(7), 575–583.

Bruggen, E. C., Hogreve, J., Holmlund, M., Kabadayi, S., & Lofgren, M. (2017). Financial wellbeing: A conceptualization and research agenda. *Journal of Business Research, 79*, 228–237.

Burroughs, J. E., & Rindfleisch, A. (2002). Materialism and wellbeing: A conflicting values perspective. *The Journal of Consumer Research, 29*(3), 348–370.

Carstensen, L. L., Isaacowitz, D. M., & Charles, S. T. (1999). Taking time seriously: A theory of socioemotional selectivity. *American Psychologist, 54*(3), 165–181.

Chan, A., Ofstedal, M. B., & Hermalin, A. (2002). Changes in subjective and objective measures of economic wellbeing and their interrelationship among the elderly in Singapore and Taiwan. *Social Indicators Research, 57*(3), 263–300.

Christopher, A. N., Lasane, T. P., Troisi, J. D., & Park, L. E. (2007). Materialism, defensive and assertive self-presentational tactics, and life satisfaction. *Journal of Social and Clinical Psychology, 26*(10), 1145–1162.

Claes, L., Bijttebier, P., Van Den Eynde, F., Mitchell, J. E., Faber, R., de Zwaan, M., & Mueller, A. (2010). Emotional reactivity and self-regulation in relation to compulsive buying. *Personality and Individual Differences, 49*, 526–530.

Clark, A. E., Frijters, P., & Shields, M. A. (2008). Relative income, happiness, and utility: An explanation for the Easterlin paradox and other puzzles. *Journal of Economic Literature, 46*(1), 95–144.

Collins, J. M., & Urban, C. (2021). Measuring financial wellbeing over the life course. In *Financial literacy and responsible finance in the Fintech era* (pp. 45–63). Routledge.

Cracolici, M. F., Giambona, F., & Cuffaro, M. (2014). Family structure and subjective economic wellbeing. *Social Indicators Research, 118*(1), 433–456.

Deaton, A. (2008). Income, health, and wellbeing around the world: Evidence from the Gallup World Poll. *Journal of Economic Perspectives, 22*(2), 53–72.

DeLeire, T., & Kalil, A. (2010). Does consumption buy happiness? Evidence from the United States. *International Review of Economics, 57*(2), 163–176.

Diener, E., & Biswas-Diener, R. (2002). Will money increase subjective wellbeing? *Social Indicators Research, 57*(2), 119–169.

Diener, E., & Oishi, S. (2000). Money and happiness: Income and subjective wellbeing across nations. In E. Diener & E. M. Suh (Eds.), *Subjective wellbeing across cultures*. MIT Press.

Diener, E., & Seligman, M. E. (2004). Beyond money: Toward an economy of wellbeing. *Psychological Science in the Public Interest, 5*(1), 1–31.

Diener, E., Sandvik, E., Seidlitz, L., & Diener, M. (1993). The relationship between income and subjective wellbeing: Relative or absolute? *Social Indicators Research, 28*(3), 195–223.

Diener, E., Kahneman, D., Tov, W., & Arora, R. (2010a). Income's association with judgements of life versus feelings. In E. Diener, J. Helliwel, & D. Kahneman (Eds.), *International differences in wellbeing* (pp. 3–15). Oxford University Press.

Diener, E., Ng, W., Harter, J., & Arora, R. (2010b). Wealth and happiness across the world: Material prosperity predicts life evaluation, whereas psychosocial prosperity predicts positive feeling. *Journal of Personality and Social Psychology, 99*(1), 52–61.

Diener, E., Tay, L., & Oishi, S. (2013). Rising income and the subjective wellbeing of nations. *Journal of Personality and Social Psychology, 104*(2), 267–276.

Dittmar, H. (2004). Understanding and diagnosing compulsive buying. In R. Coombs (Ed.), *Addictive disorders: A guide to diagnosis and treatment* (pp. 411–450). Wiley.

Dittmar, H. (2005). A new look at "compulsive buying": Self–discrepancies and materialistic values as predictors of compulsive buying tendency. *Journal of Social and Clinical Psychology, 24*(6), 832–859.

Dittmar, H., & Kapur, P. (2011). Consumerism and wellbeing in India and the UK: Identity projection and emotion regulation as underlying psychological processes. *Psychological Studies, 56*(1), 71–85.

Dittmar, H., Long, K., & Bond, R. (2007). When a better self is only a button click away: Associations between materialistic values, emotional and identity–related buying motives, and compulsive buying tendency online. *Journal of Social and Clinical Psychology, 26*(3), 334–361.

Dittmar, H., Bond, R., Hurst, M., & Kasser, T. (2014). The relationship between materialism and personal wellbeing: A meta-analysis. *Journal of Personality and Social Psychology, 107*(5), 879–924.

Dolan, P., Peasgood, T., & White, M. (2008). Do we really know what makes us happy? A review of the economic literature on the factors associated with subjective wellbeing. *Journal of Economic Psychology, 29*(1), 94–122.

Donnelly, G. E., Ksendzova, M., Howell, R. T., Vohs, K. D., & Baumeister, R. F. (2016). Buying to blunt negative feelings: Materialistic escape from the self. *Review of General Psychology, 20*(3), 272–316.

Dumludag, D. (2015). Consumption and life satisfaction at different levels of economic development. *International Review of Economics, 62*(2), 163–182.

Ekici, A., & Peterson, M. (2009). The unique relationship between quality of life and consumer trust in market-related institutions among financially constrained consumers in a developing country. *Journal of Public Policy & Marketing, 28*(1), 56–70.

Faber, R. J., & O'Guinn, T. C. (1992). A clinical screener for compulsive buying. *Journal of Consumer Research, 19*(3), 459–469.

Fafchamps, M., & Shilpi, F. (2008). Subjective welfare, isolation, and relative consumption. *Journal of Development Economics, 86*(1), 43–60.

Ferrer-i-Carbonell, A. (2005). Income and wellbeing: An empirical analysis of the comparison income effect. *Journal of Public Economics, 89*(5-6), 997–1019.

Fitzmaurice, J., & Comegys, C. (2006). Materialism and social consumption. *Journal of Marketing Theory and Practice, 14*(4), 287–299.

Fournier, S., & Richins, M. L. (1991). Some theoretical and popular notions concerning materialism. *Journal of Social Behavior and Personality, 6*(6), 403–414.

Frank, R. H. (2012). The Easterlin paradox revisited. *Emotion, 12*(6), 1188–1191.

Frost, R. O., Kyrios, M., McCarthy, K. D., & Matthews, Y. (2007). Self-ambivalence and attachment to possessions. *Journal of Cognitive Psychotherapy: An International Quarterly, 21*(3), 232–242.

Furnée, C. A., Groot, W., & Pfann, G. A. (2011). Health and income: A meta-analysis to explore cross-country, gender and age differences. *The European Journal of Public Health, 21*(6), 775–780.

Furnham, A. (1983). Attributions of affluence. *Personality and Individual Differences, 4*(1), 31–40.

Furnham, A., & Lewis, A. (1986). *The economic mind: The social psychology of economic behavior*. Wheatsheaf/Harvester.

Gino, F., & Mogilner, C. (2014). Time, money, and morality. *Psychological Science, 25*(2), 414–421.

Gokdemir, O. (2015). Consumption, savings and life satisfaction: The Turkish case. *International Review of Economics, 62*(2), 183–196.

Grable, J. E., Cupples, S., Fernatt, F., & Anderson, N. (2013). Evaluating the link between perceived income adequacy and financial satisfaction: A resource deficit hypothesis approach. *Social Indicators Research, 114*(3), 1109–1124.

Guillen-Royo, M. (2011). Reference group consumption and the subjective wellbeing of the poor in Peru. *Journal of Economic Psychology, 32*(2), 259–272.

Gutter, M., & Copur, Z. (2011). Financial behaviors and financial wellbeing of college students: Evidence from a national survey. *Journal of Family and Economic Issues, 32*(4), 699–714.

Hagerty, M. R., & Veenhoven, R. (2003). Wealth and happiness revisited–growing national income does go with greater happiness. *Social Indicators Research, 64*(1), 1–27.

Hansen, T., Slagsvold, B., & Moum, T. (2008). Financial satisfaction in old age: A satisfaction paradox or a result of accumulated wealth? *Social Indicators Research, 89*(2), 323–347.

Hayo, B., & Seifert, W. (2003). Subjective economic wellbeing in Eastern Europe. *Journal of Economic Psychology, 24*(3), 329–348.

Headey, B., Muffels, R., & Wooden, M. (2008). Money does not buy happiness: Or does it? A reassessment based on the combined effects of wealth, income and consumption. *Social Indicators Research, 87*(1), 65–82.

Hershfield, H. E., Mogilner, C., & Barnea, U. (2016). People who choose time over money are happier. *Social Psychological and Personality Science, 7*(7), 697–706.

Howell, R. T., & Howell, C. J. (2008). The relation of economic status to subjective wellbeing in developing countries: A meta-analysis. *Psychological Bulletin, 134*(4), 536–560.

Hsieh, C.-M. (2004). Income and financial satisfaction among older adults in the United States. *Social Indicators Research, 66*(3), 249–266.
Hudders, L., & Pandelaere, M. (2012). The silver lining of materialism: The impact of luxury consumption on subjective wellbeing. *Journal of Happiness Studies, 13*(3), 411–437.
Inglehart, R. (1971). The silent revolution in Europe: Intergenerational change in post-industrial societies. *American Political Science Review, 65*(4), 991–1017.
Inglehart, R. (1977). *The silent revolution: Changing values and political styles among Western publics*. Princeton University Press.
Inglehart, R. (1979). Value priorities and socioeconomic change. In S. Barnes, M. Kasse, et al. (Eds.), *Political action: Mass participation in five western democracies* (pp. 305–342). Sage.
Inglehart, R. (1990). *Culture shift in advanced industrial society*. Princeton University Press.
Jebb, A. T., Tay, L., Diener, E., & Oishi, S. (2018). Happiness, income satiation and turning points around the world. *Nature Human Behaviour, 2*(1), 33–38.
Joo, S.-H., & Grable, J. E. (2004). An exploratory framework of the determinants of financial satisfaction. *Journal of Family and Economic Issues, 25*(1), 25–50.
Kahneman, D., & Deaton, A. (2010). High income improves evaluation of life but not emotional wellbeing. *Proceedings of the National Academy of Sciences, 107*(38), 16489–16493.
Kapteyn, A., & Wansbeek, T. J. (1982). Empirical evidence on preference formation. *Journal of Economic Psychology, 2*(2), 137–154.
Kashdan, T. B., & Breen, W. E. (2007). Materialism and diminished well–being: Experiential avoidance as a mediating mechanism. *Journal of Social and Clinical Psychology, 26*(5), 521–539.
Kasser, T. (1997). *Two versions of the American dream: Which goals and values make for a high quality of life?* Paper presented at the international society for quality-of-life studies conference, Charlotte, North Carolina, November 20–22, 1997.
Kasser, T., & Ahuvia, A. (2002). Materialistic values and wellbeing in business students. *European Journal of Social Psychology, 32*(1), 137–146.
Kasser, T., & Ryan, R. M. (1993). A dark side of the American dream: Correlates of financial success as a central life aspiration. *Journal of Personality and Social Psychology, 65*(2), 410–422.
Kasser, T., & Sheldon, K. (2009). Time affluence as a path toward personal happiness and ethical business practice: Empirical evidence from four studies. *Journal of Business Ethics, 84*(2), 243–255.
Kim, H., Callan, M. J., Gheorghiu, A. I., & Matthews, W. J. (2017). Social comparison, personal relative deprivation, and materialism. *British Journal of Social Psychology, 56*(2), 373–392.
Lane, R. E. (1991). *The market experience*. Cambridge University Press.
Lathia, N., Sandstrom, G. M., Mascolo, C., & Rentfrow, P. J. (2017). Happier people live more active lives: Using smartphones to link happiness and physical activity. *PLoS ONE, 12*(1), e0160589.
Lawless, N. M., & Lucas, R. E. (2011). Predictors of regional wellbeing: A county level analysis. *Social Indicators Research, 101*(3), 341–357.
Lee, D. J., Sirgy, M. J., Larsen, V., & Wright, N. D. (2002). Developing a subjective measure of consumer wellbeing. *Journal of Macromarketing, 22*(2), 158–169.
Levin, K. A., Torsheim, T., Vollebergh, W., Richter, M., Davies, C. A., Schnohr, C. W., et al. (2011). National income and income inequality, family affluence and life satisfaction among 13-year-old boys and girls: A multilevel study in 35 countries. *Social Indicators Research, 104*(2), 179–194.
Lewin, A. C., & Stier, H. (2017). The experience of material and emotional hardship in Israel: Do some groups cope better than others? *Social Indicators Research, 134*(1), 385–402.
Lynch, J. W., Smith, G. D., Kaplan, G. A., & House, J. S. (2000). Income inequality and mortality: Importance to health of individual income, psychosocial environment, or material conditions. *British Medical Journal, 320*(7243), 1200–1204.
Lyons, A. C. (2008). Risky credit card behavior of college students. In J. J. Xiao (Ed.), *Handbook of consumer finance research* (pp. 185–208). Springer.

Lyubomirsky, S., Sheldon, K. M., & Schkade, D. (2005). Pursuing happiness: The architecture of sustainable change. *Review of General Psychology, 9*(2), 111–131.

Lyubomirsky, S., Sousa, L., & Dickerhoof, R. (2006). The costs and benefits of writing, talking, and thinking about life's triumphs and defeats. *Journal of Personality and Social Psychology, 90*(4), 692–708.

MacDonald, M., & Douthitt, R. A. (1992). Consumption theories and Consumers' assessments of subjective wellbeing. *Journal of Consumer Affairs, 26*(2), 243–261.

Madden, D. (2011). The impact of an economic boom on the level and distribution of subjective wellbeing: Ireland, 1994–2001. *Journal of Happiness Studies, 12*(4), 667–679.

Malone, K., Stewart, S. D., Wilson, J., & Korsching, P. F. (2010). Perceptions of financial wellbeing among American women in diverse families. *Journal of Family and Economic Issues, 31*(1), 63–81.

McElroy, S. L., Phillips, K. A., & Keck, P. E., Jr. (1994). Obsessive compulsive spectrum disorder. *The Journal of Clinical Psychiatry, 55*, 33–51.

Meadow, H. L., & Sirgy, M. J. (2008). Developing a measure that captures elderly's wellbeing in local marketplace transactions. *Applied Research in Quality of Life, 3*(1), 63–80.

Mogilner, C. (2010). The pursuit of happiness: Time, money, and social connection. *Psychological Science, 21*(9), 1348–1354.

Mogilner, C., & Aaker, J. (2009). "The time vs. money effect": Shifting product attitudes and decisions through personal connection. *Journal of Consumer Research, 36*(2), 277–291.

Nakano, N., MacDonald, M., & Douthitt, R. (1995). Toward consumer wellbeing: Consumer socialization effects of work experience. In M. J. Sirgy & A. C. Samli (Eds.), *New dimensions of marketing/quality-of life research* (pp. 151–175). Quorum Books.

Netemeyer, R. G., Warmath, D., Fernandes, D., & Lynch, J. G., Jr. (2018). How am I doing? Perceived financial wellbeing, its potential antecedents, and its relation to overall wellbeing. *Journal of Consumer Research, 45*(1), 68–89.

Ng, W. (2015). Processes underlying links to subjective wellbeing: Material concerns, autonomy, and personality. *Journal of Happiness Studies, 16*(6), 1575–1591.

Nickerson, C., Schwarz, N., Diener, E., & Kahneman, D. (2003). Zeroing in on the dark side of the American dream: A closer look at the negative consequences of the goal for financial success. *Psychological Science, 14*(6), 531–536.

Nickerson, C., Schwarz, N., & Diener, E. (2007). Financial aspirations, financial success, and overall life satisfaction. *Journal of Happiness Studies, 8*(4), 467–515.

Nicolao, L., Irwin, J. R., & Goodman, J. K. (2009). Happiness for sale: Do experiential purchases make consumers happier than material purchases? *Journal of Consumer Research, 36*(2), 188–198.

Noll, H. H., & Weick, S. (2015). Consumption expenditures and subjective wellbeing: Empirical evidence from Germany. *International Review of Economics, 62*(2), 101–119.

O'Guinn, T. C., & Faber, R. J. (1989). Compulsive buying: A phenomenological exploration. *Journal of Consumer Research, 16*(2), 147–157.

O'Neill, B., Sorhaindo, B., Xiao, J. J., & Garman, E. T. (2005). Financially distressed consumers: Their financial practices, financial wellbeing, and health. *Financial Counseling and Planning, 16*(1), 73–87.

Perez-Truglia, R. (2013). A test of the conspicuous–consumption model using subjective wellbeing data. *The Journal of Socioeconomics, 45*, 146–154.

Peterson, M., & Ekici, A. (2007). Consumer attitude toward marketing and subjective quality of life in the context of a developing country. *Journal of Macromarketing, 27*(4), 350–359.

Pham, T. H., Yap, K., & Dowling, N. A. (2012). The impact of financial management practices and financial attitudes on the relationship between materialism and compulsive buying. *Journal of Economic Psychology, 33*(3), 461–470.

Plagnol, A. C., & Easterlin, R. A. (2008). Aspirations, attainments, and satisfaction: Life cycle differences between American women and men. *Journal of Happiness Studies, 9*(4), 601–619.

Popova, D., & Pishniak, A. (2017). Measuring individual material wellbeing using multidimensional indices: An application using the Gender and Generation Survey for Russia. *Social Indicators Research, 130*(3), 883–910.

Prawitz, A. D., Garman, E. T., Sorhaindo, B., O'Neill, B., Kim, J., & Drentea, P. (2006). In-charge financial distress/financial wellbeing scale development, administration, and score interpretation. *Journal of Financial Counselling and Planning, 17*(1), 34–50.

Reed, A., Aquino, K., & Levy, E. (2007). Moral identity and judgments of charitable behaviors. *Journal of Marketing, 71*(1), 178–193.

Richins, M. L. (2004). The material values scale: Measurement properties and development of a short form. *Journal of consumer Research, 31*(1), 209–219.

Richins, M. L. (2011). Materialism, transformation expectations, and spending: Implications for credit use. *Journal of Public Policy & Marketing, 30*(2), 141–156.

Richins, M. L., & Dawson, S. (1992). A consumer values orientation for materialism and its measurement: Scale development and validation. *Journal of Consumer Research, 19*(3), 303–316.

Rindfleisch, A., Burroughs, J. E., & Wong, N. (2009). The safety of objects: Materialism, existential insecurity, and brand connection. *Journal of Consumer Research, 36*(1), 1–16.

Roberts, B. W., Caspi, A., & Moffitt, T. E. (2003). Work experiences and personality development in young adulthood. *Journal of Personality and Social Psychology, 84*(3), 582–593.

Rubenstein, C. (1981). Money, self-esteem, relationships, secrecy, envy, satisfaction. *Psychology Today, 15*(May), 29–44.

Ruvio, A., Somer, E., & Rindfleisch, A. (2014). When bad gets worse: The amplifying effect of materialism on traumatic stress and maladaptive consumption. *Journal of the Academy of Marketing Science, 42*(1), 90–101.

Samli, A. C. (2003). The consumer price index and consumer wellbeing: Developing a fair measure. *Journal of Macromarketing, 23*(2), 105–111.

Schnebelen, S., & Bruhn, M. (2018). An appraisal framework of the determinants and consequences of brand happiness. *Psychology & Marketing, 35*(2), 101–119.

Schroeder, J. E., & Dugal, S. S. (1995). Psychological correlates of the materialism construct. *Journal of Social Behavior and Personality, 10*(1), 243–253.

Schyns, P. (1998). Cross-national differences in happiness: Economic and cultural factors explored. *Social Indicators Research, 43*(1-2), 3–26.

Schyns, P. (2001). Income and satisfaction in Russia. *Journal of Happiness Studies, 2*(2), 173–204.

Seghieri, C., Desantis, G., & Tanturri, M. L. (2006). The richer, the happier? An empirical investigation in selected European countries. *Social Indicators Research, 79*(3), 455–476.

Shim, S., Xiao, J. J., Barber, B. L., & Lyons, A. C. (2009). Pathways to life success: a conceptual model of financial wellbeing for young adults. *Journal of Applied Developmental Psychology, 30*(6), 708–723.

Shrum, L. J., Wong, N., Arif, F., Chugani, S. K., Gunz, A., Lowrey, T. M., et al. (2013). Reconceptualizing materialism as identity goal pursuits: Functions, processes, and consequences. *Journal of Business Research, 66*(8), 1179–1185.

Sirgy, M. J. (1998). Materialism and quality of life. *Social Indicators Research, 43*(3), 227–260.

Sirgy, M. J. (2018). The psychology of material wellbeing. *Applied Research in Quality of Life, 13*(2), 273–301.

Sirgy, M. J. (2019). What determines subjective material wellbeing? In G. Brulé & C. Suter (Eds.), *Wealth(s) and subjective wellbeing*. Springer.

Sirgy, M. J. (2021a). *The Psychology of quality of life: Wellbeing and positive mental health* (3rd ed.). Springer Nature Switzerland AG.

Sirgy, M. J. (2021b). Macromarketing metrics of consumer wellbeing: An update. *Journal of Macromarketing, 41*(1), 124–131.

Sirgy, M. J., Lee, D.-J., Kosenko, R., Meadow, H. L., Rahtz, D., Cicic, M., Jin, G. X., Yarsuvat, D., Blenkhorn, D., & Wright, N. (1998). Does television viewership play a role in the perception of quality of life? *Journal of Advertising, 27*(1), 125–142.

Sirgy, M. J., Gurel-Atay, E., Webb, D., Cicic, M., Husic-Mehmedovic, M., Ekici, A., Hermann, A., Hegazy, I., Lee, D.-J., & Johar, J. S. (2013). Is materialism all that bad? Effects on satisfaction with material life, life satisfaction, and economic motivation. *Social Indicators Research, 110*(1), 349–366.

Smits, J., & Steendijk, R. (2015). The international wealth index (IWI). *Social Indicators Research, 122*(1), 65–85.

Strazdins, L., Welsh, J., Korda, R., Broom, D., & Paolucci, F. (2016). Not all hours are equal: Could time be a social determinant of health? *Sociology of Health & Illness, 38*(1), 21–42.

Tay, L., & Diener, E. (2011). Needs and subjective wellbeing around the world. *Journal of Personality and Social Psychology, 101*(2), 354–365.

Thomas, R., & Millar, M. (2013). The effects of material and experiential discretionary purchases on consumer happiness: Moderators and mediators. *The Journal of Psychology, 147*(4), 345–356.

Tsurumi, T., Yamaguchi, R., Kagohashi, K., & Managi, S. (2021). Are cognitive, affective, and eudaimonic dimensions of subjective wellbeing differently related to consumption? Evidence from Japan. *Journal of Happiness Studies, 22*(6), 2499–2522.

Van Boven, L., & Gilovich, T. (2003). To do or to have? That is the question. *Journal of Personality and Social Psychology, 85*(6), 1193–1202.

Veenhoven, R. (1991). Is happiness relative? *Social Indicators Research, 24*(1), 1–34.

Vera-Toscano, E., Ateca-Amestoy, V., & Serrano-del-Rosal, R. (2006). Building financial satisfaction. *Social Indicators Research, 77*(2), 211–243.

Vlaev, I., & Elliott, A. (2014). Financial wellbeing components. *Social Indicators Research, 118*(3), 1103–1123.

Vosloo, W., Fouche, J., & Barnard, J. (2014). The relationship between financial efficacy, satisfaction with remuneration and personal financial wellbeing. *International Business and Economics Research Journal, 13*, 1455–1470.

Walker, R., Lee, M. P., & Bubolz, M. (1990). The effects of family resources and demands on quality of life: A rural-urban comparison of women in the middle years. In H. Lee Meadow & M. J. Sirgy (Eds.), *Quality of- life studies in marketing and management* (pp. 397–411). Department of Marketing, Virginia Polytechnic Institute and State University.

Whillans, A. V., Weidman, A. C., & Dunn, E. W. (2016). Valuing time over money is associated with greater happiness. *Social Psychological and Personality Science, 7*(3), 213–222.

Williams, A. D., & Grisham, J. R. (2012). Impulsivity, emotion regulation, and mindful attentional focus in compulsive buying. *Cognitive Therapy and Research, 36*(5), 451–457.

Wu, F. (2020). An examination of the effects of consumption expenditures on life satisfaction in Australia. *Journal of Happiness Studies, 21*(8), 2735–2771.

Xiao, J. J., Sorhaindo, B., & Garman, E. T. (2006). Financial behavior of consumers in credit counseling. *International Journal of Consumer Studies, 30*(2), 108–121.

Xiao, J. J., Tang, C., & Shim, S. (2009). Acting for happiness: Financial behaviour and life satisfaction of college students. *Social Indicators Research, 92*(1), 53–68.

Xiao, J. J., Chen, C., & Chen, F. (2014). Consumer financial capability and financial satisfaction. *Social Indicators Research, 118*(1), 415–432.

Yu, G. B., Lee, D. J., Sirgy, M. J., & Bosnjak, M. (2020). Household income, satisfaction with standard of living, and subjective wellbeing. The moderating role of happiness materialism. *Journal of Happiness Studies, 21*(8), 2851–2872.

Zhang, J., & Xiong, Y. (2015). Effects of multifaceted consumption on happiness in life: A case study in Japan based on an integrated approach. *International Review of Economics, 62*(2), 143–162.

Zuzanek, J. (2013). Does being well-off make us happier? Problems of measurement. *Journal of Happiness Studies, 14*(3), 795–815.

Part II
Consumer Happiness

In Part II of the book, we will address constructs and metrics of consumer happiness, its outcomes, its antecedents, and propose ideas on how to enhance consumer happiness.

Chapter 5
Constructs and Metrics of Consumer Happiness

We live in a material world. I'm not saying that beautiful things don't enhance our lives. But in our culture, we're never happy.

—Tom Ford (https://www.brainyquote.com/topics/material-world-quotes#:~:text=We%20live%20in%20a%20material,precise%20measure%20of%20material%20things.&text=Without%20the%20spiritual%20world%20the%20material%20world%20is%20a%20disheartening%20enigma.&text=I%20can't%20see%20any,other%20than%20the%20material%20world)

Definitions and Metrics of Consumer Happiness

Consumer happiness (or wellbeing) refers to happiness in the consumer life domain. (the psychological domain that houses much of the marketplace affective experiences). Consumer happiness can be viewed through the lens of hedonic and eudaimonic happiness.

Hedonic Consumer Happiness

Hedonic happiness refers to the aspect of wellbeing that highlights temporary pleasure and pain avoidance (e.g., Ryan & Deci, 2001; Ryff, 1989; Waterman et al., 2008). Thus, hedonic consumer happiness can be defined as a preponderance of positive feelings (e.g., enjoyment, smiling, and laughing) over negative feelings (e.g., worry, sadness, depression, and anger) in the consumer life domain (cf. Kahneman & Deaton, 2010). That is, consumer happiness is a mental state of wellbeing in the consumer life domain characterized by a predominance of positive affect over negative affect related to marketplace experiences (cf. Nicolao et al., 2009; Veenhoven, 2012). As such, hedonic consumer happiness is related to satisfaction of consumer needs and wants (Baumeister et al., 2013) originating from

D.-J. Lee, M. J. Sirgy, *Happiness in the Marketplace*, Social Indicators Research Series 64, https://doi.org/10.1007/978-3-032-04443-3_5

consumers' engagement in hedonic consumption activities (e.g., engagement in recreational shopping, purchase of hedonic products, experience for fun, and immersion in hedonic experiences).

Life satisfaction is a cognitive judgment and a conscious thought (judgment) about how well one is doing in life in general (e.g., Diener et al., 2013a, b). Similarly, consumer happiness can be construed as a cognitive evaluation of how one is doing about marketplace experiences. We can break down the concept of marketplace experiences in terms of experiences related to product acquisition, product possession, product consumption, product maintenance, and product disposal (Lee et al., 2002; Sirgy, 2021).

Eudaimonic Consumer Happiness

Eudaimonia refers to the facet of individual wellbeing that highlights the long-term sense of self-fulfillment and actualization derived from seeking meaning and purpose in life (e.g., Baumeister et al., 2013; Ryan & Deci, 2001; Ryff, 1989; Ryff & Keyes, 1995; Waterman et al., 2008). Similarly, eudaimonic consumer happiness could be a state of mind that reflects a state of meaningful and flourishing consumer life. As such, eudaimonic consumer happiness reflects ethical and sustainable consumption, spending for others, personal expressiveness in consumption, meaningful consumption, and integrative thinking about the past, present, and future of marketplace experiences. In other words, eudaimonic consumer happiness emanates from spending on others, gift-giving, consumption of ethical and sustainable products, and consumption of products that benefit society at large.

Consumer Happiness (Overall)

Our view of consumer happiness is multidimensional. It covers the two dimensions of hedonic and eudaimonic happiness. In other words, consumers who report frequently feel happy in consumer life (life domain housing affective experiences related to the marketplace) tend to have high levels of positive affect in that life domain, high levels of satisfaction with marketplace experiences, as well as feelings of doing good for society at large through doing good in marketplace activities (cf. Bosnjak et al., 2016).

Both hedonic and eudaimonic consumer happiness are interrelated in that frequently experiencing short-term consumer happiness (hedonic marketplace experiences) can potentially contribute to long-term consumer happiness (eudaimonic marketplace experiences) (cf. Diener et al., 1999; Fredrickson, 2001; Lyubomirsky et al., 2005). As such, overall consumer happiness is a construct that captures both hedonic and eudaimonic dimensions of marketplace experiences.

Models and Metrics of Consumer Happiness

Consumer happiness refers to the overall evaluation of marketplace experiences housed in the consumer life domain. Specifically, consumer happiness reflects an enduring perception of hedonic and eudaimonic happiness resulting from the *consumption experiences across various goods and services.* That is, consumer happiness covers both hedonic consumer happiness (e.g., pleasurable experiences) and eudaimonic consumer happiness (e.g., meaningful and socially responsible experiences). Consumers need to engage in balanced hedonic consumption that includes both hedonic and eudemonic aspects. Irrational consumer hedonism can lead to socially irresponsible behaviors and low consumer happiness (e.g., Sameer et al., 2021).

The models of consumer happiness focus on various aspects of consumer life. These aspects include the following. First, acquisition-focused models of consumer happiness tap consumer and marketing interactions related to buying or shopping. Acquisition-focused consumer happiness models include the cost-of-living model (price level in shopping, inflation), the consumption equity model (consumption expenditure and equity), the consumption sentiment model (shopping satisfaction with marketing institutions), and the shopping satisfaction model (satisfaction with shopping in general).

Second, consumption-focused models of consumer happiness tap consumers' actual consumption experiences after purchase. These models include the possession satisfaction model (possession of material products), the consumer complaints model (consumer complaints during the use/experience), the need satisfaction model (the consequences of consumption), and the community satisfaction model (overall consumption satisfaction in the community).

Third, consumption cycle models of consumer happiness tap marketplace experiences that reflect the various stages of the entire consumption/product life cycle. These stages are acquisition (shopping and buying experiences), possession (product ownership experiences), consumption (experiences related to product use), maintenance (experiences related to product service and repair), and disposal (experiences related to getting rid of products through selling, trading, and/or dumping).

Finally, the vertical spillover models of consumer wellbeing tap into the relationship between satisfaction with consumer life and overall life satisfaction. The bottom-up spillover model focuses on how marketplace experiences impact satisfaction judgments about consumer life overall, whereas the top-down spillover model focuses on how satisfaction judgments about consumer life impact feelings that consumers experience with specific marketplace events. The collectivism vs. individualism cultural value model focuses on how cultural values influence marketplace experiences and overall consumer happiness.

There are many theoretical models explaining consumer happiness. The models and metrics of consumer happiness are discussed in detail in the following section.

The Cost-of-Living Model and Metrics

The *cost-of-living model* focuses on consumers' cost of living and argues that consumer wellbeing is high when cost of living is low (Sirgy, 2021, Lee et al., 2002). Specifically, the cost-of-living model posits that increases in prices of goods and services (i.e., inflation) tend to decrease consumers' purchasing power needed to maintain a certain consumption lifestyle (cf. Samli, 2003).

The *Consumer Price Index* (CPI) measures changes in the cost of living and inflation over time. The CPI measures changes in the cost of living over time, specifically, changes in prices of goods and services at the national level over time (https://www.bls.gov/cpi/home) (Samli, 2003). Specifically, the CPI is a measure of the average change over time in the prices paid by urban consumers for a market basket of consumer goods and services. CPI indices are available for the U.S. and various geographic areas. Average price data for certain utilities, automotive fuel, and food items are also available on the same website.

High CPI represents a state of low spending power and thus lower consumer wellbeing. Studies found that the total amount of spending, especially spending on necessities, is positively related to consumer happiness (e.g., Veenhoven et al., 2021) and that price increases tend to reduce the perceived value of goods and services (e.g., Peine et al., 2009).

While the CPI provides indirect information about general inflation and consumers' spending power, the measure does not directly capture consumers' actual disposable income, spending patterns, and consumers' consumption experiences that can impact consumer wellbeing. Consumer happiness is influenced not by the absolute amount of disposable income but also by relative income and spending behavior (cf. Dynan & Ravina, 2007; Headey et al., 2008). Furthermore, increased CPI (reduced spending power) may have a differential impact on consumers in different income brackets. Specifically, increased CPI reflects decreased spending power and real income, yet its detrimental wellbeing impact is usually greater for consumers with limited disposable income. Empirical evidence suggests that consumer happiness is positively associated with income (e.g., Aknin et al., 2009; Diener et al., 2013a, b; Sacks et al., 2012) and total spending (Veenhoven et al., 2021). Evidence also suggests that consumer happiness is negatively associated with decreases in income, especially for low-income consumers (e.g., Aknin et al., 2009). Yet, it should be noted that increased spending power does not proportionally increase consumer happiness because consumers adapt their marketplace expectations by inflating their expectations (cf. Kahneman & Deaton, 2010).

In summary, the cost-of-living model is useful in explaining consumer spending and shopping wellbeing. The detrimental effects of CPI on consumer happiness seem to be moderated by consumers' income levels. Thus, the effects of the cost of living on consumer happiness can be better captured using consumers' real income in addition to the CPI.

The Consumption Equity Model and Metrics

The *consumption equity model* argues that consumer happiness is high when there is a high level of consumption equity (Lee et al., 2002; Sirgy, 2021). While a high level of total consumption expenditure at the country level represents a high level of consumer wellbeing at the macro level, establishing a semblance of equity in the consumption of goods and services is very important. This is because a high level of consumption equity reflects the satisfaction of basic needs for human development for all. Research has shown that income inequality hurts happiness (e.g., Oishi et al., 2011; Wilkinson & Pickett, 2009).

The consumption equity model is based on the notion that consumer happiness results from social comparisons and relative spending (e.g., Dutt, 2009; Veenhoven, 1991; Veenhoven et al., 2021). Specifically, the *relative consumption hypothesis* posits that consumption happiness depends on higher levels of consumption (of certain things) than the level of consumption of others (Duesenberry, 1949). In other words, consumer happiness is high for those consumers who can consume at or above the same level as their significant others. In contrast, consumer happiness is low for those consumers who are unable to keep up with significant other's consumption level (e.g., MacDonald & Douthitt, 1992; Noll & Weick, 2015; Wang et al., 2019). Empirical evidence suggests that the relative deprivation effect is high, especially for the impoverished consumers (e.g., Hill et al., 2012) and for socially visible conspicuous products (e.g., Bertram-Hümmer & Baliki, 2015).

As such, the consumption equity model has evolved in two forms, namely *consumption expenditures* and *income inequality*. We will discuss these models in some detail below.

Consumption Expenditures

Quality-of-life researchers at the UNDP define quality of life partly in terms of satisfaction of basic needs and equity. In other words, human development, in their view, involves not only the satisfaction of basic needs but also equity in basic need satisfaction among different population segments. Researchers at the UNDP believe that countries should strive to increase or decrease consumption of goods and services to satisfy basic needs as a direct function of the ratio of total consumption expenditures and the size of the population. Thus, countries that are consuming too much (in relation to their population size) should decrease their rate of consumption, whereas countries consuming too little should increase their rate of consumption. Establishing a semblance of equity in the consumption of goods and services that meet basic needs equates with human development, ergo quality of life.

One measure of consumption inequality is the *Total Consumption Expenditure Index* (TCEI). The United Nations Development Programme (UNDP) uses various indicators and data to compare countries and world regions in their state of consumption (UNDP, 2003). The TCEI is a composite of the consumption of consumer products. Specifically, the TCEI is a composite of consumption of cars, paper products, telephone connections, electricity, total energy, meat, fish, and cereals. Thus, the TCEI score of a country refers to the summary of all expenses across various expenditure categories. The objective here is to compare the distribution of TCEI scores across various income groups. As such, the index measures equities and inequities in the consumption of goods and services that meet basic needs (Hill et al., 2007). Establishing a semblance of equity in the consumption of goods and services that meet basic needs is viewed as "just" (Sirgy, 2008). Uneven distribution of consumption expenditure in society represents a state of low consumer happiness.

As national income increases, it is important to have national prosperity trickle down to ordinary people in the country and provide all citizens with satisfaction of necessities and basic needs, thus ensuring consumption equity. As such, the TCEI provides useful information about consumption patterns in society. Yet, the information provided by the TCEI does not explain the causes of the consumption inequity and ways to improve it. In using the index to capture consumer wellbeing, one needs to consider other consumption factors affecting consumer happiness such as consumers' actual spending (absolute level of spending), choice of products (material possessions vs. experiences), degree of consumer need satisfaction, income levels, and social comparison (Howell & Hill, 2009), and among others.

Income Inequality

Most economists have customarily used objective measures to capture income inequality at the national level. A well-accepted objective measure is the *Gini Coefficient*. This measure is a summary statistic that reflects how fairly income is distributed in a population (e.g., Charles et al., 2022; Farris, 2010). The Gini coefficient (also known as the "Gini Ratio"), is a measure of statistical dispersion intended to denote the income inequality or the wealth inequality within a nation or a social group The measure rates a given society from 0 (where every person has the same income) to 1 (where one person has all the income, and others have none). See Table 5.1 for more details.

Income inequality is also regarded as the feelings of people who perceive themselves to be disadvantaged or advantaged in terms of income (Temkin, 1993).

Table 5.1 Calculating the Gini coefficient

Total disposable income = (income from employment + property income + private transfers (e.g., remittances) + public monetary transfers (e.g., social security) + public employment pensions received) – workers' contribution paid – direct tax paid).
Per capita disposable income = [total disposable income in the household / the number of household members]
The Gini index (G) is determined mathematically as the average of the absolute value of the relative mean difference in per capita disposable incomes between all possible pairs of individuals.

Source: Adapted from Charles et al. (2022)

Table 5.2 A subjective measure of income inequality

The survey asks the respondent to answer the question, "Do you think the disparity between the rich and the poor has grown in the past 5 years in this country?" on a 5-point scale (1 = no; 2 = if pressed to say, I would say no; 3 = I cannot say either way; 4 = if pressed to say, I would say yes; 5 = yes).

Source: Adapted from Oshio and Urakawa (2014)

Subjective measures of income inequality capture the extent to which an individual believes that income is distributed evenly among members of their society. Perceived income inequality thus varies among individuals within a society (e.g., Oshio & Urakawa, 2014). See Table 5.2 for an example of how this construct is typically measured in social surveys.

There is empirical evidence demonstrating that both objective and subjective measures of actual income inequality have negative effects on consumer happiness (e.g., Hagerty, 2000; Oishi et al., 2011; Oshio & Urakawa, 2014). Inequality is also found to harm life satisfaction in the OECD countries (e.g., Graafland & Lous, 2018). In addition, consumers with relative income disadvantage within the reference group tend to report lower levels of consumer happiness (e.g., Oshio et al., 2011).

In summary, consumption inequality is associated with decreased consumer happiness due to relative deprivation and perceived unfairness. While the Gini Coefficient can capture the degree of uneven distribution of consumption spending, an increase in consumption equity may not be proportionally related to increases in consumer happiness. In other words, the effect of consumption equity on consumer happiness can be negatively asymmetric in that consumption inequality decreases consumer happiness, while consumer equality may not necessarily increase happiness.

The Consumer Complaints Model and Metrics

The *consumer complaints model* focuses on consumers' negative consumption experiences that lead to consumers' complaints. Consumers are likely to be unhappy when they experience poor quality of goods and services and improper and unfair marketing practices. The model posits that consumer happiness in each country or locality is high when the number of consumer complaints is small (Lee et al., 2002; Sirgy, 2021).

The Better Business Bureau (BBB) of the U.S. developed a consumer happiness metric based on consumer complaint data (https://www.thelocalbbb.com). Consumer complaints for specific companies and brands are aggregated across all BBB communities. A high level of complaints in relation to a specific company or brand represents a lower level of consumer happiness in relation to that brand or company.

It should be noted that consumer happiness is not just about increasing positive consumer experiences (increasing organizational beneficence), but it is also about reducing negative consumer experiences (decreasing organizational malfeasance) (Sirgy & Lee, 2008). Consumers can become happier by increasing positive affect and/or decreasing negative affect (cf. Diener et al., 1999). All else being equal, preventing a negative experience is likely to provide a three to fivefold return on investment over adding a positive one (cf. Fredrickson & Losada, 2005). Furthermore, consumers adapt to positive stimuli more quickly and completely, but to negative stimuli more slowly and partially (Lucas, 2005). Thus, firms and policymakers need to take proactive measures and exert conscientious efforts to reduce consumer complaints related to marketplace experiences.

It should also be noted that the consumer complaint measure captures organizational malfeasance. While this measure captures the frequency of complaints, the measure does not capture the emotional intensity of consumer complaints or consumers' affective response to the organizational response to consumers' complaints. Furthermore, the complaints measure does not capture consumers' dissatisfaction without complaints (e.g., third-party negative word of mouth, customer exit without complaints) or consumers' illegitimate complaints (e.g., opportunistic customer claiming organizational wrongdoing without merit) (Wirtz & McColl-Kennedy, 2010). Thus, caution is warranted not to assume that absence or reduction of consumer complaints would increase consumer happiness.

Differently put, the complaint measure needs to be supplemented with other measures capturing the beneficence dimension of wellbeing (e.g., the quality or perceived value model) or other subjective measures such as the *American Customer Satisfaction Index*. Similarly, *Consumer Reports* (www.consumerreports.org), a monthly publication of the Consumer Union, provides expert assessments of product quality for a variety of goods and services. Common dimensions of quality include experts' ratings of product reliability, durability, and safety as well as owner satisfaction ratings. A high level of positive assessment for a specific product represents a higher level of consumer wellbeing (Sirgy, 2021).

The Consumer Sentiment Model and Metrics

The consumer sentiment model argues that consumer wellbeing is high when consumers have a generally positive sentiment towards marketing activities at the local level (Gaski & Etzel, 2005).

Consumers' sentiments toward key activities of marketing practices are measured using the *Index of Consumer Sentiment towards Marketing* (ICSM), a multidimensional instrument that examines consumers' sentiment towards product quality, price of products, advertising for products, and retailing/selling (Gaski & Etzel, 1986, 2005). Specifically, the measure taps consumers' attitudes towards marketing activities such as perceived value, truth in advertising, the perceived value of retail experiences, perceived fairness in pricing, and satisfaction with the provision of goods and services (Peterson & Ekici, 2007). Thus, one can say that a positive attitude towards marketing practices is reflective of satisfaction with consumer life.

Research shows that increases in prices (as reflected in the CPI) are negatively related to the consumer sentiment measure (Gaski &Etzel, 2005). Additionally, research has provided evidence suggesting the consumer sentiment measure is positively associated with other measures of consumer wellbeing (Ganglmair-Wooliscroft & Lawson, 2011).

The ICSM is the major metric used to capture consumer sentiment. The exact measure is shown in Table 5.3.

Table 5.3 The survey items of the index of consumer sentiment towards marketing

Product quality

- The quality of most products I buy today is as good as can be expected.
- *I am satisfied with most of the products I buy.
- *Most products I buy wear out too quickly. (R)
- Products are not made as well as they used to be. (R)
- *Too many of the products I buy are defective in some way. (R)
- *The companies that make products I buy don't care enough about how well they perform. (R)
- *The quality of products I buy has consistently improved over the years.

Price

- *Most products I buy are overpriced. (R)
- *Businesses could charge lower prices and still be profitable. (R)
- *Most prices are reasonable considering the high cost of doing business.
- Competition between companies keeps prices reasonable.
- Companies are unjustified in charging the prices they charge. (R)
- *Most prices are fair.
- *In general, I am satisfied with the prices I pay.

Advertising

- Most advertising provides consumers with essential information.
- *Most advertising is very annoying. (R)
- *Most advertising makes false claims. (R)
- *If most advertising was eliminated, consumers would be better off. (R)
- *I enjoy most ads.
- Advertising should be more closely regulated. (R)
- *Most advertising is intended to deceive rather than to inform consumers. (R)

Retailing or Selling

- *Most retail stores serve their customers well.
- *Because of the way retailers treat me, most of my shopping is unpleasant. (R)
- *I find most retail salespeople to be very helpful.
- Most retail stores provide an adequate selection of merchandise.
- In general, most middlemen make excessive profits. (R)
- *When I need assistance in a store, I am usually not able to get it. (R)
- *Most retailers provide adequate service.

Response scale: Five-point scale (1 = "agree strongly" to 5 = "disagree strongly."); Asterisk indicates item retained after purification. (R) indicates reverse scored.

Source: Adapted from Gaski and Etzel (1986, 2005)

The Shopping Satisfaction Model and Metrics

The shopping satisfaction model posits that consumer's cumulative experiences with retail shopping contribute significantly to consumer happiness. This model has evolved to take form in several conceptualizations with corresponding metrics.

Satisfaction with Major Retail Establishments in the Local Area

This model posits that consumer happiness is high when consumers are satisfied with the various local retail establishments from which they purchase needed goods and services (Meadow, 1983). The shopping satisfaction model measures consumer happiness with the *Overall Consumer Satisfaction Composite* (OCSC). Specifically, the measure is designed to capture consumers' expressed satisfaction with local retail institutions in purchasing food, housing, household operations, household furnishings, clothing and accessories, personal care, medical care, recreation, transportation, and education (Meadow & Sirgy, 2008). That is, this measure focuses on consumers' overall satisfaction with their various shopping experiences. The OCSC measure is based on the notion that consumers' satisfying shopping experiences spillover to the life domain housing affective experiences related to the marketplace, which in turn, spills over to influence satisfaction with life at large. *Shopping satisfaction* is commonly measured using the overall consumer satisfaction composite Index. The construct is measured with five items and responses are captured through a 5-point Likert scale. See the exact items in Table 5.4.

Table 5.4 Measures pertaining to the shopping satisfaction model (overall consumer satisfaction composite index)

Overall Consumer Satisfaction Composite Index was derived by summing the scores pertaining to the following five items.
• Overall, I am satisfied with the products I purchase from business people and firms. • Overall, I am satisfied with the services I purchase from business people and firms. • Overall, I am satisfied with the interactions I have had with business people and firms from whom I have purchased products. • Overall, I am satisfied with the interactions I have had with business people and firms whom I had purchased services. • Overall, as a CONSUMER, I am satisfied with my dealings with business people and firms from whom I purchase products and services.
Response scale: A 5-point Likert-type scale was used to capture responses to these items ("Agree ___: ___: ___: ___: ___: Disagree" "Agree" was coded as 5 all the way to "Disagree" as 1 with the in-between categories as 2, 3, and 4.

Source: Meadow and Sirgy (2008)

Table 5.5 The shopping wellbeing measure

The exact items of the shopping wellbeing measure are as follows: • Thinking about shopping, I feel that my shopping contributes significantly to my own personal wellbeing. • Thinking about shopping, my quality of life would diminish significantly if I don't shop. • Thinking about shopping, I feel that shopping makes me happy. • Thinking about shopping, I feel that shopping contributes significantly to my quality of life overall. • I feel that my shopping activities contribute significantly to my family wellbeing. • The quality of life of my family would diminish significantly if I don't shop. • I feel that shopping makes me happy because shopping contributes much to my family wellbeing. • I feel that my shopping contributes significantly to my family's quality of life overall.
Response scale: 7-point Likert scale: strongly disagree (1) – strongly agree (7)

Source: Ekici et al. (2018)

Shopping Wellbeing/Ill-Being

Shopping wellbeing/ill-being involves two dimensions: (1) wellbeing (i.e., positive beliefs regarding the degree to which shopping contributes to quality of life), and (2) ill-being (negative beliefs related to the degree to which shopping activities result in overspending time, effort, and money) (Ekici et al., 2018; Lee et al., 2014; Sirgy, Lee, & Yu, 2020).

Table 5.5 shows the measure of shopping wellbeing, whereas Table 5.6 shows the measure of shopping ill-being. These two measures were validated by demonstrating that the two dimensions are significant predictors of life satisfaction (life satisfaction is a positive function of the former dimension and negative about the latter dimension).

The Material Possessions Satisfaction Model and Metrics

The material possessions satisfaction model focuses on material possessions; the model posits that satisfaction with material possessions exerts a major and positive influence on consumer happiness (e.g., Andrews & Withey, 1976; Nakano, MacDonald, & Douthitt, 1995; Sirgy et al., 1998a, b; Smits & Steendijk, 2015). Material possessions are associated with important positive wellbeing benefits. Material products provide consumers with enduring satisfaction of consumption needs in that consumer durables are less ephemeral (Carter & Gilovich, 2010), remind people of accomplishments (Goodman et al., 2016), and are more visible for status signaling (Mandel et al., 2006).

Over the years, the *possessions satisfaction model* of consumer happiness has evolved into several offshoots with corresponding metrics.

Table 5.6 The shopping ill-being measure

The survey items for shopping ill-being measure are as follows
• Our family and close friends often complain that I spend too much time shopping. • and not enough time with the family. • Our family and close friends often complain that I spend much money on shopping causing a great deal of family strife. • Our family and close friends often complain that I spend too much energy shopping and not enough energy for family. • Our family and close friends often complain that I spend too much time shopping and not enough time for work. • Our family and close friends often complain that I spend too much money shopping and not enough money to further develop my career. • Our family and close friends often complain that I spend too much energy shopping and not enough energy to bolster my career. • Our family and close friends often complain that I spend too much time shopping and not enough time socializing with others. • Our family and close friends often complain that I spend too much money shopping and not enough money for social activities. • Our family and close friends often complain that I spend too much energy shopping and not enough energy for social activities. • Our family and close friends often complain that I spend too much time shopping and not enough time for leisure activities. • Our family and close friends often complain that I spend too much money shopping and not enough money for leisure activities. • Our family and close friends often complain that I spend too much energy shopping and not enough energy for leisure activities. • Our family and close friends often complain that I spend too much time shopping and not enough time making money by working hard. • Our family and close friends often complain that I spend too much money shopping creating havoc on financial life. • Our family and close friends often complain that I spend too much energy shopping and not enough energy for making money by working hard.
Response scale: 7-point Likert scale: strongly disagree (1) – strongly agree (7)

Source: Ekici et al. (2018)

Satisfaction with Material Possessions

The essence of the *bottom-up spillover theory of life satisfaction* (e.g., Diener, 1984; Sirgy, 2002) is the notion of a satisfaction hierarchy, and that positive and negative affect spill from concrete events in the marketplace (e.g., events related to standard of living, cost of living, and consumption of material possessions) to life domains (e.g., consumer life) to overall life.

Andrews and Withey (1976) measured *Material Possession Satisfaction* (referred to as the *Consumer Index*) in terms of people's feelings about their possessions. These scholars operationalized the *Consumer Index* in terms of people's feelings about transportation and access to work and shopping, the medical services in their area, and the goods and services they can get when they buy in their area—things like food, appliances, and clothes.

Satisfaction with Material Possessions and Standard of Living

Nakano et al. (1995) focused on *consumers' overall satisfaction with their material possessions and standard of living*. Their measure involves two survey items: "How do you feel about your standard of living — the things you have like housing, car, furniture, recreation, and the like?" and "How do you feel about the extent to which your physical needs are met?" Consumer wellbeing is computed as a composite of these two items.

Possession Satisfaction of Economic Goods

Sirgy, Lee et al. (1998a, b) focused on *possession satisfaction of economic goods*. They found that consumer happiness is high when consumers are satisfied with their material possessions. Data provided construct validation by demonstrating that (1) satisfaction with material possessions influences overall life satisfaction; (2) this effect is moderated by materialism (i.e., emotional involvement with material possessions)--satisfaction with material possessions more strongly influence life satisfaction for materialistic than for non-materialistic consumers; and (3) satisfaction with material possessions is influenced by materialism–those who are materialistic are more likely to be dissatisfied with their possessions because they have high possession expectations. See the measure in Table 5.7.

Evaluation of Standard of Living in the Context of Television Viewership

Sirgy et al. (1998a, b) found that frequent TV viewership is negatively associated with consumers' *specific evaluations of standard of living*, especially for those consumers with high materialism; and that specific evaluations of standard of living

Table 5.7 Satisfaction with material possessions

"If you own any of the following items, please indicate the extent to which you are satisfied/dissatisfied with possessing or owing something-a classic car or a piece of property-even though you never use. Or they might be pleased both to own and to use the thing. On these items, indicate only how you feel about owning the item, not how you feel about using or consuming it. Respond only to the items you own.
1. House or condominium 2. Consumer electronics (CD player, TV, VCR, computers, etc.) 3. Furniture and/or appliances 4. Private transportation (cars, trucks, motorcycles, and bicycles) 5. Clothing, accessories, and jewelry 6. Savings and investments
Response scale: 1 = awful, 2 = bad, 3 = unsatisfactory, 4 = neutral, 5 = satisfactory, 6 = good, 7 = wonderful; 0 = no opinion, missing value

Source: Sirgy et al. (1998a, b)

Table 5.8 Evaluation of standard of living measure

Specific evaluations of the standard of living: 1. I am more well off financially than most people shown on television commercials. 2. The average family we see in most ads has a higher standard of living than my own family. (reverse coded) 3. Advertisers seem to show that people are upper-middle class and happy. (reverse coded) 4. I usually find that I am materially better off than the typical family shown on television. 5. I believe that my family's standard of living is below that of the typical family shown on television. (reverse coded) 6. Most television commercials show upscale families using advertised products and services. (reverse coded). 7. I consider my family to be lower class compared to the typical family they show on television. (reverse coded).
Response scale: Five-point Likert scales ranging from "strongly disagree" (1) to "strongly agree" (5).
General evaluation of the standard of living: How do you feel about your standard of living or income as a whole?
Response scale: Seven-point rating scale ranging from "delighted" (7) to "terrible" (1)

Source: Adapted from Sirgy et al. (1998a, b)

tend to exert a positive influence on evaluations of general standard of living, which in turn plays a positive role in overall life satisfaction.

Specific evaluations of standard of living in the context of television viewership involve the belief that one is more (or less) materially well off than the average family typically shown in television advertising (Sirgy et al., 1998a, b). The measure of specific evaluation of the standard of living was operationalized through the following seven self-report items shown in Table 5.8.

Wealth

Wealth is a concept borrowed from economics and has been used to conceptualize and measure consumer happiness. For example, Smits and Steendijk (2015) define wealth as the degree to which the household possesses a basic set of assets, valued highly by people across the globe.

The measure of this construct is the *International Wealth Index* (IWI). The assets included in the IWI involve seven consumer durables (possession of a TV, refrigerator, phone, bicycle, car, cheap utensil and expensive utensil), access to two public services (water and electricity) and three housing characteristics (number of sleeping rooms, quality of floor material and quality of toilet facility). If a household owns a specific durable, has better access to public services, or has a higher value on a housing characteristic, its IWI value is raised by a specific amount (the rescaled asset weight). The IWI scale runs from 0 to 100. If a household has all durables and the highest quality housing and services, its IWI value is 100. If it has none of the durables and the lowest quality housing and services, its IWI value is 0.

Empirical studies found that consumer wellbeing is high when consumers are satisfied with their material possessions (Sirgy et al., 1998a, b). This is because material possession provides consumers with satisfaction of various consumption needs, including physiological and safety needs, symbolic needs, and social needs. Studies found that satisfaction with standard of living was a significantly stronger predictor of overall life satisfaction than of affective feelings of happiness, whereas psychological need fulfillment significantly more strongly predicted positive feelings than evaluations of life (Diener et al., 2010). The results of a review of study findings indicate that consumer happiness is positively associated with home ownership and car ownership (Veenhoven et al., 2021).

It should also be noted that too much emphasis on material possessions (i.e., high materialism) can harm consumer happiness. Research indicates that materialism has a negative influence on consumer happiness (e.g., Dittmar et al., 2014; Kasser & Ahuvia, 2002). For example, possession of material products is perceived as being materialistic (Van Boven et al., 2010); it also promotes loneliness (Pieters, 2013). Research has also shown that materialistic consumers experience low subjective wellbeing. This effect may be due to several factors. First, materialistic consumers experience less social wellbeing because of their non-generosity and competitiveness; that is people don't like to socialize much with individuals who come across as being selfish (not willing to share their wealth with others) and competitive (always wanting to prove their superiority to others) (e.g., Ahuvia, 2015; Belk, 1985; Richins & Dawson, 1992).

Second, materialistic consumers do not fully enjoy the hedonic benefits of life experiences (e.g., Zhang et al., 2014). That is, they focus on material possessions, not marketplace experiences. Experiences tend to promote happiness much more than material possessions (e.g., Van Boven & Gilovich, 2003)

Third, materialistic consumers place high priority on extrinsic goals (e.g., wealth, fame, an attractive image) rather than intrinsic goals (e.g., affiliation, personal growth, community) (e.g., Kasser, 2003; Kasser & Ahuvia, 2002). Attainment of intrinsic goals tends to be more value-laden, contributing to subjective wellbeing much more than extrinsic goals.

And finally, materialistic consumers tend to frequently evaluate their social standing with others. These social comparisons tend to be upward comparisons (i.e., evaluating their social standing with others who have higher social standing). These upward social comparisons tend to produce dissatisfaction with their social standing, which in turn takes a toll on their subjective wellbeing (Sirgy, 1998).

In summary, the material possessions model of consumer happiness focuses on the possession stage of consumption, especially in relation to material possessions (satisfaction with material possessions and satisfaction with standard of living). It should be noted that the possession model does not fully capture consumer happiness from consumption experiences. Consumer experiences are very important aspects of consumer happiness. Also, note that consumer experiences provide greater consumer happiness than material possessions.

The Acquisition/Possessions Satisfaction Model and Metrics

The *acquisition/possession satisfaction model* posits that consumer happiness is primarily influenced by acquisition and possession satisfaction (Day, 1978, 1987; Leelakulthanit et al., 1991). In this two-factor model, consumer happiness is conceptualized as satisfaction with shopping for products in the local area and satisfaction with ownership of a certain configuration of products. Specifically, acquisition satisfaction refers to satisfaction experiences related to the purchase of consumer goods and services, whereas possession satisfaction refers to satisfaction experiences related to ownership of material consumer goods.

The acquisition/possession satisfaction model has two measurement dimensions (Leelakulthanit et al., 1991). The acquisition dimension refers to shopping experiences. Examples include consumer satisfaction with assortment, quality, and price of goods available in local stores; the attractiveness of the local stores; the courtesy and helpfulness of personnel in the local stores; and after-purchase service provided by the local stores (e.g., warranty policies, return policies). The possession dimension focuses on experiences related to material possessions (e.g., ownership of house/apartment, furniture, car/truck, clothing/accessories, savings, etc.).

Research found that satisfying purchase and usage of products are positively associated with overall wellbeing (e.g., Chancellor & Lyubomirsky, 2011; Goldsmith, 2016). Research also has shown that ownership of luxury conveniences and satisfaction with the standard of living are strongly associated with life satisfaction (e.g., Diener et al., 2010).

The acquisition/possession model taps consumer need satisfaction mainly for the material products. This model is useful in explaining consumer happiness resulting from acquisition and possession of consumer durables. Yet, the model does not incorporate the effects of consumer experiences (e.g., service experiences and consumer activities) on consumer happiness. Consumer experiences can have a greater impact on consumer happiness than material possessions (e.g., Van Boven & Gilovich, 2003).

The Consumer/Product Life Cycle Model and Metrics

The consumer/product life cycle model posits that consumer happiness is influenced by consumers' product acquisition, preparation, possession, consumption, maintenance, and disposal experiences (Lee et al., 2002; Sirgy et al., 2008; Sirgy, 2021). Specifically, the consumer/product life cycle means the stages or types of marketplace experiences consumers have with goods and services, including product acquisition, product assembly for personal use, product use, product ownership, product maintenance, and product disposal (cf. Sirgy, 2008; Vadrevu, 2014). Consumers experience satisfaction and dissatisfaction about the different stages of the consumer/product life cycle, signaling how consumers feel about marketplace experiences in general, which in turn influences their overall life satisfaction (cf. Mogilner et al., 2012; Nicolao et al., 2009).

Sirgy et al. (2008) developed a metric of consumer wellbeing based on the notion that consumers experience wellbeing in their local area of residence and this experience can be captured through consumer satisfaction related to (1) shopping for desired consumer goods and services in the local area, (2) preparing locally purchased consumer durables for personal use, (3) consuming locally purchased goods and services, (4) owning consumer durables purchased in the local area, (5) using repair and maintenance services in the local area, and (6) using selling, trading-in, and disposal services in the local area. See the measure in Table 5.9.

The consumer/product life cycle model can easily be applied to measure consumer happiness in relation to consumer durables because consumer durables go through the entire consumption cycle. Some services and experiences are intangible and do not go through the entire cycle. For these products, acquisition and consumption occur simultaneously.

Furthermore, research has found that the consumer/product life cycle measure has predictive validity in relation to life satisfaction for only acquisition satisfaction, possession satisfaction, and consumption satisfaction, but not maintenance and disposal satisfaction (Lee et al., 2002).

It should be noted that the extent to which each type of experience contributes to consumer happiness depends on consumers' shopping involvement (e.g., Bergadaa et al., 1995), consumers' level of materialism (e.g., Richins & Dawson, 1992), consumers' experiential buying tendency (e.g., Howell et al., 2012), product care tendency (e.g., Ackermann et al., 2021), and environmental consciousness (e.g., Schlegelmilch et al., 1996). That is, satisfaction with marketplace experiences tends to contribute more to subjective wellbeing when consumers are more emotionally involved in their shopping, are less materialistic, are more involved with consumer services than goods, tend to be more involved in the maintenance and repair of their purchased goods, and are environmentally conscious.

The Community Satisfaction Model and Metrics

There are two models and corresponding measures of consumer happiness based on the concept of community satisfaction: (1) the model that focuses on residents' satisfaction with community services, and (2) the model that focuses on a composite of community satisfaction dimensions affecting various life domains.

Residents' Satisfaction with Community Services

The model about residents' satisfaction with community services is based on the notion that consumers experience wellbeing within the community to the extent that they are satisfied with various community services (Sirgy & Cornwell, 2001; Sirgy

Table 5.9 The consumer/product life cycle metric

Acquisition (shopping) satisfaction: Experiences related to shopping for products in your local area that you and your family need

"Please indicate how satisfied or dissatisfied you are with shopping for a variety of consumer goods and services in your local area—that is, availability and sufficiency of stores and retail outlets selling consumer goods and services as well as the quality of these retail services (e.g., store hours, courtesy of personnel, refund/exchange policy, among others). Respond to only those stores you have patronized; skip those you have not patronized.

- Satisfaction with shopping malls
- Satisfaction with shopping plazas and centers
- Satisfaction with department stores
- Satisfaction with discount stores
- Satisfaction with grocery stores
- Satisfaction with drug stores
- Satisfaction with sporting goods stores
- Satisfaction with consumer electronics stores
- Satisfaction with clothing boutiques
- Satisfaction with furniture stores
- Satisfaction with other specialty stores (e.g., toy stores, gift stores)"

Response scale: Seven-point semantic differential anchored by very dissatisfied (–3) and very satisfied (+3)

Preparation (assembly) satisfaction: Experiences related to *preparing products you bought* in the local area for personal use

"Please indicate how satisfied or dissatisfied you are with your experiences related to product assembly (or preparation of these products for personal use) of the following products you bought in the local area in the last year or so? *Respond to only those products you have purchased; skip those you have not purchased.*

- Consumer electronics (e.g., CD player, TV, computers)
- Furniture (e.g., sofas, dining sets)
- Appliances (e.g., microwave oven, refrigerator)
- Personal transportation (e.g., cars, trucks, motorcycles)
- Clothing and clothing accessories (e.g., suits, jewelry)
- Lawn and garden tools and equipment"

Response scale: Seven-point semantic differential anchored by *very dissatisfied* (–3) and *very satisfied* (+3)

Consumption (use) satisfaction: Experiences related to the *actual use of products and services* you bought in the local area

"Please indicate how satisfied or dissatisfied you are with the quality and performance of most consumer goods and services purchased in your local area in the last year or so. *Respond to only those products you have used; skip those you have not used.*

- **Consumer goods:**
  - Consumer electronics (e.g., CD player, TV, computers)
  - Furniture (e.g., sofas, dining sets)
  - Appliances (e.g., microwave oven, refrigerator)
  - Personal transportation (e.g., cars, trucks, motorcycles)
  - Clothing and clothing accessories (e.g., suits, jewelry)
  - Lawn and garden tools and equipment
- **Consumer services**:
  - Banking/savings services
  - Insurance services
  - Taxi/private transportation
  - Restaurants/night clubs
  - Health care services
  - Telephone services
  - Electric services
  - Gas/oil services
  - Real estate and realtor services
  - Day care services
  - Nursing homes/retirement community–type services
  - Primary schools
  - Secondary schools
  - Community colleges
  - Colleges and universities
  - Continuing education
  - Investment services
  - Legal services
  - Entertainment
  - Spectator sports
  - TV stations
  - Radio stations
  - Local newspaper"

Response scale: Seven-point semantic differential anchored by *very dissatisfied* (–3) and *very satisfied* (+3)

Possession (ownership) satisfaction: Experiences related to the *ownership of products* you bought in the local area

"Please indicate how satisfied or dissatisfied you are with the monetary value of owning those products you purchased in your local area over the last year or so. *Respond to only those products you own that were purchased in the local area; skip those you do not own.*

- Consumer electronics (e.g., CD player, TV, computers)
- Furniture (e.g., sofas, dining sets)
- Appliances (e.g., microwave oven, refrigerator)
- Personal transportation (e.g., cars, trucks, motorcycles)
- Clothing and clothing accessories (e.g., suits, jewelry)
- Lawn and garden tools and equipment
- Savings and investments
- Real estate
- Boat and other leisure investments"

Response scale: Seven-point semantic differential anchored by *very dissatisfied* (–3) and *very satisfied* (+3)

Maintenance (repair) satisfaction: Experiences related to the use of *repair and maintenance services* in the local area

"Please indicate how satisfied or dissatisfied you are with the quality and performance of maintenance and repair services of consumer goods you used in the last year or so. *Respond to only those products you have repaired or serviced in the local area; skip those you have not repaired or serviced.*

- Consumer electronics (e.g., CD player, TV, computers)
- Furniture (e.g., sofas, dining sets)
- Appliances (e.g., microwave oven, refrigerator)
- Personal transportation (e.g., cars, trucks, motorcycles)
- Clothing and clothing accessories (e.g., suits, jewelry)
- Lawn and garden tools and equipment"

[Seven-point semantic differential anchored by *very dissatisfied* (–3) and *very satisfied* (+3)].

Disposal satisfaction: "Experiences related to the disposal of consumer goods in the local area"

"Please indicate how satisfied or dissatisfied you are with the quality and performance of services designed to assist consumers like you to dispose of their consumed products. For example, computer stores in some local areas help computer owners dispose of their old computers, auto junk yards help car owners dispose of their junked cars, waste management disposal sites, thrift stores, and so on. *Respond to only those product categories which you actually used selling services; skip those you have not used.*

- Consumer electronics (e.g., CD player, TV, computers)
- Furniture (e.g., sofas, dining sets)
- Appliances (e.g., microwave oven, refrigerator)
- Private transportation (e.g., cars, trucks, motorcycles)
- Clothing and clothing accessories (e.g., suits, jewelry)
- Lawn and garden tools and equipment"

Response scale: Seven-point semantic differential anchored by *very dissatisfied* (–3) and *very satisfied* (+3)

Source: Adapted from Sirgy et al. (2008)

Table 5.10 A metric of consumer wellbeing based on residents' satisfaction with community services

- Satisfaction with individual government services such as fire, rescue, library, police, and sanitation services.
- Satisfaction with individual business services such as banking/ savings, insurance, restaurants/night clubs, and daycare services.
- Satisfaction with individual nonprofit services such as alcohol/drug, crisis intervention, adoption/foster care, and family planning services.
- Satisfaction with other community aspects such as quality of the environment in the community (air, water, land, etc.), the rate of change to the natural landscape (deforestation, housing/commercial development, loss of agricultural land, ridge-line development, etc.), race relations in the community, cost of living in the community, crime in the community, ties with people in the community, one's neighborhood, and one's housing situation.

Response scale: Delighted-Terrible Scale: +3 (delighted), +2 (pleased), +1 (mostly satisfied), 0 (mixed feelings), −1 (mostly dissatisfied), −2 (unhappy), and −3 (terrible)

Source: Adapted from Sirgy and Cornwell (2001)

et al., 2010). The focus here is on residents' satisfaction with local business, government services, and nonprofit organizations in the community. Specifically, this model posits that global consumer satisfaction in one's local area is a function of global satisfaction with government services, business services, and nonprofit services.

Furthermore, global consumer satisfaction with community is (1) predicted by the sum of satisfaction with individual *business services* (e.g., banking/ savings, insurance, restaurants, etc.) – weighted by the perceived importance of those business services, (2) the sum of satisfaction with individual *government services* (e.g. fire, rescue, library, etc.) – weighted by the perceived importance of those government services, (3) the sum of satisfaction with individual *nonprofit services* (e.g., alcohol/drug abuse, crisis intervention, adoption/foster care, etc.) – weighted by the perceived importance of those nonprofit services, (4) the sum of global satisfaction with quality of the environment in the community (air, water, land, etc.), rate of change to the natural landscape (deforestation, housing/commercial development, loss of agricultural land, ridge-line development, etc.), race relations in the community, cost of living in the community, crime in the community, ties with people in the community, one's neighborhood, and one's housing situation – weighted by the perceived importance of those community aspects. See selected items related to the metric underlying the residents' satisfaction with community services in Table 5.10.

Residents' Satisfaction with Life Domains Influenced by Community Services

The second model of consumer satisfaction based on community wellbeing is based on the notion that consumers experience wellbeing in their local area to the extent that they are satisfied with community services affecting various life domains (Sirgy et al., 2010). As such, the authors developed a formative index based on community satisfaction indicators affecting various life domains.

The formative index is composed of a set of community services affecting the various life domains of residents. Specifically, the formative index is composed of satisfaction with community systems affecting the residents' safety, social wellbeing, leisure wellbeing, family and home wellbeing, political wellbeing, spiritual wellbeing, neighborhood wellbeing, environmental wellbeing, transportation wellbeing, education wellbeing, health, work wellbeing, financial wellbeing, and shopping wellbeing. See the metric in Table 5.11.

The Need Satisfaction Model and Metrics

The need satisfaction model of consumer happiness posits that consumer wellbeing can be enhanced when consumers can satisfy multiple needs through marketplace experiences (El Hedhli et al., 2013; Sirgy et al., 2006, 2011). Specifically, satisfaction with an individual's needs progresses hierarchically, beginning with the most basic low-order needs such as food, clothing, and shelter, and moving sequentially on a path toward high-order psychological needs and, eventually, to self-actualization. The low-order needs (physiological needs, safety needs) are rooted in deprivation and correspond to extrinsic motivation, while the high-order "being" needs (belongingness and love, esteem, and self-actualization needs) come from within for growth and enlightenment and correspond to intrinsic motivation.

In this hierarchy of needs, the emergence of the higher-order growth needs depends on first satisfying the basic survival and safety needs. Wellbeing increases as one ascends the hierarchy up to the level of self-actualization, which is the full realization of one's potential (Maslow, 1954).

The basic premise of the need satisfaction model of consumer wellbeing is that consumer happiness is higher when consumer goods and services serve to meet the full spectrum of human development needs compared to consumer goods and services that satisfy only a small subset of needs. As such, the model argues that satisfaction in a particular domain (e.g., work life, family life) is maximized when the person experiences satisfaction about safety, economic, family, social, esteem, actualization, knowledge, and aesthetics needs – the full spectrum of human developmental needs. The greater the satisfaction, the more positive affect (the less negative affect) accumulates in that domain. For example, Sirgy et al. (2017) found that the benefits of consumers' leisure wellbeing are influenced by a set of basic need benefits and growth need benefits, and that unmet basic needs showed an inverse relation with wellbeing (cf. Diener et al., 2010).

The need satisfaction metric (Sirgy et al., 2010) is based on the notion that consumer goods and services serving to meet the full spectrum of human development needs are likely to contribute to consumer wellbeing, compared to goods and services that satisfy only a small subset of needs. For example, this metric was also employed in the context of personal transportation (Sirgy et al., 2006). The measure

Table 5.11 Residents' satisfaction with life domains influenced by community services

Overall community wellbeing index: a formative composite of the following dimensions
• Community systems affecting safety and wellbeing
• Community systems affecting social wellbeing
• Community systems affecting leisure wellbeing
• Community systems affecting family and home wellbeing
• Community systems affecting political wellbeing
• Community systems affecting spiritual wellbeing
• Community systems affecting neighborhood wellbeing
• Community systems affecting environmental wellbeing
• Community systems affecting transportation wellbeing
• Community systems affecting education wellbeing
• Community systems affecting health and wellbeing
• Community systems affecting work wellbeing
• Community systems affecting financial wellbeing
• Community systems affecting consumer wellbeing
Community systems affecting safety
• Race relations in the community area
• Your personal safety in your neighborhood
• Your personal safety in public places
• Security against break-ins to your home
• Fire protection for your neighborhood
• Police protection for your neighborhood
• Crime prevention efforts in the community area
• Small animal control
Community systems affecting social wellbeing
• Your neighbors
• The racial mix in your neighborhood
• Your friends and acquaintances in the community area
• Church-related activities

Community systems affecting leisure wellbeing
- Entertainment facilities
- Entertainment activities
- Recreational facilities
- Recreational activities
- Parks available in and near the community

Community systems affecting family and home wellbeing
- The number of children in your neighborhood
- Behavior of children in your neighborhood
- Your own family life
- The interior of your home
- The exterior of your home

Community systems affecting political wellbeing
- Community leaders
- Your local township or city government
- Local government services generally
- Property taxes in the community area

Community systems affecting spiritual wellbeing
- Church-related activities
- Church membership
- Frequency of church attendance

Community systems affecting neighborhood wellbeing
- Your neighbors
- The number of children in your neighborhood
- Behavior of children in your neighborhood
- Your personal safety in your neighborhood
- The racial mix in your neighborhood
- Security against break-ins to your home
- The number of trees in your neighborhood
- The appearance of homes in your neighborhood
- The amount of traffic on your own street

(continued)

Table 5.11 (continued)

- Fire protection for your neighborhood
- Police protection for your neighborhood
- Garbage collection in your neighborhood
- Grocery stores in your neighborhood
- Overall satisfaction with the quality of life in the community

Community systems affecting environmental wellbeing

- The number of trees in your neighborhood
- The appearance of commercial and business areas
- The appearance of public places generally
- The appearance of the residential area
- The appearance of homes in your neighborhood
- The appearance of the community area generally
- The interior of your home
- The exterior of your home
- The conditions of the street in the community area
- The climate in the community area
- Parks available in and near the community
- Garbage collection in your neighborhood

Community systems affecting transportation wellbeing

- The conditions of the street in the community area
- The amount of traffic on your street
- Traffic conditions are generally in the community area
- Public transportation in the community area

Community systems affecting education wellbeing

- Local colleges and universities
- Public schools serving your neighborhood
- Libraries in the community area

Community systems affecting health and wellbeing
- Medical doctor services are available in the community area
- Dental services are available in the community area
- Garbage collection in your neighborhood
- Hospitals in the community area

Community systems affecting work wellbeing
- Job opportunities in the community area
- Your own job
- Your husband's (wife's) job

Community systems affecting financial wellbeing
- Your family's income (husband and wife)
- Property taxes in the community area
- The cost of living in the community area

Community systems affecting shopping wellbeing
- Grocery stores in your neighborhood

Response scale: 1= strongly dissatisfied, 5= strongly satisfied

Source: Adapted from Sirgy et al. (2010)

Table 5.12 A need-based measure of consumer wellbeing in relation to personal transportation

Respondents are asked to state the make and model of their current vehicle. Then, they are presented with the following measures pertaining to satisfaction with various needs with their car. • I feel very safe in my car *(safety needs)* • My car is economical *(economic needs)* • My car satisfies my family's needs *(family needs)* • My car meets my social needs *(social needs)* • The image of my car shows status and prestige to others *(social needs)* • My car does not let me down when I use it for daily and weekly activities *(esteem needs)* • My car reflects who I am *(actualization needs)* • My car reflects who I would like to be *(actualization needs)* • I use my car a lot to explore new places *(knowledge needs)* • My car is beautiful, inside and outside *(aesthetic needs)*
Response scale: 1= strongly disagree; 5= strongly agree

Source: Adapted from Sirgy et al. (2006)

is based on the notion that the consumer's wellbeing from personal vehicles is enhanced when the consumption of the vehicle meets the full spectrum of human developmental needs (i.e., safety, economic, family, social, esteem, actualization, knowledge, and aesthetics needs). See the metric in Table 5.12.

In summary, the need satisfaction model of consumer wellbeing posits that consumers enhance their happiness by recognizing consumers' various consumption needs and effectively satisfying them through acquisition and consumption experiences (cf. Samli et al., 1987).

Summary and Conclusion

Table 5.13 shows our attempt to classify consumer happiness metrics along two dimensions, namely objective versus subjective indicators and input versus output indicators.

Objective indicators of consumer happiness require a point of view that is independent from the individual whose quality of life is being evaluated (Sumner, 1996). Objective indicators of consumer happiness include consumer price index, economic growth rate, economic stability, total consumption equity index, consumer complaints index, and integrated consumer sentiment index.

In contrast, *subjective indicators* of wellbeing tap the concept of wellbeing biased by the individual's frame of mind (i.e., values, attitudes, beliefs, motives, personality, and emotional state) (Sumner, 1996). Subjective indicators of consumer happiness include perceived financial satisfaction, shopping wellbeing/shopping ill-being, community satisfaction, satisfaction with standard of living, acquisition and possession satisfaction, and consumer product life cycle measure.

Input indicators of consumer happiness means environmental conditions affecting consumer happiness while output indicators of consumer happiness mean actual

Table 5.13 Classifying consumer happiness metrics

	Objective measures	Subjective measures
Input-focused measures (antecedents)	– Consumer Price Index – Inflation rate – Economic growth rate	– Perceived financial satisfaction
Output-focused measures (consequences)	– Total consumption equity index – Consumer Complaints Index – Consumer sentiment index	– Shopping wellbeing/shopping illbeing – Community satisfaction – Satisfaction with the standard of living – Acquisition and possession satisfaction – Consumer product life cycle measure

consumer happiness experienced (cf. Veenhoven, 2000). Input indicators of consumer happiness focus on conditional factors affecting consumer happiness. These include the consumer price index, inflation rate, economic growth rate, and perceived financial satisfaction.

In contrast, output indicators of consumer happiness focus on the evaluations of consumer life after actual consumption. These include total consumption equity index, consumer complaints index, consumer sentiment index, shopping wellbeing/shopping illbeing, community satisfaction, satisfaction with standard of living, acquisition and possession satisfaction, and consumer product life cycle measure.

References

Ackermann, L., Schoormans, J. P., & Mugge, R. (2021). Measuring consumers' product care tendency: Scale development and validation. *Journal of Cleaner Production, 295*, 126327.

Ahuvia, A. C. (2015). Nothing matters more to people than people: Brand meaning and social relationships. In *Brand meaning management* (Vol. 12, pp. 121–149). Emerald Group Publishing Limited.

Aknin, L. B., Norton, M. I., & Dunn, E. W. (2009). From wealth to wellbeing? Money matters, but less than people think. *The Journal of Positive Psychology, 4*(6), 523–527.

Andrews, F. M., & Withey, S. B. (1976). *Social indicators of wellbeing: Americans' perceptions of life quality*. Plenum Press.

Baumeister, R. F., Vohs, K. D., Aaker, J. L., & Garbinsky, E. N. (2013). Some key differences between a happy life and a meaningful life. *Journal of Positive Psychology, 8*(6), 505–516.

Belk, R. W. (1985). Materialism: Trait aspects of living in the material world. *Journal of Consumer Research, 12*(3), 265–280.

Bergadaa, M., Faure, C., & Perrien, J. (1995). Enduring involvement with shopping. *The Journal of Social Psychology, 135*(1), 17–25.

Bertram-Hümmer, V., & Baliki, G. (2015). The role of visible wealth for deprivation. *Social Indicators Research, 124*(3), 765–783.

Bosnjak, M., Brown, C. A., Lee, D. J., Yu, G. B., & Sirgy, M. J. (2016). Self-expressiveness in sport tourism: Determinants and consequences. *Journal of Travel Research, 55*(1), 125–134.

Carter, T. J., & Gilovich, T. (2010). The relative relativity of material and experiential purchases. *Journal of Personality and Social Psychology, 98*(1), 146–159.

Chancellor, J., & Lyubomirsky, S. (2011). Happiness and thrift: When spending less is hedonically more. *Journal of Consumer Psychology, 21*(2), 131–138.

Charles, V., Gherman, T., & Paliza, J. C. (2022). The Gini Index: A modern measure of inequality. In *Modern indices for international economic diplomacy* (pp. 55–84). Springer International Publishing.

Day, R. L. (1978). Beyond social indicators: Quality of life at the individual level. In F. D. Reynolds & H. C. Barksdale (Eds.), *Marketing and the quality of life* (pp. 11–18). American Marketing Association.

Day, R. L. (1987). Relationship between life satisfaction and consumer satisfaction. In A. C. Samli (Ed.), *Marketing and quality-of-life interface* (pp. 289–311). Westport, CT.

Diener, E. (1984). Subjective well-being. *Psychological Bulletin, 95*(3), 542–575.

Diener, E., Inglehart, R., & Tay, L. (2013a). Theory and validity of life satisfaction scales. *Social Indicators Research, 112*(3), 497–527.

Diener, E., Ng, W., Harter, J., & Arora, R. (2010). Wealth and happiness across the world: Material prosperity predicts life evaluation, whereas psychosocial prosperity predicts positive feeling. *Journal of Personality and Social Psychology, 99*(1), 52–61.

Diener, E., Suh, E. M., Lucas, R. E., & Smith, H. L. (1999). Subjective wellbeing: Three decades of progress. *Psychological Bulletin, 125*(2), 276–302.

Diener, E., Tay, L., & Oishi, S. (2013b). Rising income and the subjective wellbeing of nations. *Journal of Personality and Social Psychology, 104*(2), 267–276.

Dittmar, H., Bond, R., Hurst, M., & Kasser, T. (2014). The relationship between materialism and personal wellbeing: A meta-analysis. *Journal of Personality and Social Psychology, 107*(5), 879–924.

Duesenberry, J. (1949). *Income, saving and the theory of consumption behavior*. Harvard University Press.

Dutt, A. K. (2009). Happiness and the relative consumption hypothesis. In A. K. Dutt & B. Radcliff (Eds.), *Happiness, economics and politics: Towards a multi-disciplinary approach* (pp. 127–150). Edward Elgar.

Dynan, K. E., & Ravina, E. (2007). Increasing income inequality, external habits, and self-reported happiness. *American Economic Review, 97*(2), 226–231.

Ekici, A., Sirgy, M. J., Lee, D. J., Yu, G. B., & Bosnjak, M. (2018). The effects of shopping wellbeing and shopping ill-being on consumer life satisfaction. *Applied Research in Quality of Life, 13*(2), 333–353.

El Hedhli, K., Chebat, J. C., & Sirgy, M. J. (2013). Shopping wellbeing at the mall: Construct, antecedents, and consequences. *Journal of Business Research, 66*(7), 856–863.

Farris, F. A. (2010). The Gini index and measures of inequality. *The American Mathematical Monthly, 117*(10), 851–864.

Fredrickson, B. L. (2001). The role of positive emotions in positive psychology: The broaden-and-build theory of positive emotions. *American Psychologist, 56*(3), 218–226.

Fredrickson, B. L., & Losada, M. F. (2005). Positive affect and the complex dynamics of human flourishing. *American Psychologist, 60*(7), 678–686.

Ganglmair-Wooliscroft, A., & Lawson, R. (2011). Subjective wellbeing of different consumer lifestyle segments. *Journal of Macromarketing, 31*(2), 172–183.

Gaski, J. F., & Etzel, M. J. (1986). The index of consumer sentiment toward marketing. *Journal of Marketing, 50*(3), 71–81.

Gaski, J. F., & Etzel, M. J. (2005). National aggregate consumer sentiment toward marketing: A thirty-year retrospective and analysis. *Journal of Consumer Research, 31*(4), 859–867.

Goldsmith, R. (2016). The Big Five, happiness, and shopping. *Journal of Retailing and Consumer Services, 31*(July), 52–61.

Goodman, J. K., Malkoc, S. A., & Stephenson, B. L. (2016). Celebrate or commemorate? A material purchase advantage when honoring special life events. *Journal of the Association for Consumer Research, 1*(4), 497–508.

Graafland, J., & Lous, B. (2018). Economic freedom, income inequality and life satisfaction in OECD countries. *Journal of Happiness Studies, 19*(7), 2071–2093.

Hagerty, M. R. (2000). Social comparisons of income in one's community: Evidence from national surveys of income and happiness. *Journal of Personality and Social Psychology, 78*(4), 764–771.

Headey, B., Muffels, R., & Wooden, M. (2008). Money does not buy happiness: Or does it? A reassessment based on the combined effects of wealth, income and consumption. *Social Indicators Research, 87*(1), 65–82.

Hill, R. P., Felice, W. F., & Ainscough, T. (2007). International human rights and consumer quality of life: An ethical perspective. *Journal of Macromarketing, 27*(4), 370–379.

Hill, R. P., Martin, K. D., & Chaplin, L. N. (2012). A tale of two marketplaces: Consumption restriction, social comparison, and life satisfaction. *Marketing Letters, 23*(3), 731–744.

Howell, R. T., & Hill, G. (2009). The mediators of experiential purchases: Determining the impact of psychological needs satisfaction and social comparison. *The Journal of Positive Psychology, 4*(6), 511–522.

Howell, R. T., Pchelin, P., & Iyer, R. (2012). The preference for experiences over possessions: Measurement and construct validation of the Experiential Buying Tendency Scale. *The Journal of Positive Psychology, 7*(1), 57–71.

Kasser, T. (2003). *The high price of materialism*. MIT Press.

Kasser, T., & Ahuvia, A. (2002). Materialistic values and wellbeing in business students. *European Journal of Social Psychology, 32*(1), 137–146.

Kahneman, D., & Deaton, A. (2010). High income improves evaluation of life but not emotional wellbeing. *Proceedings of the National Academy of Sciences, 107*(38), 16489–16493.

Lee, D. J., Sirgy, M. J., Larsen, V., & Wright, N. D. (2002). Developing a subjective measure of consumer wellbeing. *Journal of Macromarketing, 22*(2), 158–169.

Lee, D. J., Yu, G. B., Sirgy, M. J., Ekici, A., Gurel-Atay, E., & Bahn, K. D. (2014). Shopping wellbeing and ill-being: Toward an integrated model. In *Handbook of research on retailer-consumer relationship development* (pp. 27–44). IGI Global.

Leelanuithanit, O., Day, R., & Walters, R. (1991). Investigating the relationship between marketing and overall satisfaction with life in a developing country. *Journal of Macromarketing, 11*(1), 3–23.

Lucas, R. E. (2005). Time does not heal all wounds: A longitudinal study of reaction and adaptation to divorce. *Psychological Science, 16*(12), 945–950.

Lyubomirsky, S., King, L., & Diener, E. (2005). The benefits of frequent positive affect: Does happiness lead to success? *Psychological Bulletin, 131*(6), 803–855.

MacDonald, M., & Douthitt, R. A. (1992). Consumption theories and consumers' assessments of subjective wellbeing. *Journal of Consumer Affairs, 26*(2), 243–261.

Mandel, N., Petrova, P. K., & Cialdini, R. B. (2006). Images of success and the preference for luxury brands. *Journal of Consumer Psychology, 16*(1), 57–69.

Maslow, A. (1954). *Motivation and personality*. Harper.

Meadow, H. L. (1983). *The relationship between consumer satisfaction and life satisfaction for the elderly*. Doctoral dissertation,. Virginia Polytechnic Institute and State University.

Meadow, H. L., & Sirgy, M. J. (2008). Developing a measure that captures elderly's wellbeing in local marketplace transactions. *Applied Research in Quality of Life, 3*(1), 63–80.

Mogilner, C., Aaker, J., & Kamvar, S. D. (2012). How happiness affects choice. *Journal of Consumer Research, 39*(2), 429–443.

Nakano, N., MacDonald, M., & Douthitt, R. (1995). Toward consumer wellbeing: Consumer socialization effects of work experience. In M. J. Sirgy & A. C. Samli (Eds.), *New dimensions of marketing/quality-of life research* (pp. 151–175). Quorum Books.

Nicolao, L., Irwin, J. R., & Goodman, J. K. (2009). Happiness for sale: Do experiential purchases make consumers happier than material purchases? *Journal of Consumer Research, 36*(2), 188–198.

Noll, H. H., & Weick, S. (2015). Consumption expenditures and subjective wellbeing: Empirical evidence from Germany. *International Review of Economics, 62*(2), 101–119.

Oishi, S., Kesebir, S., & Diener, E. (2011). Income inequality and happiness. *Psychological Science, 22*(9), 1095–1100.

Oshio, T., Nozaki, K., & Kobayashi, M. (2011). Relative income and happiness in Asia: Evidence from nationwide surveys in China, Japan, and Korea. *Social Indicators Research, 104*(3), 351–367.

Oshio, T., & Urakawa, K. (2014). The association between perceived income inequality and subjective wellbeing: Evidence from a social survey in Japan. *Social Indicators Research, 116*(3), 755–770.

Peine, K., Heitmann, M., & Herrmann, A. (2009). Getting a feel for price affect: A conceptual framework and empirical investigation of consumers' emotional responses to price information. *Psychology & Marketing, 26*(1), 39–66.

Peterson, M., & Ekici, A. (2007). Consumer attitude toward marketing and subjective quality of life in the context of a developing country. *Journal of Macromarketing, 27*(4), 350–359.

Pieters, R. (2013). Bidirectional dynamics of materialism and loneliness: Not just a vicious cycle. *Journal of Consumer Research, 40*(4), 615–631.

Richins, M. L., & Dawson, S. (1992). A consumer values orientation for materialism and its measurement: Scale development and validation. *Journal of Consumer Research, 19*(3), 303–316.

Ryan, R. M., & Deci, E. L. (2001). On happiness and human potential: A review of research on hedonic and eudaimonic wellbeing. *Annual Review of Psychology, 52*(1), 141–166.

Ryff, C. D. (1989). Happiness is everything, or is it? Explorations on the meaning of psychological wellbeing. *Journal of Personality and Social Psychology, 57*(6), 1069.

Ryff, C. D., & Keyes, C. L. M. (1995). The structure of psychological wellbeing revisited. *Journal of Personality and Social Psychology, 69*(4), 719–727.

Sacks, D. W., Stevenson, B., & Wolfers, J. (2012). The new stylized facts about income and subjective wellbeing. *Emotion, 12*(6), 1181–1187.

Sameer, Y. M., Elmassah, S., Mertzanis, C., & El-Maghraby, L. (2021). Are happier nations more responsible? Examining the link between happiness and sustainability. *Social Indicators Research, 158*(1), 267–295.

Samli, A. C. (2003). The consumer price index and consumer wellbeing: Developing a fair measure. *Journal of Macromarketing, 23*(2), 105–111.

Samli, A., Sirgy, M. J., & Meadow, H. L. (1987). Measuring marketing contribution to quality of life. In A. C. Samli (Ed.), *Marketing and quality of life interface* (pp. 3–14). Quorum Books.

Schlegelmilch, B. B., Bohlen, G. M., & Diamantopoulos, A. (1996). The link between green purchasing decisions and measures of environmental consciousness. *European Journal of Marketing, 30*(5), 35–55.

Sirgy, M. J. (1998). Materialism and quality of life. *Social Indicators Research, 43*(3), 227–260.

Sirgy, M. J. (2002). *The psychology of quality of life*. Kluwer Academic Publishers.

Sirgy, M. J. (2008). Ethics and public policy implications of research on consumer well-being. *Journal of Public Policy and Marketing, 27*(2), 207–212.

Sirgy, M. J. (2021). Macromarketing metrics of consumer wellbeing: An update. *Journal of Macromarketing, 41*(1), 124–131.

Sirgy, M. J., & Cornwell, T. (2001). Further validation of the Sirgy et al.'s measure of community quality of life. *Social Indicators Research, 56*(2), 125–143.

Sirgy, M. J., Kruger, P. S., Lee, D. J., & Yu, G. B. (2011). How does a travel trip affect tourists' life satisfaction? *Journal of Travel Research, 50*(3), 261–275.

Sirgy, M. J., & Lee, D. J. (2008). Wellbeing marketing: An ethical business philosophy for consumer goods firms. *Journal of Business Ethics, 77*(4), 377–403.

Sirgy, M. J., Lee, D. J., Grzeskowiak, S., Chebat, J. C., Johar, J. S., Hermann, A., et al. (2008). An extension and further validation of a community-based consumer wellbeing measure. *Journal of Macromarketing, 28*(3), 243–257.

Sirgy, M. J., Lee, D. J., Kosenko, R., Meadow, H. L., Rahtz, D., Cicic, M., Jin, G. X., Yarsuvat, D., Blenkhorn, D. L., & Wright, N. (1998a). Does television viewership influence and propagate dissatisfaction with the standard of living and overall life. *Journal of Advertising, 27*(1), 125–142.

Sirgy, M. J., Lee, D. J., & Kressmann, F. (2006). A need-based measure of consumer wellbeing (CWB) in relation to personal transportation: Nomological validation. *Social Indicators Research, 79*(2), 337–367.

Sirgy, M. J., Lee, D. J., Larsen, V., & Wright, N. D. (1998b). Satisfaction with material possessions and general wellbeing: The role of materialism. *Journal of Consumer Satisfaction, Dissatisfaction and Complaining Behavior, 11*, 103–118.

Sirgy, M. J., Lee, D. J., & Yu, G. B. (2020). Shopping-life balance: Towards a unifying framework. *Applied Research in Quality of Life, 15*(1), 17–34.

Sirgy, M. J., Uysal, M., & Kruger, S. (2017). Towards a benefits theory of leisure wellbeing. *Applied Research in Quality of Life, 12*(1), 205–228.

Sirgy, M. J., Widgery, R. N., Lee, D. J., & Yu, G. B. (2010). Developing a measure of community wellbeing based on perceptions of impact in various life domains. *Social Indicators Research, 96*(2), 295–311.

Smits, J., & Steendijk, R. (2015). The International Wealth Index (IWI). *Social Indicators Research, 122*(1), 65–85.

Sumner, L. W. (1996). *Welfare, happiness, and ethics*. Oxford University Press.

Temkin, L. S. (1993). *Inequality*. Oxford University Press.

UNDP. (2003). *Millennium development goals: A compact among nations to end human poverty: Human development report 2003*. Oxford University Press.

Vadrevu, S. K. (2014). Consumer wellbeing and life satisfaction. *International Research Journal of Management Science & Technology, 5*(6), 297–304.

Van Boven, L., Campbell, M. C., & Gilovich, T. (2010). Stigmatizing materialism: On stereotypes and impressions of materialistic and experiential pursuits. *Personality and Social Psychology Bulletin, 36*(4), 551–563.

Van Boven, L., & Gilovich, T. (2003). To do or to have? That is the question. *Journal of Personality and Social Psychology, 85*(6), 1193–1202.

Veenhoven, R. (1991). Is happiness relative? *Social Indicators Research, 24*(1), 1–34.

Veenhoven, R. (2000). The four qualities of life. *Journal of Happiness Studies, 1*(1), 1–39.

Veenhoven, R. (2012). Cross-national differences in happiness: Cultural measurement bias or effect of culture? *International Journal of Wellbeing, 2*(4), 333–353.

Veenhoven, R., Chiperi, F., Kang, X., & Burger, M. (2021). Happiness and consumption: A research synthesis using an online finding archive. *Sage Open, 11*(1), 2158244020986239.

Wang, H., Cheng, Z., & Smyth, R. (2019). Consumption and happiness. *The Journal of Development Studies, 55*(1), 120–136.

Waterman, A. S., Schwartz, S. J., & Conti, R. (2008). The implications of two conceptions of happiness (hedonic enjoyment and eudaimonia) for the understanding of intrinsic motivation. *Journal of Happiness Studies, 9*(1), 41–79.

Wilkinson, R., & Pickett, K. (2009). *The spirit level: Why equal societies almost always do 30 better*. Penguin.

Wirtz, J., & McColl-Kennedy, J. R. (2010). Opportunistic customer claiming during service recovery. *Journal of the Academy of Marketing Science, 38*(5), 654–675.

Zhang, J. W., Howell, R. T., Caprariello, P. A., & Guevarra, D. A. (2014). Damned if they do, damned if they don't: Material buyers are not happier from material or experiential consumption. *Journal of Research in Personality, 50*, 71–83.

Chapter 6
Outcomes of Consumer Happiness

The territorialism and desire to possess things come directly from the ego, which strives to own and control things. Your spirit already knows you own nothing. It is a matter of realizing that your happiness does not depend on your ownership of things. They help you in your journey, but they are not the journey itself.

—Karen Kingston (https://www.goodreads.com/quotes/tag/material-things)

Consequences of Consumer Happiness

Research has uncovered several prominent consequences of consumer happiness. These are high-level information processing, positive product evaluation, hedonic consumption and variety seeking, prosocial spending and meaningful consumption, and customer loyalty. We will discuss these outcomes of consumer happiness in some depth in the sections below.

High-Level Information Processing

One major behavioral consequence of consumer happiness is high-level information processing (e.g., abstract thinking and future-oriented time perspective). In other words, happy consumers tend to engage in high-level thinking and top-down information processing (e.g., Isen, 2001). Let's discuss this behavioral phenomenon in more detail.

Cognitive tuning theory proposes that happy consumers tend to interpret life circumstances positively, they avoid high cognitive effort, and prefer simple heuristics over effortful analyses (e.g., Bless & Burger, 2017; Bless et al., 1996; Pyone & Isen, 2011; Schwarz, 1998; Schwarz & Clore, 2007). That is, happy consumers

D.-J. Lee, M. J. Sirgy, *Happiness in the Marketplace*, Social Indicators Research Series 64, https://doi.org/10.1007/978-3-032-04443-3_6

view the purchase situation as safe and all is well, and thus they tend to use simple heuristics to organize new information. As such, happy consumers use top-down, abstract information processing strategies. Consumer happiness elevates consumers' thinking into high-level construal, helping them to see the big picture by signaling that a situation is benign. That is, happy consumers tend to reduce the amount of attention and effort toward current tasks (e.g., a more distal perspective) and engage in high-level, abstract thinking.

In contrast, a negative mood leads consumers to take a more proximal perspective, which results in concrete low-level construal by signaling danger and imminence of a situation (e.g., Labroo & Patrick, 2009). That is, a negative mood prompts the consumer to be wary, resulting in the use of more bottom-up, detail-focused information processing strategies. In sum, while a positive mood encourages a focus on the forest (i.e., abstract/global information), a negative mood encourages a focus on the trees (i.e., concrete/local information).

There are two major characteristics of happy consumers described in terms of information processing. First, happy consumers tend to take a problem-solving approach to problems and disputes and come up with the kind of solution that involves thinking creatively (e.g., Isen, 2001; Labroo & Patrick, 2009). This is because happy consumers tend to maintain psychological distance from the situation, focusing on abstract goals. Happy consumers engage in high-level abstract thinking; thus, they tend to be creative, flexible, and open to new information. Consumer happiness facilitates cognitive flexibility, the ability to switch perspectives and see things in multiple ways, and come up with viable solutions, and the ability to cope with potential problems and avoid conflict.

Second, happy consumers tend to embrace a future-oriented time perspective. This perspective helps them exert better spending control (e.g., Frey & Stutzer, 2002; Pyone & Isen, 2011). As such, they save more, spend less, and have a lower marginal propensity to consume. They take more time in making decisions, which leads them to exert more control over expenditures. More importantly, they expect to live a longer life (than average); as such, they tend to be more concerned about the future than the present (e.g., Guven, 2012). Correspondingly, they refrain from engaging in impulsive buying. We know that impulse buying might serve as an escape from stress, negative mood, or low self-esteem. In contrast, happy consumers do not feel the need to escape from those negative feelings (e.g., Silvera et al., 2008; Verplanken et al., 2005).

Positive Product Evaluation

Another behavioral consequence of consumer happiness is positive evaluation of goods and services. Specifically, happy consumers are likely to evaluate products more positively than unhappy consumers. Research found that happy consumers evaluate service quality in a more positive manner than unhappy consumers, and that overall service quality is positively associated with customer happiness (e.g., Gong & Yi, 2018; Hellén & Sääksjärvi, 2011; Schnebelen & Bruhn, 2018).

According to the *perspective on mood-as-information perspective* (Schwarz & Clore, 1983), *mood congruence theory* (Bower, 1981), and *the affect infusion model* (Forgas, 1995), emotions tend to bias information processing, evaluations, and behaviors. In other words, feelings toward a target (e.g., emotions related to a product) tend to bias subsequent thoughts about the product in question in the direction of these feelings (e.g., Pham et al., 2013). Thus, happy consumers tend to make favorable evaluations of material possessions (e.g., Forgas & Ciarrochi, 2001), services (e.g., Hellén & Sääksjärvi, 2011), and brand extensions (e.g., Barone et al., 2000).

Why do happy consumers evaluate goods and services positively? Let's explore research discerning possible mediating mechanisms. First, when consumers feel happier, they tune in to positive cognitions to be consistent with their positive feelings. Consumer happiness facilitates more ready access to positive thoughts in memory, leading to improved evaluations of neutral items (e.g., Abbe et al., 2003; Isen et al., 1978; Lyubomirsky & Tucker, 1998; Teasdale & Fogarty, 1979).

Consider the following study by Grafton and MacLeod (2017). These researchers tested the hypothesis that elevated positive affectivity causes attentional bias favoring the processing of positive information over neutral information. Study participants high in positive affectivity were found to display greater relative attention to positive information compared to neutral information than was the case for their low positive affectivity counterparts. Evidence related to services indicates that happy consumers focus on the positive side of services and perceive service quality in a more positive manner than unhappy consumers (e.g., Hellén & Sääksjärvi, 2011).

Second, happy consumers tend to reduce their cognitive effort and use simple heuristics over more effortful judgments (e.g., Schwarz & Clore, 2007). Positive moods facilitate the selective recall and use of mood-congruent information that consumers rely on when evaluating an object (e.g., Forgas & Bower, 1987).

Third, happy consumers evaluate the same events in more positive ways because they do not engage in comparative evaluations (e.g., Abbe et al., 2003). In other words, happy consumers are less sensitive to comparison information and maintain their positive emotions, engaging in social comparisons.

Fourth, happy consumers evaluate the same experiences in more positive ways because they try to reduce dissonance (i.e., they try to rationalize the purchase decision) allowing them to maintain the experience of positive emotions and heightened self-confidence after making the choice decision (e.g., Abbe et al., 2003; Forgas & Ciarrochi, 2001). In other words, happy consumers generally report high satisfaction with their choices and use rationalization to keep themselves from feelings of disappointment. As a result, happy consumers selectively recall positive, pleasurable features of the ownership experience.

Hedonic Consumption and Variety Seeking

Other behavioral consequences of consumer happiness include hedonic consumption and variety seeking. Let us explain further. First, happy consumers tend to be motivated to preserve and reinforce their positive affect by engaging in hedonic consumption (e.g., Hellén & Sääksjärvi, 2011; Zhong & Mitchell, 2010, 2012).

Second, happy consumers tend to engage in variety seeking. The broaden-and-build theory posits that experience of positive emotions broadens momentary thought–action repertoires and leads individuals to engage in various activities, which in turn serve to build their enduring personal resources (e.g., Fredrickson, 2001; Fredrickson & Branigan, 2005). As such, happy consumers are likely to consider more options and are more open to novel options (e.g., Spassova & Isen, 2013), resulting in variety seeking (e.g., Kahn & Isen, 1993). For example, research shows that happy consumers tend to engage in a variety of leisure and social activities (e.g., Zhong & Mitchell, 2012) and seek a variety of low-risk options (e.g., Lyubomirsky, Sheldon, & Schkade, 2005b).

It should be noted that happy consumers engage in variety seeking and hedonic consumption behaviors only when there is low risk involved. When the perceived risk is low, happy consumers seek variety among safe, enjoyable products and consider a wide range of options in choosing products (e.g., Isen & Geva, 1987; Isen & Patrick, 1983; Isen, 2001). When perceived risk is high, however, happy consumers do not take risks to protect their positive affect. That is, positive affect tends to increase risk aversion when the stakes are high.

Prosocial Spending and Meaningful Consumption

Another set of behavioral consequences of consumer happiness involves increased intention for pro-social spending and meaningful consumption. Happiness has been shown to foster more altruistic behavior (e.g., Lyubomirsky et al., 2005a). Happy consumers tend to be more actively engaged in donations and spending for others. Why? First, positive emotions tend to promote a helpful and generous orientation toward others. Positive affect generally leads people to be gracious, generous, and kind to others; to be socially responsible; and to take the other's perspective better in interaction while not losing sight of their perspective (e.g., Isen, 2001). As such, happy consumers are likely to engage in prosocial spending (e.g., Aknin et al., 2012) and report increased purchase intentions for ethical products such as fair-trade coffee (e.g., Hwang & Kim, 2018).

Second, research has shown a positive feedback loop between pro-social spending and consumer happiness (e.g., Aknin et al., 2012, 2013; Dunn et al., 2008). In other words, consumer acts of prosocial spending tend to lead to higher levels of consumer happiness, and consumer happiness in turn increases the likelihood of engaging in future acts of prosocial spending.

Customer Loyalty

Yet another behavioral consequence of consumer happiness is increased brand (or customer) loyalty. Customer loyalty is a deeply held commitment to re-buy or re-patronize a preferred good/service consistently in the future, thereby causing repetitive same-brand or same brand-set purchasing, despite situational influences and marketing efforts that may cause switching behavior (e.g., Oliver, 1999).

Many studies found that consumption happiness from a brand is positively associated with customer loyalty related to that brand (e.g., Bruhn & Schnebelen, 2017; Gong & Yi, 2018; Hellén & Sääksjärvi, 2011; Schnebelen & Bruhn, 2018). Specifically, consumer happiness related to a brand tends to lead to re-purchase intentions, willingness to pay a premium price, and induce greater positive word-of-mouth communications. It also should be noted that the effect of consumer happiness on brand commitment is stronger for hedonic than utilitarian services, perhaps because of the highly pleasurable character of hedonic services (Hellén & Sääksjärvi, 2011).

What are the mediating mechanisms that may help us better understand this effect? First, happy consumers tend to undertake actions to realize their goal of prolonging or re-experiencing brand happiness. The experience of a moment of happiness elicited by a brand is highly pleasurable, but also transient resulting in emotional fulfillment. This is why brand happiness prompts consumers to re-experience the purchase and consumption experience (e.g., Schnebelen & Bruhn, 2018). In sum, consumer happiness serves to increase consumers repurchase intention of the brand.

Second, happy consumers seek to prolong the experience of brand happiness via financial sacrifice. Here, consumers are willing to pay a higher price for the preferred brand than for other brands in the same product category (e.g., Schnebelen & Bruhn, 2018). In other words, consumer happiness increases consumers' willingness to pay for the brand and motivates them to stick with it time and time again.

Third, brand loyalty allows happy consumers to reinforce customer satisfaction (e.g., Belanche et al., 2013; El Hedhli et al., 2016). In other words, customer satisfaction leads to brand loyalty; and conversely, brand loyalty reinforces customer satisfaction. Evidence also suggests that consumer happiness serves to increase the subjective value of both actual and desired possessions (e.g., Forgas & Ciarrochi, 2001), motivating consumers to develop an emotional attachment with the brand (e.g., Thürridl et al., 2020).

Fourth, happy consumers become motivated to become loyal to a brand because of the emotional benefits they receive from the brand (e.g., Schnebelen & Bruhn, 2018). Specifically, positive emotions that are evoked by service experiences induce customers to reciprocate by increasing brand commitment and recommending the brand to others (e.g., DeWitt et al., 2008; Thomas & Millar, 2013).

Overall Happiness

Consumer happiness has a positive bottom-up influence on overall happiness. According to the *bottom-up theory of subjective wellbeing*, a person's domain-specific evaluation serves as a robust source of overall life satisfaction (e.g., Campbell, 1981; Diener, 1984). In other words, reduced domain satisfaction is expected to decrease overall life satisfaction, whereas increased domain satisfaction tends to boost overall life satisfaction.

Empirical evidence suggests that domain satisfaction feeds overall life satisfaction (e.g., Campbell, 1981; Tay & Kuykendall, 2013). As such, frequent experiences of consumption happiness in consumer life should have a significant and enduring effect on overall happiness (cf. Lyubomirsky, 2001; Seligman et al., 2005; Sin & Lyubomirsky, 2009).

Furthermore, this effect is amplified by consumer involvement in the marketplace event. That is, the degree of vertical spillover is likely to be high when consumers are highly involved in marketplace activities (cf. Oishi et al., 1999). The spillover is not likely to occur when consumers are not emotionally involved in the marketplace event.

Summary and Conclusion

Table 6.1 captures a summary of what was discussed in this chapter. The table makes the distinction between happy and unhappy consumers and describes several behavioral dimensions of these two consumer segments: information processing, product evaluation, consumer choice, pro-social spending, and brand loyalty.

Table 6.1 Consequences of consumer happiness

Dimension	Consequences of consumer happiness	Unhappy consumers	Happy consumers
Information processing	Construal level	Low level construal (concrete, bottom-up)	High level construal (abstract, top-down)
	Cognitive effort	High (detailed)	Low (simple heuristics)
	Purchase goal	Concrete	Abstract
	Cognitive flexibility	Low	High
	Time perspective	Present-oriented	Future-oriented
	Spending control	Low (impulsive buying) Low saving	High control High saving
Product evaluation	Product evaluation	Less positive	More positive
	Comparative evaluations	High	Low
Consumer choice	Hedonic consumption	Low	High
	Variety seeking in consumption	Low	High
Prosocial spending	Donation intention	Low	High
	Ethical spending	Low	High
Customer loyalty	Commitment to preferred brand	Low	High
	Willingness to pay for preferred brand	Low	High

References

Abbe, A., Tkach, C., & Lyubomirsky, S. (2003). The art of living by dispositionally happy people. *Journal of Happiness Studies, 4*(4), 385–404.

Aknin, L. B., Dunn, E. W., & Norton, M. I. (2012). Happiness runs in a circular motion: Evidence for a positive feedback loop between prosocial spending and happiness. *Journal of Happiness Studies, 13*(2), 347–355.

Aknin, L. B., Barrington-Leigh, C. P., Dunn, E. W., Helliwell, J. F., Burns, J., Biswas-Diener, R., et al. (2013). Prosocial spending and well-being: Cross-cultural evidence for a psychological universal. *Journal of Personality and Social Psychology, 104*(4), 635–652.

Barone, M. J., Miyazaki, A. D., & Taylor, K. A. (2000). The influence of cause-related marketing on consumer choice: Does one good turn deserve another? *Journal of the Academy of Marketing Science, 28*(2), 248–262.

Belanche, D., Casaló, L. V., & Guinaliu, M. (2013). The role of consumer happiness in relationship marketing. *Journal of Relationship Marketing, 12*(2), 79–94.

Bless, H., & Burger, A. M. (2017). Mood and the regulation of mental abstraction. *Current Directions in Psychological Science, 26*(2), 159–164.

Bless, H., Clore, G. L., Schwarz, N., Golisano, V., Rabe, C., & Wölk, M. (1996). Mood and the use of scripts: Does a happy mood really lead to mindlessness? *Journal of Personality and Social Psychology, 71*(4), 665–679.

Bower, G. H. (1981). Mood and memory. *American Psychologist, 36*(2), 129–148.

Bruhn, M., & Schnebelen, S. (2017). Integrated marketing communication–from an instrumental to a customer-centric perspective. *European Journal of Marketing, 51*(3), 464–489.

Campbell, A. (1981). *The sense of well-being in America: Recent patterns and trends*. McGraw-Hill.

DeWitt, T., Nguyen, D. T., & Marshall, R. (2008). Exploring customer loyalty following service recovery: The mediating effects of trust and emotions. *Journal of Service Research, 10*(3), 269–281.

Diener, E. (1984). Subjective well-being. *Psychological Bulletin, 95*(3), 542–575.

Dunn, E. W., Aknin, L. B., & Norton, M. I. (2008). Spending money on others promotes happiness. *Science, 319*(5870), 1687–1688.

El Hedhli, K., Zourrig, H., & Chebat, J. C. (2016). Shopping well-being: Is it just a matter of pleasure or doing the task? The role of shopper's gender and self-congruity. *Journal of Retailing and Consumer Services, 31*(July), 1–13.

Forgas, J. P. (1995). Mood and judgment: The affect infusion model (AIM). *Psychological Bulletin, 117*(1), 39–66.

Forgas, J. P., & Bower, G. H. (1987). Mood effects on person-perception judgments. *Journal of Personality and Social Psychology, 53*(1), 53–60.

Forgas, J. P., & Ciarrochi, J. (2001). On being happy and possessive: The interactive effects of mood and personality on consumer judgments. *Psychology & Marketing, 18*(3), 239–260.

Fredrickson, B. L. (2001). The role of positive emotions in positive psychology: The broaden-and-build theory of positive emotions. *American Psychologist, 56*(3), 218–226.

Fredrickson, B. L., & Branigan, C. (2005). Positive emotions broaden the scope of attention and thought-action repertoires. *Cognition & Emotion, 19*(3), 313–332.

Frey, B. S., & Stutzer, A. (2002). What can economists learn from happiness research? *Journal of Economic Literature, 40*(2), 402–435.

Gong, T., & Yi, Y. (2018). The effect of service quality on customer satisfaction, loyalty, and happiness in five Asian countries. *Psychology & Marketing, 35*(6), 427–442.

Grafton, B., & MacLeod, C. (2017). A positive perspective on attentional bias: Positive affectivity and attentional bias to positive information. *Journal of Happiness Studies, 18(August)*, 1029–1043.

Guven, C. (2012). Reversing the question: Does happiness affect consumption and savings behavior? *Journal of Economic Psychology, 33*(4), 701–717.

Hellén, K., & Sääksjärvi, M. (2011). Happiness as a predictor of service quality and commitment for utilitarian and hedonic services. *Psychology & Marketing, 28*(9), 934–957.

Hwang, K., & Kim, H. (2018). Are ethical consumers happy? Effects of ethical consumers' motivations based on empathy versus self-orientation on their happiness. *Journal of Business Ethics, 151*(2), 579–598.

Isen, A. M. (2001). An influence of positive affect on decision making in complex situations: Theoretical issues with practical implications. *Journal of Consumer Psychology, 11*(2), 75–85.

Isen, A. M., & Geva, N. (1987). The influence of positive affect on acceptable level of risk: The person with a large canoe has a large worry. *Organizational Behavior and Human Decision Processes, 39*(2), 145–154.

Isen, A. M., & Patrick, R. (1983). The effect of positive feelings on risk taking: When the chips are down. *Organizational Behavior and Human Performance, 31*(2), 194–202.

Isen, A. M., Shalker, T. E., Clark, M., & Karp, L. (1978). Affect, accessibility of material in memory, and behavior: A cognitive loop? *Journal of Personality and Social Psychology, 36*(1), 1–12.

Kahn, B. E., & Isen, A. M. (1993). The influence of positive affect on variety seeking among safe, enjoyable products. *Journal of Consumer Research, 20*(2), 257–270.

Labroo, A. A., & Patrick, V. M. (2009). Psychological distancing: Why happiness helps you see the big picture. *Journal of Consumer Research, 35*(5), 800–809.

Lyubomirsky, S. (2001). Why are some people happier than others? The role of cognitive and motivational processes in well-being. *American Psychologist, 56*(3), 239–249.

Lyubomirsky, S., & Tucker, K. L. (1998). Implications of individual differences in subjective happiness for perceiving, interpreting, and thinking about life events. *Motivation and Emotion, 22*(2), 155–186.

Lyubomirsky, S., King, L., & Diener, E. (2005a). The benefits of frequent positive affect: Does happiness lead to success? *Psychological Bulletin, 131*(6), 803–855.

Lyubomirsky, S., Sheldon, K. M., & Schkade, D. (2005b). Pursuing happiness: The architecture of sustainable change. *Review of General Psychology, 9*(2), 111–131.

Oishi, S., Diener, E., Suh, E., & Lucas, R. E. (1999). Value as a moderator in subjective well-being. *Journal of Personality, 67*(1), 157–184.

Oliver, R. L. (1999). Whence consumer loyalty? *Journal of Marketing, 63*(4_Suppl. 1), 33–44.

Pham, M. T., Geuens, M., & De Pelsmacker, P. (2013). The influence of ad-evoked feelings on brand evaluations: Empirical generalizations from consumer responses to more than 1000 TV commercials. *International Journal of Research in Marketing, 30*(4), 383–394.

Pyone, J. S., & Isen, A. M. (2011). Positive affect, intertemporal choice, and levels of thinking: Increasing consumers' willingness to wait. *Journal of Marketing Research, 48*(3), 532–543.

Schnebelen, S., & Bruhn, M. (2018). An appraisal framework of the determinants and consequences of brand happiness. *Psychology & Marketing, 35*(2), 101–119.

Schwarz, N. (1998). Warmer and more social: Recent developments in cognitive social psychology. *Annual Review of Sociology, 24*(1), 239–264.

Schwarz, N., & Clore, G. L. (1983). Mood, misattribution, and judgments of well-being: Informative and directive functions of affective states. *Journal of Personality and Social Psychology, 45*(3), 513–523.

Schwarz, N., & Clore, G. L. (2007). Feelings and phenomenal experiences. In A. Kruglanski & E. T. Higgins (Eds.), *Social psychology. Handbook of basic principles* (2nd ed.). Guilford.

Seligman, M. E., Steen, T. A., Park, N., & Peterson, C. (2005). Positive psychology progress: Empirical validation of interventions. *American Psychologist, 60*(5), 410–421.

Silvera, D. H., Lavack, A. M., & Kropp, F. (2008). Impulse buying: the role of affect, social influence, and subjective wellbeing. *Journal of Consumer Marketing, 25*(1), 23–33.

Sin, N. L., & Lyubomirsky, S. (2009). Enhancing well-being and alleviating depressive symptoms with positive psychology interventions: A practice-friendly meta-analysis. *Journal of Clinical Psychology, 65*(5), 467–487.

Spassova, G., & Isen, A. M. (2013). Positive affect moderates the impact of assortment size on choice satisfaction. *Journal of Retailing, 89*(4), 397–408.

Tay, L., & Kuykendall, L. (2013). Promoting happiness: The malleability of individual and societal subjective wellbeing. *International Journal of Psychology, 48*(3), 159–176.

Teasdale, J. D., & Fogarty, S. J. (1979). Differential effects of induced mood on retrieval of pleasant and unpleasant events from episodic memory. *Journal of Abnormal Psychology, 88*(3), 248–257.

Thomas, R., & Millar, M. (2013). The effects of material and experiential discretionary purchases on consumer happiness: Moderators and mediators. *The Journal of Psychology, 147*(4), 345–356.

Thürridl, C., Kamleitner, B., Ruzeviciute, R., Süssenbach, S., & Dickert, S. (2020). From happy consumption to possessive bonds: When positive affect increases psychological ownership for brands. *Journal of Business Research, 107*, 89–103.

Verplanken, B., Herabadi, A. G., Perry, J. A., & Silvera, D. H. (2005). Consumer style and health: The role of impulsive buying in unhealthy eating. *Psychology & Health, 20*(4), 429–441.

Zhong, J. Y., & Mitchell, V. W. (2010). A mechanism model of the effect of hedonic product consumption on well-being. *Journal of Consumer Psychology, 20*(2), 152–162.

Zhong, J. Y., & Mitchell, V. W. (2012). Does consumer well-being affect hedonic consumption? *Psychology & Marketing, 29*(8), 583–594.

Chapter 7
Determinants of Consumer Happiness

> *You can get anything you want from anywhere in the world at a bargain price, but don't [whatever you do] expect to understand how it was made or how it got to you.*
>
> *—Ed Conway, Material World: The Six Raw Materials that Shape Modern Civilization (https://search.yahoo.com/yhs/search?hspart=domaindev&hsimp=yhs-19111&p=quotation%20on%20the%20material%20world&type=1282__alt__ddc_searcho_linuxmint_com&grd=1)*

Factors Influencing Consumer Happiness

Research has uncovered several consumer-related factors that influence consumer happiness. These factors are grouped in three major categories: (1) consumption factors, (2) financial factors, and (3) market-related factors. Let's discuss these factors in some detail.

Consumption Factors

Research has shown that consumer happiness is influenced by the total amount of spending, relative consumption amount, low financial conflict, experiential consumption, savoring experiences, brand engagement, spending less on material possessions, social sharing of consumption, and pro-social spending.

D.-J. Lee, M. J. Sirgy, *Happiness in the Marketplace*, Social Indicators Research Series 64, https://doi.org/10.1007/978-3-032-04443-3_7

Total Amount of Spending

Total amount of spending is significantly associated with consumer happiness. Specifically, consumption contributes to meeting their basic needs (e.g., food, safety, health, and comfortable housing) up to a threshold and thus is more likely to lead to increased consumer happiness. In an empirical analysis on the relationship between consumption expenditures and life satisfaction, Noll and Weick (2015) found that larger consumption expenditures positively correlated with increasing levels of consumer life satisfaction. Total amount of spending, especially spending on necessities, was found to be positively related to consumer happiness (Veenhoven et al., 2021).

Relative Consumption Amount

Relative consumption amount seems to play a significant role in consumer happiness. Relative consumption refers to the perceived level and quality of one's consumption relative to that of significant others. Those who can consume at, or above, the same level as their peers tend to be more satisfied with consumer life than those who cannot (e.g., MacDonald & Douthitt, 1992). In parallel, consumers' feelings of relative deprivation of conspicuous products tend to register a negative influence on consumer happiness (e.g., Fafchamps & Shilpi, 2008; Guillen-Royo, 2011).

Relative consumption is significantly associated with consumer happiness for two reasons. First, consumer happiness is influenced by social comparison (e.g., Veenhoven, 1991; Veenhoven et al., 2021). Specifically, when consumers compare their consumption with a reference group with similar demographic characteristics, they may experience increased happiness if their consumption is greater than that of the reference group (e.g., MacDonald & Douthitt, 1992). Empirical evidence suggests that the relative deprivation effect tends to be high, especially for the impoverished consumers (e.g., Hill et al., 2012) and for socially visible conspicuous products (e.g., Bertram-Hümmer & Baliki, 2015).

Second, consumer happiness tends to be high when there is a high level of equity in consumption (e.g., Lee et al., 2002; Sirgy, 2021). Again, this may be due to social comparison. Relatedly, empirical research indicates that income inequality harms happiness (e.g., Oishi et al., 2011; Wilkinson & Pickett, 2009).

Experiential Consumption

Consumer happiness is high when consumers spend more on experiential consumption than they spend on material possessions. Compared to material possessions, consumer experiences have a stronger effect on satisfaction of psychological needs (i.e., autonomy, competency, and relatedness needs), thus inducing greater happiness (e.g., Caprariello & Reis, 2013; Gilovich et al., 2015; Howell & Hill, 2009; Weingarten & Goodman, 2021). Consider experiential leisure consumption. This type of experiential consumption strongly contributes substantially to consumer happiness (DeLeire & Kalil, 2010; Noll & Weick, 2015). Other experiential consumption behaviors, such as consumption of basic material goods (e.g., food and housing), serve to increase consumer happiness by making life easier.

Why? There are multiple reasons. First, experiences are more self-defining than material possessions (e.g., Carter & Gilovich, 2012; Nicolao et al., 2009; Thomas & Millar, 2013; Van Boven & Gilovich, 2003). In other words, consumers can easily define themselves to others by describing their consumption experiences than by making references to their material possessions. Satisfaction with experiences serves to enhance self-concept, thus contributing more to happiness.

Second, experiences tend to be more unique than possessions (e.g., Carter & Gilovich, 2010; Rosenzweig & Gilovich, 2012). In other words, consumers can easily compare alternative products and possessions. However, it is harder for consumers to compare experiences. Comparative evaluations tend to prompt more negative than positive affect.

Third, experiences are less prone to hedonic adaptation (e.g., Nicolao et al., 2009) compared to possessions. In other words, positive feelings diminish with repeated consumption of the same product, but less so with experiences. In other words, evidence suggests that consumers adapt more slowly to experiential purchases than to material purchases, if the purchase generates positive feelings to begin with.

Finally, experiences are more socially connected in that consumers actively participate in the experience process, and they become socially engaged (Caprariello & Reis, 2013; Nicolao et al., 2009; Thomas & Millar, 2013). Social engagement does make a much more significant contribution to consumer happiness than nonengagement. Consider going on a cruise (i.e., experiential, not material consumption). Most people go on a cruise with others, leading to a high level of social engagement.

Research has uncovered several moderating effects between experiential consumption and consumer happiness. Specifically, evidence suggests that the strength of association between experiential consumption and consumer happiness is high when consumers engage in:

- experiences that generate high levels of hedonic wellbeing compared to low-level hedonic experiences (e.g., Hsee & Zhang, 2004),
- diverse experiences with low hedonic adaptation (e.g., Lyubomirsky et al., 2005; Mogilner et al., 2008),
- self-expressive experiences (e.g., Waterman et al., 2008), and
- flow experiences (e.g., Csikszentmihalyi, 1990).

Savoring Experiences

Savoring refers to the individual's capacity to attend to, appreciate, and enhance the positive experiences in their lives (Bryant & Veroff, 2017). Savoring is not a positive emotion *per se,* but rather a meta-cognitive process involving an awareness of good feelings while they are unfolding.

Consumer happiness tends to be high when consumers savor their positive experiences. In other words, consumers experience heightened happiness when they anticipate savoring positive marketplace behaviors, savoring positive experiences during actual consumption, and remembering and sharing positive experiences of the past (e.g., Chun et al., 2017).

As such, savoring involves different time orientations. Besides savoring the present moment as it unfolds, consumers can savor positive experiences from the past (reminiscence) or future (anticipation). Savoring the moment, reminiscence, and anticipation all serve to generate or regulate positive feelings in the present (Smith & Bryant, 2017). In other words, consumers can enhance current positive feelings by directing attention to positive experiences, appreciating these experiences, and elaborating or enhancing the experience of these positive moments in their lives.

Brand Engagement

Consumer happiness is high when consumers engage with the brands they own. Consumers' brand engagement refers to a consumer's resource investment in their brand interactions (Kumar et al., 2019). Evidence suggests that consumer happiness is high when consumers invest their resources (time, energy, and money) they extract hedonic, self-esteem enhancing, and social benefits from such brand relationships (e.g., Gummerus et al., 2012; Kuo & Feng, 2013).

Evidence also suggests that there is a positive relationship between brand attachment and consumer happiness (e.g., Aureliano-Silva et al., 2018; Sprott et al., 2009). This is because consumers are likely to experience positive affect and self-image congruence when they actively engage in brands they possess.

It should be noted that the strength of the association between brand engagement and consumer happiness is higher for conspicuous than inconspicuous products. This is because conspicuous products can enhance a positive self-concept which in turn contributes to consumer happiness (Perez-Truglia, 2013; Wu, 2020). Supportive studies include the Hudders and Pandelaere (2012) study which demonstrated that luxury consumption leads to an enhanced positive mood, a reduced negative mood, and an increased level of consumer happiness. In addition, Wu (2020) conducted a study that showed consumers' expenditure on conspicuous products relative to those of other households significantly influences consumer happiness.

Low Financial Conflict

Research indicates that consumer happiness is high when consumers experience low financial conflict with their spending. Consumers' financial constraints limit spending opportunities that can satisfy consumption needs, which result in negative feelings (e.g., distress, guilt, and regret). Supporting this proposition are empirical studies that found a negative association between consumer debt and consumer happiness regardless of income level (e.g., Ahuvia & Friedman, 1998; Brown et al., 2005; Tatzel, 2014). This is because debt constrains consumers' buying opportunities for consumption of goods and services related to basic and growth needs. Being in debt is psychologically very harmful, and each dollar of debt is more psychologically painful (compared to the beneficial effects of a dollar of savings). In contrast, consumers' wealth and savings protect consumers from financial difficulties and provide them with the ability to purchase and own material goods (cf. Headey et al., 2008; Ruberton et al., 2016).

Spending Less on Material Possessions

Evidence also suggests that consumer happiness is high when consumers spend less on material possessions (e.g., Ozanne & Ballantine, 2010). Why? First, happy consumers tend to have a lifestyle of owning and pursuing fewer material possessions. They seek renting, leasing, and borrowing of material things instead of ownership. They manage to reduce the number of consumer durables that they own without having to sacrifice the benefits that these products confer. As such, low-ownership consumers tend to exert more control over their spending, save more, and have a low marginal propensity to spend, all of which contribute to consumer happiness.

Second, consumer happiness is high when consumers are less materialistic (e.g., Chancellor & Lyubomirsky, 2011; Kasser & Ahuvia, 2002). Research has documented much evidence showing that materialism is negatively associated with consumer happiness. Consumers with low materialism are likely to experience increased happiness because their behavior is motivated by intrinsic goals that fit their lifestyle. They do not seek extrinsic goals that reflect materialistic values. In other words, they engage in personally rewarding and meaningful activities through intrinsic goals, which in turn contribute to consumer happiness. Materialistic consumers tend to be highly concerned about their finances (e.g., Dittmar et al., 2014) and their material possessions (e.g., Richins & Dawson, 1992). They tend to engage in frequent unrealistic social comparisons (Sirgy, 1998). Evidence also shows that materialism decreases psychological need satisfaction (e.g., Kashdan & Breen, 2007) and increases depression and anxiety (e.g., Kasser & Ryan, 1993). With this said, it should be noted that materialism may not be detrimental to consumer happiness if materialism involves self-signaling (e.g., purchase material products for their true self-expression while motivated by intrinsic goals) instead of other signaling (e.g., purchase material products to make a good impression on others while motivated by extrinsic goals) (Shrum et al., 2013).

Third, consumers who spend less on material possessions tend to exert greater self-control over their spending, which contributes to a positive self-concept and in turn spills over to consumer happiness (Petersen et al., 2018). Self-control is a personality trait and is defined as the ability to monitor one's behavior against specific standards and change or interrupt undesired behavioral tendencies (Baumeister, 2002). High self-control consumers feel happy about indulgent products only when they have justifiable reasons to buy indulgent products.

Social Sharing of Consumption

Research also shows that consumer happiness is high when consumers engage in sharing their consumption experiences with others. Why? First, social sharing of material possessions allows consumers to savor their positive experiences with their possessions, which in turn amplifies positive affect (e.g., Gable et al., 2004; Langston, 1994; Lyubomirsky et al., 2006; Schnebelen & Bruhn, 2018). In other words, the experience of pleasure and positive affect from one's material possessions contributes to consumer happiness, and it is amplified through social sharing.

Second, social sharing is associated with a prolongation of positive emotions (e.g., Verduyn et al., 2011). As such, increased intensity and duration of positive affect experienced through marketplace events play a significant and positive role in consumer happiness.

Third, sharing information about one's material possessions tends to help consumers build a positive self-image (e.g., Karahanna et al., 2015), especially when consumers receive positive feedback from others. Achieving a positive self-concept serves to enhance consumer happiness.

Finally, research has demonstrated that the strength of association between consumption and consumer happiness is high when consumers become more involved with others (e.g., social spending) (Schnebelen & Bruhn, 2018). Social spending here means spending in social situations (i.e., relational products consumed with other people) and pro-social spending. This is because increased use of relational products and social spending facilitates social sharing, which in turn provides consumers with the feeling of relatedness, contributing to consumer happiness and facilitating positive social interactions, which translates into satisfaction with one's social life (cf. Lyubomirsky et al., 2006).

Prosocial Spending

Evidence suggests that spending time and money on others (prosocial spending and gift giving) is positively associated with consumer happiness (e.g., Dunn et al., 2008; Mogilner & Norton, 2016; Sääksjärvi et al., 2017; Schellong et al., 2019). Specifically, pro-social spending results in the perception of doing good for others, which in turn increases consumer happiness. Other-focused activities enhance consumer happiness more than self-focused activities do—spending money on others promotes consumer happiness more than spending money on oneself. This positive relationship between pro-social spending and consumer happiness appears to be universal and significant regardless of income (Dunn et al., 2014) and source of money (i.e., wage vs. windfall) (Geenen et al., 2014).

Pro-social spending contributes to consumer happiness for the following reasons. First, prosocial spending contributes to consumer happiness because such action provides consumers with a sense of social connection with the beneficiary, thus satisfying consumers' relatedness needs. Furthermore, the positive association between prosocial spending and consumer happiness is high when there is a strong tie between the pro-social spender and the recipients (e.g., Aknin et al., 2011; Curry et al., 2018; Dunn et al., 2014; Hui et al., 2020; Weinstein & Ryan, 2010). Prosocial spending is likely to lead to consumer happiness as the acts of generosity facilitate social connection with others (e.g., taking a friend out for dinner instead of giving a gift coupon) (Aknin et al., 2013). In sum, the positive effect of prosocial spending on consumer happiness comes about because prosocial spending provides consumers with opportunities to connect with other people, which in turn satisfies consumers' relatedness needs.

Second, prosocial spending contributes to consumer happiness when prosocial spending makes a big impact on others (Aknin et al., 2011, 2013; Hui & Kogan, 2018). For example, giving more money to charity leads to greater happiness when consumers donate to transparent causes—causes that explain how donations are used. Thus, charity organizations need to provide donors with information on how these funds are used to induce consumer happiness. Furthermore, pro-social spending perceived to produce social impact provides consumers with a sense of competence, which in turn spills over to consumer happiness.

Third, prosocial spending contributes to consumer happiness when consumers engage in prosocial spending out of their own volition (e.g., Aknin et al., 2011, 2013; Hill & Howell, 2014; Weinstein & Ryan, 2010). For example, research has documented the phenomenon linking prosocial spending and consumer happiness when prosocial spending fits with consumers' self-transcendence values (i.e., concern for others). Yet, pro-social spending does not increase happiness for those whose values do not reflect concern for others. In sum, pro-social spending guided by one's own volition provides consumers with satisfaction of autonomy needs, which in turn contributes to consumer happiness.

Financial Factors

Research has shown that consumer happiness is influenced by income, accumulated wealth, money management stress, positive financial behaviors, and financial self-efficacy.

Income

Research has demonstrated a positive relationship between income and consumer happiness. Income is likely to have a positive relationship with consumer happiness because income allows consumers to buy more material goods and experiences, which in turn serve to satisfy their consumption needs (e.g., Yu et al., 2020). Furthermore, greater income generally elevates living standards by enabling them to purchase more goods and services and save for the rainy day (e.g., Oshio et al., 2013). Empirical evidence suggests that those with high income perceive their financial situation more positively (e.g., Malone et al., 2010). They also report greater financial satisfaction (e.g., Hsieh, 2004; Seghieri et al., 2006), greater satisfaction with material possessions (e.g., Diener et al., 2013), and high levels of economic wellbeing (e.g., Hayo & Seifert, 2003).

Research has also produced evidence suggesting that consumer happiness is largely influenced not by an absolute amount of disposable income (*absolute income*) but by *relative income* and consumption spending (e.g., Dynan & Ravina, 2007; Headey et al., 2008). Evidence also suggests that consumer happiness is negatively associated with decreases in disposable income and spending, especially for consumers who have low income (e.g., Aknin et al., 2009).

Also note the moderation effect of materialism. Research has shown that materialistic consumers are likely to evaluate their marketplace experiences using ideal, inflated, and unrealistic standards (e.g., Boyce et al., 2010; Richins, 2011; Sirgy, 1998). These evaluations with ideal/inflated/unrealistic expectations are likely to result in dissatisfaction with marketplace experiences despite the increased income. In addition, materialistic consumers are likely to quickly become accustomed to their increased income. For them, the pleasure of an increase in income is quickly forgotten and replaced with a desire for more (e.g., Richins & Dawson, 1992). The net effect is a weak association between income and consumer happiness for materialistic consumers.

Accumulated Wealth

Wealth refers broadly to one's actual level of financial resources, conjoined with subjective assessments of one's level of financial resources (Tully & Sharma, 2022). *Accumulated wealth* is a financial resource that can have a positive influence on consumer happiness. Accumulated wealth provides people with more opportunities to meet their consumption needs and reduce financial anxiety and stress.

Empirical studies have shown that accumulated wealth (e.g., high financial assets and low debt) is positively associated with financial satisfaction (Hsieh, 2004), and satisfaction with financial life (Nickerson et al., 2003, 2007). These studies provide support for the notion that wealth has a considerable influence on consumer happiness (e.g., satisfaction with one's standard of living).

Money Management Stress

Research highlights a negative relationship between *money management stress* and consumer happiness. Specifically, evidence suggests that money-related stress hurts financial satisfaction (e.g., Netemeyer et al., 2018). Money management stress is associated with late payment (e.g., Hilgert et al., 2003), high levels of materialism (e.g., Richins, 2011), and lack of control in spending (e.g., Maloney et al., 2012).

In sum, when consumers experience money management stress and anxiety, they are likely to evaluate their consumer life negatively.

Positive Financial Behavior

Positive financial behavior refers to saving money, creating an emergency fund, paying bills on time, and retirement planning (Brüggen et al., 2017). Research has highlighted the relationship between positive financial behavior and consumer happiness. Specifically, current financial behavior affects perceptions of one's current financial standing, which in turn influences future financial prospects (e.g., Huston, 2010; Perry & Morris, 2005). When consumers become cognizant of their positive financial behavior (i.e., in terms of their accumulated savings and investments), they are more likely to evaluate their consumer life positively.

Perceived Financial Self-Efficacy

Perceived financial self-efficacy reflects a domain-specific belief that one can make effective financial decisions. Research indicates that the stronger one's confidence in one's financial ability, the more positive future outcomes accrue (e.g., Brüggen et al., 2017; Hadar et al., 2013). Financially knowledgeable consumers are more likely to behave in financially responsible ways (e.g., Hogarth & Hilgert, 2002). Perceived financial self-efficacy also serves to decrease financial and spending risks, leading to avoidance of negative financial behavior (e.g., Hadar et al., 2013). As such, financially skilled consumers are likely to believe that they have achieved financial security, which results in increased consumer happiness.

Market-Related Environmental Factors

Research has shown that consumer happiness is influenced by the country's level of economic development, its cost of living, its consumption equity, and its positive marketing practices.

The Country's Level of Economic Development

Research has shown that the level *of economic development* of a country plays an important role in consumer happiness (e.g., Dumludag, 2015). That is, the more the country is economically developed, the greater the consumer happiness of its citizens. The level of economic development facilitates the consumption of material products to meet basic needs (e.g., consumption for food, safety, health, and comfortable housing). Increased consumption of material goods that meet basic needs serves to enhance consumer happiness by alleviating material hardship and making life easier.

The Country's Cost of Living

The Consumer Price Index (CPI) measures changes in the cost of living and inflation over time. CPI measures changes in the cost of living over time, specifically changes in prices of goods and services at the national level over time (https://www.bls.gov/cpi/home). High CPI represents a state of low spending power which detracts from consumer happiness.

Studies found that the total amount of spending, especially spending on necessities, is positively related to consumer happiness (e.g., Veenhoven et al., 2021). Evidence also suggests that price increases reduce the perceived value and consumption of goods and services, which in turn detract from consumer happiness (e.g., Peine et al., 2009). As such, inflation harms consumer happiness (e.g., Dolan et al., 2008).

The Country's Consumption Equity

The *consumption equity index* measures equities and inequities in the consumption of goods and services that meet basic needs (e.g., Hill et al., 2007). That is, consumption inequity is associated with decreased consumer happiness. This may be due not only to relative deprivation but also to perceived unfairness. Conversely, consumption equity in society plays a positive role in consumer happiness.

An alternative to the consumption equity index is the *Gini index* (Lerman & Yitzhaki, 1984). This index is a common measure that scores a country from 0 (where every person has the same income) to 100 (where one person has all the income, and others have none). Furthermore, there are subjective measures of income inequality that capture the extent to which an individual believes that income is distributed evenly among members of their society (e.g., Gáspár et al., 2023).

Evidence suggests that consumption and income inequality exert negative effects on consumer happiness (e.g., Hagerty, 2000; Ngamaba et al., 2018; Oishi et al., 2011; Oshio & Urakawa, 2014). Three possible causes may account for this phenomenon: limited access to goods and services that can meet consumers' multiple needs, relative deprivation, and perceived unfairness.

The Country's Positive Marketing Practices

Researchers have treated the construct of *a positive attitude towards marketing practices* as a reflective and indirect indicator of satisfaction with consumer life (e.g., Peterson & Ekici, 2007). As such, consumers' attitude towards marketing practices is positive when consumers are satisfied with marketing practices, when consumers do not register many complaints about marketing practices, and when consumers perceive value and truthfulness in marketing programs.

Moreover, Ganglmair-Wooliscroft and Lawson (2012) conducted a study demonstrating that *consumer sentiment toward marketing practices* is positively associated with consumer happiness.

Summary and Conclusion

Table 7.1 captures a summary of what was discussed in this chapter. The table makes the distinction between happy and unhappy consumers and describes several sets of determinants of these two consumer segments: consumption factors, financial factors, and environmental factors.

Table 7.1 Factors influencing consumer happiness

Dimension	Factors	Low consumer happiness	High consumer happiness
Consumption factors	Total amount of spending	Low	High
	Relative consumption amount	Dissatisfied (relative deprivation)	Satisfied
	Financial conflicts	High	Low
	Experiential consumption	Low	High
	Savoring of experience	Low	High
	Brand engagement	Low	High
	Material consumption	Low	High
	Social sharing	Low	High
	Pro-social spending	Low	High
Financial factors	Income	Low	High
	Accumulated wealth	Low	High
	Money management stress	High	Low
	Positive financial behaviors	Low	High
	Financial self efficacy	Low	High
Environmental factors	Economic development	Low	High
	Cost of living	High	Low
	Consumption equality	Low	High
	Positive marketing practices	low	High

References

Ahuvia, A. C., & Friedman, D. C. (1998). Income, consumption, and subjective well-being: Toward a composite macromarketing model. *Journal of Macromarketing, 18*(2), 153–168.

Aknin, L. B., Norton, M. I., & Dunn, E. W. (2009). From wealth to well-being? Money matters, but less than people think. *The Journal of Positive Psychology, 4*(6), 523–527.

Aknin, L. B., Sandstrom, G. M., Dunn, E. W., & Norton, M. I. (2011). It's the recipient that counts: Spending money on strong social ties leads to greater happiness than spending on weak social ties. *PLoS ONE, 6*(2), e17018.

Aknin, L. B., Dunn, E. W., Sandstrom, G. M., & Norton, M. I. (2013). Does social connection turn good deeds into good feelings? On the value of putting the 'social' in prosocial spending. *International Journal of Happiness and Development, 1*(2), 155–171.

Aureliano-Silva, L., Strehlau, S., & Strehlau, V. (2018). The relationship between brand attachment and consumers' emotional well-being. *Journal of Relationship Marketing, 17*(1), 1–16.

Baumeister, R. F. (2002). Yielding to temptation: Self-control failure, impulsive purchasing, and consumer behavior. *Journal of Consumer Research, 28*(4), 670–676.

Bertram-Hümmer, V., & Baliki, G. (2015). The role of visible wealth for deprivation. *Social Indicators Research, 124*(3), 765–783.

Boyce, C. J., Brown, G. D., & Moore, S. C. (2010). Money and happiness: Rank of income, not income, affects life satisfaction. *Psychological Science, 21*(4), 471–475.

Brown, S., Taylor, K., & Price, S. W. (2005). Debt and distress: Evaluating the psychological cost of credit. *Journal of Economic Psychology, 26*(5), 642–663.

Brüggen, E. C., Hogreve, J., Holmlund, M., Kabadayi, S., & Löfgren, M. (2017). Financial well-being: A conceptualization and research agenda. *Journal of Business Research, 79*, 228–237.

Bryant, F. B., & Veroff, J. (2017). *Savoring: A new model of positive experience*. Psychology Press.

Caprariello, P. A., & Reis, H. T. (2013). To do, to have, or to share? Valuing experiences over material possessions depends on the involvement of others. *Journal of Personality and Social Psychology, 104*(2), 199–215.

Carter, T. J., & Gilovich, T. (2010). The relative relativity of material and experiential purchases. *Journal of Personality and Social Psychology, 98*(1), 146–159.

Carter, T. J., & Gilovich, T. (2012). I am what I do, not what I have: The differential centrality of experiential and material purchases to the self. *Journal of Personality and Social Psychology, 102*(6), 1304–1317.

Chancellor, J., & Lyubomirsky, S. (2011). Happiness and thrift: When (spending) less is (hedonically) more. *Journal of Consumer Psychology, 21*(2), 131–138.

Chun, H. H., Diehl, K., & MacInnis, D. J. (2017). Savoring an upcoming experience affects ongoing and remembered consumption enjoyment. *Journal of Marketing, 81*(3), 96–110.

Csikszentmihalyi, M. (1990). *Flow: The psychology of optimal experience*. Harper & Row.

Curry, O. S., Rowland, L. A., Van Lissa, C. J., Zlotowitz, S., McAlaney, J., & Whitehouse, H. (2018). Happy to help? A systematic review and meta-analysis of the effects of performing acts of kindness on the well-being of the actor. *Journal of Experimental Social Psychology, 76*, 320–329.

DeLeire, T., & Kalil, A. (2010). Does consumption buy happiness? Evidence from the United States. *International Review of Economics, 57*(2), 163–176.

Diener, E., Tay, L., & Oishi, S. (2013). Rising income and the subjective well-being of nations. *Journal of Personality and Social Psychology, 104*(2), 267–276.

Dittmar, H., Bond, R., Hurst, M., & Kasser, T. (2014). The relationship between materialism and personal well-being: A meta-analysis. *Journal of Personality and Social Psychology, 107*(5), 879–924.

Dolan, P., Peasgood, T., & White, M. (2008). Do we really know what makes us happy? A review of the economic literature on the factors associated with subjective well-being. *Journal of Economic Psychology, 29*(1), 94–122.

Dumludag, D. (2015). Consumption and life satisfaction at different levels of economic development. *International Review of Economics, 62*(2), 163–182.

Dunn, E. W., Aknin, L. B., & Norton, M. I. (2008). Spending money on others promotes happiness. *Science, 319*(5870), 1687–1688.

Dunn, E. W., Aknin, L. B., & Norton, M. I. (2014). Prosocial spending and happiness: Using money to benefit others pays off. *Current Directions in Psychological Science, 23*(1), 41–47.

Dynan, K. E., & Ravina, E. (2007). Increasing income inequality, external habits, and self-reported happiness. *American Economic Review, 97*(2), 226–231.

Fafchamps, M., & Shilpi, F. (2008). Subjective welfare, isolation, and relative consumption. *Journal of Development Economics, 86*(1), 43–60.

Gable, S. L., Reis, H. T., Impett, E. A., & Asher, E. R. (2004). What do you do when things go right? The intrapersonal and interpersonal benefits of sharing positive events. *Journal of Personality and Social Psychology, 87*(2), 228–245.

Ganglmair-Wooliscroft, A., & Lawson, R. (2012). Subjective wellbeing and its influence on consumer sentiment towards marketing: A New Zealand example. *Journal of Happiness Studies, 13*(1), 149–166.

Gáspár, A., Cervone, C., Durante, F., Maass, A., Suitner, C., Valtorta, R. R., & Vezzoli, M. (2023). A twofold subjective measure of income inequality. *Social Indicators Research, 168*(1), 25–43.

Geenen, N. Y., Hohelüchter, M., Langholf, V., & Walther, E. (2014). The beneficial effects of prosocial spending on happiness: Work hard, make money, and spend it on others? *The Journal of Positive Psychology, 9*(3), 204–208.

Gilovich, T., Kumar, A., & Jampol, L. (2015). A wonderful life: Experiential consumption and the pursuit of happiness. *Journal of Consumer Psychology, 25*(1), 152–165.

Guillen-Royo, M. (2011). Reference group consumption and the subjective wellbeing of the poor in Peru. *Journal of Economic Psychology, 32*(2), 259–272.

Gummerus, J., Liljander, V., Weman, E., & Pihlström, M. (2012). Customer engagement in a Facebook brand community. *Management Research Review, 35*(9), 857–877.

Hadar, L., Sood, S., & Fox, C. R. (2013). Subjective knowledge in consumer financial decisions. *Journal of Marketing Research, 50*(3), 303–316.

Hagerty, M. R. (2000). Social comparisons of income in one's community: Evidence from national surveys of income and happiness. *Journal of Personality and Social Psychology, 78*(4), 764–771.

Hayo, B., & Seifert, W. (2003). Subjective economic well-being in Eastern Europe. *Journal of Economic Psychology, 24*(3), 329–348.

Headey, B., Muffels, R., & Wooden, M. (2008). Money does not buy happiness: Or does it? A reassessment based on the combined effects of wealth, income and consumption. *Social Indicators Research, 87*(1), 65–82.

Hilgert, M. A., Hogarth, J. M., & Beverly, S. G. (2003). Household financial management: The connection between knowledge and behavior. *Federal Reserve Bulletin, 89*, 309–322.

Hill, G., & Howell, R. T. (2014). Moderators and mediators of pro-social spending and well-being: The influence of values and psychological need satisfaction. *Personality and Individual Differences, 69*, 69–74.

Hill, R. P., Felice, W. F., & Ainscough, T. (2007). International human rights and consumer quality of life: An ethical perspective. *Journal of Macromarketing, 27*(4), 370–379.

Hill, R. P., Martin, K. D., & Chaplin, L. N. (2012). A tale of two marketplaces: Consumption restriction, social comparison, and life satisfaction. *Marketing Letters, 23*, 731–744.

Hogarth, J. M., & Hilgert, M. A. (2002). Financial knowledge, experience and learning preferences: Preliminary results from a new survey on financial literacy. *Consumer Interest Annual, 48*(1), 1–7.

Howell, R. T., & Hill, G. (2009). The mediators of experiential purchases: Determining the impact of psychological needs satisfaction and social comparison. *The Journal of Positive Psychology, 4*(6), 511–522.

Hsee, C. K., & Zhang, J. (2004). Distinction bias: Misprediction and mischoice due to joint evaluation. *Journal of Personality and Social Psychology, 86*(5), 680–695.

Hsieh, C.-M. (2004). Income and financial satisfaction among older adults in the United States. *Social Indicators Research, 66*(3), 249–266.

Hudders, L., & Pandelaere, M. (2012). The silver lining of materialism: The impact of luxury consumption on subjective well-being. *Journal of Happiness Studies, 13*(3), 411–437.

Hui, B. P., & Kogan, A. (2018). Daily ups and downs: An event-sampling study of the mediated moderation of prosocial engagement on well-being. *Social Psychological and Personality Science, 9*(6), 675–688.

Hui, B. P., Ng, J. C., Berzaghi, E., Cunningham-Amos, L. A., & Kogan, A. (2020). Rewards of kindness? A meta-analysis of the link between prosociality and well-being. *Psychological Bulletin, 146*(12), 1084–1116.

Huston, S. J. (2010). Measuring financial literacy. *Journal of Consumer Affairs, 44*(2), 296–316.

Karahanna, E., Xu, S. X., & Zhang, N. (2015). Psychological ownership motivation and use of social media. *Journal of Marketing Theory and Practice, 23*(2), 185–207.

Kashdan, T. B., & Breen, W. E. (2007). Materialism and diminished well–being: Experiential avoidance as a mediating mechanism. *Journal of Social and Clinical Psychology, 26*(5), 521–539.

Kasser, T., & Ahuvia, A. (2002). Materialistic values and well-being in business students. *European Journal of Social Psychology, 32*(1), 137–146.

Kasser, T., & Ryan, R. M. (1993). A dark side of the American dream: Correlates of financial success as a central life aspiration. *Journal of Personality and Social Psychology, 65*(2), 410–422.

Kumar, V., Rajan, B., Gupta, S., & Pozza, I. D. (2019). Customer engagement in service. *Journal of the Academy of Marketing Science, 47*(1), 138–160.

Kuo, Y. F., & Feng, L. H. (2013). Relationships among community interaction characteristics, perceived benefits, community commitment, and oppositional brand loyalty in online brand communities. *International Journal of Information management, 33*(6), 948–962.

Langston, C. A. (1994). Capitalizing on and coping with daily-life events: Expressive responses to positive events. *Journal of Personality and Social Psychology, 67*(6), 1112–1125.

Lee, D. J., Sirgy, M. J., Larsen, V., & Wright, N. D. (2002). Developing a subjective measure of consumer well-being. *Journal of Macromarketing, 22*(2), 158–169.

Lerman, R. I., & Yitzhaki, S. (1984). A note on the calculation and interpretation of the Gini index. *Economics Letters, 15*(3-4), 363–368.

Lyubomirsky, S., Sheldon, K. M., & Schkade, D. (2005). Pursuing happiness: The architecture of sustainable change. *Review of General Psychology, 9*(2), 111–131.

Lyubomirsky, S., Sousa, L., & Dickerhoof, R. (2006). The costs and benefits of writing, talking, and thinking about life's triumphs and defeats. *Journal of Personality and Social Psychology, 90*(4), 692–708.

MacDonald, M., & Douthitt, R. A. (1992). Consumption theories and consumers' assessments of subjective well-being. *Journal of Consumer Affairs, 26*(2), 243–261.

Malone, K., Stewart, S. D., Wilson, J., & Korsching, P. F. (2010). Perceptions of financial well-being among American women in diverse families. *Journal of Family and Economic Issues, 31*(1), 63–81.

Maloney, P. W., Grawitch, M. J., & Barber, L. K. (2012). The multi-factor structure of the Brief Self-Control Scale: Discriminant validity of restraint and impulsivity. *Journal of Research in Personality, 46*(1), 111–115.

Mogilner, C., & Norton, M. I. (2016). Time, money, and happiness. *Current Opinion in Psychology, 10*, 12–16.

Mogilner, C., Rudnick, T., & Iyengar, S. S. (2008). The mere categorization effect: How the presence of categories increases choosers' perceptions of assortment variety and outcome satisfaction. *Journal of Consumer Research, 35*(2), 202–215.

Netemeyer, R. G., Warmath, D., Fernandes, D., & Lynch, J. G., Jr. (2018). How am I doing? Perceived financial well-being, its potential antecedents, and its relation to overall well-being. *Journal of Consumer Research, 45*(1), 68–89.

Ngamaba, K. H., Panagioti, M., & Armitage, C. J. (2018). Income inequality and subjective well-being: A systematic review and meta-analysis. *Quality of Life Research, 27*, 577–596.

Nickerson, C., Schwarz, N., Diener, E., & Kahneman, D. (2003). Zeroing in on the dark side of the American dream: A closer look at the negative consequences of the goal for financial success. *Psychological Science, 14*(6), 531–536.

Nickerson, C., Schwarz, N., & Diener, E. (2007). Financial aspirations, financial success, and overall life satisfaction. *Journal of Happiness Studies, 8*(4), 467–515.

Nicolao, L., Irwin, J. R., & Goodman, J. K. (2009). Happiness for sale: Do experiential purchases make consumers happier than material purchases? *Journal of Consumer Research, 36*(2), 188–198.

Noll, H. H., & Weick, S. (2015). Consumption expenditures and subjective well-being: Empirical evidence from Germany. *International Review of Economics, 62*(2), 101–119.

Oishi, S., Kesebir, S., & Diener, E. (2011). Income inequality and happiness. *Psychological Science, 22*(9), 1095–1100.

Oshio, T., & Urakawa, K. (2014). The association between perceived income inequality and subjective well-being: Evidence from a social survey in Japan. *Social Indicators Research, 116*(3), 755–770.

Oshio, T., Umeda, M., & Fujii, M. (2013). The association of life satisfaction and self-rated health with income dynamics among male employees in Japan. *Japan and the World Economy, 28*, 143–150.

Ozanne, L. K., & Ballantine, P. W. (2010). Sharing as a form of anti-consumption? An examination of toy library users. *Journal of Consumer Behavior, 9*(6), 485–498.

Peine, K., Heitmann, M., & Herrmann, A. (2009). Getting a feel for price affect: A conceptual framework and empirical investigation of consumers' emotional responses to price information. *Psychology & Marketing, 26*(1), 39–66.

Perez-Truglia, R. (2013). A test of the conspicuous–consumption model using subjective well-being data. *The Journal of Socio-Economics, 45*, 146–154.

Perry, V. G., & Morris, M. D. (2005). Who is in control? The role of self-perception, knowledge, and income in explaining consumer financial behavior. *Journal of Consumer Affairs, 39*(2), 299–313.

Petersen, F. E., Dretsch, H. J., & Loureiro, Y. K. (2018). Who needs a reason to indulge? Happiness following reason-based indulgent consumption. *International Journal of Research in Marketing, 35*(1), 170–184.

Peterson, M., & Ekici, A. (2007). Consumer attitude toward marketing and subjective quality of life in the context of a developing country. *Journal of Macromarketing, 27*(4), 350–359.

Richins, M. L. (2011). Materialism, transformation expectations, and spending: Implications for credit use. *Journal of Public Policy & Marketing, 30*(2), 141–156.

Richins, M. L., & Dawson, S. (1992). A consumer values orientation for materialism and its measurement: Scale development and validation. *Journal of Consumer Research, 19*(3), 303–316.

Rosenzweig, E., & Gilovich, T. (2012). Buyer's remorse or missed opportunity? Differential regrets for material and experiential purchases. *Journal of Personality and Social Psychology, 102*(2), 215–223.

Ruberton, P. M., Gladstone, J., & Lyubomirsky, S. (2016). How your bank balance buys happiness: The importance of "cash on hand" to life satisfaction. *Emotion, 16*(5), 575–580.

Sääksjärvi, M., Hellén, K., & Desmet, P. (2017). The "you and I" of happiness: Investigating the long-term impact of self-and other-focused happiness-enhancing activities. *Psychology & Marketing, 34*(6), 623–630.

Schellong, M., Kraiczy, N. D., Malär, L., & Hack, A. (2019). Family firm brands, perceptions of doing good, and consumer happiness. *Entrepreneurship Theory and Practice, 43*(5), 921–946.

Schnebelen, S., & Bruhn, M. (2018). An appraisal framework of the determinants and consequences of brand happiness. *Psychology & Marketing, 35*(2), 101–119.

Seghieri, C., Desantis, G., & Tanturri, M. L. (2006). The richer, the happier? An empirical investigation in selected European countries. *Social Indicators Research, 79*(3), 455–476.

Shrum, L. J., Wong, N., Arif, F., Chugani, S. K., Gunz, A., Lowrey, T. M., et al. (2013). Reconceptualizing materialism as identity goal pursuits: Functions, processes, and consequences. *Journal of Business Research, 66*(8), 1179–1185.

Sirgy, M. J. (1998). Materialism and quality of life. *Social Indicators Research, 43*(3), 227–260.

Sirgy, M. J. (2021). Macromarketing metrics of consumer well-being: An update. *Journal of Macromarketing, 41*(1), 124–131.

Smith, J. L., & Bryant, F. B. (2017). Savoring and well-being: Mapping the cognitive-emotional terrain of the happy mind. In *The happy mind: Cognitive contributions to well-being* (pp. 139–156). Springer.

Sprott, D., Czellar, S., & Spangenberg, E. (2009). The importance of a general measure of brand engagement on market behavior: Development and validation of a scale. *Journal of Marketing Research, 46*(1), 92–104.

Tatzel, M. (2014). *Consumption and well-being in the material world.* Springer.

Thomas, R., & Millar, M. (2013). The effects of material and experiential discretionary purchases on consumer happiness: Moderators and mediators. *The Journal of Psychology, 147*(4), 345–356.

Tully, S. M., & Sharma, E. (2022). Consumer wealth. *Consumer. Psychology Review, 5*(1), 125–143.

Van Boven, L., & Gilovich, T. (2003). To do or to have? That is the question. *Journal of Personality and Social Psychology, 85*(6), 1193–1202.

Veenhoven, R. (1991). Is happiness relative? *Social Indicators Research, 24*(1), 1–34.

Veenhoven, R., Chiperi, F., Kang, X., & Burger, M. (2021). Happiness and consumption: A research synthesis using an online finding archive. *Sage Open, 11*(1), 2158244020986239.

Verduyn, P., Van Mechelen, I., & Tuerlinckx, F. (2011). The relation between event processing and the duration of emotional experience. *Emotion, 11*(1), 20–28.

Waterman, A. S., Schwartz, S. J., & Conti, R. (2008). The implications of two conceptions of happiness (hedonic enjoyment and eudaimonia) for the understanding of intrinsic motivation. *Journal of Happiness Studies, 9*(1), 41–79.

Weingarten, E., & Goodman, J. K. (2021). Re-examining the experiential advantage in consumption: A meta-analysis and review. *Journal of Consumer Research, 47*(6), 855–877.

Weinstein, N., & Ryan, R. M. (2010). When helping helps: Autonomous motivation for prosocial behavior and its influence on well-being for the helper and recipient. *Journal of Personality and Social Psychology, 98*(2), 222–244.

Wilkinson, R. G., & Pickett, K. E. (2009). Income inequality and social dysfunction. *Annual Review of Sociology, 35*(1), 493–511.

Wu, F. (2020). An examination of the effects of consumption expenditures on life satisfaction in Australia. *Journal of Happiness Studies, 21*(8), 2735–2771.

Yu, G. B., Lee, D. J., Sirgy, M. J., & Bosnjak, M. (2020). Household income, satisfaction with standard of living, and subjective well-being. The moderating role of happiness materialism. *Journal of Happiness Studies, 21*(8), 2851–2872.

Chapter 8
How to Enhance Consumer Happiness

Money is only a tool. It will take you wherever you wish, but it will not replace you as the drive

—Ayn Rand (https://wellbeing.gmu.edu/famous-quotes-on-financial-stability-and-well-being/)

Ways to Enhance Consumer Happiness

Research has uncovered several interventions deemed successful in enhancing consumer happiness. These are (1) increase consumption to meet the full spectrum of human needs, (2) spend on variety of products and experiences, (3) spend more on experiences, (4) increase social spending, (5) reduce social comparisons, (6) increase income and wealth, (7) increase financial efficacy and positive financial behaviors, and (8) reduce materialism. Let's discuss these personal strategies in some detail.

Increase Consumption to Meet the Full Spectrum of Human Needs

Consumer happiness can be enhanced when consumers experience *satisfaction with the full spectrum of needs*. Consumer happiness is high when consumers experience satisfaction of various needs including needs for having, loving, and being (Allardt, 1973), needs for being, belonging, and becoming (Raphael et al., 1996), physical, social, self-actualization needs (Arndt, 1981), basic psychological needs (autonomy, competency, and relatedness) (Ryan & Deci, 2000), the need for positive emotion, engagement, relationships, meaning, and accomplishment (Seligman, 2011).

The basic premise of the need-satisfaction model is that consumer happiness is likely to be greater when consumer goods and services serve to meet the full

D.-J. Lee, M. J. Sirgy, *Happiness in the Marketplace*, Social Indicators Research Series 64, https://doi.org/10.1007/978-3-032-04443-3_8

spectrum of human development needs than when the same goods and services satisfy only a small subset of needs (e.g., Sirgy et al., 2011). Specifically, the *need satisfaction model* argues that satisfaction in a particular domain is maximized when the person experiences satisfaction in relation to safety, economic, family, social, esteem, actualization, knowledge, and aesthetics needs—the full spectrum of human developmental needs. The greater the need satisfaction, the more positive affect (the less negative affect) accumulates in the life domain in question (e.g., Diener et al., 2010; Sirgy et al., 2006).

For example, in the context of leisure consumption, research has revealed that leisure wellbeing is influenced by a set of benefits related to basic and growth needs (Lee et al., 2023; Sirgy et al., 2017). Said differently, lack of need satisfaction derived from the have-want discrepancies in the consumer life domain is negatively associated with consumer happiness (Wu, 2008).

Consumption does contribute to meeting consumers' basic needs (e.g., food, safety, health, and comfortable housing) up to a certain threshold point; thus, consumption that meets consumers' needs is likely to lead to enhanced consumer happiness (e.g., Noll & Weick, 2015). Specifically, evidence suggests that consumers spending on necessities is positively related to consumer happiness (e.g., Veenhoven et al., 2021), especially for consumers with low income (e.g., Aknin et al., 2009).

However, it should also be noted that increased consumption of basic material goods (e.g., food and housing) enhances consumer happiness by making life easier, yet consumption of material products has a diminishing marginal utility (e.g., Dolan et al., 2008).

Spend on Variety of Products and Experiences

Consumer happiness can be enhanced when consumers engage in *variety seeking* and looking for more options in the marketplace (e.g., Kahn & Isen, 1993). For example, research has demonstrated that consumer happiness is enhanced when they engage in a variety of leisure experiences and social activities (e.g., Zhong & Mitchell, 2012), and through variety of the low-risk alternatives (e.g., Lyubomirsky et al., 2005). That is, variety seeking can increase consumer happiness only when there is low risk involved (e.g., variety among safe, enjoyable products). Conversely, variety seeking among the high-risk options can increase anxiety and decrease consumer happiness (e.g., Isen & Geva, 1987).

In addition, variety seeking can increase consumer happiness by reducing hedonic adaptation (e.g., Galak et al., 2009; Redden, 2008; Yang et al., 2017). That is, variety seeking slows down the rate of hedonic adaptation by introducing novelty in consumption (e.g., Dunn et al., 2011).

Spend More on Experiences

Consumer happiness can be increased by *spending more on experiences* than on material possessions. Research has documented the finding that experience consumption contributes to consumer happiness much more than consumption of material goods, and it does so by elevating consumers' positive self-concept and satisfaction of social needs (this phenomenon is referred to in the research literature as "experiential advantage") (e.g., Thomas & Millar, 2013; Nicolao et al., 2009; Van Boven & Gilovich, 2003). That is, experiences help consumers increase their self-esteem, mostly through social activities that allow them to satisfy their social needs.

For example, in the context of leisure studies, evidence suggests that leisure experiences strongly contribute to consumer happiness (e.g., De Leire & Kalil, 2010; Noll & Weick, 2015). Much research in travel and tourism has provided much documentation about the notion that travel and tourism activities that can be considered mostly "experiential consumption" contribute significantly to consumer happiness (e.g., Uysal et al., 2012; Uysal & Sirgy, 2023)

Increase Social Spending

Consumer happiness can be increased through *social spending*. Social spending involves spending on activities with others, like relational products used together, and pro-social spending. Social spending increases consumer happiness because social spending facilitates social sharing and helps consumers meet their social needs. Social sharing about goods that consumers own (and services that they often experience) allows consumers to savor these experiences, which ultimately serves to generate positive affect, feeding into consumer happiness (e.g., Lyubomirsky et al., 2006; Schnebelen & Bruhn, 2018).

Prosocial spending is also more likely to lead to consumer happiness when acts of generosity facilitate social connection with others (e.g., taking a friend out for dinner) (e.g., Aknin et al., 2013). The positive effect of pro-social spending on consumer happiness is greater when their pro-social spending provides them with opportunities to connect with other people, which in turn serves to satisfy their *relatedness* needs.

Reduce Social Comparisons

Consumption equity refers to the perception that most people consume the same amounts of goods and services. Consumer happiness is influenced by *social comparison* and *consumption equity* (e.g., Veenhoven, 1991; Veenhoven et al., 2021; Lee et al., 2002; Sirgy, 2021). Why?

First, evidence suggests that consumer happiness is high when there is a high level of consumption equity (e.g., Lee et al., 2002; Sirgy, 2021). This is because a high level of consumption equity reflects the fact that most people consume enough goods and services to meet their basic needs. Consider the research on *income inequality* (e.g., Oishi et al., 2011; Wilkinson & Pickett, 2009). This research shows that income inequality results in consumption inequity, which in turn detracts from wellbeing and happiness.

Second, evidence suggests that consumer happiness is low when consumers experience relative deprivation. Specifically, increased consumption of a reference group (i.e., people with similar demographic characteristics) tend to reduce consumer happiness because of social comparisons (e.g., MacDonald & Douthitt, 1992; Noll & Weick, 2015; Wang et al., 2019)—consumers compare themselves to others who are better off or less deprived of material possessions. Furthermore, empirical studies found that the relative deprivation effect is high especially among the impoverished (e.g., Hill et al., 2012) and is particularly more pronounced for conspicuous products (those that are consumed with a great deal of social visibility such automobiles and homes and neighborhoods) (e.g., Bertram-Hümmer & Baliki, 2015).

Third, consumer happiness can be heightened when consumers refrain from comparison shopping (comparing alternative products before and after purchase). When consumers engage in comparative evaluations, they are likely to experience negative feelings such as feelings of regret (e.g., Rosenzweig & Gilovich, 2012), which decrease consumer happiness. That is, when consumers engage in comparative evaluations, they tend to experience "buyer's remorse" and "missed opportunities." Research also indicates that consumers tend to have "action regrets" (feelings that one has chosen the wrong alternative) for purchased material goods because it is much easier to make direct comparisons between different possible material purchases than between different services. Consumers tend to have "inaction regrets" for missed experiences because opportunities for experiences are rare, and each experience is unique. When consumers engage in comparative evaluations of consumer goods, they are likely to experience more negative affect than when making comparative evaluations with services, which plays a significant role in consumer happiness over time (e.g., Hsee et al., 2009; Tu & Hsee, 2018).

Fourth, research has demonstrated that consumer happiness is high when consumers do not engage in frequent social comparisons with other consumers (e.g., Howell & Hill, 2009). To reiterate, social comparison of consumption results in negative affect (i.e., dissatisfaction with the purchased products and feelings of regret) (e.g., Carter & Gilovich, 2010), which often spills over to negative evaluations about self. Research has also documented evidence suggesting that consumers motivated by eudaimonia (those who seek meaning related to self- and social development in the purchase of consumer durables and services) are less likely to engage in social comparisons, and as such they are likely to experience greater consumer happiness (e.g., Yang et al., 2021).

Increase Income and Wealth

Income can contribute significantly to consumer happiness because income allows people to buy more material goods and experiences that serve to satisfy consumers' needs. Simply put, higher income provides people with more options and opportunities to satisfy their needs, resulting in greater consumer happiness (e.g., Yu et al., 2020). Higher income generally increases consumer happiness by allowing consumers to save for a rainy day (e.g., Oshio et al., 2013). Research has shown that income is positively associated with consumers' positive perceptions of their financial situation (e.g., Malone et al., 2010). Research has also documented the findings that consumers with higher income report higher levels of financial satisfaction (e.g., Diener et al., 2013; Hayo & Seifert, 2003; Hsieh, 2004; Seghieri et al., 2006).

In addition to income, *accumulated wealth* (e.g., high financial assets and low debt) is positively associated with consumer happiness. Specifically, accumulated wealth is positively associated with financial satisfaction (e.g., Hsieh, 2004) and satisfaction with financial life (e.g., Nickerson et al., 2003, 2007). Research has documented that a broad measure of wealth and consumption (e.g., housing, business assets, equity and cash investments, bank accounts, accumulated pension holdings, vehicles and collectibles, housing debt, credit cards, student and personal debt, as well as food expenditure) is a stronger predictor of life satisfaction than income alone (Headey et al., 2008). These results support the notion that income, wealth, and consumption have a considerable influence on both satisfaction with the standard of living and life satisfaction.

Increase Financial Efficacy and Positive Financial Behaviors

Financial efficacy is likely to contribute significantly to consumer happiness. This is because financial self-efficacy serves to protect consumers from risks related to overspending. Consumers who perceive themselves to be financially efficacious tend to avoid taking unnecessary financial risk (e.g., Hadar et al., 2013). As such, financially skilled consumers are likely to believe that they can maintain financial security in their lives resulting in increased consumer happiness.

Positive financial behavior also has a positive effect on consumer happiness because positive financial behavior creates conditions that lead to financial wellbeing. Examples of positive financial behavior include saving, creating an emergency fund, paying bills on time, and positive retirement planning (Brüggen et al., 2017). In sum, positive financial behavior serves to increase satisfaction with one's financial situation, reducing financial risk, resulting in increased consumer happiness (e.g., Gutter & Copur, 2011; Xiao et al., 2006). In contrast, *compulsive buying behavior* has a negative influence on consumer happiness. Consumers afflicted with the urge to buy and buy compulsively (i.e., experience buying as irresistible urges) tend to lose control over their buying behavior despite being aware of the harmful consequences of such behavior (e.g., Dittmar, 2004; Faber & O'Guinn, 1992; McElroy et al., 1994; O'Guinn & Faber, 1989; Williams & Grisham, 2012).

Reduce Materialism

Consumer *materialism* hurts consumer happiness. As such, consumer happiness can be increased by reducing materialistic proclivities. Materialistic consumers are likely to experience more dissatisfaction with material life than non-materialistic. That is, they are less satisfied with their material possessions (material wellbeing). This may account for the negative relationship between materialism and consumer happiness (e.g., Ahuvia, 2001; Dittmar et al., 2014; Sirgy, 1998; Sirgy et al., 1998). Two explanations. First, materialism induces consumers to make frequent evaluations of their standard of living based on *ideal expectations*, which in turn induces dissatisfaction with the standard of living (e.g., Sirgy et al., 1998). In other words, materialistic consumers tend to evaluate their standard of living against unrealistically high expectations of "becoming rich," which ultimately leads to feelings of disappointment.

Second, materialistic consumers tend to frequently engage in social comparisons, which results in feelings of dissatisfaction with their standard of living (e.g., Sirgy, 1998). Yet. It needs to be noted that consumer materialism is detrimental to consumer happiness only when materialistic consumers engage in other signaling (i.e., purchase material goods to make a good impression on others), more so than self-signaling (i.e., purchase material goods to express their true self) (Shrum et al., 2013). On the other hand, materialism can play a positive role in consumer happiness by motivating consumers to excel in the economic arena, which in time may lead to a higher standard of living (e.g., Sirgy et al., 2013). In other words, materialism can motivate consumers to work hard to purchase luxury products that can meet esteem needs, which in turn contributes positively to satisfaction with material life (e.g., Hudders & Pandelaere, 2012).

Summary and Conclusion

Table 8.1 captures a summary of what was discussed in this chapter. The table shows all the possible interventions that have been researched and proved to be effective. The table also captures a brief description of each intervention as well as the reasons for why the intervention works.

Table 8.1 How to enhance consumer happiness

Dimension	Ways to enhance consumer happiness	Reasons
Consumption & spending	Increase consumption need satisfaction (consumer happiness is higher when consumer goods and services serve to meet the full spectrum of human development needs than when consumer goods and services serve to satisfy only a small subset of needs)	The greater the need satisfaction, the more positive affect (the less negative affect) accumulates in the consumer life domain
	Spend on a variety of products and experiences (consumer happiness is enhanced when consumers engage in variety seeking among the low-risk alternatives)	Variety seeking slows down the rate of hedonic adaptation by introducing uncertainty and novelty in consumption
	Spend more on experiences (consumer happiness can be increased by spending more on experiences than on material possessions)	Experiences provide consumers with a positive self-concept and increase satisfaction in social life
	Increase social spending (consumer happiness can be increased through spending with others and spending for others)	Social spending facilitates social sharing, allowing consumers to meet their social needs
	Reduce social comparisons (consumer happiness is high when consumers do not engage in comparative evaluation with other alternative products or other consumers)	Social comparison in consumption results in negative affect (e.g., feelings of regret and missed opportunities)
Financial resources	Increase income and wealth (consumer happiness is high when consumers have high income and wealth)	Higher income and wealth provide consumers with more options and opportunities to satisfy their needs
	Increase financial efficacy and positive financial behaviors (consumer happiness is high for consumers with high financial efficacy and positive financial behaviors)	Financial self-efficacy serves to protect consumers from financial and spending risks
Consumption value	Reduce materialism (consumer happiness is low for consumers with high materialism)	Materialism induces social comparisons, leading to dissatisfaction with the standard of living

References

Ahuvia, A. C. (2001). Individualism/collectivism and cultures of happiness: A theoretical conjecture on the relationship between consumption, culture and subjective well-being at the national level. *Journal of Happiness Studies, 3*(1), 23–36.

Aknin, L. B., Norton, M. I., & Dunn, E. W. (2009). From wealth to well-being? Money matters, but less than people think. *The Journal of Positive Psychology, 4*(6), 523–527.

Aknin, L. B., Dunn, E. W., Sandstrom, G. M., & Norton, M. I. (2013). Does social connection turn good deeds into good feelings? On the value of putting the 'social' in prosocial spending. *International Journal of Happiness and Development, 1*(2), 155–171.

Allardt, E. (1973). *About dimensions of welfare—Research group for comparative sociology*. (Research Report No. 1). University of Helsinki.

Arndt, H. W. (1981). Economic development: a semantic history. *Economic Development and Cultural Change, 29*(3), 457–466.

Bertram-Hümmer, V., & Baliki, G. (2015). The role of visible wealth for deprivation. *Social Indicators Research, 124*(3), 765–783.

Brüggen, E. C., Hogreve, J., Holmlund, M., Kabadayi, S., & Löfgren, M. (2017). Financial well-being: A conceptualization and research agenda. *Journal of Business Research, 79*, 228–237.

Carter, T. J., & Gilovich, T. (2010). The relative relativity of material and experiential purchases. *Journal of Personality and Social Psychology, 98*(1), 146–159.

De Leire, T., & Kalil, A. (2010). Does consumption buy happiness? Evidence from the United States. *International Review of Economics, 57*(2), 163–176.

Diener, E., Ng, W., Harter, J., & Arora, R. (2010). Wealth and happiness across the world: material prosperity predicts life evaluation, whereas psychosocial prosperity predicts positive feeling. *Journal of Personality and Social Psychology, 99*(1), 52–61.

Diener, E., Tay, L., & Oishi, S. (2013). Rising income and the subjective well-being of nations. *Journal of Personality and Social Psychology, 104*(2), 267–276.

Dittmar, H. (2004). Understanding and diagnosing compulsive buying. In R. Coombs (Ed.), *Addictive disorders: A guide to diagnosis and treatment* (pp. 411–450). Wiley.

Dittmar, H., Bond, R., Hurst, M., & Kasser, T. (2014). The relationship between materialism and personal well-being: A meta-analysis. *Journal of Personality and Social Psychology, 107*(5), 879–924.

Dolan, P., Peasgood, T., & White, M. (2008). Do we really know what makes us happy? A review of the economic literature on the factors associated with subjective well-being. *Journal of Economic Psychology, 29*(1), 94–122.

Dunn, E. W., Gilbert, D. T., & Wilson, T. D. (2011). If money doesn't make you happy, then you probably aren't spending it right. *Journal of Consumer Psychology, 21*(2), 115–125.

Faber, R. J., & O'Guinn, T. C. (1992). A clinical screener for compulsive buying. *Journal of Consumer Research, 19*(3), 459–469.

Galak, J., Redden, J. P., & Kruger, J. (2009). Variety amnesia: Recalling past variety can accelerate recovery from satiation. *Journal of Consumer Research, 36*(4), 575–584.

Gutter, M., & Copur, Z. (2011). Financial behaviors and financial well-being of college students: Evidence from a national survey. *Journal of Family and Economic Issues, 32*(4), 699–714.

Hadar, L., Sood, S., & Fox, C. R. (2013). Subjective knowledge in consumer financial decisions. *Journal of Marketing Research, 50*(3), 303–316.

Hayo, B., & Seifert, W. (2003). Subjective economic well-being in Eastern Europe. *Journal of Economic Psychology, 24*(3), 329–348.

Headey, B., Muffels, R., & Wooden, M. (2008). Money does not buy happiness: or does it? A reassessment based on the combined effects of wealth, income and consumption. *Social Indicators Research, 87*(May), 65–82.

Hill, R. P., Martin, K. D., & Chaplin, L. N. (2012). A tale of two marketplaces: Consumption restriction, social comparison, and life satisfaction. *Marketing Letters, 23*(3), 731–744.

Howell, R. T., & Hill, G. (2009). The mediators of experiential purchases: Determining the impact of psychological needs satisfaction and social comparison. *The Journal of Positive Psychology, 4*(6), 511–522.

Hsee, C. K., Yang, Y., Li, N., & Shen, L. (2009). Wealth, warmth, and well-being: Whether happiness is relative or absolute depends on whether it is about money, acquisition, or consumption. *Journal of Marketing Research, 46*(3), 396–409.

Hsieh, C.-M. (2004). Income and financial satisfaction among older adults in the United States. *Social Indicators Research, 66*(3), 249–266.

Hudders, L., & Pandelaere, M. (2012). The silver lining of materialism: the impact of luxury consumption on subjective well-being. *Journal of Happiness Studies, 13*(3), 411–437.

Isen, A. M., & Geva, N. (1987). The influence of positive affect on acceptable level of risk: The person with a large canoe has a large worry. *Organizational Behavior and Human Decision Processes, 39*(2), 145–154.

Kahn, B. E., & Isen, A. M. (1993). The influence of positive affect on variety seeking among safe, enjoyable products. *Journal of Consumer Research, 20*(2), 257–270.

Lee, D. J., Sirgy, M. J., Larsen, V., & Wright, N. D. (2002). Developing a subjective measure of consumer well-being. *Journal of Macromarketing, 22*(2), 158–169.

Lee, D. J., Yu, G. B., & Sirgy, M. J. (2023). Testing the benefits theory of leisure wellbeing. *Applied Research in Quality of Life, 18*(5), 2705–2748.

Lyubomirsky, S., Sheldon, K. M., & Schkade, D. (2005). Pursuing happiness: The architecture of sustainable change. *Review of General Psychology, 9*(2), 111–131.

Lyubomirsky, S., Sousa, L., & Dickerhoof, R. (2006). The costs and benefits of writing, talking, and thinking about life's triumphs and defeats. *Journal of Personality and Social Psychology, 90*(4), 692–708.

MacDonald, M., & Douthitt, R. A. (1992). Consumption theories and consumers' assessments of subjective well-being. *Journal of Consumer Affairs, 26*(2), 243–261.

Malone, K., Stewart, S. D., Wilson, J., & Korsching, P. F. (2010). Perceptions of financial well-being among American women in diverse families. *Journal of Family and Economic Issues, 31*(1), 63–81.

McElroy, S. L., Phillips, K. A., & Keck, P. E., Jr. (1994). Obsessive compulsive spectrum disorder. *The Journal of Clinical Psychiatry, 55*, 33–51.

Nickerson, C., Schwarz, N., Diener, E., & Kahneman, D. (2003). Zeroing in on the dark side of the American dream: A closer look at the negative consequences of the goal for financial success. *Psychological Science, 14*(6), 531–536.

Nickerson, C., Schwarz, N., & Diener, E. (2007). Financial aspirations, financial success, and overall life satisfaction. *Journal of Happiness Studies, 8*(4), 467–515.

Nicolao, L., Irwin, J. R., & Goodman, J. K. (2009). Happiness for sale: Do experiential purchases make consumers happier than material purchases? *Journal of Consumer Research, 36*(2), 188–198.

Noll, H. H., & Weick, S. (2015). Consumption expenditures and subjective well-being: Empirical evidence from Germany. *International Review of Economics, 62*(2), 101–119.

O'Guinn, T. C., & Faber, R. J. (1989). Compulsive buying: A phenomenological exploration. *Journal of Consumer Research, 16*(2), 147–157.

Oishi, S., Kesebir, S., & Diener, E. (2011). Income inequality and happiness. *Psychological Science, 22*(9), 1095–1100.

Oshio, T., Umeda, M., & Fujii, M. (2013). The association of life satisfaction and self-rated health with income dynamics among male employees in Japan. *Japan and the World Economy, 28*, 143–150.

Raphael, D., Renwick, R., Brown, I., & Rootman, I. (1996). Quality of life indicators and health: Current status and emerging conceptions. *Social Indicators Research, 39*(1), 65–88.

Redden, J. P. (2008). Reducing satiation: The role of categorization level. *Journal of Consumer Research, 34*(5), 624–634.

Rosenzweig, E., & Gilovich, T. (2012). Buyer's remorse or missed opportunity? Differential regrets for material and experiential purchases. *Journal of Personality and Social Psychology, 102*(2), 215–223.

Ryan, R. M., & Deci, E. L. (2000). Self-determination theory and the facilitation of intrinsic motivation, social development, and well-being. *American Psychologist, 55*(1), 68–78.

Schnebelen, S., & Bruhn, M. (2018). An appraisal framework of the determinants and consequences of brand happiness. *Psychology & Marketing, 35*(2), 101–119.

Seghieri, C., Desantis, G., & Tanturri, M. L. (2006). The richer, the happier? An empirical investigation in selected European countries. *Social Indicators Research, 79*(3), 455–476.

Seligman, M. E. P. (2011). *Flourish: A visionary new understanding of happiness and well-being*. The Free Press.

Shrum, L. J., Wong, N., Arif, F., Chugani, S. K., Gunz, A., Lowrey, T. M., et al. (2013). Reconceptualizing materialism as identity goal pursuits: Functions, processes, and consequences. *Journal of Business Research, 66*(8), 1179–1185.

Sirgy, M. J. (1998). Materialism and quality of life. *Social Indicators Research, 43*(3), 227–260.

Sirgy, M. J. (2021). Macromarketing metrics of consumer well-being: An update. *Journal of Macromarketing, 41*(1), 124–131.

Sirgy, M. J., Lee, D.-J., Kosenko, R., Meadow, H. L., Rahtz, D., Cicic, M., Jin, G. X., Yarsuvat, D., Blenkhorn, D., & Wright, N. (1998). Does television viewership play a role in the perception of quality of life? *Journal of Advertising, 27*(1), 125–142.

Sirgy, M. J., Lee, D. J., & Kressmann, F. (2006). A need-based measure of consumer wellbeing (CWB) in relation to personal transportation: Nomological validation. *Social Indicators Research, 79*(2), 337–367.

Sirgy, M. J., Kruger, P. S., Lee, D. J., & Yu, G. B. (2011). How does a travel trip affect tourists' life satisfaction? *Journal of Travel Research, 50*(3), 261–275.

Sirgy, M. J., Gurel-Atay, E., Webb, D., Cicic, M., Husic-Mehmedovic, M., Ekici, A., Hermann, A., Hegazy, I., Lee, D.-J., & Johar, J. S. (2013). Is materialism all that bad? Effects on satisfaction with material life, life satisfaction, and economic motivation. *Social Indicators Research, 110*(1), 349–366.

Sirgy, M. J., Uysal, M., & Kruger, S. (2017). Towards a benefits theory of leisure wellbeing. *Applied Research in Quality of Life, 12*(1), 205–228.

Thomas, R., & Millar, M. (2013). The effects of material and experiential discretionary purchases on consumer happiness: Moderators and mediators. *The Journal of Psychology, 147*(4), 345–356.

Tu, Y., & Hsee, C. K. (2018). Hedonomics: On subtle yet significant determinants of happiness. In E. Diener, S. Oishi, & L. Tay (Eds.), *Handbook of well-being* (pp. 1–12). DEF Publishers. nobascholar.com.

Uysal, M., & Sirgy, M. J. (Eds.). (2023). *Handbook of tourism and quality-of-life research II: Enhancing the lives of tourists, residents of host communities, and service providers*. Springer Nature.

Uysal, M., Perdue, R., & Sirgy, M. J. (Eds.). (2012). *Handbook of tourism and quality-of-life research: Enhancing the lives of tourists and residents of host communities*. Springer.

Van Boven, L., & Gilovich, T. (2003). To do or to have? That is the question. *Journal of Personality and Social Psychology, 85*(6), 1193–1202.

Veenhoven, R. (1991). Is happiness relative? *Social Indicators Research, 24*, 1–34.

Veenhoven, R., Chiperi, F., Kang, X., & Burger, M. (2021). Happiness and consumption: A research synthesis using an online finding archive. *Sage Open, 11*(1), 2158244020986239.

Wang, H., Cheng, Z., & Smyth, R. (2019). Consumption and happiness. *The Journal of Development Studies, 55*(1), 120–136.

Wilkinson, R., & Pickett, K. (2009). *The spirit level: Why equal societies almost always do better*. Penguin.

Williams, A. D., & Grisham, J. R. (2012). Impulsivity, emotion regulation, and mindful attentional focus in compulsive buying. *Cognitive Therapy and Research, 36*(5), 451–457.

Wu, C.-H. (2008). The role of perceived discrepancy in satisfaction evaluation. *Social Indicators Research, 88*(3), 423–436.

Xiao, J. J., Sorhaindo, B., & Garman, E. T. (2006). Financial behavior of consumers in credit counseling. *International Journal of Consumer Studies, 30*(2), 108–121.

Yang, Y., Gu, Y., & Galak, J. (2017). When it could have been worse, it gets better: How favorable uncertainty resolution slows hedonic adaptation. *Journal of Consumer Research, 43*(5), 747–768.

Yang, W., Zhang, Y., & So, K. K. F. (2021). Tourism experiences vs. material purchases: Effects of eudaimonic consumption motive on consumers' reactions to invidious comparisons. *Tourism Management, 83*, 104247.

Yu, G. B., Lee, D. J., Sirgy, M. J., & Bosnjak, M. (2020). Household income, satisfaction with standard of living, and subjective well-being. The moderating role of happiness materialism. *Journal of Happiness Studies, 21*(8), 2851–2872.

Zhong, J. Y., & Mitchell, V. W. (2012). Does consumer well-being affect hedonic consumption? *Psychology & Marketing, 29*(8), 583–594.

Part III
Consumption Happiness

In Part III of the book, we will address constructs and metrics of consumption happiness, its outcomes, its antecedents, and propose ideas on how to enhance consumption happiness.

Chapter 9
Constructs and Metrics of Consumption Happiness

We are what we consume. If we look deeply into the items that we consume every day, we will come to know our own nature very well.

—Thich Nhat Hanh (https://www.google.com/search?q=quotation+on+consuming&rlz=1C1GCEB_enUS960US960&oq=quotation+on+consuming&gs_lcrp=EgZjaHJvbWUyBggAEEUYOTIHCAEQIRigATIHCAIQIRigAdIBCTE0NTg1ajBqN6gCALACAA&sourceid=chrome&ie=UTF-8#vhid=zephyr:0&vssid=atritem)

Definitions and Dimensions of Consumption Happiness

The research literature on consumption happiness alludes to several constructs and different definitions. These include "consumption happiness," "momentary consumption happiness," "anticipated consumption happiness," and "remembered consumption happiness." We'll describe these constructs and their dimensions in the sections below.

Consumption Happiness

Consumption happiness refers to an overall satisfaction rating and positive/negative emotional reflection of their consumption activities (Desmeules, 2002). Specifically, consumption happiness is defined as a state of happiness related to a specific consumption activity (e.g., Laros & Steenkamp, 2005; Merunka & Sirgy, 2011; Mogilner et al., 2012; Richins, 1997; van Boven & Gilovich, 2003). Consumption happiness is different from consumer happiness in that consumption happiness is momentary happiness resulting from a consumption activity about a consumer good or service. Frequent consumption experiences will ultimately spill over to consumer happiness, a more stable and enduring happiness, capturing affect and satisfaction

D.-J. Lee, M. J. Sirgy, *Happiness in the Marketplace*, Social Indicators Research Series 64, https://doi.org/10.1007/978-3-032-04443-3_9

associated with the consumer life domain (i.e., the life domain that houses affective experiences related to marketplace events). As such, consumption happiness is viewed as a positive emotion experienced—joy, pleasure, and satisfaction.

Consumption happiness is typically measured by asking how happy one feels or how happy a product or a marketplace situation makes one feel (e.g., Merunka & Sirgy, 2011; Nicolao et al., 2009; Thomas & Millar, 2013; van Boven & Gilovich, 2003; Weidman & Dunn, 2016). For example, Merunka and Sirgy (2011) captured consumption happiness from a brand in terms of a judgment made by consumers regarding the extent to which the focal brand/company makes a significant contribution to his or her quality of life.

The research literature on consumption happiness points to three distinct forms of consumption happiness, namely momentary happiness (consumption happiness from consuming a purchase in the present), anticipatory happiness (consumption happiness from looking forward to a purchase) and remembered happiness (consumption happiness from looking back on a purchase, or afterglow.

Momentary Consumption Happiness

The first dimension of consumption happiness is *momentary consumption* happiness. Momentary consumption happiness is defined as the pleasure consumers feel during actual consumption (e.g., Dunn & Weidman, 2015). Specifically, momentary consumption happiness is situation-specific happiness induced by marketplace events such as positive experiences related to shopping, buying, consumption, service, and maintenance etc. Momentary consumption happiness is an affective state that is temporal and short-term in nature.

For example, Weidman and Dunn (2016) examined momentary consumption happiness regarding consumer purchase using a novel data collection method (daily diary and experiential sampling over two weeks). Their results indicate that material and experiential purchases deliver consumption happiness in two distinct ways: (1) material purchases provide more frequent momentary happiness over time than experiential purchases, and (2) experiential purchases provide more intense momentary happiness on individual occasions than material purchases.

A similar study by Carter and Gilovich (2010) showed that consumption happiness is higher for experiential purchases than for material purchases. Momentary consumption happiness from material purchases declines over time because of hedonic adaptation and feelings of regret. That is, consumption happiness ratings for material goods dropped off more steeply over time, reflecting more rapid adaptation than experiences (cf. Nicolao et al., 2009). In contrast, consumption happiness with experiential purchases did not decline much over time and tended to last longer. Why? Gilovich et al. (2015) explained: It seems like happiness related to marketplace experiences does not decline much because experiential purchases tend to be closely aligned with consumers' self-concept, which in turn serves to facilitate social connections through conversations and storytelling. In addition, consumers tend to feel far less regret in experiential purchases compared to material purchases.

Anticipated Consumption Happiness

The second dimension of consumption happiness is *anticipated consumption happiness*. There is a conceptual difference between anticipated consumption happiness and *anticipatory consumption happiness*. Anticipated consumption happiness represents a forecast of *future* positive consumption emotions (e.g., consumption happiness) that may arise when consumers imagine or simulate product consumption (Baumgartner et al., 2008). Research has shown that anticipated happiness requires a cognitive effort of imagining future events (Bettiga & Lamberti, 2020). Furthermore, evidence suggests that anticipated consumption happiness leads consumers to focus on future gains (Higgins, 1997) and influences the formation of purchase intentions (Bettiga & Lamberti, 2020).

In contrast, anticipatory consumption happiness involves feelings of consumption happiness *currently* experienced due to the prospect of a future consumption event (Baumgartner et al., 2008). That is, anticipatory consumption happiness involves feelings of consumption happiness experienced in the present about future consumption events. Anticipatory consumption happiness is commonly captured by asking participants how much happiness they are currently feeling while thinking about a future purchase and consumption (e.g., Kumar et al., 2014). While both anticipated and anticipatory consumption happiness do play a positive role in the formation of purchase intentions, anticipated consumption happiness seems to have a stronger effect on purchase intention than anticipatory consumption happiness (Bettiga & Lamberti, 2020).

Research has revealed that consumers overestimate the impact (both intensity and duration) of a future affective event (e.g., Buehler & McFarland, 2001; Gilbert et al., 1998; Gilbert et al., 2004; Mitchell et al., 1997; Wilson et al., 2000). While consumers believe that they will often think and converse about their experiences in the future, they tend to overestimate the frequency and intensity of the anticipated positive affect. This is because consumers respond with greater emotional intensity to future events than to past events (Caruso et al., 2008). In other words, the emotional experience of anticipating an event is more intense than relevant post-event emotional experiences (cf. van Boven & Ashworth, 2007).

Research has also discovered that consumers derive more happiness from the anticipation of experiential purchases than from the anticipation of material goods (e.g., Kumar et al., 2014). Why? Consumers tend to think about future experiential consumption at a higher level of construal, which serves to amplify positive feelings (Trope & Liberman, 2003). For example, waiting for future experiences increases the positive feeling of anticipation, but waiting for material goods tends to increase frustration.

Research has also uncovered the tendency to overestimate anticipated happiness from purchase to be greater for consumers in countries high on individualism than countries high on collectivism (e.g., Lam et al., 2005). This is because individuals in a collectivistic culture tend to think more holistically than individuals in an individualistic culture—they do not focus their attention narrowly on upcoming positive events. In contrast, individuals in a collectivistic culture tend to employ a holistic thinking style, and they tend to be sensitive to background stimuli and context. Said differently, individuals in an individualistic culture tend to view positive events in isolation and expect these events to have an enduring effect (Nisbett et al., 2001).

Remembered Consumption Happiness

The third dimension of consumption happiness is *remembered consumption happiness*. Remembered consumption happiness related to a marketplace event is the consumer's retrospective global assessment of the consumption experiences. Remembered consumption happiness (afterglow) can be captured by asking participants how much a past purchase contributes to their overall happiness or how happy they feel about the purchase when they think back on it (e.g., Howell & Hill, 2009; van Boven & Gilovich, 2003).

Research has shown that consumers remember events as being better or worse than the actual momentary experience (e.g., Buehler & McFarland, 2001; Mitchell et al., 1997; Wirtz et al., 2003). In other words, consumers tend to overestimate the intensity of their recollections of positive and negative affect. Furthermore, consumers' repeat purchase intention seems to be strongly influenced by remembered happiness.

Why are positive experiences reconstructed more favorably in memory, more so than during the experience? Perhaps this may be due to the possibility that positive events' peak and end experiences are better recalled at the time of retrospective evaluation than when they occur (cf. Fredrickson & Kahneman, 1993; Hsee & Hastie, 2006; Wirtz et al., 2003).

Remembered consumption happiness also seems to be influenced by cultural values. Consumers from individualistic countries tend to report higher retrospective experiential happiness than those from collectivistic cultures, even when there were no differences in real-time experiences (Oishi, 2002). This may be because individuals from an individualistic culture tend to maintain a strong belief that "life is good." They also value high-arousal positive affect (e.g., excitement). In contrast, consumers from a collectivistic culture have a belief that "good and bad things happen in life," and value low arousal positive affect (e.g., calm) (cf. Oishi et al., 1998; Tsai et al., 2006).

Models and Metrics of Consumption Happiness

Consumption happiness refers to perceptions, evaluations, and actions in the marketplace that contribute to positive emotions and ultimately increase (or decrease) satisfaction in the life domain, housing affective experiences related to the marketplace (e.g., Mogilner et al., 2012; Sirgy et al., 2008). Arnould et al. (2002) identified several consumption happiness dimensions related to consumer goods and services. Specifically, consumers interact with material goods they possess in different ways: anticipated consumption experiences (e.g., searching and planning for future purchases), purchase experiences (e.g., brand choice, payment, and service encounter), consumption experiences (e.g., sensory experiences, satiation, arousal/flow, and transformation); and remembered consumption (e.g., reliving past experiences by telling stories and remembering the experience along with memorabilia and souvenirs).

The models of consumption happiness can be grouped into several categories related to the stage of the consumption life cycle: acquisition-focused models, possession-focused models, and experience-focused models (see Table 9.2).

The first set of consumption happiness models involves the acquisition of consumer goods and services. Acquisition-focused models of consumption happiness include satisfaction with a local shopping mall (or center), shopping wellbeing, perceived shopping value (utilitarian and hedonic), and purchase happiness. Possession-focused models include brand relationships and brand community. Experience-focused models include self-congruity, extended self, positive self, self-expressiveness, perceived quality-of-life impact, perceived quality of consumer goods and services, perceived value (functional, social, and emotional), benefits and need satisfaction, personal values, positive social interactions, experiential advantage, and hedonic adaptation.

In summary, the models of consumption happiness explain the mechanisms that consumers experience happiness from their acquisition, possession, and marketplace experiences.

Acquisition-Focused Models

To reiterate, acquisition-focused models are consumer behavior models that focus on shopping and purchase activities. We identified four major models in that regard: satisfaction with a local shopping mall (or center), shopping wellbeing, perceived shopping value (utilitarian and hedonic), and purchase happiness.

Satisfaction with a Local Shopping Mall (or Center)

The focus here is satisfaction with the local shopping mall or market area. In other words, consumer happiness can be viewed in terms of satisfaction with one's shopping mall or market area located in one's neighborhood (e.g., Day, 1987; Meadow & Sirgy, 2008; Sirgy & Lee, 2006). As such, shopping wellbeing focuses on one aspect of consumers' experience in the marketplace, namely, experiences related to product acquisition. As such, shopping wellbeing is defined as a shopper's perceived impact of a shopping mall in contributing to satisfaction in important life domains (e.g., consumer life, social life, leisure life, and community life) resulting in a global judgment that the mall contributes significantly to one's overall quality of life (El Hedhli et al., 2013). Research has shown that shopping wellbeing is positively associated with mall functionality, mall convenience, mall safety, mall leisure, mall atmospherics, and shoppers' self-identification (El Hedhli et al., 2013) and that functional congruity has a stronger effect than self-congruity on shopping wellbeing (El Hedhli et al., 2021).

See Tables 9.1 and 9.2 for a measure of satisfaction with a local shopping mall or center.

Shopping Wellbeing and Ill-Being

The *shopping wellbeing* concept captures perceived impact of shopping on one's quality of life; it is composed of two dimensions: positive beliefs regarding the degree to which shopping contributes to quality of life (shopping wellbeing), and

Table 9.1 Capturing the concept of satisfaction with a local shopping mall (or center)

For shopping wellbeing, respondents are prompted by the following question: "Does shopping at (mall name) contribute to your quality of life?"
Then, respondents are presented with 7-point differential scales involving four items: • This mall does not satisfy/satisfies my overall shopping needs. • This mall does not play a role/plays a role in my social wellbeing. • This mall does not play a role/plays a very important role in my leisure wellbeing. • This mall does not play a role/plays an important role in enhancing the quality of life in my community.

Source: Adapted from El Hedhli et al. (2013)

Table 9.2 Modified measure of satisfaction with a shopping center

• The shopping center X satisfies my general purchasing needs. • The shopping center X plays an important role in my social wellbeing. • The shopping center X plays an important role in the leisure activities. • The shopping center X plays an important role in improving the quality of life in my community.
Response scale: 1 = strongly disagree; 7 = strongly agree

Source: adapted from de Rezende Pinto et al. (2018)

negative beliefs related to the degree to which shopping activities result in overspending of time, effort, and money (shopping illbeing) (e.g., Ekici et al., 2018; Lee et al., 2014; Sirgy et al., 2020).

It should be noted that consumers often focus on positive experiences they have during shopping, yet they may end up with negative experiences during the actual consumption of the purchased products (e.g., Hsee & Hastie, 2006). Furthermore, consumers may overestimate the intensity or duration of positive emotions from the products during their shopping. Thus, it is necessary to measure consumers' actual consumption experiences after purchase. In addition, it is important to evaluate happiness in a shopping context along with consumers' financial situation because overspending on shopping can lead to reduced consumer wellbeing (e.g., Netemeyer et al., 2018).

Shopping wellbeing can be construed to the extent to which shopping increases positive affect in a variety of life domains (e.g., social life, leisure life, community life, cultural life). An increase in positive affect in life domains is then assumed to contribute to increases in consumer life satisfaction (El Hedhli et al., 2013).

It should be noted that shopping wellbeing does not contribute to consumer wellbeing when shopping activities result in role conflict due to overspending time, effort, and money (shopping ill-being) (Ekici et al., 2018). As such, shopping ill-being refers to a consumer's investment of too much time, money, and energy in shopping at the expense of meeting one's needs in other life domains. Shopping ill-being reduces consumer happiness as shopping ill-being results in role conflict by making role responsibilities in one life domain incompatible with other life domains. Thus, it is important to measure shopping wellbeing along with shopping ill-being. The resultant construct is *shopping life balance,* which refers to a state of balanced satisfaction between shopping life and other life domains. This state involves a high level of engagement in shopping life (i.e., high shopping wellbeing) along with minimal role conflict (low shopping ill-being) (Sirgy et al., 2020). See a measure of shopping life balance in Table 9.3.

Perceived Shopping Value: Utilitarian and Hedonic

Shopping happiness is construed in terms of consumers' perceived value from shopping events and activities. These events and activities provide consumers with utilitarian and hedonic shopping value that contributes to shopping happiness (e.g., Babin et al., 1994; Babin & Attaway, 2000; El Hedhli et al., 2013).

Perceived shopping value is customarily broken down in terms of two dimensions: utilitarian and hedonic (e.g., Babin et al., 1994; Voss et al., 2003). *Utilitarian value* is associated with task completion, and it is derived from the functions performed by products. *Hedonic value,* on the other hand, is associated with entertainment and fun, and it results from sensations derived from the experience of using products. To reiterate, utilitarian shopping reflects the acquisition of products and/or information in an efficient manner and can be viewed as reflecting a more task-oriented, cognitive, and non-emotional outcome of shopping. In contrast, hedonic

Table 9.3 Measure of shopping wellbeing and shopping illbeing

Shopping Wellbeing (Belief that Shopping Contributes to Personal and One's Family Quality of Life) • Thinking about shopping, I feel that my shopping contributes significantly to my wellbeing. • Thinking about shopping, my quality of life would diminish significantly if I didn't shop. • Thinking about shopping, I feel that shopping makes me happy. • Thinking about shopping, I feel that shopping contributes significantly to my quality of life overall. • I feel that my shopping activities contribute significantly to my family's wellbeing. • The quality of life of my family would diminish significantly if I didn't shop. • I feel that shopping makes me happy because shopping contributes much to my family's wellbeing. • I feel that my shopping contributes significantly to my family's quality of life overall.
Response scale: 1 = strongly disagree; 7 = strongly agree
Shopping Ill-being (Investment of Too Much Time, Money, Energy in Shopping at the Expense Family, Work, Social, Leisure, and Financial Life) • Our family and close friends often complain that I spend too much time shopping and not enough time with the family. • Our family and close friends often complain that I spend a lot of money on shopping, causing a great deal of family strife. • Our family and close friends often complain that I spend too much energy shopping and not enough energy on family. • Our family and close friends often complain that I spend too much time shopping and not enough time on work. • Our family and close friends often complain that I spend too much money shopping and not enough money on further developing my career. • Our family and close friends often complain that I spend too much energy shopping and not enough energy to bolster my career. • Our family and close friends often complain that I spend too much time shopping and not enough time socializing with others. • Our family and close friends often complain that I spend too much money shopping and not enough money for social activities. • Our family and close friends often complain that I spend too much energy shopping and not enough energy for social activities. • Our family and close friends often complain that I spend too much time shopping and not enough time for leisure activities. • Our family and close friends often complain that I spend too much money shopping and not enough money for leisure activities. • Our family and close friends often complain that I spend too much energy shopping and not enough energy for leisure activities. • Our family and close friends often complain that I spend too much time shopping and not enough time making money by working hard. • Our family and close friends often complain that I spend too much money shopping creating havoc on financial life. • Our family and close friends often complain that I spend too much energy shopping and not enough energy for making money by working hard.
Response scale: 1 = strongly disagree; 7 = strongly agree

Source: Adapted from Ekici et al. (2018)

Table 9.4 Measure of utilitarian and hedonic value in shopping

Hedonic shopping value

- This shopping trip was truly a joy.
- I continued to shop, not because I had to, but because I wanted to.
- This shopping trip truly felt like an escape.
- Compared to other things I could have done, the time spent shopping was truly enjoyable.
- I enjoyed being immersed in exciting new products.
- I enjoyed this shopping trip for its own sake, not just for the items I may have purchased.
- I had a good time because I was able to act on the "spur-of-the-moment."
- During the trip, I felt the excitement of the hunt.
- While shopping, I was able to forget my problems.
- While shopping, I felt a sense of adventure.
- This shopping trip was not a very nice time out.

Utilitarian shopping value:

- I accomplished just what I wanted to on this shopping trip.
- I couldn't buy what I really needed.
- While shopping, I found just the item(s) I was looking for.
- I was disappointed because I had to go to another store(s) to complete my shopping.

Response scale: 1 = strongly disagree; 5 = strongly agree

Source: Adapted from Babin et al. (1994)

shopping reflects the value received from the multisensory, fantasy, and emotive aspects of the shopping experience. That is, hedonic shopping reflects the value found in the shopping experience itself, independent of task-related activities (cf. Babin & Attaway, 2000). See Table 9.4 for an example of a measure capturing utilitarian and hedonic shopping value.

Research has shown that shopping wellbeing is strongly influenced by both hedonic and utilitarian value of a shopping center, but much more so by hedonic than utilitarian value (e.g., El Hedhli et al., 2016). In sum, shopping happiness tends to be high when consumers perceive utilitarian and hedonic values in their shopping events and activities. Shopping wellbeing in turn contributes to customer loyalty and life satisfaction (e.g., El Hedhli et al., 2013; de Rezende Pinto et al. 2018).

Purchase Happiness

Purchase happiness refers to positive feelings experienced from having purchased a specific consumer good or service. The focus is how the consumer felt about the focal purchase (e.g., Howell & Hill, 2009; Nicolao et al., 2009; Thomas & Millar, 2013; van Boven & Gilovich, 2003).

Specifically, purchase happiness is a state of happiness related to a specific purchase activity. Purchase happiness is consumption happiness at the acquisition stage. Purchase happiness can be measured by asking how happy one feels or how happy a product or a marketplace situation makes one feel (e.g., Nicolao et al., 2009; Thomas & Millar, 2013; van Boven & Gilovich, 2003; Weidman & Dunn, 2016).

Table 9.5 Selected measures of purchase happiness

Purchase happiness (van Boven & Gilovich, 2003)

1. "When you think about this purchase, how happy does it make you?" (1 = not happy, 9 = very happy)
2. "How much does this purchase contribute to your happiness in life?" (1 = not at all 9 = very much)
3. "To what extent would you say this purchase is money well-spent?" (1 = not very well-spent, 9 = very well spent)
4. "To what extent do you think the money spent on this purchase would have been better spent on something else—some other type of purchase that would have made you happier?" (1 = not at all, 5 = moderately, 9 = very much).

Purchase happiness (Thomas & Millar, 2013; Nicolao et al., 2009 as adapted from van Boven and Gilovich, 2003)

1. "When you think about this purchase, how happy does it make you?" (1 = not happy, 9 = very happy)
2. "How much does this purchase contribute to your happiness in life?" (1 = not at all 9 = very much)
3. "To what extent do you think the money spent on this purchase would have been better spent on something else—some other type of purchase that would have made you happier?" (1 = not at all, 5 = moderately, 9 = very much)

Purchase happiness (Howell & Hill, 2009)

1. "I am happy with the purchase I made." (1 = strongly disagree, 7 = strongly agree)
2. "This money was well spent." (1 = strongly disagree, 7 = strongly agree)
3. "The purchase has made me happier." (1 = strongly disagree, 7 = strongly agree)
4. "The purchase has made others happier." (1 = strongly disagree, 7 = strongly agree)

To measure consumption happiness, respondents are asked to reflect on a purchase within the last three months and write a short paragraph describing the purchase, as well as their feelings and the environmental cues surrounding the purchase. Specifically, participants rate their happiness with a purchase ("I am happy with the purchase I made"), their satisfaction with purchase ("This money in the purchase was well-spent"), if the purchase had made them happier ("The purchase has made me happier"), and if the purchase had made others in their life happier ("The purchase has made others happier"). Each item begins with the phrase: "Specifically, when I reflect on this purchase ..." and is anchored between two polar responses: 1 (strongly disagree) and 7 (strongly agree) (Van Boven & Gilovich, 2003; Howell & Hill, 2009). See Table 9.5 for more examples of measures of purchase happiness.

Possession-Focused Models

Possession-focused models are consumer behavior models that focus on the psychology of product ownership. We identified four major models in that regard: brand relationship, brand community, extended self, and positive self.

Brand Relationship

The *brand relationship* model posits that consumption happiness from a brand is high when there is a close consumer-brand relationship (e.g., Bruhn & Schnebelen, 2017). Consumer interactions with brands result in several forms of consumer-brand relationships: *brand attitude* (object-centered engagements with brands), *brand attachment* (self-centered engagements with brands), and *brand community* (interpersonal and socio-cultural engagements with the brand) (Schmitt, 2012). As such, consumption happiness related to a specific brand is high when there is a close consumer-brand relationship in the form of positive brand attitude, high brand attachment, and engagement in the brand community.

The gist of the brand relationship models involves brand attachment. Let's discuss this concept a little more. Specifically, a strong brand relationship reflects brand attachment, which is a self-related engagement with the brand and expresses a consumer's connection with the brand (Thomson et al., 2005). The concept of brand attachment has been used interchangeably with related concepts such as *brand love* (degree of passionate emotional attachment a satisfied consumer has for a particular trade name) (Carroll & Ahuvia, 2006), *self-brand connection* (the extent to which individuals have incorporated brands into their self-concepts) (Escalas & Bettman, 2003), and *brand identification* (a consumer's perceived state of oneness with a brand) (Stokburger-Sauer et al., 2012). See measures related to these concepts in Table 9.6.

Brand attachment develops when the brand is perceived as an active contributor to a dyadic relationship when brands are animated, humanized or somehow personalized (Cohen, 2014; Fournier, 1998). Consumers establish deep, meaningful

Table 9.6 Measures of consumer-brand relationship

Construct	Measurement items
Emotional brand attachment (emotion-laden target-specific bond between a person and a specific brand)	Respondents use a 7-point rating scale, ranging from 1 (not at all) to 7 (very well), to describe "the extent to which the following words describe your typical feelings toward the brand." *Affection* • Affectionate • Friendly • Loved • Peaceful *Passion* • Passionate • Delighted • Captivated *Connection* • Connected • Bonded • Attached

(continued)

Table 9.6 (continued)

Construct	Measurement items
Brand love (degree of passionate emotional attachment a satisfied consumer has for a particular trade name)	Respondents are asked to recall a specific brand of packaged goods (and their product category) with which they were satisfied. Respondents then completed the questionnaire concerning the brand they had identified. • This is a wonderful brand. • This brand makes me feel good. • This brand is totally awesome. • I have neutral feelings about this brand. (R) • This brand makes me very happy. • I love this brand! • I have no particular feelings about this brand. (R) • This brand is a pure delight. • I am passionate about this brand. • I'm very attached to this brand.
	Response scale: 1 = strongly disagree; 5 = strongly agree
Self-brand connection (the extent to which individuals have incorporated brands into their self-concepts)	Participants rate the degree to which they themselves had formed self-brand connections with the focal brand. • Brand X reflects who I am (not at all/extremely well). • I can identify with Brand X (not at all/extremely well). • I feel a personal connection to Brand X (not at all/very much so). • I (can) use Brand X to communicate who I am to other people (not at all/extremely well). • I think Brand X (could) help(s) me become the type of person I want to be (not at all/extremely well). • I consider Brand X to be "me" (it reflects who I consider myself to be or the way that I want to present myself to others) (not "me"/"me"). • Brand X suits me well (not at all/extremely well).
Consumer-brand identification (a consumer's perceived state of oneness with a brand)	Respondents are first asked to name a brand that they had last consumed, or had last visited, or currently used most often. Then they are asked to respond to the survey questions with the specific brand (brand X) in mind. • I feel a strong sense of belonging to brand X. • I identify strongly with brand X. • Brand X embodies what I believe in. • Brand X is like a part of me. • Brand X has a great deal of personal meaning for me.
	Response scale: 1 = completely disagree; 7 = completely agree

Source: Adapted from Thomson et al. (2005), Carroll and Ahuvia (2006), Escalas and Bettman (2003), and Stokburger-Sauer et al. (2012)

relationships with brands (Fournier, 1998), become emotionally attached to them (Thomson et al., 2005), and use them to express their personality and self-image (Escalas & Bettman, 2005; Swaminathan et al., 2009). As such, brand attachment reflects a stronger connection than brand attitude (Thomson et al., 2005) and is viewed as an antecedent of true brand loyalty (Fournier & Yao, 1997).

Research indicates that close brand relationships contribute to consumption happiness. Why? Several reasons. First, a close brand relationship enhances consumption happiness because it provides consumers with hedonic benefits (e.g., emotions related to pleasure). Evidence suggests that consumers with close brand relationships derive hedonic benefits from the frequent and close interactions with the brand (e.g., Gummerus et al., 2012; Kuo & Feng, 2013).

Second, close brand relationships enhance consumption happiness because they serve to enhance consumers' self-esteem (e.g., Kuo & Feng, 2013). Consumers with close brand relationships are likely to experience satisfaction with needs such as self-confirmation, self-enhancement, and belongingness. Satisfaction of self-related needs serves to collectively generate a more positive self-concept that, in turn, contributes to consumption happiness (Bruhn & Schnebelen, 2017).[1]

Third, close brand relationships enhance consumption happiness because they facilitate social interactions. In other words, close brand relationships make consumers feel less lonely by facilitating social interactions with brand community members and other brand users (e.g., Lastovicka & Fernandez, 2005; Rosenbaum et al., 2007).

Fourth, a close brand relationship facilitates the positive effects of material brand purchase on consumption happiness. Research has established that consumers derive much happiness from experiential marketplace activities compared to material goods (e.g., Nicolao et al., 2009; Thomas & Millar, 2013; Van Boven & Gilovich, 2003). Yet, consumers with close brand relationships derive similar levels of consumption happiness from both experiential and material purchases (Razmus et al., 2022). That is, close brand relationships serve to amplify the positive effect of material purchase on consumption happiness.

In summary, the brand relationship model posits that consumption happiness from a brand is high when consumers have a close relationship with the brand that provides consumers with satisfaction of experiential, symbolic, and emotional needs (Arnould & Thompson, 2005).

Brand Community

The *brand community* model posits that consumption happiness is high when consumers are voluntarily engaged and experience much satisfaction from the social engagement in the context of a brand community. Brand communities are a "specialized, non-geographically bound community, based on a structured set of social relations among admirers of a brand" (Muniz & O'Guinn, 2001, p. 412).

Evidence suggests that brand communities can increase customer engagement (e.g., Algesheimer et al., 2005; Bagozzi & Dholakia, 2002). This comes about because communication with other members enhances the customer interaction

[1] Research has also shown that self-esteem and happiness are highly correlated especially in countries with strong individualistic values (e.g., Baumeister et al., 2003; Diener & Diener, 1995; Lyubomirsky et al., 2006).

with the focal brand, and all members can actively take part in the creation of the brand image (Prahalad & Ramaswamy, 2000). Brand communities also accentuate a sense of emotional involvement and connection with the group—create shared goals among members, who may engage in joint actions to accomplish collective goals (Bagozzi & Dholakia, 2006). Consumers in brand communities provide aid and support, and recommendations to others. Communities also facilitate social interaction with like-minded consumers and promote community activities.

Research shows that customer engagement in a brand community exerts a significant positive effect on consumption happiness (Niedermeier et al., 2019). Why? First, engagement in a brand community increases satisfaction of various consumption needs. Consumer engagement with brand community provides consumers with many benefits, such as information benefits (e.g., feedback, product knowledge), social benefits (e.g., interactive communications, social connectedness, sense of belongingness), entertainment benefits (e.g., fun, relaxation), and economic benefits (e.g., discounts, time saving) (Gummerus et al., 2012). All these benefits contribute to need satisfaction, thereby enhancing consumption happiness.

Second, engagement in brand communities contributes to hedonic feelings (e.g., pleasure). Research has shown that consumers' engagement with their favorite brand community can generate high levels of hedonic happiness (e.g., Lianopoulos et al., 2020; Prayag et al., 2020). For example, consumers who are actively engaged in the community of their favorite sports team are likely to enjoy the sports game and social interactions with other fans.

Third, consumer engagement in a brand community serves to satisfy psychological needs (e.g., autonomy, competence, and relatedness), which in turn fosters consumers' psychological wellbeing (cf. Ryan & Deci, 2000). That is, participation in a brand community serves to satisfy autonomy needs (i.e., voluntary participation and sharing of information), competence needs (i.e., provision of useful information and creative ideas for others), and relatedness needs (i.e., social support and sense of belongingness), all contributing to consumption happiness.

Research also indicates that consumers who are members of a brand community are likely to play the role of brand influencer due to their passion for the brand. They seek assistance from other members and provide aid to other members through information sharing and discussions. Moreover, through active engagement in a brand community, consumers are likely to experience utilitarian benefits (up-to-date product information, reduced product risk, time saving, and monetary incentives), hedonic benefits (e.g., pleasure from experiences and social interactions), and self-expressive benefits (e.g., self-expression and positive self-image), all of which contribute to consumption happiness (e.g., Baldus et al., 2015; Harmeling et al., 2017; Kozlenkova et al., 2017; Nambisan & Baron, 2007). See Table 9.7 for a metric of brand community engagement.

Table 9.7 Measure of brand community engagement

Engagement dimensions	Measurement items
Brand influence (the degree to which a community member wants to influence the brand)	• I am motivated to participate in this brand community because I can help improve the brand and its products. • I like to know that my comments and suggestions can influence the brand and its products. • Increasing the influence I have on the brand and its products makes me want to participate more in this brand community. • I hope to improve the brand or product through my participation and expression in this brand community.
Brand passion (the ardent affection a community member has for the brand)	• I am motivated to participate in this brand community because I am passionate about the brand. • I participate in this brand community because I care about the brand. • I would not belong to a brand community if I did not have passion for the brand. • My passion for this brand's products makes me want to participate in this brand community.
Connecting (the extent to which a community member feels that being a member of the brand community connects them to some good thing bigger than themselves)	• Increasing the strength of the connection I have with this brand community makes me want to participate more in the community. • Being part of this brand community makes me feel more connected to the brand. • Being part of this brand community makes me feel more connected to other consumers of the brand.
Seeking assistance (the degree to which a community member wants to receive help from fellow community members who share their knowledge, experience, or time with them.)	• I am motivated to participate in this brand community because I can receive help from other community members. • I am motivated to participate in this brand community because community members can use their knowledge to help me. • I like participating in this brand community because it gives me an opportunity to receive help from other community members. • It is important to me to be able to use this. community to find answers to my questions about the brand.

(continued)

Table 9.7 (continued)

Engagement dimensions	Measurement items
Helping (the degree to which a community member wants to help fellow community members by sharing knowledge, experience, or time.)	• I like participating in the brand community because I can use my experience to help other people. • I like to share my experience and knowledge with others in this brand community to help them be more educated about the brand. • I really like helping other community members with their questions. • I feel good when I can help answer other community members' questions.
Like-minded discussion (the extent to which a community member is interested in talking with people like themselves about the brand)	• I look forward to discussing my opinions about the brand with others who share the same interest as me. • I enjoy conversing with people similar to myself in this brand community. • I look to this brand community when I want to discuss a topic with people who have similar interests. • Having conversations with people in this brand community who share the same views about this brand is important to me.
Utilitarian reward (the degree to which the community member wants to gain utilitarian rewards (e.g., monetary rewards, time savings, deals or incentives, merchandise, and prizes) through their participation in the community)	• I am motivated to participate in this brand community because I can earn money. • If it weren't for the money, I wouldn't participate in this brand community. • Receiving more money makes me want to participate more in this brand community.
Up-to-date information (the degree to which a community member feels that the brand community helps them to stay informed or keep up-to date with brand and product related information)	• This brand community is my critical connection for new and important information about the brand and its products. • When I want up-to-date information about this brand, I look to this brand community. • This community keeps me on the leading edge of information about the brand. • This community is the best way to stay informed about new developments with this brand.
Hedonic reward (the degree to which the community member wants to gain hedonic rewards (e.g., fun, enjoyment, entertainment, friendly environment, and social status) through their participation in the community)	• I like participating in this brand community because it is entertaining. • Having fun is my main reason for participating in this brand community. • I participate in this brand community because I think it is fun. • I find participating in this brand community to be very entertaining.

(continued)

Table 9.7 (continued)

Engagement dimensions	Measurement items
Self-expression (the degree to which a community member feels that the community provides them with a forum where they can express their true interests and opinions)	• I feel that I can freely share my interests in the brand community. • I would express any opinion or idea I had about this brand in this brand community. • I can always be myself when interacting with others in this community. • This community makes it easy for me to express my true beliefs about the brand.
Validation (a community member's feeling of the extent to which other community members affirm the importance of their opinions, ideas, and interests)	• Receiving more affirmation of the value of my comments makes me want to participate more in the brand community. • I feel good about myself when other community members share my ideas. • I appreciate it when others agree with the ideas I express in this brand community. • When others support my ideas and opinions in this brand community, I feel better about myself.
Response scale: (0 = strongly disagree and 10 = strongly agree)	

Source: Adapted from Baldus et al. (2015)

Experience-Focused Models

Experience-focused models are consumer behavior models that focus on the psychology of marketplace activities and services (i.e., experiences). We identified twelve prominent models in that regard: self-congruity, extended self, positive self, self-expressiveness, perceived quality-of-life impact, perceived quality of consumer goods and services, perceived value (functional, social, and emotional), benefits and need satisfaction, personal values, positive social interactions, experiential advantage, and hedonic adaptation.

Self-Congruity

Concerning *self-congruity*, the basic tenet is that consumption happiness is high when consumers are satisfied with consumer goods and services that fit well with their self-concept. Self-concept is the totality of the individual's thoughts and feelings with reference to the self as an object (Rosenberg, 1989). Consumers develop self-knowledge through activities and experiences that explore and deepen their sense of self. Consumer memories of these activities and experiences are the building blocks of consumer self-concept.

Specifically, self-congruity is a psychological process and outcome in which consumers compare their perception of a brand image (more specifically, brand personality or brand-user image) with their self-concept (e.g., actual self, ideal self, social self) (Sirgy, 2018). That is, the consumer's self-congruity reflects the match between the consumer's self-concept and brand personality or brand user image. In other words, self-congruity with brand-user image refers to perceived similarity a potential buyer sees between the typical user of a brand and himself or herself.

The consumer self-concept involves four dimensions: (1) *actual self-image*, (2) *ideal self-image*, (3) *social self-image*, and (4) *ideal social self-image* (Sirgy, 1982). The actual self-image is how a consumer describes himself or herself in personal terms (e.g., attractive, old, vivacious, generous, compassionate, family person, etc.). The ideal self-image is how a consumer describes his or her aspired self in personal terms (e.g., would like to become more attractive, young, vivacious, less temperamental, more independent, etc.). The social self-image is how a consumer believes he is viewed by others (e.g., I believe that others think of me as obnoxious, recluse, envious, temperamental, etc.). The ideal social self-image is how a consumer would like to be viewed by others (e.g., I would like people to think of me as generous, compassionate, sociable, friendly, etc.). Consumers experience high levels of self-congruity when they perceive a match between the brand-user image (the stereotypic image of the typical consumer using the brand in question) and the four dimensions of the self-concept (actual self, ideal self, social self, and ideal social self).

Let's illustrate by focusing on a particular brand of automobile, let's say the Tesla Model S luxury car. The *brand-user image* of this brand may be rich and environmentally conscious. That is, a consumer may think that the typical person driving a Tesla Model S luxury car is "rich and environmentally conscious." *Actual self-congruity* is experienced when the consumer sees himself or herself as "rich and environmentally conscious" (i.e., match between the brand-user image and actual self-image). Similarly, *ideal self-congruity* occurs when the consumer aspires to see himself or herself as "rich and environmentally" (i.e., match between the brand-user image and the ideal self-image). By the same token, *social self-congruity* occurs when the consumer believes that others think of him or her as "rich and environmentally" (i.e., match between the brand-user image and the social self-image). The same can be said concerning *ideal social self-congruity*. That is, *ideal social self-congruity* occurs when the consumer aspires to have others think of him or her as "rich and environmentally" (i.e., match between the brand-user image and the ideal social self-image). See Table 9.8 for examples of self-congruity measures.

Much research demonstrated that self-congruity with brand-user image (and brand personality) is a strong predictor of brand attitude and brand loyalty concerning various products (Sirgy, 1982; Kressmann et al., 2006; Rodriguez et al., 2012). Self-congruity (actual, ideal, social, and ideal social self-congruity) influences consumers' pre-purchase behavior (e.g., brand preference and choice) and post-purchase behavior (e.g., consumer satisfaction, word-of-mouth communication, and brand loyalty) (Sirgy et al., 2016a, b). Empirical studies found that self-image congruence positively affects brand loyalty directly and indirectly through functional congruity (Kressmann et al., 2006; Sirgy & Su, 2000). Self-congruity enhances consumption happiness because it serves to meet consumers' needs for self-consistency, self-enhancement, social consistency, and social approval (e.g., Grzeskowiak &

Table 9.8 Selected measures of self-congruity

Actual self-congruity (Sirgy et al., 1997) • People who use (focal brand) are much more like me than people who use (referent brand). • I can identify with those people who prefer a (focal brand) over a (referent brand). • I am very much like the typical person who prefers to use (focal brand) rather than a (referent brand). • The image of the user of (focal brand) is highly consistent with how I see myself
Response scale: 1 = strongly disagree; 7 = strongly agree
Actual self-congruence (Japutra et al., 2019) • This brand is consistent with how I see myself. • This brand is a mirror image of me. • This brand is similar to me.
Response scale: 1 = strongly disagree; 7 = strongly agree
Ideal self-congruence (Japutra et al., 2019) • This brand is a mirror image of the person I would like to be. • This brand is similar to the person I would like to be. • This brand is consistent with how I would like to be.
Response scale: 1 = strongly disagree; 7 = strongly agree

Source: Adapted from Sirgy et al. (1997), Japutra et al. (2019), Williams et al. (2022)

Sirgy, 2007; Grzeskowiak et al., 2016; Sirgy, 1982; Sirgy, 1985; Sirgy et al., 2016a, b, 2000).

Consumption happiness is high when material products enhance consumer self-concept through image and value congruence. That is, consumption happiness is high when there is image congruence between consumer self-concept and brand-user image (Aaker, 1999; Sirgy, 1982). To reiterate, self-congruity is the psychological process that reflects how consumers compare themselves (their self-concept) with a brand image (brand personality or brand-user image). By consuming a brand that is congruent with their self-concept (e.g., actual self, ideal self, social self, ideal social self), consumers can express their identity to others. Self-expression is often a key motive for the consumption of a brand, and satisfying this need is emotionally pleasing (Fournier, 1998). Studies found that consumer spending on self-congruent brands increases consumption happiness (Matz et al., 2016; Veenhoven et al., 2021). Ownership of *self-congruent products* contributes to consumption happiness by reducing consumers' discrepancies between consumers' actual and ideal self (cf. Michalos, 1985; Higgins et al., 1997), matching the product-user image with their ideal self-image (cf. Sirgy, 1982), enhancing self-esteem (cf. Diener, 1984; Rosenberg, 1965), and prompting positive self-evaluations (cf. Campbell et al., 1976).

Self-Expressiveness

Self-expressiveness refers to feelings that the consumption experiences are in harmony with the true self (daimon) and one's intrinsic values—feelings of fulfillment from engaging meaningful activities towards personal growth and self-actualization

(Deci & Ryan, 2008; Waterman, 1990; Waterman et al., 2008). In other words, feelings of self-expressiveness reflect feelings from realizing one's full personal potential and progressing toward achieving one's true nature. For example, self-expressiveness in shopping is defined as the degree to which consumers think shopping activity is an important part of their self-concept (Sirgy et al., 2016a, b).

Research has uncovered a set of antecedents to self-expressiveness in the marketplace. First, consumers experience self-expressiveness when they engage in activities that are important to the self-concept, moderately challenging, require substantial effort, and have a high potential for self-actualization (e.g., Bosnjak et al., 2016; Waterman et al., 2008). In other words, consumers experience feelings of self-expressiveness when they engage in self-defining activities. For example, research has demonstrated that self-expressiveness in a sport activity experienced by a tourist depends on the activity's perceived difficulty, perceived effort, perceived importance, and potential for self-realization (Bosnjak et al., 2016). Furthermore, evidence suggests that self-expressiveness in shopping increases overall life satisfaction, mediated by perceived impact of shopping on life satisfaction (Sirgy et al., 2016a, b). Second, consumers experience self-expressiveness when they engage in activities with intrinsic value (Waterman, 1990). Third, consumers experience self-expressiveness when there is a high level of self-congruity with the activity. That is, consumers experience feelings of self-expressiveness when the market-related activity serves to reduce the gap between actual and ideal self (Sharma et al., 2022).

Research also uncovered a set of consequences arising from the experience of self-expressiveness in general. First, feelings of self-expression from an activity have a positive impact on attitude toward the market-related activity and its corresponding behavioral intention (Thorbjørnsen et al., 2007). Second, self-expressiveness is positively related to positive affect and eudaimonic wellbeing. Research has shown that self-expressiveness is positively associated with improved health, positive affect, satisfaction of basic psychological needs, and meaning and vitality in their lives (Ryan et al., 2008; Waterman et al., 2008). These outcomes can easily translate into the context of the marketplace.

Perceived Quality-of-Life Impact

The *perceived quality-of-life impact* model posits that consumption happiness (satisfaction impact of a consumer good or service) is a function of perceived product benefits and costs within various life domains. In other words, a consumer good or service can have an impact on various life domains by increasing or decreasing satisfaction in those domains (e.g., Sirgy et al., 2006a, 2008). That is, consumption happiness derived from a product is high when consumers perceive significant benefits from the product is high with low costs contributing to domain satisfaction, which in turn contributes to subjective wellbeing.

Sirgy and Lee (2003) developed a measure of the perceived quality-of-life impact of a product. Using this measure, the authors found that consumers' perceived quality-of-life impact of one's current vehicle is largely determined by satisfaction

Table 9.9 Selected measures of perceived quality-of-life impact

Perceived quality-of-life impact (Grzeskowiak et al., 2014)
1. "How do you feel about the way your ____ contributes to your overall quality of life?" (1 = not satisfied, 5 = very satisfied)
2. "How do you feel about the way the purchase of your _____ contributes to your overall quality of life?" (1 = not satisfied, 5 = very satisfied)
3. "How do you feel about the way that owning your ____ contributes to your overall quality of life?" (1 = not satisfied, 5 = very satisfied)
4. "How do you feel about the way that using of your ____ contributes to your overall quality of life?" (1 = not satisfied, 5 = very satisfied)
Perceived quality-of-life impact (Sirgy et al., 2008)
1. "My ___ has significantly improved my quality of life." (1 = strongly disagree, 5 = strongly agree)
2. "My ___ has enhanced my social wellbeing." (1 = strongly disagree, 5 = strongly agree)
3. "My ___ has significantly helped me with my work." (1 = strongly disagree, 5 = strongly agree)
Perceived quality-of-life impact (Sirgy et al., 2006b)
1. "I feel very safe in my ___." (1 = strongly disagree, 5 = strongly agree)
2. "My ___ is economical." (1 = strongly disagree, 5 = strongly agree)
3. "My ___ satisfies my family needs." (1 = strongly disagree, 5 = strongly agree)
4. "My ___ meets my social needs." (1 = strongly disagree, 5 = strongly agree)
5. "The image of my ___ shows status and prestige to others." (1 = strongly disagree, 5 = strongly agree)
6. "My ___ does not let me down when I use it for daily and weekly activities." (1 = strongly disagree, 5 = strongly agree)
7. "My ___ reflects who I am." (1 = strongly disagree, 5 = strongly agree)
8. "My ___ reflects who I would like to be." (1 = strongly disagree, 5 = strongly agree)
9. "I use my ____ a lot to explore new places." (1 = strongly disagree, 5 = strongly agree)
10. "My ___ is beautiful, inside and out." (1 = strongly disagree, 5 = strongly agree)

Source: Adapted from Grzeskowiak et al. (2014) and Sirgy et al. (2006b)

with purchase, preparation for personal use, ownership, use, and maintenance. Similarly, Grzeskowiak et al. (2006) found that consumers' overall wellbeing is influenced by home resident's overall wellbeing is influenced by residents' cumulative positive and negative affect associated with house purchase, use, maintenance, ownership, and selling. Empirical research related to consumption happiness includes studies on consumer happiness resulting from the consumption of a residential housing unit such as a house (Grzeskowiak et al., 2006), consumer durable products (Grzeskowiak et al., 2014), an automobile (Sirgy et al., 2006b), and from a smartphone (Sirgy et al., 2008). Selected measures of perceived quality-of-life impact are shown in Table 9.9.

Perceived Quality

The *quality* model of consumption happiness focuses on consumers' evaluation of a consumer good or service. The implicit notion here is that consumption happiness is high when consumers purchase and consume high-quality consumer goods and services (e.g., Sirgy et al., 2007). In other words, the model posits that consumption of high-quality consumer goods or services is likely to lead to happiness in consumption.

How does this come about? Several reasons. First, high-quality goods and services can boost consumer happiness by meeting consumers' material needs, bestowing status and prestige, and/or strengthening social relations (e.g., De Leire & Kalil, 2010).

Second, high-quality goods and services can boost consumer happiness by prompting consumers to experience satisfaction with material possessions. For instance, empirical research has shown that consumption happiness is influenced by the qualities of material objects in one's possession (e.g., Schmitt et al., 2015).

Third, high-quality goods and services can boost consumer happiness through experiential satisfaction. For example, empirical research has shown that consumption happiness is influenced by the quality of the service outcomes (e.g., De Keyser & Lariviere, 2014; Dagger & Sweeney, 2006) and by the quality of the service encounter as well as the service delivery process (e.g., Dagger & Sweeney 2006; Gong & Yi, 2018; Sweeney et al., 2015). Furthermore, consumption happiness increases when consumers experience progressively increasing quality of experiences—compared to a stable or declining quality of experiences (e.g., Loewenstein & Prelec, 1993).[2]

How do consumers evaluate product quality? Many consumers rely on the news media and product quality rating companies to learn about the quality of a particular set of products contemplated for purchase. One such publication outlet is *Consumer Reports*. This publication measures product quality and customer satisfaction. Faulty and unsafe products influence consumption happiness adversely. As such, consumers avoid brands that are faulty and unsafe in their alternative evaluations of a product set (Sirgy et al., 2007).

Another proxy metric of product quality is information involving customer satisfaction. The National Quality Research Center at the University of Michigan (www.theacsi.org) reports *American Consumer Satisfaction Index* (ACSI) levels quarterly in major manufacturing durables. In the survey, perceived product quality is measured in terms of overall evaluation of quality experience, evaluation of customization experience (e.g., how well the product fits the customer's requirements), and evaluation of reliability experience (e.g., how often things have gone wrong) (e.g., Fornell, 1992; Fornell et al., 1996).

Now let's turn to consumer services. How do consumers determine service quality? Several methods for measuring service quality have been reported in the service research literature. First, Grönroos (1984) defined service quality in terms of two dimensions: technical quality and functional quality. *Technical quality* refers to what customers receive because of their interactions with a service firm (e.g.,

[2]Interestingly, the reader should note that the effects of the quality of consumer goods and the quality of services on consumption happiness are additive. Nevertheless, experiential quality (from consumer services) tends to register stronger effects on consumption happiness than material quality (from consumer goods) (e.g., Weingarten et al., 2023).

outcome quality). In contrast, functional quality represents how the service is delivered (i.e., interaction quality).

Second, Parasuraman et al. (1988) have proposed five dimensions of service quality: (1) *tangibility* (appearances of physical elements), (2) *reliability* (dependable and accurate performance), (3) *responsiveness* (promptness and helpfulness), (4) *assurance* (credibility, security, competence, and courtesy), and (5) *empathy* (easy access, good communication, and customer understanding). They developed a measure of service quality (referred to as SERVQUAL) capturing gaps between expectations and perceived performance.

Cronin and Taylor (1992) developed the performance-only measure of service quality (SERPERF) and found that the SERVPERF scale is equally valid relative to the SERVQUAL measure. Specifically, they made the case that the measurement of expectations adds limited information beyond what is gained from measuring perceptions of performance alone (cf. Babakus & Boller, 1992; Dabholkar et al., 2000). See the SERVPERF measure in Table 9.10 and SERVQUAL in Table 9.11.

Third, Brady and Cronin (2001) conceptualized overall service quality in terms of outcome quality, interaction quality, and physical environment quality. That is, overall service quality is a higher-order construct, composed of three service quality dimensions: the outcome quality (e.g., waiting time, tangibles, valence), the

Table 9.10 The SERVPERF measure

The following set of statements relates to your feelings about the XTZ. For each statement, please show the extent to which you believe XYZ has the feature described by the statement.

- XYZ has up-to-date equipment.
- XYZ's physical facilities are visually appealing.
- XYZ's employees are well-dressed and appear neat.
- The appearance of the physical facilities of XYZ is in keeping with the type of service provided.
- When XYZ promises to do something by a certain time, it does so.
- When you have problems, XYZ is sympathetic and reassuring.
- XYZ is dependable.
- XYZ provides its services at the time it promises to do so.
- XYZ keeps its records accurately.
- XYZ does not tell its customers exactly when services will be performed.
- You do not receive prompt service from XYZ employees.
- Employees of XYZ are not always willing to help customers.
- Employees of XYZ are too busy to respond to customer requests promptly.
- You can trust employees of XYZ
- You can feel safe in your transactions with XYZ's employees.
- Employees of XYZ are polite.
- Employees get adequate support from XYZ to do their jobs well.
- XYZ does not give you individual attention.
- Employees of XYZ do not give you personal attention.
- Employees of XYZ do not know what your needs are.
- XYZ does not have your best interests at heart.
- XYZ does not have operating hours convenient to all their customers

Response scale: 1 = strongly disagree; 7 = strongly agree

Source: Adapted from Cronin and Taylor (1992)

Table 9.11 The SERVQUAL measure

Expectations:

1. They should have up-to-date equipment.
2. Their physical facilities should be visually appealing.
3. Their employees should be well-dressed and appear neat.
4. The appearance of the physical facilities of these firms should be in keeping with the type of services provided.
5. When these firms promise to do something by a certain time, they should do so.
6. When customers have problems, these firms should be sympathetic and reassuring.
7. These firms should be dependable.
8. They should provide their services at the time they promise to do so.
9. They should keep their records accurately.
10. They shouldn't be expected to tell customers exactly when services will be performed (reverse).
11. It is not realistic for customers to expect prompt service from employees of these firms (reverse).
12. Their employees don't always have to be willing to help customers (reverse).
13. It is okay if they are too busy to respond to customer requests promptly (reverse).
14. Customers should be able to trust employees of these firms.
15. Customers should be able to feel safe in their transactions with these firms' employees.
16. Their employees should be polite.
17. Their employees should get adequate support from these firms to do their jobs well.
18. These firms should not be expected to give customers individual attention (reverse).
19. Employees of these firms cannot be expected to give customers personal attention (reverse).
20. It is unrealistic to expect employees to know what the needs of their customers are (reverse).
21. It is unrealistic to expect these firms to have their customers' best interests at heart (reverse).
22. They shouldn't be expected to have operating hours convenient to all their customers (reverse).

Response scale: 1 = strongly disagree; 7 = strongly agree

Perceptions:

1. XYZ has up-to-date equipment.
2. XYZ's physical facilities are visually appealing
3. XYZ's employees are well-dressed and appear neat.
4. The appearance of the physical facilities of XYZ is in keeping with the type of services provided.
5. When XYZ promises to do something by a certain time, it does so.
6. When you have problems, XYZ is sympathetic and reassuring.
7. XYZ is dependable.
8. XYZ provides its services at the time it promises to do so.
9. XYZ keeps its records accurately.
10. XYZ does not tell customers exactly when services will be performed (reverse).
11. You do not receive prompt service from XYZ's employees (reverse).
12. Employees of XYZ are not always willing to help customers (reverse).
13. Employees of XYZ are too busy to respond to customer requests promptly (reverse).
14. You can trust the employees of XYZ.
15. You feel safe in your transactions with XYZ's employees.
16. Employees of XYZ are polite.
17. Employees get adequate support from XYZ to do their jobs well.
18. XYZ does not give you individual attention (reverse).
19. Employees of XYZ do not give your attention (reverse)
20. Employees of XYZ do not know what their needs are (reverse).
21. XYZ does not have your best interests at heart (reverse).
22. XYZ does not have operating hours convenient for all its customers (reverse).

Response scale: 1 = strongly disagree; 7 = strongly agree

Source: Adapted from Parasuraman et al. (1988)

Table 9.12 A measure of health service quality

Respondents rate the clinic's performance on each scale item using a 7-point scale (1 = strongly disagree, 7 = strongly agree).
The items below are grouped by dimension for expositional convenience; they appear in random order in the survey questionnaire.

Perceived service quality (overall higher-order construct)

- The overall quality of the service provided by the clinic is excellent.
- The quality of the service provided at the clinic is impressive.
- The service provided by the clinic is of a high standard.
- I believe the clinic offers service that is superior in every way.

Primary service quality dimensions

Outcome (technical) quality

- The quality of care I receive at the clinic is excellent.
- The care provided by the clinic is of a high standard.
- I am impressed by the care provided at the clinic.

Interaction (Interpersonal) quality

- The interaction I have with the staff at the clinic is of a high standard.
- The interaction I have with the staff at the clinic is excellent.
- I feel good about the interaction I have with the staff at the clinic.

Quality of the environment

- I believe the physical environment at the clinic is excellent.
- I am impressed with the quality of the clinic's physical environment.
- The physical environment at the clinic is of a high standard.

Administrative quality

- The administration system at the clinic is excellent.
- The administration at the clinic is of a high standard.
- I have confidence in the clinic's administration system.

Response scale: 1 = strongly disagree, 7 = strongly agree

Source: Adapted from Dagger et al. (2007)

customer-employee interaction quality (e.g., attitude, behavior, expertise), and the physical environment quality (e.g., ambient conditions, design, social factors) (cf., Dagger et al., 2007; Pollack, 2009). See Table 9.12 for a measure of service quality in the context of healthcare

Benefits and Need Satisfaction

Perceived product attributes are associated in the mind of the consumer with abstract benefits and values (cf. Gutman, 1982; Reynolds & Olson, 2001). For example, an automobile tends to be evaluated in terms of style, power, reliability, cost, gas mileage, durability, etc. These attributes are associated with a set of benefits serving certain needs. Some needs are basic in the sense that they are important to daily function and survival (e.g., safety, health, economic, sensory, escape, and sensation needs), while other needs are related to personal growth and flourishing (e.g., symbolic, aesthetic, moral, mastery, social, and distinctiveness needs). A product that satisfies a larger set of both basic and growth needs is likely to generate much more consumption happiness than a product satisfying a smaller set of basic needs (e.g., Lee et al., 2023; Sirgy et al., 2017).

In the context of leisure services, this model posits that leisure benefits contribute to leisure wellbeing by satisfying a set of basic needs and growth needs (Lee et al., 2023). The authors provided empirical evidence suggesting that leisure benefits contribute to consumer wellbeing by satisfying a set of basic needs (benefits related to safety, health, economic, sensory, escape, and sensation) and growth needs (symbolic, aesthetic, moral, mastery, relatedness, and distinctiveness). The study results also show that perceived leisure benefits effects on leisure wellbeing are mediated by a set of corresponding personal characteristics related to basic needs (safety consciousness, health consciousness, price sensitivity, hedonism, escapism, and sensation seeking) and growth needs (status consciousness, aestheticism, moral sensitivity, mastery seeking, extroversion, and need for distinction), respectively. See Table 9.13 for a measure of basic needs and benefits.

Additionally, consumption happiness from material products tends to be high when consumers choose products with functional attributes that can be translated into personal and meaningful experiential benefits. Personally meaningful experiences are experiences that provide individuals with satisfaction with psychological needs (autonomy, competence, and belongingness) playing an important role in subjective wellbeing (e.g., Baumeister & Leary, 1995; Carter & Gilovich, 2010; Deci & Ryan, 2000; Eakman, 2013; Hooker et al., 2020; Hsee et al., 2009; Kasser & Ryan, 1996; Tu & Hsee, 2016). Satisfaction of psychological needs is inherently rewarding, which serves to enhance consumption happiness.

Personal Values

Personal values are desirable goals that can be ordered by importance (Rokeach & Regan, 1980; Schwartz, 2012, 2015). Schwartz (2012) suggested ten personal values (universalism, benevolence, tradition, conformity, security, power, achievement, hedonism, stimulation, self-direction), which are later grouped into four higher-order values (self-enhancement, self-transcendence, conservation, and openness to change). Personal values guide one's intentional activities and provide means of altering one's happiness level (Lyubomirsky et al., 2005).

The relationship between personal values and wellbeing can be examined through two perspectives, person-environment fit and "healthy values" (Sagiv et al., 2004). The *person-environment fit perspective posits that* values and lifestyles that are congruent with those prevailing in the environment can lead to greater wellbeing (Oishi et al., 1999). The *healthy values* perspective posits that holding certain values (which leads to goal formulation) is likely to lead to positive wellbeing. For example, self-determination theory (Ryan & Deci, 2000), holds that intrinsic values (e.g., self-transcendence value), reflecting psychological growth and self-actualization needs, promote wellbeing, while extrinsic values (e.g., self-enhancement values) prompt the individual to seek others' approval, admiration and praise, undermining wellbeing.

Table 9.13 Measure of leisure benefits providing satisfaction of basic and growth needs

Basic needs/benefits

Safety benefits

- This leisure activity is safe.
- The chance of physical injury is low during leisure activities.
- The chances of being ill are low during leisure activity.

Health benefits

- My leisure activities are physically challenging.
- I do leisure activities which develop my physical fitness.
- I participate in my leisure to restore me physically.
- My leisure activities help me to stay healthy.

Economic benefits

- Compared to other leisure activities, participating in this leisure activity is financially affordable.
- Compared to other leisure activities, the equipment required for this leisure activity is financially affordable.
- Overall, this leisure activity is financially affordable.

Sensory benefits

- In general, leisure activity pleases my physical senses (sight, sound, touch, scent).
- In general, the leisure activity environment pleases my physical senses (sight, sound, touch, scent).
- The leisure activity provides me with sensory pleasure.

Escape benefits

- This leisure activity allows me to forget about work.
- This leisure activity allows me to distance myself from the demands of work.
- This leisure activity allows me to get a break from the demands of work.

Sensation benefits

- This leisure activity helps me get involved with exciting activities.
- This leisure activity helps me manage to do exciting things and experience a lot of thrills.

Growth needs/benefits

Symbolic benefits

- This leisure activity reflects how I see myself.
- This leisure activity reflects how I like to see myself.
- This leisure activity reflects how I believe others see me.
- This leisure activity reflects how I would like others to see me.

Aesthetic benefits

- The areas or places where I engage in my leisure activities are fresh and clean.
- The areas or places where I engage in my leisure activities are interesting.
- The areas or places where I engage in my leisure activities are beautiful.
- The areas or places where I engage in my leisure activities are well designed.

Moral benefits

- I think this leisure activity is helpful for many people.
- Through this leisure activity, I was able to contribute to my community.
- I think this leisure activity is socially responsible.

Mastery benefits

- Through this leisure activity, I was able to challenge myself to learn new things.
- Through this leisure activity, I feel like I have mastered the art of doing this activity.
- Through this leisure activity, I feel that I was able to sharpen my skill of doing this activity.

Relatedness benefits

- Through this leisure activity, I was able to make new friends.
- Through this leisure activity, I was able to build strong relationships with others.
- Through this leisure activity, I was able to spend time with someone special.

Distinctiveness benefits

- How much do you feel like you stand out within this group?
- How much do you feel unique as you participate in this group?
- How distinct and separate do you feel within this group?

Response scale: 1 = not at all, 7 = very much so

Source: Lee et al. (2023)

Concerning the *person-environment value congruence* perspective suggests that holding values that are congruent with those prevailing in the environment leads to greater happiness (Sagiv et al., 2004). Oishi et al. (1999) found that value-congruent domain satisfaction (self-congruent goal attainment) was more strongly related to overall life satisfaction. As such, this perspective asserts that attainment of values that are socially desired leads to higher levels of consumption happiness, while values that conflict undermine consumption happiness (Sagiv & Schwartz, 2000; Burroughs & Rindfleisch, 2002). In sum, the *personal values and lifestyle* model posits that consumption happiness is high when consumers have values that enhance consumption happiness and when consumers obtain satisfaction from goods and services that fit with their personal values and lifestyle.

To further elaborate on the notion of value congruence, one can argue that consumption happiness is effectively enhanced when consumers obtain satisfaction from goods and services that fit well with their consumption values. When the delivered experience is at odds with the consumer's closely held values, the mismatch creates cognitive dissonance, resulting in reduced happiness. When there is value congruence between consumers' marketplace experiences and their values, consumers are likely to consider these experiences as intrinsically satisfying. For example, evidence suggests that the effect of pro-social spending on consumption happiness is moderated by consumers' self-transcendence value (Hill & Howell, 2014). Values related to self-transcendence include social justice, protecting the environment, and broad-mindedness, while values related to self-enhancement include social status, ambition, and social influence (Schwartz, 1994). Because pro-social spending necessarily entails a contribution to others, the effect of pro-social spending on consumption happiness is stronger for those consumers with self-transcendence values than for those with self-enhancement values (Hill & Howell, 2014). Additionally, evidence suggests that spending more on others does not increase happiness for those whose values do not emphasize a concern for others (Hill & Howell, 2014).

With respect to the *perspective of healthy values*, the basic tenet is that consumption happiness is enhanced when consumers engage in marketplace activities guided by healthy rather than unhealthy values. For example, research found that consumers' values related to ethics and universalism (i.e., healthy values) contribute to consumer happiness. Specifically, consumers motivated by the universalism value (i.e., appreciation, tolerance, and protection for the welfare of all people and nature) (cf. Schwartz et al., 2012) are likely to engage in ethical and sustainable consumption (e.g., Ganglmair-Wooliscroft & Wooliscroft, 2019; Matz et al., 2016). In contrast, research found that materialism (i.e., unhealthy value) (cf. Richins & Dawson, 1992) and material beliefs (cf. Mitchell & Mickel, 1999) produce a negative impact on consumer happiness (e.g., Dittmar et al., 2014). The negative effect of materialism-related values on consumption happiness has been explained as follows: Materialism-related values have detrimental effects on establishing and developing relationships with others and on self-esteem (cf. Moldes & Ku, 2020). As such, too much emphasis on material goals may decrease consumption happiness

Table 9.14 Measures of self-transcendence and self-enhancement values

Participants rate the degree to which each value serves as a guiding principle in their lives.
Self-transcendence values • Social justice • Honest • Unity with nature • Loyal • Equality • Helpful *Self-enhancement values* • Social power • Successful • Wealth • Social recognition • Ambitious • Influential
Response scale: 9-point Likert scale ranging from −1 (opposed to my values) to 7 (of supreme importance)

Source: Adapted from Schwartz (1994)

(cf. Dittmar et al., 2014; Sirgy, 1998). See measures of self-transcendence and self-enhancement values in Table 9.14.

Positive Social Interactions

Research found that wellbeing is associated with close relationships—number of close others, time spent with close others (e.g., Lucas & Dyrenforth, 2006), lack of loneliness and satisfaction with friendships (e.g., Lyubomirsky et al., 2006), close social connections (e.g., Helliwell et al., 2010a, b), and social capital (e.g., Coleman, 1988; Putnam, 2001). Evidence also suggests that positive social relationships tend to enhance personal happiness (e.g., Argyle, 1987; Diener, 1984; Ryff, 1989; Myers & Diener, 1995) and help buffer stress and avert distress due to loneliness, anxiety, boredom, and loss of self-esteem (e.g., Argyle, 1987). See examples of measures of positive social interaction in Table 9.15.

As such, the *positive social interaction* model posits that consumption happiness is high when consumers experience positive social interactions with marketplace activities and events. That is, sharing positive experiences in the marketplace increases positive affect, happiness, and life satisfaction. Why?

First, social interactions during shopping and leisure experiences are likely to create and reinforce positive social connections and strengthen social bonds. For example, research has demonstrated that consumers' leisure experiences provide satisfaction of relatedness needs, which in turn contributes to consumption happiness (e.g., De Leire & Kali, 2010).

Second, a study by Grzeskowiak and Sirgy (2007) suggests that social sharing following a positive marketplace experience serves to satisfy the need of belongingness (Baumeister & Leary, 1995; Caprariello & Reis, 2013) and emotional

Table 9.15 Measures of positive social interactions

Sharing of positive experiences (Lambert et al., 2013)
- I am the type of person who loves to share it with others when something good happens to me.
- I almost always let the people that I'm close to know when I feel good and why.
- I usually keep good feelings bottled up and don't share them very often. (R)
- I'm constantly telling people my good news.

Conversational value of object/experience (Bastos & Brucks, 2017)
- That object/experience makes for a good conversation.
- I want to talk to others about that object/experience.
- That object/experience is a good topic to talk about.
- I desire to talk to people about that object/experience.
- I feel excited about telling others about that object/experience.

Response scale: 1 = strongly disagree; 7 = strongly agree

Source: Adapted from Bastos and Brucks (2017) and Lambert et al. (2013)

Table 9.16 Mediators of the relationship between sharing positive experiences and consumption happiness

Mediators	Study findings
Satisfaction of relatedness needs	Sharing positive experiences satisfies the relatedness need (e.g., strengthening social connections and social bonds), which in turn enhances consumer happiness
Satisfaction of belonging needs	Sharing positive of positive experiences satisfies the need for belongingness (e.g., enhanced emotional attachment), which in turn enhances consumer happiness
Enhanced self-image	Sharing positive experiences enhances positive self-image, which in turn positively influences consumer happiness

attachment (Aureliano-Silva et al., 2018), all of which contribute to consumption happiness.

Third, social sharing following a positive marketplace experience serves to enhance a positive self-image. Positive feedback on shared experiences enhances the self-esteem of the sharer when the relationship partner provides an active-constructive response (e.g., Lambert et al., 2013; Valkenburg & Peter, 2007; Zhan & Zhou, 2018). In the case of online sharing of experiences, research also indicates that the number of "likes" individuals received on their Facebook profile pictures was positively associated with self-esteem (Burrow & Rainone, 2017). See a summary of the mediators in Table 9.16.

Please note that there are moderators involved with the positive effect of social interaction on consumption happiness. First, the effect of social interaction on consumption happiness *is stronger for experiential purchase* than for material purchase (e.g., Bastos & Brucks, 2017). Experiences have higher conversational value and are more conducive to social interactions than material purchases. In addition, consumers are more likely to share their experiences (versus material possessions) with others and feel closer to others with whom they share their experiences (e.g., Bastos

& Brucks, 2017; Kumar & Gilovich, 2015), which in turn increases consumption happiness. That is, consumers derive much happiness from social interactions and communications *about their experiences.*

Second, the effect of social interaction on consumption happiness is weaker *for materialistic consumers.* Materialism distracts consumers from social relationships and social engagement, thereby reducing consumption happiness (cf. Kasser, 2002). Materialistic consumers tend to be extrinsically motivated and believe that happiness can be achieved through the acquisition of money and material possessions. Thus, materialistic consumers have less satisfying social relationships because of their materialistic desires and the negative impressions people have of materialistic consumers (e.g., van Boven et al., 2010).

Third, the effect of social interaction with new acquaintances on consumption happiness is stronger for the *young* than for the old. Young consumers feel happy when they interact with interesting new acquaintances. For young consumers, the value of spending time with interesting new acquaintances is high (e.g., Aaker et al., 2011). Self-definition is malleable at a younger age. Younger consumers seek experiences of active social interactions (motivated by relatedness needs) and develop their sense of self (Berezan et al., 2018). As one gets old, however, the value of spending time with interesting new acquaintances decreases, and the value of spending time with familiar friends and family increases (Carstensen, 2006). Older consumers already have a well-established self-concept and feel little social pressure to be anything other than what and who they perceive themselves to be. They desire social interactions with close others and want to move away from frequent social interactions with new acquaintances (Berezan et al., 2018).

Fourth, the effect of social interaction with others on consumption happiness is stronger for those with *secure attachment style* than those with insecure attachment (Mikulincer & Shaver, 2007). Attachment style shapes people's feelings, beliefs, and expectations about relationships. Attachment styles are commonly measured along dimensions of anxiety and avoidance, with secure attachment characterized by low levels of both anxiety and avoidance. Individuals with secure attachment style hold more positive beliefs about self and others, use more effective affect-regulation strategies, and enjoy higher levels of psychological wellbeing than those with attachment avoidance or anxiety. Those consumers with secure attachment style are likely to experience more frequent and prolonged positive affect are more resilient in times of stress (cf. Berant et al., 2001).

See a summary of the moderators in Table 9.17.

Experiential Advantage

The model of *experiential advantage* posits that consumption happiness is greater with experience purchases compared to material purchases (e.g., Nicolao et al., 2009; Thomas & Millar, 2013; van Boven & Gilovich, 2003; van Boven, 2005). Experiential purchases allow consumers to acquire a memorable life experience,

Table 9.17 Factors moderating the relationship between sharing positive experiences and consumption happiness

Moderators	Study findings
Experiential purchases	The effect of social interaction on consumption happiness is stronger for experiential purchases than for material purchases.
Consumers low on materialism	The effect of social interaction on consumption happiness is weaker for materialistic consumers than their non-materialistic counterparts.
Young consumers	The effect of social interaction with new acquaintances on consumption happiness is stronger for the young than for the old.
Consumers with a secure attachment style	The effect of social interaction with others on consumption happiness is stronger for those with secure attachment style compared to the insecure.

Table 9.18 Measuring experiential advantage

Experiential purchase vs. material purchase (Thomas & Millar, 2013)
Participants are randomly assigned to either material purchase or experiential purchase conditions. In the material purchase condition, the instructions prompt participants to recall their most recent material purchase for more than $100. That is, think about a recent discretionary purchase of an object that you obtained and kept in your possession. In the experiential purchase condition, the instructions prompt participants to recall their most recent experiential purchase for more than $100 where the primary purpose of the purchase was to acquire life experience. That is, think about some recent discretionary activities you paid to participate in.
Experiential advantage (Chu, 2022)
Participants are asked to think about their discretionary spending, or "money spent with the intent of furthering your happiness." They are then given brief definitions of material and experiential purchases

- *Material purchase*: Material purchase is a purchase that you made with the primary intention of acquiring a material possession—tangible object that you obtain, use, and keep in your possession, such as electronics.
- *Experiential purchase*: An experiential purchase is a purchase that you made with the primary intention of acquiring a life experience—an event or series of events that you personally encounter or live through, such as visiting a museum.

Participants are then asked to take a moment to recall a significant material purchase and a significant experiential purchase above $50 "that you made in order to make yourself happy." Participants then are prompted to indicate which purchase made them happier by answering on a 7-point scale from −3 (definitely experiential purchase) to +3 (definitely material purchase), which is reverse-coded in the analysis so that positive numbers signify an experiential advantage and negative numbers point to a material advantage

Source: Adapted from van Boven and Gilovich (2003), Thomas and Millar (2013), and Chu (2022)

while material purchases serve the only purpose of acquiring the material product. As such, "experiential advantage" refers to a psychological state that describes that, compared to material purchases, experiential purchases produce greater happiness for consumers. See Table 9.18 for an example of how experiential advantage is measured.

Why does this occur? For several reasons. Frist, consumers associated with experiences are frequently seen more favorably than those associated with material objects (e.g., van Boven et al., 2010), and consumer experiences tend to be more closely related to a positive self-concept (e.g., Carter & Gilovich, 2012; Thomas & Millar, 2013; van Boven & Gilovich, 2003).

A second reason involves the notion that consumer experiences are unique and less subject to social comparisons (e.g., Carter & Gilovich, 2010; Howell & Hill, 2009). Uniqueness tends to produce positive affect, whereas social comparisons tend to generate negative affect (because of upward comparisons—comparing one's situation to a superior other).

Third, consumer experiences tend to register slower hedonic adaptation (e.g., Carter & Gilovich, 2010; Nicolao et al., 2009). Compared to material possessions, the memories related to positive affect associated with marketplace experiences do not diminish as fast.

Finally, consumer experiences facilitate social interactions, which in turn contribute significantly to positive affect and satisfaction with social life (e.g., Caprariello & Reis, 2013; van Boven et al., 2010; van Boven & Gilovich, 2003). That is, experiences in the marketplace tend to deal mostly with associates, friends, and family members. These interactions are likely to be positive, which induce positive feelings in social life. Such feelings may capture a significant chunk of consumption happiness.

In summary, compared to material products, experiences are close to self-concept (positive self-concept), unique (less comparison and slow adaptation), and involve social interactions (social satisfaction). These experiential qualities in the experience purchase contribute to consumption happiness. See Table 9.19.

How about moderation effect? It should be noted that the experiential advantage effect does not hold under the following conditions. The experiential advantage effect does not hold when the material product has experiential qualities. Material products can have both material and experiential qualities (Guevarra & Howell, 2015). Specifically, the experiential advantage effect does not hold when:

- Material products also have a high level of experiential qualities (Weingarten et al., 2023),
- Material purchase and experiential purchase have similar hedonic qualities (Kousi et al., 2023),

Table 9.19 Mediators related to experiential advantage

Mediators	Findings
Positive self-concept	Consumers associated with experiences are frequently seen more favorably than those associated with material objects
Low social comparisons	Experiences are unique and less subject to social comparisons
Slow hedonic adaptation	Experiences tend to register a slower rate of hedonic adaptation
Increased social interactions	Experiences facilitate social interactions which in turn contribute significantly to positive affect and satisfaction with social life

- Material products are purchased to commemorate important life events, and the material purchase is close to the self-concept of the consumers (Goodman et al., 2016),
- Consumers treat material brands as an important part of their self-concept (e.g., self-congruent brand) (Razmus et al., 2022),
- Material purchases are imbued with human-like characteristics (e.g., anthropomorphized brand) that facilitate social interactions and emotional attachment (Lee et al., 2022), and
- Material purchases also facilitate involvement with others and social interactions (e.g., game machine for multiple players) (Caprariello & Reis, 2013).

These are moderators that focus on product-related conditions. There are also moderators related to consumer-related conditions. Specifically, the experiential advantage effect does not hold when:

- Consumers end up with a negative outcome related to experiential purchase (e.g., negative service experiences) (Nicolao et al., 2009),
- Consumers are highly materialistic and value material possessions (Millar & Thomas, 2009),
- Consumers are identified as low in socioeconomic status, making material products highly valued (Thomas & Millar, 2013), and
- Consumers' financial constraints are high making material products highly valued (Spiller, 2011; Tully et al., 2015).

See a summary of these moderators in Table 9.20.

In summary, the model of experiential advantage is well-established in relation to consumption happiness and is supported by much evidence, yet the model should be understood along with its various constraints.

Hedonic Adaptation

The model of *hedonic adaptation* posits that consumption happiness is high when hedonic adaptation in consumption is low. The *hedonic treadmill theory* makes the case that our emotional system adjusts to almost anything that happens in our lives, good or bad; therefore, we adapt to new circumstances (e.g., Brickman et al., 1978). In 1978, the study by Brickman, Coates, and Janoff-Bulman offered initial empirical support for the treadmill concept. Lottery winners were not found to be happier than nonwinners, and people with paraplegia were not substantially less happy than those who can walk. In addition, the theory explained that people with substantial resources are sometimes no happier than those with few resources and that people with severe problems are sometimes quite happy (cf. Diener et al., 2006). Relatedly, *set-point theory* posits that major life events affect a person's happiness only temporarily, after which the person's happiness level regresses to a default determined by heritable factors (Lykken & Tellegen, 1996). Research shows that wellbeing is

Table 9.20 Moderators related to experiential advantage

Product-related moderators	Study findings
Products with high experiential properties	When a material product has high levels of experiential qualities, the effect of material purchase on consumption happiness is high
Hedonic quality of the material product	When material purchase has similar hedonic qualities to experiential purchase, material purchase can result in similar level of consumption happiness
Commemorative products	When material products are purchased to commemorate important life events (making the material purchase important to self-concept), commemorative material goods can lead to high consumption happiness
Self-congruent brand	When a material brand is an important part of their self-concept (i.e., self-congruent brand), the purchase of the brand can result in high consumption happiness
Anthropomorphized brand	When material purchases are imbued with human-like characteristics (e.g., anthropomorphized brand), these purchases can result in high consumption happiness
Products with involvement of others and social interactions	When material purchase facilitates involvement of others and social interactions (e.g., game machine for multiple players), material purchase can result in high consumption happiness
Consumer-related moderators	**Study findings**
Consumer experiences with negative outcomes	When consumers end up with negative outcomes associated with the experiential purchase (e.g., negative service experiences), that purchase does not lead to consumption happiness
Consumers high on materialism	When consumers are highly materialistic (i.e., value material possessions), material purchases can result in high consumption happiness
Consumers with low socioeconomic status	Consumers low in socioeconomic status and material possessions, material purchases can result in high consumption happiness
High financial constraints	The effect of material purchases on consumption happiness is high for consumers with financial constraints

reasonably stable over time (e.g., Eid & Diener, 2004) and is strongly correlated with personality and heritable factors (e.g., Diener & Lucas, 1999)

Initially, consumers tend to overestimate the duration and intensity of their affective reactions to positive events (Buehler & McFarland, 2001; Wilson et al., 2000). This is because consumers focus too much on the event and not enough on the consequences of other future events (Wilson et al., 2000). However, over time, consumers experience the attenuation of affective reactions resulting from ongoing and repetitive ownership and usage of a particular product (e.g., Wang et al., 2009; Yang et al., 2017).

Consumers gradually adapt to positive events, as the positive episodes become less novel and more numerous, thus decreasing the amount and intensity of resultant positive emotions. For example, one may experience many positive events after buying a new convertible, but those occasions will become less and less numerous, and the positive emotions (excitement, happiness, pride, etc.) will become less frequent. In addition, consumers tend to jack up their aspirations about the positive event. As such, they need even more positive events to experience future increases in happiness. That is, consumers experience hedonic adaptation of their consumption happiness because of decreased positive affect and increased expectations over time (cf. Sheldon & Lyubomirsky, 2012). See Table 9.21 for an example of a method and measure related to hedonic adaptation in relation to marketplace activities and events.

Research has shown that hedonic adaptation of consumption happiness is *greater for material purchases* than for experiential purchases. Why? Perhaps this may be due to the possibility that consumption happiness with material purchase declines fast because of hedonic adaptation (Carter & Gilovich, 2010). Consumers adapt more quickly to material products than to experiences. This is because material products are static, and pleasure derived from material products is subject to relatively rapid adaptation and satiation (Nicolao et al., 2009).

Additionally, evidence suggests that consumption happiness with experiential purchases declines slowly (e.g., Frank, 2004). This is because (1) experiences are unique and memorable and thus the benefits of experiential purchases are enduring over time in consumer stories and memories (e.g., Carter & Gilovich, 2010; Nicolao et al., 2009), (2) experiential purchases are strongly connected to the self (e.g., Nicolao et al., 2009) and consumers can continue to enjoy past pleasant experiences via memories (e.g., Frederick & Loewenstein, 1999), and (3) experiential purchases facilitate savoring of the experiences through storytelling and social sharing (e.g., Bryant, 1989; Gilovich et al., 2015).

How do consumers need to respond to hedonic adaptation of material products and experiences? Research shows that consumers' hedonic adaptation can be mitigated in several ways. First, hedonic adaptation of a material product is likely to be weakened when consumers are highly engaged in the material products (e.g., Carter & Gilovich, 2010), because engaged consumers view each material product as novel and unique.

Table 9.21 Method and measure of hedonic adaptation

Hedonic adaptation (Carter & Gilovich, 2010) In the survey context, respondents are first asked to recall either a material or an experiential purchase that had cost at least \$50 (to ensure that it was of sufficient importance to generate continued thought). They are then asked to provide a brief description of the purchase and to indicate how much it cost, and how long ago it was made. Participants are then asked about both their initial and current satisfaction with the purchase using the following 7-point response scale: 1= not at all satisfied, 7 = very satisfied
Hedonic adaptation (Yang et al., 2017)
Participants are instructed to eat a food item (e.g., M&M's Chocolates) and indicate their happiness on a slider scale ("Just now, how did you feel?" 0 = not happy at all; 100 = very happy) after each of the 10 iterations

Source: Adapted from Carter and Gilovich (2010) and Yang et al. (2017)

Second, hedonic adaptation can be decreased when consumers engage in social discourse related to their positive marketplace experiences (e.g., Chugani et al., 2015; Yang & Galak, 2015). Social sharing prompts consumers to savor positive experiences and consolidate memorable experiences.

Third, hedonic adaptation to marketplace experiences can be mitigated when consumers indulge in a variety of novel experiences instead of a string of the same experiences (e.g., Dunn et al., 2011; Galak et al., 2009; Redden, 2008; Yang et al., 2017). That is, consumers can prevent decreased satisfaction from repetition by seeking novel experiences instead of habitual experiences.

Fourth, hedonic adaptation to marketplace experiences can be mitigated when consumers experience a series of smaller positive experiences instead of one substantial positive experience (e.g., Nelson & Meyvis, 2008). When consumers experience a "big" positive experience, their sensitivity to the positive experience wanes because of hedonic adaptation. Consumers can extract more happiness when they experience several "little" positive experiences instead of a "big" one.

Fifth, hedonic adaptation to marketplace experiences can be mitigated when consumers slow down the rate of consumption (e.g., Galak et al., 2013). In other words, consumers can reduce satiation and fully savor the positive experience by slowing down the speed of consumption.

Summary and Conclusion

In summary, consumption happiness is a micro psychological process and outcomes that feed into the more macro construct of consumer happiness. Consumers' experience of immediate happiness can increase happiness in the life domain, housing marketplace affective experiences, and their overall happiness at the most abstract level of the satisfaction hierarchy (e.g., Kivetz & Keinan, 2006). That is, repeated momentary positive consumption experiences result in long-term consumer happiness (Chancellor & Lyubomirsky, 2011) because of increased levels of positive affect (Ryan & Deci, 2001) and increased social connectedness (Gilovich et al., 2015).

It should be noted that momentary evaluations during positive experiences do not simply add up to consumers' retrospective evaluations of the positive experiences. Positive consumption experiences are often subject to hedonic adaptation, mispredictions, and forgetting. Consumers may hedonically adapt to positive consumption experiences after the experiences (e.g., Nawijn et al., 2010). Consumers may overpredict the amount of consumption happiness before and after the actual experience (Mitchell et al., 1997). Consumers may not remember positive experiences they experienced because consumers' peak and end moments largely determine how the positive experiences are remembered (Diener et al., 2001; Fredrickson & Kahneman, 1993; Wirtz et al., 2003).

Despite the mitigating effects of hedonic adaptation, mispredictions, and forgetting of experiences, positive consumption experiences over the consumption life cycle play a significant role in influencing consumer happiness over time and across marketplace activities and events (Sirgy, 2021; Lee et al., 2002; Neal et al., 1999). That is, frequent and positive consumption experiences tend to register a positive influence on consumer happiness (cf. Seligman et al., 2005; Sin & Lyubomirsky, 2009).

Below is a summary of the models of consumption happiness. See Table 9.22.

Table 9.22 Models of consumption happiness

Classification	Consumption model	Conditions for high consumption happiness
Acquisition-focused models	Satisfaction with a local shopping mall (or center)	High satisfaction with local shopping mall (or center)
	Shopping wellbeing and ill-being	High shopping wellbeing and low shopping ill-being
	Perceived shopping value	High utilitarian and hedonic value in shopping
	Purchase happiness	High purchase happiness
Possession-focused models	Brand relationship	Positive relationship with a brand
	Brand community	Voluntary engagement with the community and satisfaction of social needs derived from engagement
Experience-focused models	Self-congruity	High fit between the band-user image and the four dimensions of consumers' self-concept (actual self, ideal self, social self, and ideal social self)
	Self-expressiveness	Consumer goods and services producing high levels of self-expressiveness
	Perceived quality-of-life impact	Consumer goods/services and other marketplace activities and events perceived to have a high quality-of-life impact
	Perceived quality	Consumer goods/services and other marketplace activities and events that have high functional, social, and emotional value
	Benefits and need satisfaction	Consumer goods/services that provide benefits meeting basic and growth needs
	Personal values	Consumer goods/services and other marketplace activities and events that are congruent with consumer positive values
	Positive social interaction	High satisfaction with social interactions in the context of marketplace activities and events
	Experiential advantage	Increased spending on purchases of experiences instead of purchases of material possessions
	Hedonic adaptation	Low hedonic adaptation from consumption

References

Aaker, J. L. (1999). The malleable self: The role of self-expression in persuasion. *Journal of Marketing Research, 36*(1), 45–57.

Aaker, J. L., Rudd, M., & Mogilner, C. (2011). If money does not make you happy, consider time. *Journal of Consumer Psychology, 21*(2), 126–130.

Algesheimer, R., Dholakia, U. M., & Herrmann, A. (2005). The social influence of brand community: Evidence from European car clubs. *Journal of Marketing, 69*(3), 19–34.

Argyle, M. (1987). *The psychology of happiness*. Methuen and Co.

Arnould, E. J., & Thompson, C. J. (2005). Consumer culture theory (CCT): Twenty years of research. *Journal of Consumer Research, 31*(4), 868–882.

Arnould, E. J., Price, L. L., & Zinkhan, G. (2002). *Consumers*. McGraw-Hill.

Aureliano-Silva, L., Strehlau, S., & Strehlau, V. (2018). The relationship between brand attachment and consumers' emotional well-being. *Journal of Relationship Marketing, 17*(1), 1–16.

Babakus, E., & Boller, G. W. (1992). An empirical assessment of the SERVQUAL scale. *Journal of Business Research, 24*(3), 253–268.

Babin, B. J., & Attaway, J. S. (2000). Atmospheric affect as a tool for creating value and gaining share of customer. *Journal of Business Research, 49*(2), 91–99.

Babin, B. J., Darden, W. R., & Griffin, M. (1994). Work and/or fun: Measuring hedonic and utilitarian shopping value. *Journal of Consumer Research, 20*(4), 644–656.

Bagozzi, R. P., & Dholakia, U. M. (2002). Intentional social action in virtual communities. *Journal of Interactive Marketing, 16*(2), 2–21.

Bagozzi, R. P., & Dholakia, U. M. (2006). Antecedents and purchase consequences of customer participation in small group brand communities. *International Journal of Research in Marketing, 23*(1), 45–61.

Baldus, B. J., Voorhees, C., & Calantone, R. (2015). Online brand community engagement: Scale development and validation. *Journal of Business Research, 68*(5), 978–985.

Bastos, W., & Brucks, M. (2017). How and why conversational value leads to happiness for experiential and material purchases. *Journal of Consumer Research, 44*(3), 598–612.

Baumeister, R. F., & Leary, M. R. (1995). The need to belong: Desire for interpersonal attachments as a fundamental human motivation. *Psychological Bulletin, 117*(3), 497–529.

Baumeister, R. F., Campbell, J. D., Krueger, J. I., & Vohs, K. D. (2003). Does high self-esteem cause better performance, interpersonal success, happiness, or healthier lifestyles? *Psychological Science in the Public Interest, 4*(1), 1–44.

Baumgartner, H., Pieters, R., & Bagozzi, R. P. (2008). Future-oriented emotions: Conceptualization and behavioral effects. *European Journal of Social Psychology, 38*(4), 685–696.

Berant, E., Mikulincer, M., & Florian, V. (2001). Attachment style and mental health: A 1-year follow-up study of mothers of infants with congenital heart disease. *Personality and Social Psychology Bulletin, 27*(8), 956–968.

Berezan, O., Krishen, A. S., Agarwal, S., & Kachroo, P. (2018). The pursuit of virtual happiness: Exploring social media experience across generations. *Journal of Business Research, 89*(August), 455–461.

Bettiga, D., & Lamberti, L. (2020). Future-oriented happiness: Its nature and role in consumer decision-making for new products. *Frontiers in Psychology, 11*, 929.

Bosnjak, M., Brown, C. A., Lee, D. J., Yu, G. B., & Sirgy, M. J. (2016). Self-expressiveness in sport tourism: Determinants and consequences. *Journal of Travel Research, 55*(1), 125–134.

Brady, M. K., & Cronin, J. J., Jr. (2001). Some new thoughts on conceptualizing perceived service quality: A hierarchical approach. *Journal of Marketing, 65*(3), 34–49.

Brickman, P., Coates, D., & Janoff-Bulman, R. (1978). Lottery winners and accident victims: Is happiness relative? *Journal of Personality and Social Psychology, 36*(8), 917–927.

Bruhn, M., & Schnebelen, S. (2017). Integrated marketing communication–from an instrumental to a customer-centric perspective. *European Journal of Marketing, 51*(3), 464–489.

Bryant, F. B. (1989). A four-factor model of perceived control: Avoiding, coping, obtaining, and savoring. *Journal of Personality, 57*(4), 773–797.

Buehler, R., & McFarland, C. (2001). Intensity bias in affective forecasting: The role of temporal focus. *Personality and Social Psychology Bulletin, 27*(11), 1480–1493.

Burroughs, J. E., & Rindfleisch, A. (2002). Materialism and well-being: A conflicting values perspective. *Journal of Consumer Research, 29*(3), 348–370.

Burrow, A. L., & Rainone, N. (2017). How many likes did I get? Purpose moderates links between positive social media feedback and self-esteem. *Journal of Experimental Social Psychology, 69*(March), 232–236.

Campbell, A., Converse, P. E., & Rodgers, W. L. (1976). *The quality of American life: Perceptions, evaluations, and satisfactions*. Russell Sage.

Caprariello, P. A., & Reis, H. T. (2013). To do, to have, or to share? Valuing experiences over material possessions depends on the involvement of others. *Journal of Personality and Social Psychology, 104*(2), 199–215.

Carroll, B. A., & Ahuvia, A. C. (2006). Some antecedents and outcomes of brand love. *Marketing Letters, 17*(2), 79–89.

Carstensen, L. L. (2006). The influence of a sense of time on human development. *Science, 312*(5782), 1913–1915.

Carter, T. J., & Gilovich, T. (2010). The relative relativity of material and experiential purchases. *Journal of Personality and Social psychology, 98*(1), 146–159.

Carter, T. J., & Gilovich, T. (2012). I am what I do, not what I have: The differential centrality of experiential and material purchases to the self. *Journal of Personality and Social Psychology, 102*(6), 1304–1317.

Caruso, E. M., Gilbert, D. T., & Wilson, T. D. (2008). A wrinkle in time: Asymmetric valuation of past and future events. *Psychological Science, 19*(8), 796–801.

Chancellor, J., & Lyubomirsky, S. (2011). Happiness and thrift: When (spending) less is (hedonically) more. *Journal of Consumer Psychology, 21*(2), 131–138.

Chu, C. K. (2022). Savoring and the experiential advantage: Savoring beliefs determine consumer happiness from experiential versus material purchases. *Personality and Individual Differences, 195*, 111636.

Chugani, S. K., Irwin, J. R., & Redden, J. P. (2015). Happily ever after: The effect of identity-consistency on product satiation. *Journal of Consumer Research, 42*(4), 564–577.

Cohen, R. J. (2014). Brand personification: Introduction and overview. *Psychology & Marketing, 31*(1), 1–30.

Coleman, J. S. (1988). Social capital in the creation of human capital. *The American Journal of Sociology, 94*, S95–S120.

Cronin, J. J., Jr., & Taylor, S. A. (1992). Measuring service quality: Reexamination and extension. *Journal of Marketing, 56*(3), 55–68.

Dabholkar, P. A., Shepherd, C. D., & Thorpe, D. I. (2000). A comprehensive framework for service quality: An investigation of critical conceptual and measurement issues through a longitudinal study. *Journal of Retailing, 76*(2), 139–173.

Dagger, T. S., & Sweeney, J. C. (2006). The effect of service evaluations on behavioral intentions and quality of life. *Journal of Service Research, 9*(1), 3–18.

Dagger, T. S., Sweeney, J. C., & Johnson, L. W. (2007). A hierarchical model of health service quality: Scale development and investigation of an integrated model. *Journal of Service Research, 10*(2), 123–142.

Day, R. L. (1987). Relationships between life satisfaction and consumer satisfaction. In A. C. Samli (Ed.), *Marketing and quality-of-life interface* (pp. 289–311). Greenwood.

De Keyser, A., & Lariviere, B. (2014). How technical and functional service quality drive consumer happiness: Moderating influences of channel usage. *Journal of Service Management, 25*(1), 30–48.

De Leire, T., & Kalil, A. (2010). Does consumption buy happiness? Evidence from the United States. *International Review of Economics, 57*(2), 163–176.

de Rezende Pinto, M., Leite, R. S., de Andrade, M. L., & de Mendonça Joaquim, A. (2018). Shopping well-being: A study with the elderly people in shopping centers. *Revista Pensamento Contemporâneo em Administração, 12*(4), 124–141.

Deci, E. L., & Ryan, R. M. (2000). The "what" and "why" of goal pursuits: Human needs and the self-determination of behavior. *Psychological Inquiry, 11*(4), 227–268.

Deci, E. L., & Ryan, R. M. (2008). Self-determination theory: A macrotheory of human motivation, development, and health. *Canadian Psychology/Psychologie Canadienne, 49*(3), 182–185.

Desmeules, R. (2002). The impact of variety on consumer happiness: Marketing and the tyranny of freedom. *Academy of Marketing Science Review, 12*(1), 1–18.

Diener, E. (1984). Subjective well-being. *Psychological Bulletin, 95*(3), 542–575.

Diener, E., & Diener, M. (1995). Cross-cultural correlates of life satisfaction and self-esteem. *Journal of Personality and Social Psychology, 68*(4), 653–663.

Diener, E., & Lucas, R. E. (1999). Personality and subjective well-being. In D. Kahneman, E. Diener, & N. Schwarz (Eds.), *Well-being: The foundations of a hedonic psychology* (pp. 213–229). Russell Sage Foundation.

Diener, E., Wirtz, D., & Oishi, S. (2001). End effects of rated life quality: The James Dean effect. *Psychological Science, 12*(2), 124–128.

Diener, E., Lucas, R. E., & Scollon, C. N. (2006). Beyond the hedonic treadmill: Revising the adaptation theory of well-being. *American Psychologist, 61*(4), 305–314.

Dittmar, H., Bond, R., Hurst, M., & Kasser, T. (2014). The relationship between materialism and personal well-being: A meta-analysis. *Journal of Personality and Social Psychology, 107*(5), 879–924.

Dunn, E. W., & Weidman, A. C. (2015). Building a science of spending: Lessons from the past and directions for the future. *Journal of Consumer Psychology, 25*(1), 172–178.

Dunn, E. W., Gilbert, D. T., & Wilson, T. D. (2011). If money doesn't make you happy, then you probably aren't spending it right. *Journal of Consumer Psychology, 21*(2), 115–125.

Eakman, A. M. (2013). Relationships between meaningful activity, basic psychological needs, and meaning in life: Test of the meaningful activity and life meaning model. *OTJR: Occupation, Participation and Health, 33*(2), 100–109.

Eid, M., & Diener, E. (2004). Global judgments of subjective well-being: Situational variability and long-term stability. *Social Indicators Research, 65*(3), 245–277.

Ekici, A., Sirgy, M. J., Lee, D. J., Yu, G. B., & Bosnjak, M. (2018). The effects of shopping well-being and shopping ill-being on consumer life satisfaction. *Applied Research in Quality of Life, 13*(June), 333–353.

El Hedhli, K., Chebat, J. C., & Sirgy, M. J. (2013). Shopping well-being at the mall: Construct, antecedents, and consequences. *Journal of Business Research, 66*(7), 856–863.

El Hedhli, K., Zourrig, H., & Chebat, J. C. (2016). Shopping well-being: Is it just a matter of pleasure or doing the task? The role of shopper's gender and self-congruity. *Journal of Retailing and Consumer Services, 31*(July), 1–13.

El Hedhli, K., Becheur, I., Zourrig, H., & Chaouali, W. (2021). Shopping well-being: The role of congruity and shoppers' characteristics. *Journal of Consumer Marketing, 38*(3), 293–304.

Escalas, J. E., & Bettman, J. R. (2003). You are what they eat: The influence of reference groups on consumers' connections to brands. *Journal of Consumer Psychology, 13*(3), 339–348.

Escalas, J. E., & Bettman, J. R. (2005). Self-construal, reference groups, and brand meaning. *Journal of Consumer Research, 32*(3), 378–389.

Fornell, C. (1992). A national customer satisfaction barometer: The Swedish experience. *Journal of Marketing, 56*(1), 6–21.

Fornell, C., Johnson, M. D., Anderson, E. W., Cha, J., & Bryant, B. E. (1996). The American customer satisfaction index: Nature, purpose, and findings. *Journal of Marketing, 60*(4), 7–18.

Fournier, S. (1998). Consumers and their brands: Developing relationship theory in consumer research. *Journal of Consumer Research, 24*(4), 343–373.

Fournier, S., & Yao, J. L. (1997). Reviving brand loyalty: A reconceptualization within the framework of consumer-brand relationships. *International Journal of Research in Marketing, 14*(5), 451–472.

Frank, R. H. (2004). How not to buy happiness. *Daedalus, 133*(2), 69–79.

Frederick, S., & Loewenstein, G. (1999). Hedonic adaptation. In D. Kahneman, E. Diener, & N. Schwarz (Eds.), *Well-being The foundations of hedonic psychology* (pp. 302–329). Russell Sage Foundation.

Fredrickson, B. L., & Kahneman, D. (1993). Duration neglect in retrospective evaluations of affective episodes. *Journal of Personality and Social Psychology, 65*(1), 45–55.

Galak, J., Redden, J. P., & Kruger, J. (2009). Variety amnesia: Recalling past variety can accelerate recovery from satiation. *Journal of Consumer Research, 36*(4), 575–584.

Galak, J., Kruger, J., & Loewenstein, G. (2013). Slow down! Insensitivity to rate of consumption leads to avoidable satiation. *Journal of Consumer Research, 39*(5), 993–1009.

Ganglmair-Wooliscroft, A., & Wooliscroft, B. (2019). Well-being and everyday ethical consumption. *Journal of Happiness Studies, 20*(1), 141–163.

Gilbert, D. T., Pinel, E. C., Wilson, T. D., Blumberg, S. J., & Wheatley, T. P. (1998). Immune neglect: A source of durability bias in affective forecasting. *Journal of Personality and Social Psychology, 75*(3), 617–638.

Gilbert, D. T., Morewedge, C. K., Risen, J. L., & Wilson, T. D. (2004). Looking forward to looking backward: The misprediction of regret. *Psychological Science, 15*(5), 346–350.

Gilovich, T., Kumar, A., & Jampol, L. (2015). A wonderful life: Experiential consumption and the pursuit of happiness. *Journal of Consumer Psychology, 25*(1), 152–165.

Gong, T., & Yi, Y. (2018). The effect of service quality on customer satisfaction, loyalty, and happiness in five Asian countries. *Psychology & Marketing, 35*(6), 427–442.

Goodman, J. K., Malkoc, S. A., & Stephenson, B. L. (2016). Celebrate or commemorate? A material purchase advantage when honoring special life events. *Journal of the Association for Consumer Research, 1*(4), 497–508.

Grönroos, C. (1984). A service quality model and its marketing implications. *European Journal of Marketing, 18*(4), 36–44.

Grzeskowiak, S., & Sirgy, M. J. (2007). Consumer well-being (CWB): The effects of self-image congruence, brand-community belongingness, brand loyalty, and consumption recency. *Applied research in Quality of Life, 2*(4), 289–304.

Grzeskowiak, S., Sirgy, M. J., Lee, D. J., & Claiborne, C. B. (2006). Housing well-being: Developing and validating a measure. *Social Indicators Research, 79*(3), 503–541.

Grzeskowiak, S., Lee, D. J., Yu, G. B., & Sirgy, M. J. (2014). How do consumers perceive the quality-of-life impact of durable goods? A consumer well-being model based on the consumption life cycle. *Applied Research in Quality of Life, 9*(3), 683–709.

Grzeskowiak, S., Sirgy, M. J., Foscht, T., & Swoboda, B. (2016). Linking retailing experiences with life satisfaction: The concept of story-type congruity with shopper's identity. *International Journal of Retail & Distribution Management, 44*(2), 124–138.

Guevarra, D. A., & Howell, R. T. (2015). To have in order to do: Exploring the effects of consuming experiential products on well-being. *Journal of Consumer Psychology, 25*(1), 28–41.

Gummerus, J., Liljander, V., Weman, E., & Pihlström, M. (2012). Customer engagement in a Facebook brand community. *Management Research Review, 35*(9), 857–877.

Gutman, J. (1982). A means-end chain model based on consumer categorization processes. *Journal of Marketing, 46*(2), 60–72.

Harmeling, C. M., Moffett, J. W., Arnold, M. J., & Carlson, B. D. (2017). Toward a theory of customer engagement marketing. *Journal of the Academy of Marketing Science, 45*(3), 312–335.

Helliwell, J. F., Barrinton-Leigh, C., Harris, A., & Huang, H. (2010a). International evidence on the social context of well-being. In E. Diener, J. Helliwell, & D. Kahneman (Eds.), *International differences in well-being* (pp. 291–327). Oxford University Press.

Helliwell, J., et al. (2010b). International differences in the social context of well-being. In E. Diener, J. Helliwell, & D. Kahneman (Eds.), *International differences in well-being* (pp. 291–327). Oxford University Press.

Higgins, E. T. (1997). Beyond pleasure and pain. *American Psychologist, 52*(12), 1280–1300.

Higgins, E. T., Shah, J., & Friedman, R. (1997). Emotional response to goal attainment: Strength of regulatory focus as moderator. *Journal of Personality and Social Psychology, 72*(3), 515–525.

Hill, G., & Howell, R. T. (2014). Moderators and mediators of pro-social spending and well-being: The influence of values and psychological need satisfaction. *Personality and Individual Differences, 69*, 69–74.

Hooker, S. A., Masters, K. S., Vagnini, K. M., & Rush, C. L. (2020). Engaging in personally meaningful activities is associated with meaning salience and psychological well-being. *The Journal of Positive Psychology, 15*(6), 821–831.

Howell, R. T., & Hill, G. (2009). The mediators of experiential purchases: Determining the impact of psychological needs satisfaction and social comparison. *The Journal of Positive Psychology, 4*(6), 511–522.

Hsee, C. K., & Hastie, R. (2006). Decision and experience: Why don't we choose what makes us happy? *Trends in Cognitive Sciences, 10*(1), 31–37.

Hsee, C. K., Yang, Y., Li, N., & Shen, L. (2009). Wealth, warmth, and well-being: Whether happiness is relative or absolute depends on whether it is about money, acquisition, or consumption. *Journal of Marketing Research, 46*(3), 396–409.

Japutra, A., Ekinci, Y., & Simkin, L. (2019). Self-congruence, brand attachment and compulsive buying. *Journal of Business Research, 99*(June), 456–463.

Kasser, T. (2002). *The high price of materialism*. MIT Press.

Kasser, T., & Ryan, R. M. (1996). Further examining the American dream: Differential correlates of intrinsic and extrinsic goals. *Personality and Social Psychology Bulletin, 22*(3), 280–287.

Kivetz, R., & Keinan, A. (2006). Repenting hyperopia: An analysis of self-control regrets. *Journal of Consumer Research, 33*(2), 273–282.

Kousi, S., Halkias, G., & Kokkinaki, F. (2023). Hedonic objects and utilitarian experiences: The overriding influence of hedonism in driving consumer happiness. *Psychology & Marketing, 40*(8), 1634–1645.

Kozlenkova, I. V., Palmatier, R. W., Fang, E., Xiao, B., & Huang, M. (2017). Online relationship formation. *Journal of Marketing, 81*(3), 21–40.

Kressmann, F., Sirgy, M. J., Herrmann, A., Huber, F., Huber, S., & Lee, D. J. (2006). Direct and indirect effects of self-image congruence on brand loyalty. *Journal of Business Research, 59*(9), 955–964.

Kumar, A., & Gilovich, T. (2015). Some "thing" to talk about? Differential story utility from experiential and material purchases. *Personality and Social Psychology Bulletin, 41*(10), 1320–1331.

Kumar, A., Killingsworth, M. A., & Gilovich, T. (2014). Waiting for merlot: Anticipatory consumption of experiential and material purchases. *Psychological Science, 25*(10), 1924–1931.

Kuo, Y. F., & Feng, L. H. (2013). Relationships among community interaction characteristics, perceived benefits, community commitment, and oppositional brand loyalty in online brand communities. *International Journal of Information Management, 33*(6), 948–962.

Lam, K. C., Buehler, R., McFarland, C., Ross, M., & Cheung, I. (2005). Cultural differences in affective forecasting: The role of focalism. *Personality and Social Psychology Bulletin, 31*(9), 1296–1309.

Lambert, N. M., Stillman, T. F., Hicks, J. A., Kamble, S., Baumeister, R. F., & Fincham, F. D. (2013). To belong is to matter: Sense of belonging enhances meaning in life. *Personality and Social Psychology Bulletin, 39*(11), 1418–1427.

Laros, F. J., & Steenkamp, J. B. E. (2005). Emotions in consumer behavior: A hierarchical approach. *Journal of Business Research, 58*(10), 1437–1445.

Lastovicka, J. L., & Fernandez, K. V. (2005). Three paths to disposition: The movement of meaningful possessions to strangers. *Journal of Consumer Research, 31*(4), 813–823.

Lee, D. J., Sirgy, M. J., Larsen, V., & Wright, N. D. (2002). Developing a subjective measure of consumer well-being. *Journal of Macromarketing, 22*(2), 158–169.

Lee, D. J., Yu, G. B., Sirgy, M. J., Ekici, A., Gurel-Atay, E., & Bahn, K. D. (2014). Shopping well-being and ill-being: Toward an integrated model. In *Handbook of research on retailer-consumer relationship development* (pp. 27–44). IGI Global.

Lee, J. C., Kim, S., & Wang, P. X. (2022). Anthropomorphizing makes material goods as happiness-inducing as experiences. *Marketing Letters, 33*(1), 61–73.

Lee, D. J., Yu, G. B., & Sirgy, M. J. (2023). Testing the benefits theory of leisure well-being. *Applied Research in Quality of Life, 18*(5), 2705–2748.

Lianopoulos, Y., Theodorakis, N. D., Tsigilis, N., Gardikiotis, A., & Koustelios, A. (2020). Elevating self-esteem through sport team identification: A study about local and distant sport fans. *International Journal of Sports Marketing and Sponsorship, 21*(4), 695–718.

Loewenstein, G. F., & Prelec, D. (1993). Preferences for sequences of outcomes. *Psychological Review, 100*(1), 91–108.

Lucas, R. E., & Dyrenforth, P. S. (2006). Does the existence of social relationships matter for subjective well-being? In K. D. Vobs & E. J. Finkel (Eds.), *Self and relationships: Connecting intrapersonal and interpersonal processes* (pp. 254–273). Guilford Press.

Lykken, D., & Tellegen, A. (1996). Happiness is a stochastic phenomenon. *Psychological Science, 7*(3), 186–189.

Lyubomirsky, S., Sheldon, K. M., & Schkade, D. (2005). Pursuing happiness: The architecture of sustainable change. *Review of General Psychology, 9*(2), 111–131.

Lyubomirsky, S., Tkach, C., & DiMatteo, M. R. (2006). What are the differences between happiness and self-esteem. *Social Indicators Research, 78*(3), 363–404.

Matz, S. C., Gladstone, J. J., & Stillwell, D. (2016). Money buys happiness when spending fits our personality. *Psychological Science, 27*(5), 715–725.

Meadow, H. L., & Sirgy, M. J. (2008). Developing a measure that captures elderly's well-being in local marketplace transactions. *Applied Research in Quality of Life, 3*(July), 63–80.

Merunka, D. R., & Sirgy, M. J. (2011). Distinguishing consumer satisfaction from consumer well-being in brand post-purchase behavior: A positive psychology perspective. In *Proceedings for the inaugural conference on positive marketing, center for positive marketing, New York, NY* (pp. 21–22).

Michalos, A. C. (1985). Multiple discrepancies theory (MDT). *Social Indicators Research, 16*(4), 347–413.

Mikulincer, M., & Shaver, P. R. (2007). *Attachment in adulthood: Structure, dynamics, and change*. Guilford Press.

Millar, M., & Thomas, R. (2009). Discretionary activity and happiness: The role of materialism. *Journal of Research in Personality, 43*(4), 699–702.

Mitchell, T. R., & Mickel, A. E. (1999). The meaning of money: An individual-difference perspective. *Academy of Management Review, 24*(3), 568–578.

Mitchell, T. R., Thompson, L., Peterson, E., & Cronk, R. (1997). Temporal adjustments in the evaluation of events: The "rosy view". *Journal of Experimental Social Psychology, 33*(4), 421–448.

Mogilner, C., Aaker, J., & Kamvar, S. D. (2012). How happiness affects choice. *Journal of Consumer Research, 39*(2), 429–443.

Moldes, O., & Ku, L. (2020). Materialistic cues make us miserable: A meta-analysis of the experimental evidence for the effects of materialism on individual and societal well-being. *Psychology & Marketing, 37*(10), 1396–1419.

Muniz, A. M., Jr., & O'guinn, T. C. (2001). Brand community. *Journal of Consumer Research, 27*(4), 412–432.

Myers, D. G., & Diener, E. (1995). Who is happy? *Psychological Science, 6*(1), 10–19.

Nambisan, S., & Baron, R. A. (2007). Interactions in virtual customer environments: Implications for product support and customer relationship management. *Journal of Interactive Marketing, 21*(2), 42–62.

Nawijn, J., Marchand, M. A., Veenhoven, R., & Vingerhoets, A. J. (2010). Vacationers happier, but most not happier after a holiday. *Applied Research in Quality of Life, 5*(1), 35–47.

Neal, J. D., Sirgy, M. J., & Uysal, M. (1999). The role of satisfaction with leisure travel/tourism services and experience in satisfaction with leisure life and overall life. *Journal of Business Research, 44*(3), 153–163.

Nelson, L. D., & Meyvis, T. (2008). Interrupted consumption: Disrupting adaptation to hedonic experiences. *Journal of Marketing Research, 45*(6), 654–664.

Netemeyer, R. G., Warmath, D., Fernandes, D., & Lynch, J. G., Jr. (2018). How am I doing? Perceived financial well-being, its potential antecedents, and its relation to overall well-being. *Journal of Consumer Research, 45*(1), 68–89.

Nicolao, L., Irwin, J. R., & Goodman, J. K. (2009). Happiness for sale: Do experiential purchases make consumers happier than material purchases? *Journal of Consumer Research, 36*(2), 188–198.

Niedermeier, A., Albrecht, L., & Jahn, B. (2019). "Happy together": Effects of brand community engagement on customer happiness. *Journal of Relationship Marketing, 18*(1), 54–76.

Nisbett, R. E., Peng, K., Choi, I., & Norenzayan, A. (2001). Culture and systems of thought: Holistic versus analytic cognition. *Psychological Review, 108*(2), 291–310.

Oishi, S. (2002). The experiencing and remembering of well-being: A cross-cultural analysis. *Personality and Social Psychology Bulletin, 28*(10), 1398–1406.

Oishi, S., Schimmack, U., Diener, E., & Suh, E. M. (1998). The measurement of values and individualism–collectivism. *Personality and Social Psychology Bulletin, 24*(11), 1177–1189.

Oishi, S., Diener, E., Suh, E., & Lucas, R. E. (1999). Value as a moderator in subjective well-being. *Journal of Personality, 67*(1), 157–184.

Parasuraman, A., Zeithaml, V. A., & Berry, L. L. (1988). SERVQUAL: A multiple-item scale for measuring customer perceptions of service quality. *Journal of Retailing, 64*(1), 12–40.

Pollack, L. B. (2009). Linking the hierarchical service quality model to customer satisfaction and loyalty. *Journal of Services Marketing, 23*(1), 42–50.

Prahalad, C. K., & Ramaswamy, V. (2000). Co-opting customer competence. *Harvard Business Review, 78*(1), 79–90.

Prayag, G., Mills, H., Lee, C., & Soscia, I. (2020). Team identification, discrete emotions, satisfaction, and event attachment: A social identity perspective. *Journal of Business Research, 112*, 373–384.

Putnam, R. D. (2001). *Bowling alone: The collapse and revival of the American community*. Simon & Schuster.

Razmus, W., Grabner-Kräuter, S., Kostyra, M., & Zawadzka, A. M. (2022). Buying happiness: How brand engagement in self-concept affects purchase happiness. *Psychology & Marketing, 39*(11), 2096–2109.

Redden, J. P. (2008). Reducing satiation: The role of categorization level. *Journal of Consumer Research, 34*(5), 624–634.

Reynolds, T. J., & Olson, J. C. (Eds.). (2001). *Understanding consumer decision making: The means-end approach to marketing and advertising strategy*. Psychology Press.

Richins, M. L. (1997). Measuring emotions in the consumption experience. *Journal of Consumer Research, 24*(2), 127–146.

Richins, M. L., & Dawson, S. (1992). A consumer values orientation for materialism and its measurement: Scale development and validation. *Journal of Consumer Research, 19*(3), 303–316.

Rodriguez, A., Bosnjak, M., & Sirgy, M. J. (2012). Moderators of the self-congruity effect on consumer decision-making: A meta-analysis. *Journal of Business Research, 65*(8), 1179–1188.

Rokeach, M., & Regan, J. F. (1980). The role of values in the counseling situation. *The Personnel and Guidance Journal, 58*(9), 576–582.

Rosenbaum, M. S., Ward, J., Walker, B. A., & Ostrom, A. (2007). A cup of coffee with a dash of love: An investigation of commercial social support and third place attachment. *Journal of Service Research, 10*(1), 43–59.

Rosenberg, M. (1965). *Society and the adolescent self-image*. Princeton University Press.

Rosenberg, M. (1989). Self-concept research: A historical overview. *Social Forces, 68*(1), 34–44.

Ryan, R. M., & Deci, E. L. (2000). Self-determination theory and the facilitation of intrinsic motivation, social development, and well-being. *American Psychologist, 55*(1), 68–78.

Ryan, R. M., & Deci, E. L. (2001). On happiness and human potentials: A review of research on hedonic and eudaimonic well-being. *Annual Review of Psychology, 52*(1), 141–166.

Ryan, R. M., Huta, V., & Deci, E. L. (2008). Living well: A self-determination theory perspective on eudaimonia. *Journal of Happiness Studies, 9*(1), 139–170.

Ryff, C. D. (1989). Happiness is everything, or is it? Explorations on the meaning of psychological well-being. *Journal of Personality and Social Psychology, 57*(6), 1069–1081.

Sagiv, L., & Schwartz, S. H. (2000). Value priorities and subjective well-being: Direct relations and congruity effects. *European Journal of Social Psychology, 30*(2), 177–198.

Sagiv, L., Roccas, S., & Hazan, O. (2004). Value pathways to well-being: Healthy values, valued goal attainment, and environmental congruence. In A. Linley & J. Stephen (Eds.), *Positive psychology in practice* (pp. 68–85). John Wiley.

Schmitt, B. (2012). The consumer psychology of brands. *Journal of Consumer Psychology, 22*(1), 7–17.

Schmitt, B., Brakus, J. J., & Zarantonello, L. (2015). From experiential psychology to consumer experience. *Journal of Consumer Psychology, 25*(1), 166–171.

Schwartz, S. H. (1994). Are there universal aspects in the structure and contents of human values? *Journal of Social issues, 50*(4), 19–45.

Schwartz, S. H. (2012). An overview of the Schwartz theory of basic values. *Online Readings in Psychology and Culture, 2*(1) article 11. https://doi.org/10.9707/2307-0919.1116

Schwartz, S. H. (2015). Basic individual values: Sources and consequences. In D. Sander & T. Brosch (Eds.), *Handbook of value* (pp. 63–84). Oxford University Press.

Schwartz, S. H., Cieciuch, J., Vecchione, M., Davidov, E., Fischer, R., Beierlein, C., et al. (2012). Refining the theory of basic individual values. *Journal of Personality and Social Psychology, 103*(4), 663.

Seligman, M. E., Steen, T. A., Park, N., & Peterson, C. (2005). Positive psychology progress: Empirical validation of interventions. *American Psychologist, 60*(5), 410–421.

Sharma, T. G., Hamari, J., Kesharwani, A., & Tak, P. (2022). Understanding continuance intention to play online games: Roles of self-expressiveness, self-congruity, self-efficacy, and perceived risk. *Behaviour & Information Technology, 41*(2), 348–364.

Sheldon, K. M., & Lyubomirsky, S. (2012). The challenge of staying happier: Testing the hedonic adaptation prevention model. *Personality and Social Psychology Bulletin, 38*(5), 670–680.

Sin, N. L., & Lyubomirsky, S. (2009). Enhancing well-being and alleviating depressive symptoms with positive psychology interventions: A practice-friendly meta-analysis. *Journal of Clinical Psychology, 65*(5), 467–487.

Sirgy, M. J. (1982). Self-concept in consumer behavior: A critical review. *Journal of Consumer Research, 9*(3), 287–300.

Sirgy, M. J. (1985). Using self-congruity and ideal congruity to predict purchase motivation. *Journal of Business Research, 13*(3), 195–206.

Sirgy, M. J. (1998). Materialism and quality of life. *Social Indicators Research, 43*(3), 227–260.

Sirgy, M. J. (2018). Self-congruity theory in consumer behavior: A little history. *Journal of Global Scholars of Marketing Science, 28*(2), 197–207.

Sirgy, M. J. (2021). Macromarketing metrics of consumer well-being: An update. *Journal of Macromarketing, 41*(1), 124–131.

Sirgy, M. J., & Lee, D. J. (2003). Developing a measure of consumer well-being in relation to personal transportation. *Yonsei Business Review, 40*(1), 73–101.

Sirgy, M. J., & Lee, D. J. (2006). Macro measures of consumer well-being (CWB): A critical analysis and a research agenda. *Journal of Macromarketing, 26*(1), 27–44.

Sirgy, M. J., & Su, C. (2000). Destination image, self-congruity, and travel behavior: Toward an integrative model. *Journal of Travel Research, 38*(4), 340–352.

Sirgy, M. J., Grewal, D., Mangleburg, T. F., Park, J. O., Chon, K. S., Claiborne, C. B., et al. (1997). Assessing the predictive validity of two methods of measuring self-image congruence. *Journal of the Academy of Marketing Science, 25*(3), 229–241.

Sirgy, M. J., Grewal, D., & Mangleburg, T. (2000). Retail environment, self-congruity, and retail patronage: An integrative model and a research agenda. *Journal of Business Research, 49*(2), 127–138.

Sirgy, M. J., Lee, D. J., & Bae, J. (2006a). Developing a measure of internet well-being: Nomological (predictive) validation. *Social Indicators Research, 78*(2), 205–249.

Sirgy, M. J., Lee, D. J., & Kressmann, F. (2006b). A need-based measure of consumer well-being (CWB) in relation to personal transportation: Nomological validation. *Social Indicators Research, 79*(2), 337–367.

Sirgy, M. J., Lee, D. J., & Rahtz, D. (2007). Research on consumer well-being (CWB): Overview of the field and introduction to the special issue. *Journal of Macromarketing, 27*(4), 341–349.

Sirgy, M. J., Lee, D. J., Kamra, K., & Tidwell, J. (2008). What determines the perceived quality-of-life impact of mobile phones? A model based on the consumption life cycle. *Applied Research in Quality of Life, 3*(4), 251–268.

Sirgy, M. J., Lee, D. J., & Yu, G. B. (2016a). Revisiting self-congruity theory in consumer behaviour: Making sense of the research so far. In *Routledge international handbook of consumer psychology* (pp. 203–219). Routledge.

Sirgy, M. J., Lee, D. J., Yu, G. B., Gurel-Atay, E., Tidwell, J., & Ekici, A. (2016b). Self-expressiveness in shopping. *Journal of Retailing and Consumer Services, 30*(5), 292–299.

Sirgy, M. J., Uysal, M., & Kruger, S. (2017). Towards a benefits theory of leisure well-being. *Applied Research in Quality of Life, 12*(1), 205–228.

Sirgy, M. J., Lee, D. J., & Yu, G. B. (2020). Shopping-life balance: Towards a unifying framework. *Applied Research in Quality of Life, 15*(1), 17–34.

Spiller, S. A. (2011). Opportunity cost consideration. *Journal of Consumer Research, 38*(4), 595–610.

Stokburger-Sauer, N., Ratneshwar, S., & Sen, S. (2012). Drivers of consumer–brand identification. *International Journal of Research in Marketing, 29*(4), 406–418.

Swaminathan, V., Stilley, K. M., & Ahluwalia, R. (2009). When brand personality matters: The moderating role of attachment styles. *Journal of Consumer Research, 35*(6), 985–1002.

Sweeney, J. C., Danaher, T. S., & McColl-Kennedy, J. R. (2015). Customer effort in value cocreation activities: Improving quality of life and behavioral intentions of health care customers. *Journal of Service Research, 18*(3), 318–335.

Thomas, R., & Millar, M. (2013). The effects of material and experiential discretionary purchases on consumer happiness: Moderators and mediators. *The Journal of Psychology, 147*(4), 345–356.

Thomson, M., MacInnis, D. J., & Park, C. W. (2005). The ties that bind: Measuring the strength of consumers' emotional attachments to brands. *Journal of Consumer Psychology, 15*(1), 77–91.

Thorbjørnsen, H., Pedersen, P. E., & Nysveen, H. (2007). "This is who I am": Identity expressiveness and the theory of planned behavior. *Psychology & Marketing, 24*(9), 763–785.

Trope, Y., & Liberman, N. (2003). Temporal construal. *Psychological Review, 110*(3), 403–421.

Tsai, J. L., Knutson, B., & Fung, H. H. (2006). Cultural variation in affect valuation. *Journal of Personality and Social Psychology, 90*(2), 288–307.

Tu, Y., & Hsee, C. K. (2016). Consumer happiness derived from inherent preferences versus learned preferences. *Current Opinion in Psychology, 10*(August), 83–88.

Tully, S. M., Hershfield, H. E., & Meyvis, T. (2015). Seeking lasting enjoyment with limited money: Financial constraints increase preference for material goods over experiences. *Journal of Consumer Research, 42*(1), 59–75.

Valkenburg, P. M., & Peter, J. (2007). Online communication and adolescent well-being: Testing the stimulation versus the displacement hypothesis. *Journal of Computer-Mediated Communication, 12*(4), 1169–1182.

Van Boven, L. (2005). Experientialism, materialism, and the pursuit of happiness. *Review of General Psychology, 9*(2), 132–142.

Van Boven, L., & Ashworth, L. (2007). Looking forward, looking back: Anticipation is more evocative than retrospection. *Journal of Experimental Psychology: General, 136*(2), 289–300.

Van Boven, L., & Gilovich, T. (2003). To do or to have? That is the question. *Journal of Personality and Social Psychology, 85*(6), 1193–1202.

Van Boven, L., Campbell, M. C., & Gilovich, T. (2010). Stigmatizing materialism: On stereotypes and impressions of materialistic and experiential pursuits. *Personality and Social Psychology Bulletin, 36*(4), 551–563.

Veenhoven, R., Chiperi, F., Kang, X., & Burger, M. (2021). Happiness and consumption: A research synthesis using an online finding archive. *Sage Open, 11*(1), 2158244020986239.

Voss, K. E., Spangenberg, E. R., & Grohmann, B. (2003). Measuring the hedonic and utilitarian dimensions of consumer attitude. *Journal of Marketing Research, 40*(3), 310–320.

Wang, J., Novemsky, N., & Dhar, R. (2009). Anticipating adaptation to products. *Journal of Consumer Research, 36*(2), 149–159.

Waterman, A. S. (1990). Personal expressiveness: Philosophical and psychological foundations. *The Journal of Mind and Behavior, 11*(1), 47–73.

Waterman, A. S., Schwartz, S. J., & Conti, R. (2008). The implications of two conceptions of happiness (hedonic enjoyment and eudaimonia) for the understanding of intrinsic motivation. *Journal of Happiness Studies, 9*(1), 41–79.

Weidman, A. C., & Dunn, E. W. (2016). The unsung benefits of material things: Material purchases provide more frequent momentary happiness than experiential purchases. *Social Psychological and Personality Science, 7*(4), 390–399.

Weingarten, E., Duke, K., Liu, W., Hamilton, R. W., Amir, O., Appel, G., et al. (2023). What makes people happy? Decoupling the experiential-material continuum. *Journal of Consumer Psychology, 33*(1), 97–106.

Williams, P., Escalas, J. E., & Morningstar, A. (2022). Conceptualizing brand purpose and considering its implications for consumer eudaimonic well-being. *Journal of Consumer Psychology, 32*(4), 699–723.

Wilson, T. D., Wheatley, T., Meyers, J. M., Gilbert, D. T., & Axsom, D. (2000). Focalism: A source of durability bias in affective forecasting. *Journal of Personality and Social Psychology, 78*(5), 821–836.

Wirtz, D., Kruger, J., Scollon, C. N., & Diener, E. (2003). What to do on spring break? The role of predicted, on-line, and remembered experience in future choice. *Psychological Science, 14*(5), 520–524.

Yang, Y., & Galak, J. (2015). Sentimental value and its influence on hedonic adaptation. *Journal of Personality and Social Psychology, 109*(5), 767–790.

Yang, Y., Gu, Y., & Galak, J. (2017). When it could have been worse, it gets better: How favorable uncertainty resolution slows hedonic adaptation. *Journal of Consumer Research, 43*(5), 747–768.

Zhan, G., & Zhou, Z. (2018). Mobile internet and consumer happiness: The role of risk. *Internet Research, 28*(3), 785–803.

Chapter 10
Outcomes of Consumption Happiness

Children will not remember you for the material things you provided, but for the feeling that you cherished them.

—Richard L. Evans (https://www.azquotes.com/quotes/topics/material-things.html)

Evidence-Based Outcomes of Consumption Happiness

The research on the outcomes of consumption happiness suggests that there are consumer behavior outcomes, namely positive brand evaluation, brand loyalty, positive word-of-mouth communication, brand trust, altruistic behavior, positive self-image, and satisfaction in consumer life.

Positive Brand Evaluation

Research has shown that consumers with dispositional happiness tend to evaluate service quality in a positive light (Hellén & Sääksjärvi, 2011). Happiness tends to bias information processing, evaluation, and behaviors in a consistent manner (Pham et al., 2013). In Hellén and Sääksjärvi (2011)'s study, participants were first asked to recall the service quality of their most recent visit to each company. Then respondents were asked to answer the measure of subjective happiness (Lyubomirsky & Lepper, 1999) and the measure of service quality (Dagger et al., 2007). The study results indicate that happier customers evaluate service quality in a more positive manner than do less happy customers.

Happiness tends to facilitate access to positive materials in memory and leads to more positive evaluations of neutral items (Isen et al., 1978; Teasdale & Fogarty, 1979). Specifically, those who experience high levels of happiness evaluate the same events in more positive ways because they are motivated to maintain the

D.-J. Lee, M. J. Sirgy, *Happiness in the Marketplace*, Social Indicators Research Series 64, https://doi.org/10.1007/978-3-032-04443-3_10

Table 10.1 Dispositional happiness and service quality evaluation

Subjective Happiness Scale (Lyubomirsky & Lepper, 1999). • Compared to most of my peers, I consider myself (1 = not at all as a happy person; 7 = as a very happy person). • Some people are generally very happy. They enjoy life regardless of what is going on, getting the most out of everything. To what extent does this characterization describe you? (1 = not at all; 7 = great deal) • In general, I consider myself (1 = not at all as a happy person; 7 = as a very happy person). • Some people are generally not very happy. Although they are not depressed, they never seem as happy as they might be. To what extent does this characterization describe you? (1 = not at all; 7 = great deal) Service Quality (Dagger et al., 2007) • I believe that the firm offers a service that is superior to other firms. • The overall quality of the firm is excellent. • The quality of the firm is impressive. • The firm is of a high standard.
Response scale: (1 = strongly disagree; 7 = strongly agree)

Source: Adapted from Lyubomirsky and Lepper (1999) and Dagger et al. (2007)

experience of positive emotions (Abbe et al., 2003), they do not engage in comparative evaluations (Abbe et al., 2003), and they use simple heuristics instead of effortful judgments (Forgas & Bower, 1987). As a result, consumers who experience high-levels of consumption happiness tend to make favorable evaluations of material products (Forgas & Ciarrochi, 2001) and services (Hellén & Sääksjärvi, 2011). See measures of the constructs in question in Table 10.1.

Brand Loyalty

Brand happiness is viewed as consumers' greatest emotional fulfillment, a moment-based experience of pleasant high and low arousal emotions, induced at different brand contact points (Schnebelen & Bruhn, 2018). That is, brand happiness is consumption happiness elicited by a brand and a moment-based emotional construct (Bruhn & Schnebelen, 2017).

To measure brand happiness, consumers are asked to choose a brand that makes them happy and are asked to evaluate how well the emotional adjectives describe their happy brand. The brand happiness measure had four affective factors such as joy, vigor, pride, and serenity (Schnebelen & Bruhn, 2018).

There is a positive association between brand happiness and *brand loyalty*. This may be due to several reasons. First, the experience of momentary consumption happiness elicited by a brand is highly pleasurable and provides consumers with hedonic value in the form of high-level emotional fulfillment. This is why consumption happiness from a brand generates a consumer's desire to re-experience it (Bruhn & Schnebelen, 2017). Second, brand happiness leads consumers to increase their willingness to pay (Bruhn & Schnebelen, 2017). Brand happiness also motivates consumers to reciprocate the affective benefits received from a brand by committing to remain loyal to that brand (Schnebelen & Bruhn, 2018). Third, brand happiness increases *positive word-of-mouth*. Consumers who have experienced happiness about a specific brand are likely to hold a positive attitude towards the brand through affect transfer (Pham et al., 2013). This positive brand attitude is likely to increase self-disclosure and enhance positive social interactions with others (Cunningham, 1988; Diener & Seligman, 2004). The outcome of all of this is positive word-of-mouth communications about the brand.

Many studies found that brand happiness is positively associated with brand loyalty (Gong & Yi, 2018; Bruhn & Schnebelen, 2017). Consumer happiness with a brand strongly predicts re-purchase intention, willingness to pay a premium price, and positive word-of-mouth communications (Bruhn & Schnebelen, 2017). Evidence suggests that, compared to other affective constructs (e.g., brand attachment, brand love), brand happiness shows a stronger influence on purchase intention, willingness to pay a price premium, and positive word-of-mouth communications (Bruhn & Schnebelen, 2017). Evidence also suggests that brand happiness has a positive influence on brand evangelism, an emotion-focused proselytizing behavior based on which consumers try to convince others to use their favorite brands (Mansoor & Paul, 2022). This is because the pleasure associated with brand happiness motivates consumers to share the brand information with others and strongly recommend the brand (Schnebelen & Bruhn, 2018). See the measure of brand happiness and brand evangelism in Table 10.2.

Table 10.2 Measure of Brand Happiness and Brand Evangelism

Brand Happiness (Mansoor & Paul, 2022 adapted from Schnebelen & Bruhn, 2018)

- I feel glad buying/using this brand
- I feel cheerful buying/using this brand.
- I feel joyful buying/using this brand.
- Buying/using this brand makes me feel lively.
- Buying/using this brand makes me feel peppy.
- Buying/using this brand makes me feel vigorous.
- Buying/using this brand makes me feel proud.
- Buying/using this brand makes me feel superior.
- Buying/using this brand makes me feel worthy.
- Buying/using this brand makes me feel relaxed.
- I feel myself at ease buying/using this brand.
- Buying/using this brand makes me feel comfortable.

Brand evangelism (Mansoor & Paul, 2022 adapted from Matzler et al., 2007).

- I have proselytized several of my friends to this brand.
- I try to convince as many people as possible to buy this brand.
- I feel the need to tell everybody that this is the most appealing brand.

Response scale: (1 = strongly disagree; 7 = strongly agree)

Source: Schnebelen and Bruhn (2018), Matzler et al. (2007), Mansoor and Paul (2022)

Brand Trust

People's feelings of happiness foster interpersonal trust. Individuals who experience happiness are likely to think about other people in a more positive light and perceive other people as more trustworthy (e.g., Tov & Diener, 2009). As a result, happy individuals are not only more trusting than unhappy consumers, but they are also trusted more by others (e.g., Dunn & Schweitzer, 2005).

The *affect-as-information model* suggests that people often misattribute their mood to the judgment at hand. Specifically, Schwarz and Clore (1988) have argued that when people make evaluative judgments, they unconsciously ask themselves, "How do I feel about (the judgment)?" In responding to this question, a person may use the valence of his or her unrelated feelings to inform the judgment. Thus, trust judgments of unfamiliar trustees (e.g., acquaintances) are frequently influenced by the affect-as-information heuristic. That is, positive mood increases positive thoughts, which may lead to more favorable evaluations of others. In an experimental study, Dunn and Schweitzer (2005) found that participants in the happy condition were significantly more trusting than participants in the angry condition and significantly more trusting than participants in the sad condition.

Brand trust is defined as the willingness to rely on a brand, based on beliefs about that brand, despite the risk or uncertainty associated with that brand (Chaudhuri & Holbrook, 2001; Delgado-Ballester et al., 2003). Brand trust is composed of cognitive beliefs as well as affective perceptions about the brand. Cognitive brand trust beliefs include expectations of brand reliability, consistency, competence, and/or predictability of performance across all products sold under that brand (Chaudhuri & Holbrook, 2001; Delgado-Ballester et al., 2003). The affective or emotional elements that can lead to brand trust include expectations of brand integrity, honesty, and/or benevolence, which encompass expectations that the brand will act in the consumers' best interest in mind across all products sold under that brand (Delgado-Ballester et al., 2003).

Research suggests that there is a positive association between brand happiness and brand trust. This association can be explained as follows. First, brand happiness facilitates positive evaluations of the brand. Brand happiness facilitates access to positive materials in memory and leads to more positive evaluations of neutral items (Isen et al., 1978; Teasdale & Fogarty, 1979). Thus, consumers who are high on brand happiness are likely to have cognitive brand trust (e.g., positive expectations about brand reliability, consistency, competence, and/or predictability of the brand). Second, brand happiness represents a consumer's emotional fulfillment with a brand (Schnebelen & Bruhn, 2018); as such, brand happiness is likely to spill over to brand trust through affect transfer. That is, consumers high on brand happiness are also likely to hold affective brand trust (e.g., positive expectations about brand integrity, honesty, and/or benevolence) through affect transfer). As such, brand-induced happiness leads consumers to trust and advocate the brand to others (Schnebelen & Bruhn, 2018). See measures of brand happiness and trust in Table 10.3.

Table 10.3 Brand happiness and brand trust

Incidental Emotion (Feelings of Happiness) (Dunn & Schweitzer, 2005)
The emotion induction exercise asked participants to first "briefly describe three to five things that make you most [angry/sad/happy]." The following page asked participants to "describe in detail the one situation that has made you the most [angry/sad/happy] you have been in your life and describe it such that a person reading the description would become [angry/sad/happy] just from hearing about the situation."
Interpersonal trust (Dunn & Schweitzer, 2005)
Participants identified a specific trustee (e.g., coworker or acquaintance) and responded to the trustworthiness of that specific trustee.

- I would give ___ an important letter to mail after s/he mentions that s/he is stopping by the post office today.
- If ___ promised to copy a presentation for me, s/he would follow through.
- If ___ and I decided to meet for coffee, I would be certain s/he would be there.
- I would expect ___ to tell me the truth if I asked him/her for feedback on an idea related to my job.
- If ___ was late for a meeting, I would guess there was a good reason for the delay.
- ___ would never intentionally misrepresent my point of view to others.
- I would ___ expect to pay me back if I loaned him/her $40.
- If ___ laughed unexpectedly at something I did or said, I would know s/he was not being unkind.
- If ___ gave me a compliment on my haircut, I would believe s/he meant what was said.
- If ___ borrowed something of value and returned it broken, s/he would offer to pay for the repairs.

Response scale: (1 = not at all likely. to 7 = very likely)

Brand Trust (Chaudhuri & Holbrook, 2001; Delgado-Ballester et al., 2003).

- I trust the brand
- I rely on the brand
- The brand is trustworthy
- The brand is safe
- The brand is honest

Response scale: (1 = not at all likely. to 7 = very likely).

Source: Dunn and Schweitzer (2005); Chaudhuri and Holbrook (2001); Delgado-Ballester et al. (2003)

Altruistic Behavior

Generally, happiness fosters *altruistic behaviors* (for a review, see Lyubomirsky et al., 2005). Individuals who score high on overall happiness report a relatively greater interest in helping people, a tendency to act in a prosocial or cooperative manner (e.g., enjoying sharing or helping others), and intentions to perform specific altruistic, courteous, or conscientious behaviors at work (Lyubomirsky et al., 2005).

Through two experiments, Aknin et al. (2012) explored whether recalling a previous act of prosocial spending leads to an increase in happiness, and whether higher levels of happiness, in turn, lead consumers to want to spend on others again shortly (Aknin et al., 2012; Dunn et al., 2008).

The first experiment was conducted to examine whether recalling a previous act of prosocial spending leads to an increase in happiness. Participants were asked to recall and describe in as much detail as possible the last time they spent either $20 or $100 on either themselves or for someone else (pro-social spending). After describing this memory, participants reported their happiness on the Subjective Happiness Scale (Lyubomirsky & Lepper, 1999). The results indicate that consumers felt happier when they thought about a time when they had spent money on others rather than themselves, and this effect was consistent across smaller ($20) and larger ($100) purchases. The results indicate that consumers' prosocial spending leads to higher levels of happiness because it fosters positive social relations.

The second experiment was conducted to examine whether higher levels of happiness lead people to want to spend on others again in the near future. Experiment participants were told they could spend the windfall money on personal spending (e.g., a bill, expense, or gift for themselves) or prosocial spending (e.g., a gift for someone else or donation to charity). The results indicate that consumers who felt happier after the recollection task were more likely to choose to engage in prosocial spending in the future.

In the context of the consumption of consumer goods or services, we posit that consumption happiness is positively associated with consumers' altruistic behavior. Evidence suggests that a brand's corporate social responsibility is positively associated with consumption happiness related to the brand because consumption of the brand serves to induce perceptions of doing good (Schellong et al., 2019). In a similar vein, research has shown that consumption of fair-trade products is positively associated with consumer happiness (Hwang & Kim, 2018). The general principle is that as overall happiness increases, intention to engage in helping and prosocial behavior also increases (Lyubomirsky et al., 2005). If so, one can argue that consumption happiness from a brand motivates consumers to engage in altruistic spending to enhance their positive self-image and gain social approval from significant others.

Positive Self-Image

In general, happy individuals tend to perceive themselves more positively than unhappy individuals (e.g., DeNeve & Cooper, 1998; Dunning et al., 1995; Steel et al., 2008). Studies found that general happiness and positive self-image are highly correlated, especially in countries with an individualistic culture. This may be due to the possibility that positive self-image tends to make a significant contribution to general happiness (e.g., Baumeister et al., 2003; Diener & Diener, 1995; Lyubomirsky et al., 2006).

In the context of consumption happiness, one can argue that consumption happiness related to a particular consumer good or service is positively associated with *positive self-image*. This may occur for the following reasons. First, positive self-image from brand use contributes to consumption happiness. *Conspicuous consumption theory* supports the notion that the usage of brands conspicuously is positively associated with consumption happiness (e.g., Perez-Truglia, 2013). In an empirical survey on the use of mass prestige products, Kumar et al. (2021) found that the use of prestige brands (e.g., iPhone) is positively associated with feelings of happiness from the brand. Consumption happiness from a good or service is positively associated with a *positive self-image* because product use provides experiences that help consumers stay true to their desired identity (Arnould & Thompson, 2005). Second, happy consumption experiences serve to reinforce consumers' positive self-concept through the satisfaction of self-related needs (i.e., needs related to self-confirmation, self-enhancement, and belonging. In other words, satisfaction with self-related needs reinforces a positive self-concept and boosts self-esteem (Bruhn & Schnebelen, 2017).

Satisfaction with Consumer Life

Consumption happiness from goods and services tends to contribute to consumer happiness (i.e., happiness in consumer life). According to the *bottom-up theory of subjective wellbeing* (Lyubomirsky, 2001; Seligman et al., 2005; Sin & Lyubomirsky, 2009), a person's domain-specific experiences serve as a source of life domain satisfaction. Frequent experiences of consumption happiness in the consumer life domain tend to aggregate and spill over into the consumer life domain, thus contributing to satisfaction with consumer life, which in turn is likely to influence overall happiness. Specifically, consumer happiness is cumulative, long-term happiness in the life domain, and housing marketplace affective experiences. In other words, consumer happiness is significantly influenced by a host of cumulative short-term consumption happiness—a host of cumulative consumption experiences, including shopping, material possession, and experiences over time.

Empirical studies found that need satisfaction with automobiles (Sirgy et al., 2006) and need satisfaction with housing (Grzeskowiak et al., 2006) contribute to happiness in consumer life. Evidence also suggests that frequent consumption of hedonic products vertically spillover to overall wellbeing through satisfaction in related life domains (Zhong & Mitchell, 2010). Another example of study finding is positive travel experiences spills over to various life domains (e.g., satisfaction with leisure life, social life, family life), which in turn contribute to overall life satisfaction (Neal et al., 1999; Sirgy et al., 2011).

Summary and Conclusion

Table 10.4 summarizes much of the research discussed in this chapter. As shown in the table, the outcomes of consumption happiness can play an important role at both the individual, organizational, and societal levels. At the individual level, consumption happiness contributes to overall happiness through increased satisfaction in the

Table 10.4 Outcomes of consumption happiness

The effect of consumption happiness on:	Details
Positive brand evaluations	Customers who feel happier evaluate service quality more positively than do less happy customers. This is because feelings of happiness tend to bias information processing, evaluation, and behaviors in a consistent manner.
Customer loyalty	Individuals high on consumption happiness are likely to be high on brand loyalty, high on willingness to pay, and high on intention to engage in positive word-of-mouth communications. Why? First, consumption happiness related to a brand generates a desire to re-experience it. Second, consumers who have experienced happiness about a specific brand are likely to hold a positive attitude towards the brand through affect transfer.
Brand trust	There is a positive association between brand happiness and brand trust. Why? Brand happiness facilitates access to positive events in memory which in turn leads to more positive evaluations of neutral items. Thus, consumers high on brand happiness are likely to trust the brand through positive expectations about the brand reliability, consistency, and competence. Furthermore, brand happiness may reflect consumers' emotional fulfillment with a brand, which in turn contributes to brand trust through affect transfer (through positive expectations about brand integrity, honesty, and benevolence).
Altruistic behaviors (e.g., pro-social spending)	Consumption happiness and consumers' altruistic behavior (e.g., pro-social spending) are positively related. Why? Consumers' prosocial spending leads to increased happiness because it fosters positive social relations. Consumers feel happier when recalling events involving prosocial spending. Consumers high on consumption happiness have a great interest in helping people.
Positive self-image	Consumption happiness related to a good or service is positively associated with positive self-image. Why? The use of a prestige brand (e.g., iPhone) is positively associated with feelings of happiness from the brand. Happy consumption experiences serve to reinforce consumers' positive self-concept.
Satisfaction in the consumer life domain	Frequent satisfying consumption experiences spill over to happiness in the consumer life domain. Why? Consumption serves to satisfy human needs (e.g., need satisfaction with automobiles, housing, and travel), which in turn contributes to happiness in the consumer life domain.

consumer life domain, which in turn spills over to overall life satisfaction. At the organizational level, consumption happiness contributes significantly to positive brand evaluations, brand trust, and brand loyalty. At the societal level, consumption happiness contributes to altruistic behavior. All these outcomes are positive to the individual consumer, to organizations marketing consumer goods and services, and to society at large. These positive outcomes highlight the importance of consumption happiness an important social phenomenon worthy of study.

References

Abbe, A., Tkach, C., & Lyubomirsky, S. (2003). The art of living by dispositionally happy people. *Journal of Happiness Studies, 4*(4), 385–404.

Aknin, L. B., Dunn, E. W., & Norton, M. I. (2012). Happiness runs in a circular motion: Evidence for a positive feedback loop between prosocial spending and happiness. *Journal of Happiness Studies, 13*(2), 347–355.

Arnould, E. J., & Thompson, C. J. (2005). Consumer culture theory (CCT): Twenty years of research. *Journal of Consumer Research, 31*(4), 868–882.

Baumeister, R. F., Campbell, J. D., Krueger, J. I., & Vohs, K. D. (2003). Does high self-esteem cause better performance, interpersonal success, happiness, or healthier lifestyles? *Psychological Science in the Public Interest, 4*(1), 1–44.

Bruhn, M., & Schnebelen, S. (2017). Integrated marketing communication—From an instrumental to a customer-centric perspective. *European Journal of Marketing, 51*(3), 464–489.

Cunningham, M. R. (1988). Does happiness mean friendliness? Induced mood and heterosexual self-disclosure. *Personality and Social Psychology Bulletin, 14*(2), 283–297.

Chaudhuri, A., & Holbrook, M. B. (2001). The chain of effects from brand trust and brand affect to brand performance: The role of brand loyalty. *Journal of Marketing, 65*(2), 81–93.

Dagger, T. S., Sweeney, J. C., & Johnson, L. W. (2007). A hierarchical model of health service quality: Scale development and investigation of an integrated model. *Journal of Service Research, 10*(2), 123–142.

Delgado-Ballester, E., Munuera-Aleman, J. L., & Yague-Guillen, M. J. (2003). Development and validation of a brand trust scale. *International Journal of Market Research, 45*(1), 35–54.

DeNeve, K. M., & Cooper, H. (1998). The happy personality: A meta-analysis of 137 personality traits and subjective well-being. *Psychological Bulletin, 124*(2), 197–229.

Diener, E., & Diener, M. (1995). Cross-cultural correlates of life satisfaction and self-esteem. *Journal of Personality and Social Psychology, 68*(4), 653–663.

Diener, E., & Seligman, M. E. P. (2004). Beyond money: Toward an economy of well-being. *Psychological Science in the Public Interest, 5*, 1–31. Republished in E. Diener (Ed.). (2009). *The science of well-being: The collected works of Ed Diener* (pp. 201–265). Dordrecht, The Netherlands: Springer.

Dunn, E. W., Aknin, L. B., & Norton, M. I. (2008). Spending money on others promotes happiness. *Science, 319*(5870), 1687–1688.

Dunn, J. R., & Schweitzer, M. E. (2005). Feeling and believing: The influence of emotion on trust. *Journal of Personality and Social Psychology, 88*(5), 736–748.

Dunning, D., Leuenberger, A., & Sherman, D. A. (1995). A new look at motivated inference: Are self-serving theories of success a product of motivational forces? *Journal of Personality and Social Psychology, 69*(1), 58–68.

Forgas, J. P., & Bower, G. H. (1987). Mood effects on person-perception judgments. *Journal of Personality and Social Psychology, 53*(1), 53–60.

Forgas, J. P., & Ciarrochi, J. (2001). On being happy and possessive: The interactive effects of mood and personality on consumer judgments. *Psychology & Marketing, 18*(3), 239–260.

Gong, T., & Yi, Y. (2018). The effect of service quality on customer satisfaction, loyalty, and happiness in five Asian countries. *Psychology & Marketing, 35*(6), 427–442.

Grzeskowiak, S., Sirgy, M. J., Lee, D. J., & Claiborne, C. B. (2006). Housing well-being: Developing and validating a measure. *Social Indicators Research, 79*(3), 503–541.

Hellén, K., & Sääksjärvi, M. (2011). Happiness as a predictor of service quality and commitment for utilitarian and hedonic services. *Psychology & Marketing, 28*(9), 934–957.

Hwang, K., & Kim, H. (2018). Are ethical consumers happy? Effects of ethical consumers' motivations based on empathy versus self-orientation on their happiness. *Journal of Business Ethics, 151*(2), 579–598.

Isen, A. M., Shalker, T. E., Clark, M., & Karp, L. (1978). Affect, accessibility of material in memory, and behavior: A cognitive loop? *Journal of Personality and Social Psychology, 36*(1), 1–12.

Kumar, A., Paul, J., & Starčević, S. (2021). Do brands make consumers happy? A masstige theory perspective. *Journal of Retailing and Consumer Services, 58*(January), 102318.

Lyubomirsky, S. (2001). Why are some people happier than others? The role of cognitive and motivational processes in well-being. *American Psychologist, 56*(3), 239–249.

Lyubomirsky, S., King, L., & Diener, E. (2005). The benefits of frequent positive affect: Does happiness lead to success? *Psychological Bulletin, 131*(6), 803–855.

Lyubomirsky, S., & Lepper, H. S. (1999). A measure of subjective happiness: Preliminary reliability and construct validation. *Social Indicators Research, 46*(2), 137–155.

Lyubomirsky, S., Tkach, C., & DiMatteo, M. R. (2006). What are the differences between happiness and self-esteem. *Social Indicators Research, 78*(3), 363–404.

Mansoor, M., & Paul, J. (2022). Mass prestige, brand happiness and brand evangelism among consumers. *Journal of Business Research, 144*, 484–496.

Matzler, K., Pichler, E. A., & Hemetsberger, A. (2007). Who is spreading the word? The positive influence of extraversion on consumer passion and brand evangelism. *Marketing Theory and Applications, 18*(1), 25–32.

Neal, J. D., Sirgy, M. J., & Uysal, M. (1999). The role of satisfaction with leisure travel/tourism services and experience in satisfaction with leisure life and overall life. *Journal of Business Research, 44*(3), 153–163.

Perez-Truglia, R. (2013). A test of the conspicuous–consumption model using subjective well-being data. *The Journal of Socio-Economics, 45*, 146–154.

Pham, M. T., Geuens, M., & De Pelsmacker, P. (2013). The influence of ad-evoked feelings on brand evaluations: Empirical generalizations from consumer responses to more than 1000 TV commercials. *International Journal of Research in Marketing, 30*(4), 383–394.

Schellong, M., Kraiczy, N. D., Malär, L., & Hack, A. (2019). Family firm brands, perceptions of doing good, and consumer happiness. *Entrepreneurship Theory and Practice, 43*(5), 921–946.

Schnebelen, S., & Bruhn, M. (2018). An appraisal framework of the determinants and consequences of brand happiness. *Psychology & Marketing, 35*(2), 101–119.

Schwarz, N., & Clore, G. L. (1988). How do I feel about it? Informative functions of affective states. In K. Fiedler & J. Forgas (Eds.), *Affect, cognition, and social behavior* (pp. 44–62). Hogrefe.

Seligman, M. E., Steen, T. A., Park, N., & Peterson, C. (2005). Positive psychology progress: Empirical validation of interventions. *American Psychologist, 60*(5), 410–421.

Sin, N. L., & Lyubomirsky, S. (2009). Enhancing well-being and alleviating depressive symptoms with positive psychology interventions: A practice-friendly meta-analysis. *Journal of Clinical Psychology, 65*(5), 467–487.

Sirgy, M. J., Kruger, P. S., Lee, D. J., & Yu, G. B. (2011). How does a travel trip affect tourists' life satisfaction? *Journal of Travel Research, 50*(3), 261–275.

Sirgy, M. J., Lee, D. J., & Kressmann, F. (2006). A need-based measure of consumer wellbeing (CWB) in relation to personal transportation: Nomological validation. *Social Indicators Research, 79*(2), 337–367.

Steel, P., Schnnidt, J., & Shultz, J. (2008). Refining the relationship between personality and subjective well-being. *Psychological Bulletin, 134*(1), 138–161.

Teasdale, J. D., & Fogarty, S. J. (1979). Differential effects of induced mood on retrieval of pleasant and unpleasant events from episodic memory. *Journal of Abnormal Psychology, 88*(3), 248–257.

Tov, W., & Diener, E. (2009). The well-being of nations: Linking together trust, cooperation, and democracy. In E. Diener (Ed.), *The science of well-being: The collected works of Ed Diener* (pp. 155–173). Springer.

Zhong, J. Y., & Mitchell, V. W. (2010). A mechanism model of the effect of hedonic product consumption on well-being. *Journal of Consumer Psychology, 20*(2), 152–162.

Chapter 11
Antecedents of Consumption Happiness

Simplicity makes me happy.

—Alicia Keys (https://declutterthemind.com/blog/happiness-quotes/)

Factors Influencing Consumption Happiness

The research on the antecedents of consumption happiness suggests that there are several prominent factors that play a significant role: perceived value, perceived quality, intrinsically enjoyable and meaningful experiential benefits, satisfaction from goods and services that fit well with personal values, a positive self, and social satisfaction.

Perceived Value

The perceived value of a product is positively correlated with consumption happiness, given product use. Why? First, the perceived value of a product leads consumers to feel that they obtained what they want, which in turn induces consumption happiness (Varey, 2010). Goals achieved through the consumption of a consumer good or service generate positive affect, thereby positively influencing consumption happiness.

Second, perceived value contributes to consumption happiness by allowing consumers to satisfy of a set of basic needs (benefits related to safety, health, economic, sensory, escape, and sensation) and growth needs (symbolic, aesthetic, moral, mastery, relatedness, and distinctiveness) (Sirgy et al., 2017). For example, according to the *benefit theory of leisure wellbeing* (Sirgy et al., 2017) consumption happiness from a leisure experience is increased when the leisure experience provides consumers with benefits related to basic needs and growth needs. For example, benefits of basic needs in a racquetball game experience include benefits related to safety

D.-J. Lee, M. J. Sirgy, *Happiness in the Marketplace*, Social Indicators Research Series 64, https://doi.org/10.1007/978-3-032-04443-3_11

(e.g., safety measures are taken such wearing of protective eyewear), health (e.g., the game enhances cardio-vascular health and helps with weight control), economics (e.g., the service fee is affordable), sensory (e.g., after the game the patrons enjoy a soothing massage followed by a hot shower and a delicious snack), escape (e.g., the game is scheduled mid-day to allow the patrons to temporarily escape the stress of their job), and/or sensation/stimulation (e.g., the game allows the patrons to experience a high level of sensation/stimulation perhaps by matching players with competitors of equal skill level. Benefits of growth needs in a racquetball game experience include benefits related to the self (e.g., the patrons can identify with one another, perhaps in terms of age, gender, and occupational status), aesthetics (e.g., the racquetball courts are aesthetically pleasing), morality (e.g., the game is sponsored by a charity organization), mastery (e.g., a racquetball mentor oversees the game to provide tips and guidance to foster performance excellence), relatedness (e.g., the game is offered through a social club to allow players to socialize before and after the game), and/or distinctiveness (e.g., each play is encouraged to develop his or her winning strategies and to share this knowledge with selected others) (Sirgy et al., 2017).

Third, consumption happiness is high when consumers experience various benefits from the use of a consumer good or service. These benefits include functional benefits (high quality and monetary value), emotional benefits (e.g., positive affect), and social benefits (enhancement of social self-concept) (Sheth et al., 1991; Sweeney & Soutar, 2001). Research has shown that consumers' perception of various benefits in using the product is positively associated with consumption happiness. Examples of benefits in internet shopping include convenience shopping, comparison shopping, finding an offer that matches needs, finding rare and novel items, and being able to examine the product in virtual reality (Sirgy et al., 2006). Research has shown that consumption happiness is positively related to perceived product benefits (Sirgy et al., 2006, 2008) and leisure benefits (Sirgy et al., 2011). Concerning shopping, El Hedhli et al. (2016) provided evidence suggesting that shopping happiness is largely driven by perceived hedonic value of the shopping mall more than perceived utilitarian value.

Perceived Quality

The perceived quality of a consumer good or service is likely to contribute to consumption happiness (e.g., Dagger & Sweeney, 2006; De Leire & Kalil, 2010; De Keyser & Lariviere, 2014; Loewenstein & Prelec, 1993; Weingarten et al., 2023). Research found that quality of service encounters enhances consumption happiness (Dagger & Sweeney, 2006; De Keyser & Lariviere, 2014; Gong & Yi, 2018; Sweeney et al., 2015). High-quality products provide consumers with strong product benefits, which serve to meet consumption needs. Satisfying consumption needs in turn serves to boost consumption happiness.

Moderators? Yes, consumption happiness is high when consumers experience high-quality goods and services under the following conditions. First, consumption happiness is likely to be high when a high-quality product serves to satisfy a variety of consumption needs. For example, consumption happiness is high when high-quality goods and services can boost consumer happiness by reducing material difficulties, by increasing brand prestige, or by strengthening social relations (De Leire & Kalil, 2010).

Second, consumption happiness is high when the products have high material qualities and high experience qualities (Schmitt et al., 2015). Both tangible material qualities and experiential service qualities positively contribute to consumption happiness (Weingarten et al., 2023). In a study by Weingarten et al. (2023), respondents were asked to recall four recent purchases that increased their happiness. They then were asked to rate experiential quality of each purchase they made (e.g., To what extent is each purchase list an experiential purchase: 1 = not at all, 7 = very much) and material quality of each purchase they made (e.g., To what extent is each purchase list a material purchase: 1 = not at all, 7 = very much). Study findings indicate that experiential service qualities have stronger effects on consumption happiness than material product qualities, and that tangible material qualities and experiential service qualities positively contribute to consumption happiness.

Third, consumption happiness is high when the high-quality product provides consumers with progressively increasing quality of experiences, compared with a stable or declining quality of experiences (Loewenstein & Prelec, 1993). Increasingly high quality can help overcome hedonic adaptation and better meet consumer expectations. In an experiment by Loewenstein and Prelec (1993), respondents were first asked to express their restaurant preferences (a fancy French restaurant vs. a local Greek restaurant). The majority of respondents (86%) expressed their preference for a French restaurant over a Greek restaurant. Of most respondents who preferred the fancy French dinner, 80% preferred a more immediate French dinner over a more delayed French dinner. However, when the French dinner was put into a sequence with the Greek dinner, giving subjects the option of having Greek and then French, or French and then Greek, most respondents (57%) preferred to defer the French dinner. The results indicate that when the sequence context is highlighted (e.g., having both dinners in sequence), consumers prefer options that provide improved satisfaction over time. In a similar study, Ross and Simonson (1991) presented subjects with a series of hypothetical choices between sequences that ended with a loss (e.g., win \$85, then lose \$15) or a gain (lose \$15, then win \$85). Subjects overwhelmingly preferred sequences that ended with a gain. When a series of services is presented to customers, consumption happiness was found to be high when consumers experience progressively increasing service quality. This is because progressively increasing service quality better meets increased consumer expectations, reduces hedonic adaptations, and provides consumers with feelings of gain.

Intrinsically Enjoyable and Meaningful Experiential Benefits

Consumption happiness can be increased when consumers can derive intrinsically enjoyable and meaningful experiential benefits from the products they consume. Why? Consumption happiness is high when consumers choose products that provide intrinsically enjoyable experiential benefits (e.g., good picture quality and pleasant music) (Carter & Gilovich, 2010; Hsee et al., 2009; Tu & Hsee, 2016). Intrinsically enjoyable experiential benefits provide consumers with positive affect and are less subject to hedonic adaptation or social comparison (Hsee et al., 2009; Tu & Hsee, 2016).

Relatedly, consumption happiness can be increased when consumers experience personally meaningful marketplace events. Personally meaningful experiences are experiences that provide individuals with satisfaction with basic psychological needs (autonomy, competence, and belongingness) that contribute to consumption happiness (Eakman, 2013; Hooker et al., 2020). Satisfaction of basic psychological needs is inherently rewarding and likely to serve to enhance consumer happiness (Baumeister & Leary, 1995; Deci & Ryan, 2000; Kasser & Ryan, 1996).

Moderator effects? Yes, there are several. Consumption happiness from experiences can be amplified under the following conditions. The effects of experiential benefits on consumption happiness is especially high (1) when the outcome of experiential purchase is positive (Nicolao et al., 2009), (2) when experience facilitates involvement of others (Caprariello & Reis, 2013; Van Boven et al., 2010; Van Boven & Gilovich, 2003), (3) when consumers do not have financial constraints with the experiential purchase (Spiller, 2011; Tully et al., 2015), and (4) when consumer experiences are closely related to a positive self-concept (Carter & Gilovich, 2012; Thomas & Millar, 2013; Van Boven & Gilovich, 2003), and (5) when consumers have low materialism (Millar & Thomas, 2009; Nicolao et al., 2009).

First, the effect of consumption happiness is high when the experiential outcome is positive (Nicolao et al., 2009). In a between-subjects experiment by Nicolao et al. (2009), respondents were asked to recall a personal purchase of $300 (experiential or material) and purchase outcome (positive or negative). Then they responded to the scale of consumption happiness (Van Boven & Gilovich, 2003). The consumption happiness items include "When you think about this purchase, how happy does it make you?" (1 = not happy; 7 = very happy), "How much does this purchase contribute to your happiness in life?" (1 = not at all; 7 = very much), "To what extent do you think the money spent on this purchase would have been better spent on something else—some other type of purchase that would have made you happier?" (1 = not at all; 7 = very much). The results indicate that experiential purchases induced significantly more reported happiness than did material purchases. If the purchase did not turn out positively, however, the effect did not hold. That is, there was no significant difference in happiness between experiential and material purchases. Experiential advantage over material possession is held only when the purchase outcome is positive.

Second, the effect of consumption happiness from experiences is high when the experience facilitates the involvement of others (Caprariello & Reis, 2013; Van Boven et al., 2010; Van Boven & Gilovich, 2003). Experience with others provides consumers with social satisfaction, and it is the social aspect of these experiences that provides greater happiness relative to material goods. Increases in social interactions are associated with increases in happiness. In a representative panel study by Caprariello and Reis (2013), 1424 respondents were given definitions of material, solitary, and social purchases, asked to think of a time that they spent money on each kind, reported how happy each of the purchases made them on a scale from 1 (neutral) to 5 (exceptionally happy), and ranked the three purchases in terms of happiness. The results indicate that social experiences were rated as making consumers the happiest, material purchases the next happiest, and solitary experiences the least happy. On average, social experiential purchases were ranked significantly higher than material purchases and solitary experiences.

Third, the effect of consumption happiness from experiences is high when consumers are not financially constrained with the experiential purchase (Spiller, 2011; Tully et al., 2015). The effect of consumption happiness from material goods is high when consumers are financially constrained by the material purchase. This is because feelings related to financial constraint increase consumers' concern about the lasting utility of their purchases, which in turn increases their preference for material goods over experiences. Consumers who were asked to consider their financial constraints were more likely to prefer material goods, even when the intangible long-term benefits of experiences were made explicit. In other words, the more consumers considered their financial constraints, the more likely they were to prefer the material good over the experience. This relationship was mediated by an increased concern about the longevity of their purchase.

Fourth, the effect of consumption happiness from experiences is high when consumer experiences are closely related to a positive self-concept (Carter & Gilovich, 2012; Thomas & Millar, 2013; Van Boven & Gilovich, 2003). Experiential purchases are more central to positive self-identity than material purchases because a large part of one's self-concept is made-up of experiences. When consumers' experiences are closely related to their self-concept, satisfaction from the experiences are likely to result in positive self-esteem, which is positively associated with consumption happiness. In an experiment by Thomas and Millar (2013), participants were asked to recall their most recent material purchase for more than \$100 or experiential purchase for more than \$100. Then participants were asked to indicate how happy the purchase made them feel on a nine–point scale with endpoints of 1 (not happy) and 9 (very happy). In addition, participants were asked about the impact of the purchase on self (e.g., how much the purchase contributed to their self-concept, how meaningful the purchase was to them, and if the purchase made them feel more positive about themselves). The study results indicate that the impact on self mediates the relationship between purchase type and consumption happiness. Thus, one can argue that the effect of consumption happiness from experiences is high when consumer experiences are closely related to a positive self-concept.

Fifth, the effect of consumption happiness is high when consumers are low on materialism (Millar & Thomas, 2009; Nicolao et al., 2009). At a low level of materialism, positive experiences led to higher consumption happiness than material possessions, but only for the positive experiences. However, for individuals who were rated high on materialism, experiential and material purchases did not differentially affect consumption happiness regardless of the outcome of the purchase. Experiential and material purchases were not different in consumption happiness because respondents with high materialism tend to be highly involved with their material possessions (Richins, 1994).

Satisfaction from Products That Fit Well with Personal Values

Consumption happiness can be increased when consumers obtain satisfaction from products that fit well with their personal values.

Consumption happiness is high when consumers have values that enhance consumption happiness and when consumers obtain satisfaction from products that fit with their personal values. This is because the degree of spillover from positive experiences to consumption happiness is high when the positive experience is valued by consumers (Oishi et al., 1999). In contrast, when the delivered experience is at odds with the customer's closely held beliefs and values, the mismatch creates cognitive dissonance, which detracts from consumption happiness.

Personal values are desirable goals that can be ordered by importance (Rokeach & Regan, 1980; Schwartz, 2012, 2015). Schwartz (2012) suggested ten personal values (universalism, benevolence, tradition, conformity, security, power, achievement, hedonism, stimulation, self-direction), which are later grouped into four higher-order values (self-enhancement, self-transcendence, conservation, and openness to change). Personal values guide one's intentional activities and provide means of altering one's happiness level (Lyubomirsky et al., 2005). The relationship between consumer values and consumption happiness can also be examined through the following perspective. Consumers' *values and lifestyles* (*VALS*) are related to the availability of resources and linked to consumers' needs and spending patterns (Kahle et al., 1986). The VALS model posits that consumption happiness can be enhanced when consumers engage in consumption behaviors that fit well with their consumption values.

Consumption happiness is effectively enhanced when consumers obtain satisfaction from products that fit well with their consumption values. When the delivered experience is at odds with the customer's closely held beliefs and values, the mismatch creates cognitive dissonance and reduced happiness. When there is a fit between consumers' positive experiences and consumption values (e.g., positive experiences are valued by consumers), consumers are likely to think the positive experiences are intrinsically satisfying and place high importance on positive experiences.

Evidence also suggests that personal values moderate the relationship between consumption behavior and consumption happiness. Consider the following evidence. First, the effect of pro-social spending on consumption happiness is moderated by consumers' self-transcendence value (Hill & Howell, 2014). Self-transcendence values (e.g., social justice, protecting the environment, broad-mindedness) represent a concern for people and entities outside of the individual, while self-enhancement values (e.g., social status, ambition, social influence) represent a tendency toward promotion of the self within the societal hierarchy (cf. Schwartz, 1994). Because pro-social spending necessarily entails a contribution to others, the effect of pro-social spending on consumption happiness is greater for those consumers with self-transcendence values (e.g., concern for persons and entities outside of the individual) (Hill & Howell, 2014). Second, spending more on others and ethical consumption does not increase consumption happiness for those whose values do not emphasize a concern for others. Third, the positive effect of consumer experiences on consumption happiness is high when consumer materialism is low. That is, positive consumer experiences can effectively be translated into consumption happiness when dealing with consumers who are less materialistic (Millar & Thomas, 2009). For consumers with high levels of materialism, experiential and material purchases did not differentially affect consumption happiness (Nicolao et al., 2009).

A Positive Self

Consumption happiness is high when the consumption experience serves to boost a positive self-concept. This may be the case for the following reasons. Consumption happiness is high when product ownership contributes to a positive self-concept (Lyubomirsky et al., 2006). Specifically, ownership of self-congruent products contributes to consumption happiness by reducing consumers' discrepancies with their ideal self (Michalos, 1985; Higgins et al., 1997), matching the product user image with ideal self-image (Sirgy, 1982), enhancing self-esteem (Diener, 1984), and providing positive evaluations about self (Campbell et al., 1976).

Much research has provided evidence showing that happiness and *self-esteem* are highly correlated (e.g., Dunn et al., 2011; Gilovich et al., 2015; Lyubomirsky et al., 2006; Van Boven & Gilovich, 2003). Self-esteem refers to a global feeling of self-worth or adequacy as a person, or generalized feelings of self-acceptance, goodness, and self-respect (Crocker & Major, 1989). That is, it is an individual's global positive or negative attitude toward oneself (Rosenberg, 1965). Individuals who feel good about themselves feel happy, and those consumers who lack self-worth and self-respect are generally unhappy (Diener & Diener, 1995; Lyubomirsky & Lepper, 1999; Lyubomirsky et al., 2006).

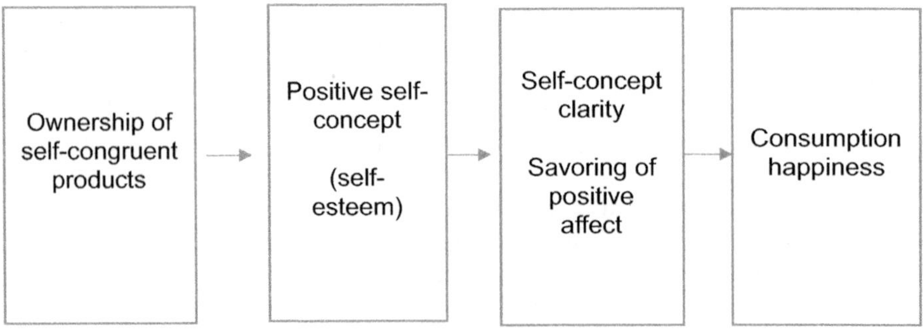

Fig. 11.1 Positive self-concept and consumption happiness

How does self-esteem contribute to happiness? First, high self-esteem consumers are likely to have high *self-concept clarity* (Campbell et al., 1996), which contributes to happiness. Self-concept clarity refers to the extent to which the contents of an individual's self-concept are clearly and confidently defined, internally consistent, and temporally stable (Campbell et al., 1996). Examples of self-concept clarity measurement items include "I seldom experience conflict between the different aspects of my personality," and "In general, I have a clear sense of who I am and what I am" (Campbell et al., 1996). Self-concept clarity plays a protective role against important life stressors because individuals with a clear self-concept may be less affected by and more able to cope with negative events (Lee-Flynn et al., 2011). High self-concept clarity is positively associated with high self-esteem (Campbell et al., 1996) and reduces negative affect (Lee-Flynn et al., 2011; Usborne & Taylor, 2010), which contributes to consumption happiness. Second, high self-esteem is associated with the *savoring* of positive affect and its amplification, which contributes to happiness. High self-esteem is associated with *affect regulation*. When people experience positive affect, those low in self-esteem are especially likely to dampen that affect, whereas those high in self-esteem are especially likely to savor it (Bryant, 1989; Wood et al., 2003).

In sum, the entire process of how ownership of self-congruent products influence consumption happiness is shown in Fig. 11.1. Specifically, ownership of self-congruent products leads to consumption happiness through positive self-concept, self-concept clarity, and savoring of positive affect.

Social Satisfaction

Consumption happiness is high when consumption experience facilitates positive social interactions and resultant satisfaction with others. Consumption happiness is high when consumers experience positive social interactions and satisfaction during their consumption. Why?

First, consumption happiness is high when consumption experience facilitates positive social interactions because positive social interactions provide consumers with satisfaction of the need for belonging. Research found that positive social relationships enhance happiness and help buffer stress and avert distress due to loneliness, anxiety, boredom, and loss of self-esteem (e.g., Argyle, 1987; Diener, 1984; Ryff, 1989; Myers & Diener, 1995). In the consumption context, consumer engagement with brand community provides customers with social benefits (e.g., interactive communications, social connectedness, and sense of belongingness) (Gummerus et al., 2012). For example, consumers who are actively engaged in the community of their favorite sports team are likely to enjoy the sports game and social interactions with other fans (Lianopoulos et al., 2020). Research has demonstrated that consumers' leisure experience with others provides satisfaction of relatedness needs, which in turn contributes to consumption happiness (De Leire & Kalil, 2010). Evidence also suggests that customer engagement in brand community exerts a significant positive effect on consumption happiness (Niedermeier et al., 2019). The results of a survey on consumers in an automobile brand community indicate that consumers' active social interactions with others increased consumer happiness.

Second, consumption happiness is high when consumption experience facilitates positive social interactions because consumers can experience positive affect during their social sharing (Jose et al., 2012). Using experience sampling methodology, Jose et al. (2012) found that momentary positive events were positively related to momentary savoring, and momentary savoring responses, in turn, were positively related to momentary happy mood.

Thus, it can be said that consumption happiness is high when consumption experience facilitates positive social interactions and resultant satisfaction with others.

Summary and Conclusion

Table 11.1 summarizes much of the discussion related to the antecedents of consumption happiness. As shown in the table, consumption happiness can be increased when the product is perceived to have high value, when the product is perceived to have high quality, when the marketplace event is experienced positively, when the marketplace experience is self-congruent, when the marketplace experience helps boost a positive self-image, and when the marketplace event is replete with social interaction resulting in increased satisfaction in social life.

Table 11.1 Factors influencing consumption happiness

Factor characteristics	Factors affecting consumption happiness.	Mediating mechanisms.
High perceived value	Consumption happiness is high when consumers experience high perceived value.	Goals achieved through the consumption of a product/service derive positive affect.
High perceived quality	Consumption happiness is high when consumers experience high-quality products and services.	High-quality products and services will provide consumers with high product benefits and satisfaction of consumption needs.
Positive experiences	Consumption happiness is high when consumers can derive intrinsically enjoyable and meaningful experiential benefits from the products and services they consume.	Intrinsically enjoyable experiential benefits lead to positive affect and are less subject to hedonic adaptation or social comparison. Personally meaningful experiences provide consumers with satisfaction with basic psychological needs (autonomy, competence, and belongingness).
Self congruent experiences	Consumption happiness is high when consumers get satisfaction from products and services that fit well with their personal values.	The degree of spillover from positive experiences to consumption happiness is high when the positive experiences are valued by consumers.
Positive self-image	Consumption happiness is high when the consumption experience facilitates a positive self-concept.	Ownership of self-congruent products contributes to consumption happiness by providing positive evaluations of self.
Social satisfaction	Consumption happiness is high when the consumption experience facilitates social satisfaction with others.	Sharing experience provides consumers with the satisfaction of belonging and social connectedness benefits.

References

Argyle, M. (1987). *The psychology of happiness*. Methuen and Co.

Baumeister, R. F., & Leary, M. R. (1995). The need to belong: Desire for interpersonal attachments as a fundamental human motivation. *Psychological Bulletin, 117*(3), 497–529.

Bryant, F. B. (1989). A four-factor model of perceived control: Avoiding, coping, obtaining, and savoring. *Journal of Personality, 57*(4), 773–797.

Campbell, A., Converse, P. E., & Rodgers, W. L. (1976). *The quality of American life: Perceptions, evaluations, and satisfactions*. Russell Sage.

Campbell, J. D., Trapnell, P. D., Heine, S. J., Katz, I. M., Lavallee, L. F., & Lehman, D. R. (1996). Self-concept clarity: Measurement, personality correlates, and cultural boundaries. *Journal of Personality and Social Psychology, 70*(1), 141–156.

Caprariello, P. A., & Reis, H. T. (2013). To do, to have, or to share? Valuing experiences over material possessions depends on the involvement of others. *Journal of Personality and Social Psychology, 104*(2), 199–215.

Carter, T. J., & Gilovich, T. (2010). The relative relativity of material and experiential purchases. *Journal of Personality and Social Psychology, 98*(1), 146–159.

Carter, T. J., & Gilovich, T. (2012). I am what I do, not what I have: The differential centrality of experiential and material purchases to the self. *Journal of Personality and Social Psychology, 102*(6), 1304–1317.
Crocker, J., & Major, B. (1989). Social stigma and self-esteem: The self-protective properties of stigma. *Psychological Review, 96*(4), 608–630.
Dagger, T. S., & Sweeney, J. C. (2006). The effect of service evaluations on behavioral intentions and quality of life. *Journal of Service Research, 9*(1), 3–18.
De Keyser, A., & Lariviere, B. (2014). How technical and functional service quality drive consumer happiness: Moderating influences of channel usage. *Journal of Service Management, 25*(1), 30–48.
De Leire, T., & Kalil, A. (2010). Does consumption buy happiness? Evidence from the United States. *International Review of Economics, 57*(2), 163–176.
Deci, E. L., & Ryan, R. M. (2000). The "what" and "why" of goal pursuits: Human needs and the self-determination of behavior. *Psychological Inquiry, 11*(4), 227–268.
Diener, E. (1984). Subjective well-being. *Psychological Bulletin, 95*(3), 542–575.
Diener, E., & Diener, M. (1995). Cross-cultural correlates of life satisfaction and self-esteem. *Journal of Personality and Social Psychology, 68*(4), 653–663.
Dunn, E. W., Gilbert, D. T., & Wilson, T. D. (2011). If money doesn't make you happy, then you probably aren't spending it right. *Journal of Consumer Psychology, 21*(2), 115–125.
Eakman, A. M. (2013). Relationships between meaningful activity, basic psychological needs, and meaning in life: Test of the meaningful activity and life meaning model. *OTJR: Occupation, Participation and Health, 33*(2), 100–109.
El Hedhli, K., Zourrig, H., & Chebat, J. C. (2016). Shopping well-being: Is it just a matter of pleasure or doing the task? The role of shopper's gender and self-congruity. *Journal of Retailing and Consumer Services, 31*(July), 1–13.
Gilovich, T., Kumar, A., & Jampol, L. (2015). A wonderful life: Experiential consumption and the pursuit of happiness. *Journal of Consumer Psychology, 25*(1), 152–165.
Gong, T., & Yi, Y. (2018). The effect of service quality on customer satisfaction, loyalty, and happiness in five Asian countries. *Psychology & Marketing, 35*(6), 427–442.
Gummerus, J., Liljander, V., Weman, E., & Pihlström, M. (2012). Customer engagement in a Facebook brand community. *Management Research Review, 35*(9), 857–877.
Higgins, E. T., Shah, J., & Friedman, R. (1997). Emotional response to goal attainment: Strength of regulatory focus as moderator. *Journal of Personality and Social Psychology, 72*(3), 515–525.
Hill, G., & Howell, R. T. (2014). Moderators and mediators of pro-social spending and well-being: The influence of values and psychological need satisfaction. *Personality and Individual Differences, 69*(October), 69–74.
Hooker, S. A., Masters, K. S., Vagnini, K. M., & Rush, C. L. (2020). Engaging in personally meaningful activities is associated with meaning salience and psychological well-being. *The Journal of Positive Psychology, 15*(6), 821–831.
Hsee, C. K., Yang, Y., Li, N., & Shen, L. (2009). Wealth, warmth, and well-being: Whether happiness is relative or absolute depends on whether it is about money, acquisition, or consumption. *Journal of Marketing Research, 46*(3), 396–409.
Jose, P. E., Lim, B. T., & Bryant, F. B. (2012). Does savoring increase happiness? A daily diary study. *The Journal of Positive Psychology, 7*(3), 176–187.
Kahle, L. R., Beatty, S. E., & Homer, P. (1986). Alternative measurement approaches to consumer values: The list of values (LOV) and values and life style (VALS). *Journal of Consumer Research, 13*(3), 405–409.
Kasser, T., & Ryan, R. M. (1996). Further examining the American dream: Differential correlates of intrinsic and extrinsic goals. *Personality and Social Psychology Bulletin, 22*(3), 280–287.
Lee-Flynn, S. C., Pomaki, G., DeLongis, A., Biesanz, J. C., & Puterman, E. (2011). Daily cognitive appraisals, daily affect, and long-term depressive symptoms: The role of self-esteem and self-concept clarity in the stress process. *Personality and Social Psychology Bulletin, 37*(2), 255–268.

Lianopoulos, Y., Theodorakis, N. D., Tsigilis, N., Gardikiotis, A., & Koustelios, A. (2020). Elevating self-esteem through sport team identification: A study about local and distant sport fans. *International Journal of Sports Marketing and Sponsorship, 21*(4), 695–718.
Loewenstein, G. F., & Prelec, D. (1993). Preferences for sequences of outcomes. *Psychological Review, 100*(1), 91–108.
Lyubomirsky, S., & Lepper, H. S. (1999). A measure of subjective happiness: Preliminary reliability and construct validation. *Social Indicators Research, 46*(2), 137–155.
Lyubomirsky, S., Sheldon, K. M., & Schkade, D. (2005). Pursuing happiness: The architecture of sustainable change. *Review of General Psychology, 9*(2), 111–131.
Lyubomirsky, S., Tkach, C., & DiMatteo, M. R. (2006). What are the differences between happiness and self-esteem. *Social Indicators Research, 78*(3), 363–404.
Michalos, A. C. (1985). Multiple discrepancies theory (MDT). *Social Indicators Research, 16*(4), 347–413.
Millar, M., & Thomas, R. (2009). Discretionary activity and happiness: The role of materialism. *Journal of Research in Personality, 43*(4), 699–702.
Myers, D. G., & Diener, E. (1995). Who is happy? *Psychological Science, 6*(1), 10–19.
Nicolao, L., Irwin, J. R., & Goodman, J. K. (2009). Happiness for sale: Do experiential purchases make consumers happier than material purchases? *Journal of Consumer Research, 36*(2), 188–198.
Niedermeier, A., Albrecht, L., & Jahn, B. (2019). "Happy together": Effects of brand community engagement on customer happiness. *Journal of Relationship Marketing, 18*(1), 54–76.
Oishi, S., Diener, E., Suh, E., & Lucas, R. E. (1999). Value as a moderator in subjective well-being. *Journal of Personality, 67*(1), 157–184.
Richins, M. L. (1994). Special possessions and the expression of material values. *Journal of Consumer Research, 21*(3), 522–533.
Rokeach, M., & Regan, J. F. (1980). The role of values in the counseling situation. *The Personnel and Guidance Journal, 58*(9), 576–582.
Rosenberg, M. (1965). *Society and the adolescent self-image*. Princeton University Press.
Ross, W. T., & Simonson, I. (1991). Evaluations of pairs of experiences: A preference for happy endings. *Journal of Behavioral Decision Making, 4*(4), 273–282.
Ryff, C. D. (1989). Happiness is everything, or is it? Explorations on the meaning of psychological well-being. *Journal of Personality and Social Psychology, 57*(6), 1069–1081.
Schmitt, B., Brakus, J. J., & Zarantonello, L. (2015). From experiential psychology to consumer experience. *Journal of Consumer Psychology, 25*(1), 166–171.
Schwartz, S. H. (1994). Are there universal aspects in the structure and contents of human values? *Journal of Social Issues, 50*(4), 19–45.
Schwartz, S. H. (2012). An overview of the Schwartz theory of basic values. *Online Readings in Psychology and Culture, 2*(1), Article 11.
Schwartz, B. (2015). *Why we work*. Simon and Schuster.
Sheth, J. N., Newman, B. I., & Gross, B. L. (1991). Why we buy what we buy: A theory of consumption values. *Journal of Business Research, 22*(2), 159–170.
Sirgy, M. J. (1982). Self-concept in consumer behavior: A critical review. *Journal of Consumer Research, 9*(3), 287–300.
Sirgy, M. J., Lee, D. J., & Bae, J. (2006). Developing a measure of internet well-being: Nomological (predictive) validation. *Social Indicators Research, 78*(2), 205–249.
Sirgy, M. J., Lee, D. J., Kamra, K., & Tidwell, J. (2008). What determines perceived quality-of-life impact of mobile phones? A model based on the consumption life cycle. *Applied Research in Quality of Life, 3*(4), 251–268.
Sirgy, M. J., Kruger, P. S., Lee, D. J., & Yu, G. B. (2011). How does a travel trip affect tourists' life satisfaction? *Journal of Travel Research, 50*(3), 261–275.
Sirgy, M. J., Uysal, M., & Kruger, S. (2017). Towards a benefits theory of leisure well-being. *Applied Research in Quality of Life, 12*(1), 205–228.

Spiller, S. A. (2011). Opportunity cost consideration. *Journal of Consumer Research, 38*(4), 595–610.

Sweeney, J. C., & Soutar, G. N. (2001). Consumer perceived value: The development of a multiple item scale. *Journal of Retailing, 77*(2), 203–220.

Sweeney, J. C., Danaher, T. S., & McColl-Kennedy, J. R. (2015). Customer effort in value cocreation activities: Improving quality of life and behavioral intentions of health care customers. *Journal of Service Research, 18*(3), 318–335.

Thomas, R., & Millar, M. (2013). The effects of material and experiential discretionary purchases on consumer happiness: Moderators and mediators. *The Journal of Psychology, 147*(4), 345–356.

Tu, Y., & Hsee, C. K. (2016). Consumer happiness derived from inherent preferences versus learned preferences. *Current Opinion in Psychology, 10*, 83–88.

Tully, S. M., Hershfield, H. E., & Meyvis, T. (2015). Seeking lasting enjoyment with limited money: Financial constraints increase preference for material goods over experiences. *Journal of Consumer Research, 42*(1), 59–75.

Usborne, E., & Taylor, D. M. (2010). The role of cultural identity clarity for self-concept clarity, self-esteem, and subjective well-being. *Personality and Social Psychology Bulletin, 36*(7), 883–897.

Van Boven, L., & Gilovich, T. (2003). To do or to have? That is the question. *Journal of Personality and Social Psychology, 85*(6), 1193–1202.

Van Boven, L., Campbell, M. C., & Gilovich, T. (2010). Stigmatizing materialism: On stereotypes and impressions of materialistic and experiential pursuits. *Personality and Social Psychology Bulletin, 36*(4), 551–563.

Varey, R. J. (2010). Marketing means and ends for a sustainable society: A welfare agenda for transformative change. *Journal of Macromarketing, 30*(2), 112–126.

Weingarten, E., Duke, K., Liu, W., Hamilton, R. W., Amir, O., Appel, G., et al. (2023). What makes people happy? Decoupling the experiential-material continuum. *Journal of Consumer Psychology, 33*(1), 97–106.

Wood, J. V., Heimpel, S. A., & Michela, J. L. (2003). Savoring versus dampening: Self-esteem differences in regulating positive affect. *Journal of Personality and Social Psychology, 85*(3), 566–580.

Part IV
How to Enhance Happiness in the Marketplace

In Part IV of the book, we will focus on research findings to make specific recommendations on how to enhance happiness in the marketplace. Chapter 12 will address interventions that can increase happiness in the marketplace, in general. The subsequent chapters focus on three contexts related to consumption happiness, namely happiness in a shopping context, happiness in the context of product ownership, and happiness in the context of marketplace experiences. These three contexts involving consumption happiness can be viewed as capturing different stages of the consumption life cycle. Acquisition, possession, and consumption. Specifically, happiness in a shopping context occurs during the acquisition stage, happiness in the context of product ownership occurs during the possession stage, and happiness in the context of marketplace experiences occurs during the consumption stage.

Chapter 12
How to Enhance Consumption Happiness

> *I am convinced that material things can contribute a lot to making one's life pleasant, but, basically, if you do not have very good friends and relatives who matter to you, life will be really empty and sad, and material things cease to be important.*
>
> *—David Rockefeller (https://www.brainyquote.com/quotes/david_rockefeller_253678?src=t_material_things)*

Enhancing Consumption Happiness

There are several guiding principles in consuming consumer goods and services that can effectively enhance consumption happiness. Specifically, based on the research evidence, consumption happiness can be increased by (1) increasing satisfaction in multiple life domains in consumption, (2) reducing hedonic adaptation in consumption, (3) refraining from comparative product evaluation, (4) evaluating products with low expectations, (5) spending more on experiences than material products, (6) increasing consumption spending on others, (7) increasing spending on time-saving products, (8) boosting a positive self-concept through consumption, and (9) increasing social interactions in consumption

Increase Satisfaction in Multiple Life Domains in Consumption

Consumption happiness can be increased when consumers take action in the marketplace to increase satisfaction from multiple life domains (i.e., the full spectrum of consumption needs). Consumption happiness is high when consumers derive needs for having, loving, and being (Allardt, 1973), needs for being, belonging, and becoming (Raphael et al., 1996), physical, social, self-actualization needs (Arndt,

D.-J. Lee, M. J. Sirgy, *Happiness in the Marketplace*, Social Indicators Research Series 64, https://doi.org/10.1007/978-3-032-04443-3_12

1981), basic psychological needs (autonomy, competency, and relatedness) (Ryan & Deci, 2000), the need for positive emotion, engagement, relationships, meaning, and accomplishment (Seligman, 2011). Regardless of the number of needs, theorists agree that the satisfaction of the full spectrum of human needs is related to wellbeing (e.g., Maslow, 1970; Omodei & Wearing, 1990; Lyubomirsky et al., 2006).

Let us focus on a prominent theory of motivation, namely, *self-determination theory*. This theory predicts that psychological wellbeing can be increased when three basic psychological needs are met. Those needs are autonomy, competence, and relatedness (Deci & Ryan, 2000; Deci et al., 2001). *Autonomy* refers to self-government or to the extent to which people feel self-directed in their actions. *Competence* entails the sense that one has control over desired outcomes and feels competent to deliver them. *Relatedness* refers to the need for human beings to belong, to feel connected, and to be understood by others. Research has shown that satisfaction of basic psychological needs is positively related to intrinsic motivation, psychological health, and wellbeing (Deci et al., 2001; Heppner et al., 2008; Howell & Hill, 2009; Patrick et al., 2007).

Let's consider research on consumption happiness more specifically. Evidence suggests that consumption happiness is high when consumers derive satisfaction of high- and low-order needs (El Hedhli et al., 2013). This is because consumers who buy and consume goods and services capable of satisfying the full spectrum of needs are more likely to feel good about themselves, which in turn translates into consumption happiness (Lyubomirsky et al., 2006). In simple terms, consumers can achieve satisfaction of multiple needs by engaging in a variety of positive marketplace experiences (Etkin & Mogilner, 2016).

Reduce Hedonic Adaptation in Consumption

Consumption happiness can be increased when consumers experience a low degree of hedonic adaptation or satiation in product consumption. Hedonic adaptation is the psychological process by which people become accustomed to a positive or negative stimulus, such that the emotional effects of that stimulus are attenuated over time (Frederick & Loewenstein, 1999). Under hedonic adaptation, better things become "less good" over time, and worse things become better. Research has shown that hedonic adaptation is faster in response to positive experiences than in response to negative experiences because negative information is weighted more heavily (Lyubomirsky, 2010).

Focusing on consumption happiness, research shows that a high degree of hedonic adaptation or satiation does not increase consumption happiness (Dunn et al., 2011; Gilovich et al., 2015; Nicolao et al., 2009). As such, hedonic adaptation from positive consumption experiences can be reduced through the following interventions. First, hedonic adaptation be reduced by separating the positive experiences (e.g., presenting two separate gains) (Thaler, 1985). Consumers can seek a variety of products and experiences and avoid repetition. By providing two separate benefits rather than one big benefit, hedonic adaptation can be reduced, and consumers can achieve increased levels of happiness. For example, hedonic adaptation is reduced by adding interruptions to the flow of consumption (Tu & Hsee, 2018). Adding a break time (e.g., half-time break during the show) during positive consumption experience reduces hedonic adaptation (Nelson & Meyvis, 2008) and satiation (Galak et al., 2013). Evidence also suggests that frequent consumption of low-cost hedonic products, rather than the infrequent consumption of high-cost products, relates positively to consumers' wellbeing (Zhong & Mitchell, 2010).

Second, consumers can reduce hedonic adaptation by slowing down the speed of consumption (Tu & Hsee, 2018). Hedonic adaptation is reduced by delaying actual consumption. In addition, delayed consumption (e.g., reservation long before the actual marketplace experience) can increase anticipated consumption happiness and reduce hedonic adaptation and satiation. This is because people can gain anticipated utility or savoring value by imagining positive experiences before the actual occurrence (Kahneman, 1999).

Third, consumers can reduce hedonic adaptation by spending more on a variety of experiences. Compared to material purchases, experiential purchases are subject to slower rates of hedonic adaptation (Nicolao et al., 2009) because experiences are more unique and harder to compare with forgone alternatives (Carter & Gilovich, 2010). In addition, consumers can reduce hedonic adaptation by choosing material products with limited availability. Limited availability slows hedonic adaptation and satiation because consumers' perception of limited availability triggers a focus more on the value of the product and less on the quantity consumed. This lack of attention to the quantity consumed subsequently reduces the rate of satiation (Sevilla & Redden, 2014).

Fourth, consumers can reduce hedonic adaptation by choosing products that are consistent with their identity. When consumers make associations between their self-concept and experienced goods, they may encounter more dissonance during satiation. Thus, hedonic adaptation from repeatedly consuming a product is likely to be diminished when that product is made consistent with a salient self-image (Chugani et al., 2015).

Fifth, consumers can reduce hedonic adaptation and satiation by choosing products that have sentimental value (e.g., association with a special person or special events such as gifts, commemorative goods). The sentimental value of objects is less likely to decline with time because consumers focus more on the emotional associations the product evokes and less on the functional qualities (Yang & Galak, 2015).

Refrain from Comparative Product Evaluations and Social Comparisons

Consumption happiness can be increased when consumers do not engage in *comparative product evaluation*. Why? First, when consumers engage in comparative evaluations with other alternatives, they are likely to experience negative affect such as regret (Rosenzweig & Gilovich, 2012), that detracts from consumption happiness.

Specifically, when consumers engage in comparative evaluations with other alternatives, their material purchase decisions are more likely to generate regrets of action (e.g., buyer's remorse). In contrast, their experiential purchase decisions are more likely to lead to regrets of inaction (e.g., missed opportunities) (Rosenzweig & Gilovich, 2012). Consumers tend to have action regrets for material goods because it is much easier to make direct comparisons between different possible material purchases than between different experiences. Consumers tend to have inaction regrets for experiences because opportunities for experiences are rare, and each experience is unique. However, when consumers engage in comparative evaluations with other alternatives (e.g., price comparison of a stereo), they are likely to experience negative affect, such as feelings of regret. To reiterate, when consumers do not engage in comparative evaluations and focus on the inherent quality of the products (e.g., sound quality of a stereo), they are likely to experience high consumption happiness (Hsee et al., 2009; Tu & Hsee, 2018).

Second, consumption happiness is high when consumers do not engage in frequent *social comparisons* with other consumers (Howell & Hill, 2009). In most cases, social comparisons related to marketplace-type events tend to produce negative affect, such as dissatisfaction or regret (Carter & Gilovich, 2010), which often results in negative evaluations of self. Research also suggests that consumers with eudaimonic consumption motive (e.g., those who seek meanings in the purchase) are less likely to engage in social comparisons (i.e., be less disturbed and have less diminished satisfaction due to price comparisons) (Yang et al., 2021).

Evaluate Products with Low Expectations

Consumption happiness can be increased when consumers do not have too high expectations in product evaluation. Some consumers have insatiable financial and material aspirations. They have ever-rising standards of what is enough and what is good enough, while what they already have is taken for granted. Why? First, financial aspirations (pursuit of money) hurt wellbeing. However, financial aspirations do not hurt wellbeing if financial aspirations are achieved. Yet consumers with high financial aspirations without much achievement are likely to suffer from their financial aspirations (Nickerson et al., 2003). Thus, consumers need to have achievable financial aspirations.

Second, consumption happiness decreases when consumers have unrealistically high material expectations (Sirgy, 1998). Consumers often overestimate the intensity and duration of an affective event as they fail to consider environmental conditions of their actual experience, hedonic adaptation, social comparisons, present bias, and others (Hsee & Hastie, 2006; Tu & Hsee, 2018). Thus, consumers need to have realistic expectations about material products and not have too high expectations.

Spend More on Experiences Than Material Products

Consumption happiness can be increased when consumers spend money on experiences (e.g., an event or series of events that consumers personally encounter or live through such as trip or movie watching) than on material things (e.g., a tangible object that consumers obtain and keep in your possession) (Van Boven & Gilovich, 2003). This is because experiential consumption is central to one's self-concept. It leads to inherent evaluations and facilitates social interactions.

Why? For several reasons. First, experiential consumption is more important than material consumption to one's identity. Experiences constitute a larger proportion of, and are more central to, one's identity. As the saying goes, we are what we do, not what we have (Carter & Gilovich, 2012). Consumers' experiential purchases contribute more to their sense of self, something they carry with them all the time.

Second, consumers are likely to derive more consumption happiness from experiential consumption than from material consumption. That is, although material goods may have physical longevity and can continue to be consumed over time, the momentary happiness one derives from using them is quite noticeably lower than that derived from experiential purchases (Kumar et al., 2020). In addition, consumers are less likely to engage in alternative or social comparisons after making experiential purchases than material purchases (Carter & Gilovich, 2010; Howell & Hill, 2009). This is because experiences are more inherently evaluable, making comparison unnecessary (Carter & Gilovich, 2010).

Third, consumers are likely to feel more satisfaction in social life from experiences because experiences are likely to involve social interactions and sharing (Caprariello & Reis, 2013; Van Boven et al., 2010). Experiential purchases do more to build social capital than material purchases. Shared experiences make consumers feel closer to others than shared material goods do. Consumers are more likely to talk to others about their experiences, and listeners get more enjoyment when they do (Kumar & Gilovich, 2015; Van Boven et al., 2010).

Experiential purchases tend to be more social and help consumers fulfill the basic psychological need for belonging. Thus, consumption happiness is high when consumers have a positive self-concept from the consumption, do not engage in alternative or social comparisons, and derive much social satisfaction from their consumption.

Empirical studies found that, compared to buying material possessions, purchasing experiences result in greater anticipatory, remembered, and experienced consumption happiness for all subcategories of experiential purchases (Kumar et al., 2020). While material purchase contributes to consumption happiness only up to a certain threshold, experiential purchase contributes to consumption happiness without clear upper bounds. Experiential purchases provide more remembered happiness and enduring satisfaction than material purchases (Gilovich et al., 2015). In addition, experiential purchases also provide more anticipatory consumption happiness in that waiting to consume an experience is more pleasurable than waiting to receive a material good (Kumar et al., 2014; Kumar & Gilovich, 2016).

Increase Consumption Spending on Others

Consumption happiness can be increased when consumers engage in spending for others. Research has shown that consumption happiness is higher when consumers engage in other-focused consumption activities (e.g., donation, social interactions, purchase for others) than in self-focused consumption activities (purchase for self) (Sääksjärvi et al., 2017). Through a nationally representative survey and a field study, Dunn et al. (2008) also demonstrated that spending money on other individuals has a greater impact on the happiness of individuals than spending money on oneself.

Research has also demonstrated that *prosocial spending* is likely to boost happiness under the following conditions. First, prosocial spending is likely to produce greater happiness when givers feel their *spending was volitional and not coerced* (Weinstein & Ryan, 2010; Lok & Dunn, 2020). A study by Weinstein and Ryan (2010) showed that consumers' prosocial spending has a greater impact on happiness when consumers were allowed to choose how much money they would like to give, but prosocial spending did not contribute to happiness when prosocial spending was required (Weinstein & Ryan, 2010). In other words, the positive effect of pro-social spending on consumer happiness is higher when consumers voluntarily engage in pro-social spending because such conditions allow consumers to satisfy their *autonomy needs* (Aknin et al., 2013b).

Second, prosocial spending is likely to increase happiness when one feels as *if they have made a positive impact on others*. That is, prosocial spending is likely to produce greater happiness when consumers can see the difference their pro-social spending made on others (Aknin et al., 2013c). The positive effect of pro-social spending on consumer happiness is higher when their pro-social spending makes a significant impact on others because their pro-social spending allows consumers to satisfy their *competence needs* (Aknin et al., 2013b).

Third, prosocial spending is also more likely to lead to greater happiness when the act of generosity serves to facilitate social connection with others (e.g., taking a friend out for dinner instead of giving a gift coupon) (Aknin et al., 2013b). In other words, the positive effect of pro-social spending on consumer happiness is higher when their pro-social spending provides them with opportunities to connect with other people; as such, pro-social spending allows them to satisfy their *relatedness needs* (Aknin et al., 2013b). Additional evidence suggests that when consumers have a greater feeling for those in need, they are likely to increase their intention to donate to charity. Consumers have reported higher levels of positive affect after recalling a time they spent on a strong tie (e.g., those with intimate relationships) versus a weak tie (Aknin et al., 2013b) Furthermore, evidence suggests that pro-social spending has a positive influence on happiness when consumers have self-transcendence values (i.e., a concern for persons and entities outside of the individual) (Hill & Howell, 2014).

Research also suggests that the positive impact of pro-social spending is not affected by the *income of the giver*. That is, the effect of pro-social spending on consumer happiness is not affected by the level of income. Also, consumers in poor and rich countries alike reported greater happiness if they engaged in prosocial spending. Consider the study by Aknin et al. (2013a, b, c). They examined the correlation between charitable giving and happiness in 136 countries. In 120 out of 136 countries, they found a positive and significant relationship between giving and happiness (controlling for income and other demographic variables).

Finally, pro-social spending enhances the life satisfaction of the receiver of the gift when the *receiver views the gift as attractive and perceives the giver's intention positively* (Zhang et al., 2018). To examine the effect of pro-social spending on the happiness of the receiver, a large-scale survey was conducted. Survey respondents were first asked to recall the latest prosocial spending in which somebody else bought some product (a material item or an experience) for them. Then, they responded to the measures of gift attractiveness, perceived giver intention, their willingness to accept, and happiness. The results indicate that both gift attractiveness and positive perceived intention of the giver are positively related to the recipients' willingness to accept the gift, and that the recipient's willingness to accept is positively associated with recipients' happiness (Zhang et al., 2018). The results indicate that pro-social spending enhances the happiness of the receiver as well as the happiness of the giver.

Increase Spending on Time-Saving Products

Consumption happiness can be increased when consumers spend money on time-saving devices (e.g., spending money to save time). Time and money are finite resources that influence consumption happiness. Spending money for time (e.g., consumer spending on time-saving products and services) effectively contributes to the enhancement of consumer happiness (Aknin et al., 2018). When people were asked whether they would want more money or more time, the majority stated they would prefer money. Yet, the minority of people who stated that they would prefer more time were significantly happier than those who stated they would prefer money (Hershfield et al., 2016; Whillans et al., 2016). That is, consumers can be happier by spending more money on time-saving products. Supporting this, research has found that consumers were happier, on average, after using money to save time (e.g., house cleaner, dog walker, and preprepared meal) than after making a material purchase (e.g., a book, air freshener, and groceries), and that these hedonic benefits were mediated by lower feelings of stress that day (Whillans et al., 2017). Spending more money on time provides consumers with hedonic benefits and reduced stress.

Boost a Positive Self-Concept Through Consumption

Consumption happiness can be increased when consumers' experiences of goods and services help create a *positive boost to their self-concept*. Specifically, consumption happiness is high when consumption experiences fit well with consumers' identity (Bhattacharjee & Mogilner, 2014; Carter & Gilovich, 2012; Mogilner et al., 2011). Research has shown that consumers who spent more of their monthly income on products that matched their personality (e.g., extroverts at the bookstore and introverts at the bar) reported higher levels of life satisfaction (Matz et al., 2016). Satisfaction of *self-consistency and self-enhancement needs* serves to maintain and boost a positive self-concept.

Consumption happiness is high when consumers' self-esteem is heightened because of the consumption experience (Dunn et al., 2011; Gilovich et al., 2015; van Boven & Gilovich, 2003). For example, a study demonstrated that consumption of certain conspicuous goods can enhance consumers' feeling of status and consumption happiness (Charles et al., 2009; Veblen, 1899).

Increase Social Interactions in Consumption

Consumption happiness can be increased when consumers' experiences with the product help them increase opportunities for social interaction, resulting in social satisfaction. Evidence suggests that consumption happiness is high when consumer experiences social satisfaction from consumption experiences (Dunn et al., 2011; van Boven & Gilovich, 2003). In general, people experience more positive feelings on average when they are with others than when alone (Pavot et al., 1990; Diener & Seligman, 2002), and interventions aimed at increasing social engagement tend to generate higher levels of happiness (Zelenski et al., 2012). As such, consumption happiness is higher for socially shared experiences than for solitary experiences (Caprariello & Reis, 2013).

Moderator effects? Yes, there are several. *Socioemotional selectivity theory* argues that younger people are more future-oriented and prioritize knowledge goals, often seeking novel social interactions to develop future-ready selves. In contrast, older people are more present-oriented and prioritize emotional goals, *often seeking emotionally fulfilling social interactions with familiar others* (Carstensen, 1992, 2006).

Additionally, research suggests that consumption happiness is high when consumers experience close social interactions online. Online communication stimulates consumption happiness via its positive effect on close social interactions that contribute to relationship quality (Stepanikova et al., 2010). That is, online communications facilitate online social interactions and allow the expression of a positive self-image, thereby enhancing consumption happiness (Valkenburg & Peter, 2007).

Summary and Conclusion

Table 12.1 summarizes much of the discussion of this chapter. All the strategies for enhancing consumption happiness are spelled out under "Action." The impact on consumption happiness for each strategy is spelled out under "Impact on Consumption Happiness." The Mechanism column shows the underlying psychological principles designed to explain the impact of each intervention.

Table 12.1 Enhancing consumption happiness

Action	Impact on consumption happiness	Mechanism
Increase satisfaction in multiple life domains in consumption	Consumption happiness is high when the consumption experience serves to meet a large spectrum of consumer needs—the more needs a product satisfies, the higher the consumption happiness.	Need satisfaction is a major factor in consumption happiness.
Reduce hedonic adaptation in consumption	Consumption happiness is high when consumers experience a low degree of hedonic adaptation or satiation. Means of intervention: Separate consumption experiences, slow down consumption speed, seek variety, and engage in experiences that are self-congruent with high sentimental value.	A high degree of hedonic adaptation or satiation works against consumption happiness.
Refrain from comparative evaluations and social comparisons	Consumption happiness is high when consumers do not engage in comparative product evaluation and social comparisons.	When consumers engage in comparative evaluations with other alternatives, they are likely to experience negative affect in the form of regret Upward social comparisons lead to unhappiness.
Evaluate products with low expectations	Consumption happiness is high when consumers do not have too high expectations.	Consumption happiness is reduced when consumers have high and rising financial aspirations. The greater the gap between the actual and desired situation, the greater the dissatisfaction.
Spend more on experiences than material products	Consumption happiness is high and more enduring when consumers spend money on experiences than on material products.	Experiential consumption is central to one's self-concept, prompting consumers to focus on inherent evaluations and facilitating social interactions.
Increase consumption spending on others	Consumption happiness is high when consumers engage in spending on others.	Prosocial spending provides consumers with the satisfaction of autonomy, competence, and relatedness needs.
Increase spending on time-saving products	Consumer happiness is higher when consumers spend money to save time.	Spending more money on time provides consumers with hedonic benefits while reducing stress.
Boost a positive self-concept through consumption	Consumption happiness is high when consumers' experiences of goods and services help boost consumers' positive self-concept.	Consumption happiness is associated with satisfaction of self-consistency and enhancement needs.

(continued)

Table 12.1 (continued)

Action	Impact on consumption happiness	Mechanism
Increase social interactions in consumption	Consumption happiness is high when consumers' experiences of products provide consumers with opportunities for social interaction, resulting in heightened satisfaction in social life.	Consumption happiness is higher for socially shared experiences than for solitary experiences. Social and belonging needs are met through shared experiences.

References

Aknin, L. B., Barrington-Leigh, C. P., Dunn, E. W., Helliwell, J. F., Burns, J., Biswas-Diener, R., et al. (2013a). Prosocial spending and well-being: Cross-cultural evidence for a psychological universal. *Journal of Personality and Social Psychology, 104*(4), 635–652.

Aknin, L. B., Dunn, E. W., Sandstrom, G. M., & Norton, M. I. (2013b). Does social connection turn good deeds into good feelings? On the value of putting the 'social' in prosocial spending. *International Journal of Happiness and Development, 1*(2), 155–171.

Aknin, L. B., Dunn, E. W., Whillans, A. V., Grant, A. M., & Norton, M. I. (2013c). Making a difference matters: Impact unlocks the emotional benefits of prosocial spending. *Journal of Economic Behavior & Organization, 88*, 90–95.

Aknin, L. B., Wiwad, D., & Hanniball, K. B. (2018). Buying well-being: Spending behavior and happiness. *Social and Personality Psychology Compass, 12*(5), e12386.

Allardt, E. (1973). *About dimensions of welfare—Research Group for Comparative Sociology*. (Research Report (Vol. No. 1)). University of Helsinki.

Arndt, J. (1981). Marketing and the quality of life. *Journal of Economic Psychology, 1*(4), 283–301.

Bhattacharjee, A., & Mogilner, C. (2014). Happiness from ordinary and extraordinary experiences. *Journal of Consumer Research, 41*(1), 1–17.

Caprariello, P. A., & Reis, H. T. (2013). To do, to have, or to share? Valuing experiences over material possessions depends on the involvement of others. *Journal of Personality and Social Psychology, 104*(2), 199–215.

Carstensen, L. L. (1992). Social and emotional patterns in adulthood: Support for socioemotional selectivity theory. *Psychology and Aging, 7*(3), 331–338.

Carstensen, L. L. (2006). The influence of a sense of time on human development. *Science, 312*(5782), 1913–1915.

Carter, T. J., & Gilovich, T. (2010). The relative relativity of material and experiential purchases. *Journal of Personality and Social Psychology, 98*(1), 146–159.

Carter, T. J., & Gilovich, T. (2012). I am what I do, not what I have: The differential centrality of experiential and material purchases to the self. *Journal of Personality and Social Psychology, 102*(6), 1304–1317.

Charles, K. K., Hurst, E., & Roussanov, N. (2009). Conspicuous consumption and race. *The Quarterly Journal of Economics, 124*(2), 425–467.

Chugani, S. K., Irwin, J. R., & Redden, J. P. (2015). Happily ever after: The effect of identity-consistency on product satiation. *Journal of Consumer Research, 42*(4), 564–577.

Deci, E. L., & Ryan, R. M. (2000). The "what" and "why" of goal pursuits: Human needs and the self-determination of behavior. *Psychological Inquiry, 11*(4), 227–268.

Deci, E. L., Ryan, R. M., Gagné, M., Leone, D. R., Usunov, J., & Kornazheva, B. P. (2001). Need satisfaction, motivation, and well-being in the work organizations of a former eastern bloc country: A cross-cultural study of self-determination. *Personality and Social Psychology Bulletin, 27*(8), 930–942.

Diener, E., & Seligman, M. E. (2002). Very happy people. *Psychological Science, 13*(1), 81–84.

Dunn, E. W., Aknin, L. B., & Norton, M. I. (2008). Spending money on others promotes happiness. *Science, 319*(5870), 1687–1688.

Dunn, E. W., Gilbert, D. T., & Wilson, T. D. (2011). If money doesn't make you happy, then you probably aren't spending it right. *Journal of Consumer Psychology, 21*(2), 115–125.

El Hedhli, K., Chebat, J. C., & Sirgy, M. J. (2013). Shopping well-being at the mall: Construct, antecedents, and consequences. *Journal of Business Research, 66*(7), 856–863.

Etkin, J., & Mogilner, C. (2016). Does variety among activities increase happiness? *Journal of Consumer Research, 43*(2), 210–229.

Frederick, S., & Loewenstein, G. (1999). Hedonic adaptation. In D. Kahneman & E. Diener (Eds.), *Well-being. The foundations of hedonic psychology* (pp. 302–329). Russell Sage Foundation.

Galak, J., Kruger, J., & Loewenstein, G. (2013). Slow down! Insensitivity to rate of consumption leads to avoidable satiation. *Journal of Consumer Research, 39*(5), 993–1009.

Gilovich, T., Kumar, A., & Jampol, L. (2015). A wonderful life: Experiential consumption and the pursuit of happiness. *Journal of Consumer Psychology, 25*(1), 152–165.

Heppner, W. L., Kernis, M. H., Nezlek, J. B., Foster, J., Lakey, C. E., & Goldman, B. M. (2008). Within-person relationships among daily self-esteem, need satisfaction, and authenticity. *Psychological Science, 19*(11), 1140–1145.

Hershfield, H. E., Mogilner, C., & Barnea, U. (2016). People who choose time over money are happier. *Social Psychological and Personality Science, 7*(7), 697–706.

Hill, G., & Howell, R. T. (2014). Moderators and mediators of pro-social spending and well-being: The influence of values and psychological need satisfaction. *Personality and Individual Differences, 69*, 69–74.

Howell, R. T., & Hill, G. (2009). The mediators of experiential purchases: Determining the impact of psychological needs satisfaction and social comparison. *The Journal of Positive Psychology, 4*(6), 511–522.

Hsee, C. K., & Hastie, R. (2006). Decision and experience: Why don't we choose what makes us happy? *Trends in Cognitive Sciences, 10*(1), 31–37.

Hsee, C. K., Yang, Y., Li, N., & Shen, L. (2009). Wealth, warmth, and well-being: Whether happiness is relative or absolute depends on whether it is about money, acquisition, or consumption. *Journal of Marketing Research, 46*(3), 396–409.

Kahneman, D. (1999). Objective happiness. In D. Kahneman, E. Diener, & N. Schwarz (Eds.), *Wellbeing: The foundations of hedonic psychology* (pp. 3–25). Russell Sage Foundation.

Kumar, A., & Gilovich, T. (2015). Some "thing" to talk about? Differential story utility from experiential and material purchases. *Personality and Social Psychology Bulletin, 41*(10), 1320–1331.

Kumar, A., & Gilovich, T. (2016). To do or to have, now or later? The preferred consumption profiles of material and experiential purchases. *Journal of Consumer Psychology, 26*(2), 169–178.

Kumar, A., Killingsworth, M. A., & Gilovich, T. (2014). Waiting for merlot: Anticipatory consumption of experiential and material purchases. *Psychological Science, 25*(10), 1924–1931.

Kumar, A., Killingsworth, M. A., & Gilovich, T. (2020). Spending on doing promotes more moment-to-moment happiness than spending on having. *Journal of Experimental Social Psychology, 88*, 103971.

Lok, I., & Dunn, E. W. (2020). Under what conditions does prosocial spending promote happiness?. *Collabra. Psychology, 6*(1), 5.

Lyubomirsky, S. (2010). *Della Porta. Boosting happiness, buttressing resilience. Handbook of adult resilience*. Gilford Press.

Lyubomirsky, S., Tkach, C., & DiMatteo, M. R. (2006). What are the differences between happiness and self-esteem. *Social Indicators Research, 78*(3), 363–404.

Maslow, A. (1970). *Motivation and personality* (2nd ed.). Harper.

Matz, S. C., Gladstone, J. J., & Stillwell, D. (2016). Money buys happiness when spending fits our personality. *Psychological Science, 27*(5), 715–725.

Mogilner, C., Kamvar, S. D., & Aaker, J. (2011). The shifting meaning of happiness. *Social Psychological and Personality Science, 2*(4), 395–402.

Nelson, L. D., & Meyvis, T. (2008). Interrupted consumption: Disrupting adaptation to hedonic experiences. *Journal of Marketing Research, 45*(6), 654–664.

Nickerson, C., Schwarz, N., Diener, E., & Kahneman, D. (2003). Zeroing in on the dark side of the American dream: A closer look at the negative consequences of the goal for financial success. *Psychological Science, 14*(6), 531–536.

Nicolao, L., Irwin, J. R., & Goodman, J. K. (2009). Happiness for sale: Do experiential purchases make consumers happier than material purchases? *Journal of Consumer Research, 36*(2), 188–198.

Omodei, M. M., & Wearing, A. J. (1990). Need satisfaction and involvement in personal projects: Toward an integrative model of subjective well-being. *Journal of Personality and Social Psychology, 59*(4), 762–769.

Patrick, H., Knee, C. R., Canevello, A., & Lonsbary, C. (2007). The role of need fulfillment in relationship functioning and well-being: A self-determination theory perspective. *Journal of Personality and Social Psychology, 92*(3), 434–457.

Pavot, W., Diener, E. D., & Fujita, F. (1990). Extraversion and happiness. *Personality and Individual Differences, 11*(12), 1299–1306.

Raphael, D., Renwick, R., Brown, I., & Rootman, I. (1996). Quality of life indicators and health: Current status and emerging conceptions. *Social Indicators Research, 39*(1), 65–88.

Rosenzweig, E., & Gilovich, T. (2012). Buyer's remorse or missed opportunity? Differential regrets for material and experiential purchases. *Journal of Personality and Social Psychology, 102*(2), 215–223.

Ryan, R. M., & Deci, E. L. (2000). Self-determination theory and the facilitation of intrinsic motivation, social development, and well-being. *American Psychologist, 55*(1), 68–78.

Sääksjärvi, M., Hellén, K., & Desmet, P. (2017). The "You and I" of happiness: Investigating the long-term impact of self-and other-focused happiness-enhancing activities. *Psychology & Marketing, 34*(6), 623–630.

Seligman, M. E. P. (2011). *Flourish: A visionary new understanding of happiness and well-being*. The Free Press.

Sevilla, J., & Redden, J. P. (2014). Limited availability reduces the rate of satiation. *Journal of Marketing Research, 51*(2), 205–217.

Sirgy, M. J. (1998). Materialism and quality of life. *Social Indicators Research, 43*(3), 227–260.

Stepanikova, I., Nie, N. H., & He, X. (2010). Time on the Internet at home, loneliness, and life satisfaction: Evidence from panel time-diary data. *Computers in Human Behavior, 26*(3), 329–338.

Thaler, R. (1985). Mental accounting and consumer choice. *Marketing Science, 4*(3), 199–214.

Tu, Y., & Hsee, C. K. (2018). Hedonomics: On subtle yet significant determinants of happiness. In E. Diener, S. Oishi, & L. Tay (Eds.), *Handbook of well-being* (pp. 1–12). DEF Publishers. nobascholar.com.

Valkenburg, P. M., & Peter, J. (2007). Online communication and adolescent well-being: Testing the stimulation versus the displacement hypothesis. *Journal of Computer-Mediated Communication, 12*(4), 1169–1182.

Van Boven, L., & Gilovich, T. (2003). To do or to have? That is the question. *Journal of Personality and Social Psychology, 85*(6), 1193–1202.

Van Boven, L., Campbell, M. C., & Gilovich, T. (2010). Stigmatizing materialism: On stereotypes and impressions of materialistic and experiential pursuits. *Personality and Social Psychology Bulletin, 36*(4), 551–563.

Veblen, T. (1899). The barbarian status of women. *American Journal of Sociology, 4*(4), 503–514.

Weinstein, N., & Ryan, R. M. (2010). When helping helps: Autonomous motivation for prosocial behavior and its influence on well-being for the helper and recipient. *Journal of Personality and Social Psychology, 98*(2), 222–244.

Whillans, A. V., Weidman, A. C., & Dunn, E. W. (2016). Valuing time over money is associated with greater happiness. *Social Psychological and Personality Science, 7*(3), 213–222.

Whillans, A. V., Dunn, E. W., Smeets, P., Bekkers, R., & Norton, M. I. (2017). Buying time promotes happiness. *Proceedings of the National Academy of Sciences, 114*(32), 8523–8527.
Yang, Y., & Galak, J. (2015). Sentimental value and its influence on hedonic adaptation. *Journal of Personality and Social Psychology, 109*(5), 767–790.
Yang, W., Zhang, Y., & So, K. K. F. (2021). Tourism experiences vs. material purchases: Effects of eudaimonic consumption motive on consumers' reactions to invidious comparisons. *Tourism Management, 83*(April), 104247.
Zelenski, J. M., Santoro, M. S., & Whelan, D. C. (2012). Would introverts be better off if they acted more like extraverts? Exploring emotional and cognitive consequences of counter-dispositional behavior. *Emotion, 12*(2), 290–303.
Zhang, W., Chen, M., Xie, Y., & Zhao, Z. (2018). Prosocial spending and subjective well-being: The recipient perspective. *Journal of Happiness Studies, 19*(8), 2267–2281.
Zhong, J. Y., & Mitchell, V. W. (2010). A mechanism model of the effect of hedonic product consumption on well-being. *Journal of Consumer Psychology, 20*(2), 152–162.

Chapter 13
Happiness in Relation to Shopping

There are always flowers for those who want to see them.

Henri Matisse (https://www.countryliving.com/life/g4815/happy-life-quotes/?utm_source=google&utm_medium=cpc&utm_campaign=mgu_ga_clv_md_pmx_hybd_mix_us_18709966696&gad_source=1&gclid=EAIaIQobChMI8OXhxdeIiAMV-F1HAR2dfhJnEAAYASAAEgIEKPD_BwE)

What Is Happiness in Relation to Shopping?

Consumption wellbeing during the acquisition stage is shopping happiness. Shopping happiness (or purchase happiness) refers to an affective judgment of how much a purchase contributes to one's overall consumer happiness (Dias et al., 2022). It is a feeling of happiness resulting from shopping activities (El Hedhli et al., 2013; Ekici et al., 2018; Lee et al., 2014; Sirgy et al., 2020).

Shopping activity provides consumers with shopping values that contribute to shopping happiness. Research found that shopping provides two types of benefits for the consumer: hedonic and utilitarian (e.g., Babin et al., 1994), which contribute to happiness. That is, engagement in shopping activities facilitates the acquisition of products and/or information in an efficient manner. In addition, engagement in shopping activities provides opportunities for social exchange, offers relaxation and distraction, and gives variety and pleasure to everyday life (Zulauf & Wagner, 2022).

Engagement in online shopping also enhances happiness. First, consumers can browse different online shops, compare prices, and learn the attributes and functions of various products simultaneously. Thus, compared with shopping in physical stores, online shopping improves shopping efficiency and saves time (Chiu et al., 2019). Second, online shopping enables consumers to purchase products without time and place restrictions, which enhances consumer happiness. Third, posting purchases on online social media positively influences consumers' happiness via the mediating roles of the perceived impact of purchases on self and interpersonal relationships (Duan & Dholakia, 2017).

D.-J. Lee, M. J. Sirgy, *Happiness in the Marketplace*, Social Indicators Research Series 64, https://doi.org/10.1007/978-3-032-04443-3_13

Happiness in a shopping context is consumption happiness during the acquisition stage. Shopping happiness refers to an affective judgment of how much a purchase contributes to one's overall consumer happiness (Dias et al., 2022). It is a feeling of happiness resulting from shopping activities. Shopping happiness is also called *shopping wellbeing* (El Hedhli et al., 2016).

How do the benefits of utilitarian and hedonic values of shopping contribute to happiness? First, utilitarian shopping value reflects the acquisition of products and/or information in an efficient manner and can be viewed as reflecting a more task-oriented, cognitive, and non-emotional outcome of shopping (Babin et al., 1994). Utilitarian value in shopping reflects the task-related value of a shopping experience (Babin & Attaway, 2000); thus, increases in utilitarian shopping value contribute to happiness.

Second, hedonic shopping values reflect the value received from the multisensory, fantasy, and emotive aspects of the shopping experience (Babin et al., 1994). Hedonic shopping value reflects the value found in the shopping experience itself, independent of task-related activities (Babin & Attaway, 2000); thus, increases in hedonic shopping value contribute to happiness.

Third, it should be noted that happiness is greatly influenced by hedonic values than by utilitarian values in shopping (El Hedhli et al., 2016).

Finally, happiness in relation to shopping can be increased when consumers have a sense of accomplishment on the shopping trip (e.g., need satisfaction and positive self-esteem in shopping) and when consumers enjoy the recreational aspects of shopping.

Shopping Engagement

Consumers' frequent engagement in shopping activities contributes to happiness. This may be for the following reasons. First, engagement in shopping activities allows consumers to escape from the stressors of daily life (Gilovich & Gallo, 2020; Vieira et al., 2018). Engagement in shopping activities provides opportunities for social exchange, offers relaxation and distraction, and offers opportunities for variety and pleasure in everyday life (Zulauf & Wagner, 2022). The hedonic value of shopping enhances happiness (El Hedhli et al., 2016). That is, engagement in shopping activities allows consumers to experience positive affect and pleasure, thereby enhancing happiness.

Second, shopping engagement contributes to happiness because shopping helps consumers increase their self-esteem (Arnold & Reynolds, 2003; Horváth & Adıgüzel, 2018). Consumers who are highly engaged in shopping consider shopping activity as a central aspect in their lives, providing not only hedonic value but also self-expressive value (Beaton et al., 2011; Schulz et al., 2018). Self-expressiveness concerning shopping is typically manifested when consumers think that shopping activity is an important part of their self-concept and perceive themselves as making progress towards the realization of their best potential through shopping. Consumers with self-expressiveness in shopping have increased happiness (Sirgy et al., 2016).

Third, shopping engagement can be characterized in terms of three dimensions: shopping frequency, shopping intensity, and shopping diversity. As happiness is largely influenced by frequency rather than intensity (Diener et al., 2009), one can argue that the frequency of shopping engagement has a greater effect on happiness than intensity or diversity of shopping engagement. It should be noted that shopping happiness declines when consumers are excessively engaged in shopping. Excessive shopping participation deteriorates shopping satisfaction and happiness. Specifically, the positive effect of shopping engagement on happiness is finite, and at some point, shopping satiation occurs. Excessive engagement in shopping may result in compulsive buying behaviors that lead to distress. Research has shown that the positive effect of shopping engagement on consumer happiness is higher for young consumers, especially when they engage in exciting shopping activities (e.g., Mogilner et al., 2012) and social shopping activities (e.g., Aaker et al., 2011; Berezan et al., 2018), and online shopping activities (Dabholkar & Bagozzi, 2002).

Shopping Passion

Happiness can be increased when consumers engage in shopping activities with harmonious passion rather than obsessive passion (Vallerand et al., 2003; Stenseng, 2008). Consumers with harmonious shopping passion are autonomous and self-determined in their shopping engagement (Mageau et al., 2009; Vallerand et al., 2003). Their shopping engagement does not conflict with roles in other life domains (Seguin-Levesque et al., 2003). Shopping for consumers with *harmonious passion* is in line with their self-concept (Stenseng, 2008). As such, they often experience positive affect and flow during shopping (Curran et al., 2015; Stenseng, 2008; Vallerand, 2015). Thus, one can argue that the effect of shopping engagement on wellbeing (flow and pleasure) is strong when consumers engage in shopping with harmonious passion.

In contrast, consumers motivated by *obsessive passion* are driven by interpersonal pressure or controlled intrapersonal reasons, and their shopping engagement often results in role conflict (i.e., the shopping role conflicting with other roles in other life domains) (Seguin-Levesque et al., 2003). Shopping for consumers with obsessive passion is not an activity consistent with their self-concept (Stenseng, 2008). As such, they often experience negative feelings and ruminate during shopping (Curran et al., 2015; Stenseng, 2008). In sum, one can argue that the effect of shopping engagement on shopping illbeing (regret, rumination) is high when consumers are motivated by obsessive shopping passion.

Enhancing Happiness in Relation to Shopping

Research on happiness in relation to shopping can be grouped into two categories, namely what products to buy and how to spend money.

What Products to Buy

There is some research on the type of products that consumers purchase that serve to enhance happiness in relation to shopping. These are hedonic products, sustainable and ethical products, products that fit their personal values, experiential products, memorable products, and time-saving products.

Hedonic Products

Happiness concerning shopping can be increased when consumers purchase hedonic products more than functional products. Functional products are products that consumers purchase for functional, utilitarian, and physical performance. Hedonic products are products that consumers purchase for pleasure and sensory satisfaction—consumption is primarily characterized by an affective and sensory experience of aesthetic or sensual pleasure, fantasy, and fun (Dhar & Wertenbroch, 2000; Hirschman & Holbrook, 1982; Sheth et al., 1991).

Happiness can be increased when consumers buy more hedonic than functional products because consumers are likely to experience strong positive affect from hedonic products (e.g., delight and excitement) but weak positive affect from functional products (e.g., relief and satisfaction) (Chitturi et al., 2008). For example, consumers experience high levels of happiness buying aesthetic products because products designed to be aesthetically pleasing deliver emotional value (e.g., pleasure from attractive stimuli), social value (e.g., positive self-image), and epistemic value (knowledge need satisfaction) (Chaouali et al., 2020). Similarly, El Hedhli et al. (2016) found that shopping wellbeing is influenced more strongly by hedonic value than utilitarian value. This suggests that shoppers are likely to experience a sense of wellbeing because they enjoy their shopping experiences rather than simply meeting their functional shopping goals. Frequent hedonic pleasurable experiences in shopping spill over to consumer life, enhancing consumer happiness (Zhong & Mitchell, 2010). Research found that the effect of exciting hedonic products on consumer happiness is greater for young consumers who seek excitement for their happiness (e.g., Mogilner et al., 2012).

It should be noted that frequent shopping for indulgent products can decrease rather than increase happiness because doing so causes role conflict (i.e., conflict with other goals such as spending within a budget which is important to financial wellbeing—momentary pleasure versus long-term harm) (Hu & Min, 2022;

Ramanathan & Williams, 2007). Indulgent consumption represents time-inconsistent preferences, or a tendency to overweigh short-term rewards relative to more distant ones and a tendency in the short term to ignore the costs of one's actions (e.g., Prelec & Loewenstein, 1991; Ramanathan & Williams, 2007; Thaler & Shefrin, 1981).

Sustainable and Ethical Products

Sustainable consumer behavior is defined as consumer actions in purchasing, using, and disposing of products that minimize damage to the natural environment and society (Rowe et al., 2019). Sustainable consumption involves environmental concerns and is related to long-term benefits for others and the environment (White et al., 2019).

Happiness in a shopping context can be increased when consumers purchase sustainable and ethical products. There is evidence suggesting that the purchase of sustainable and ethical products may induce positive emotions, reduce guilty feelings, and reinforce consumers' moral identity and a positive self-image (Ramos-Hidalgo et al., 2022). In addition, the purchase of environmental and ethical products can also enhance eudaimonic happiness by aligning their consumption behaviors with meaningful life values (Schröder & McEachern, 2004). Engaging in sustainable consumption helps to create consumers' environmentally friendly self-identity, or the extent to which consumers see themselves as environmentally friendly person (Van der Werff et al., 2014). Environmental and prosocial behaviors provide consumers with intrinsic satisfactions that bolster happiness (De Young, 2000; Brown & Kasser, 2005). Research found that the purchase of sustainable products increases consumer happiness, especially for those consumers with self-transcendence values (i.e., a concern for persons and entities outside of the individual) (Hill & Howell, 2014).

To reiterate, research has demonstrated that the purchase of sustainable products increases positive emotions and reduces negative emotions (Onwezen et al., 2013; Sun & Trudel, 2017). That is, the purchase and consumption of sustainable products lead consumers to feel good about using the green products and have enhanced enjoyment of the accompanying consumption experiences (Giebelhausen et al., 2016; Tezer & Bodur, 2020). Research has also shown that ethical and sustainable consumption has a stronger association with eudaimonic happiness than with hedonic happiness (Ganglmair-Wooliscroft & Wooliscroft, 2019).

Products That Fit Consumers' Personality and Values

Shopping happiness can be increased when consumers buy products that match their personality and values. Research indicates that consumers tend to spend more money on products that match their personality/values, and this personality/values-matched spending increases consumers' happiness (Matz et al., 2016; Veenhoven et al., 2021). Evidence indicates that consumers who spend more of their income on products that are aligned with their personalities/values tend to report a high level of life satisfaction (e.g., extroverts spending more at a bar, introverts spending at a bookstore) (Matz et al., 2016). In addition, consumption happiness is increased when consumers get much satisfaction from products that fit well with their values and lifestyles (Ganglmair-Wooliscroft & Lawson, 2011). Research found that the effect of value shopping on shopping happiness is high for those consumers with smart shopper identity (Babin et al., 1994) while the effect of recreational shopping on shopping happiness is high for those consumers with recreational shopper identity (Arnold & Reynolds, 2003; Guiry et al., 2006). Consumer happiness is effectively enhanced by having shopping experiences that match consumers' identity.

Shopping happiness is high when consumers buy products with personality and value fit. This is because the fit between personality/value and the consumer leads to satisfaction of fundamental consumer needs and positive self-concept, which in turn enhances consumer happiness. This effect of personality and value fit on consumer happiness was stronger than the effect of an individual's total income or their total spending (Matz et al., 2016). For example, one can argue that green product shopping is positively associated with eudaimonic happiness for consumers with environmentally friendly self-identity.

Experiential Products

Shopping happiness is higher when consumers purchase *experiential products* than when they purchase material products. Experiential products are material products that provide experience (e.g., a book or guitar) (Guevarra & Howell, 2015). In contrast, experiential products provide similar levels of wellbeing compared to other life experiences and more wellbeing than material items (Guevarra & Howell, 2015).

However, defining products as experiential versus material is somewhat elusive. Purchases can be perceived as either experiential or material depending on individuals' primary intentions to consume their purchases (Schmitt et al., 2015). Experiential purchases are defined as those made with the primary intention of acquiring a life experience: an event or series of events that one lives through, while material purchases are those made with the primary intention of acquiring a material good: a tangible object that is kept in one's possession (Van Boven & Gilovich, 2003).

Relative to possessions, experiences elicit greater *in-the-moment happiness* (Kumar et al., 2020). Yet, it should be noted that higher level of happiness is associated with experiential purchases rather than material purchases when consumers have covered their basic needs such as adequate clothing, housing, or nourishment (Gilovich & Gallo, 2020; Gilovich et al., 2015; Kumar & Gilovich, 2016; Nicolao et al., 2009; Van Boven & Gilovich, 2003). For example, the results of a national survey indicate that consumers derive higher levels of happiness from experiential purchases than from material purchases when consumers have income resources to meet their basic needs, such as adequate clothing, housing, or nourishment (Van Boven & Gilovich, 2003). Research also found that leisure spending has a positive and significant association with consumer happiness when consumers are already satisfied with basic needs (DeLeire & Kalil, 2010). The notion of experiential advantage is more relevant to those consumers who have the resources to meet their basic needs and ponder whether to spend their discretionary resources on experiences or possessions (Van Boven & Gilovich, 2003). In sum, we conclude that shopping happiness is high when consumers purchase experiential products. Much evidence suggests that the effect of experiential purchase on consumer happiness is high for consumers with low financial constraints (Tully et al., 2015), consumers with high socio-economic status (Van Boven & Gilovich, 2003), and consumers with low subjective debt (Netemeyer et al., 2018; Tay et al., 2017).

Memorable Products

Shopping happiness tends to be high when consumers purchase memorable goods and services. Memorable goods and services allow consumers to effectively maintain memories of good experiences (Tully & Meyvis, 2017).

Specifically, people tend to overestimate how much they will reflect on their experiences. This overestimation results from people focusing on their desire to reflect on experiences while failing to consider the experience's limited enduring accessibility in memory (Tully & Meyvis, 2017). Obtaining physical reminders (e.g., memorable goods) of an experience reduces the overestimation of retrospection by increasing how much people retrospect, bringing their realized retrospection more in line with their forecasts and aspirations. As a result, shopping happiness is elevated when consumers purchase memorable goods.

How does the purchase of memorable products enhance happiness in shopping? Two explanations. First, memorable products contribute to happiness in shopping because consumers will always be able to revisit the memories of their positive experiences (Howell & Hill, 2009). In the absence of physical reminders (e.g., memorable products), the accessibility and salience of those memories are likely to wane over time (Van Boven & Gilovich, 2003). For example, research found that commemorative products for one's graduation (e.g., graduation ring) enhance the strength of positive feelings experienced when consumers think back to their special and meaningful event (Goodman et al., 2016). Memorable products enable consumers to be transported back to their positive emotions at the time of the special life event, thus connecting the emotions from a person's past self to his/her future self. The lasting memories of positive experiences through memorable products effectively contribute to consumer happiness (cf. Gilovich et al., 2015; Van Boven & Gilovich, 2003).

Second, memorable products contribute to happiness in shopping because memorable products facilitate communication about the positive event. Talking about positive past experiences with the help of physical reminders can increase positive affect, improve social satisfaction, and improve interpersonal relationships (Lambert et al., 2013; Reis et al., 2010). Thus, the purchase of memorable products contributes to happiness in the shopping context.

Time-Saving Products

Consumers are happier when they spend on *time-saving goods and services* (Whillans et al., 2017). In other words, they feel happier after spending money on time-saving products (e.g., house cleaner services, pre-prepared meals) compared to material purchases that do not allow time saving. This is because time-saving goods and services serve to reduce the feelings of stress arising from a lack of time to get things done.

When asked whether they would want more money or more time, most of the consumers stated that they would prefer money. Yet, studies found that those consumers with preferences for time over money are significantly happier than consumers with a preference for money over time (Hershfield et al., 2016; Whillans et al., 2016).

Yes indeed. The tendency to prioritize time over money has a positive effect on happiness. Time-focused consumers tend to seek emotional meaning by spending time with friends and family (Mogilner, 2010) and others (Liu & Aaker, 2008). Thus, the tendency to prioritize time is positively related to greater happiness (Whillans et al., 2016; Hershfield et al., 2016).

How to Spend Money

Research on how to spend money highlights the role of the following factors: shopping from many alternatives, online/mobile shopping, gift giving, pro-social spending, frugal spending, and justifiable spending.

Many Alternatives in Shopping

Shopping happiness can be increased when consumers make choices out of many alternatives. *Choices from many alternatives* serve to define, express, and reify the distinct individual identity (Markus & Schwartz, 2010; Schwartz, 2004). An abundance of options means choice freedom and autonomy, which contributes to consumer happiness (Markus & Schwartz, 2010; Schwartz, 2004). An abundance of options is good in that many alternatives enable consumers to have the opportunity to live the kinds of lives they want and help consumers to express their desired self-image. For example, it is possible to imagine that when jeans come in only a few styles, one's choice of jeans says little about the self because there is not enough variety to differentiate among the many different possible selves. However, when jeans come in thousands of styles, brands, and colors, it becomes possible for one's choice of jeans to say something about who one is (Markus & Schwartz, 2010).

Many alternatives tend to enhance happiness, especially for high variety-seeking consumers. This may be due to the possibility that an increased number of alternatives tends to increase the chance of finding the best product that meets consumers' needs (Desmeules, 2002). Additionally, an increased number of alternatives may slow hedonic adaptation and satiation from the same products over time (Sevilla et al., 2019).

It should be noted that shopping happiness decreases when consumers make choices out of *too many* alternatives. Consumers with too many alternatives may feel overwhelmed and less satisfied with their decision because they might regret their choice (Roets et al., 2012). An abundance of options (i.e., choice overload) can lead to negative outcomes such as decision paralysis, regret, and decreased satisfaction (Iyengar & Lepper, 2000). Research has demonstrated that consumers are more likely to purchase gourmet jams or chocolates or to undertake optional class essay assignments when offered a limited array of 6 choices rather than a more extensive array of 24 or 30 choices (Iyengar & Lepper, 2000). Consumers can reduce the plethora of alternatives by grouping them into a manageable number to avoid information overload and choice regret.

Online/Mobile Shopping

Shopping happiness can be increased when consumers engage in *online or mobile shopping*. Why? Four reasons. First, online shopping provides consumers with custom tailored products and services that can effectively meet consumer needs; thus, this mode of shopping can induce higher levels of positive feelings compare to retail shopping where the shopper may not find the right product but may settle for the "next best thing" (Pappas et al., 2014). In other words, shopping happiness is likely to be high when shoppers find products that meet their needs.

Second, online or mobile shopping increases the utilitarian value of a shopping expedition. That is, online/mobile shopping is more efficient than brick-and-mortar shopping. Specifically, the interactive nature of online shopping offers greater utilitarian value for saving time/effort, reduced risk, and increased chance of finding a better choice, compared to brick-and-mortar shopping (Klein, 1998). Consider the following study finding: Online shopping significantly increases consumer happiness in rural areas by increasing consumer accessibility to goods and services (Zheng & Ma, 2021).

Third, online shopping can increase shopping happiness through a *virtual environment* with optimal stimulation and enjoyment—sensory, emotional, and cognitive stimulation (Fiore et al., 2005). As such, such an environment is more capable of contributing to shopping happiness compared to a brick-and-mortar environment.

Fourth, the interactive nature of online shopping reduces possible negative feelings arising from *social exclusion* and may facilitate interactions characterized as high in *social inclusion* (Dennis et al., 2016). As such, online shopping can strengthen social interactions by stimulating online and offline social interactions, especially for consumers with mobility/disability issues.

Gift Giving

Gift giving serves to increase consumer happiness. Gift giving creates happiness because it helps people meet what *self-determination theory* considers to be their basic psychological needs (Dunn et al., 2014). That is, gift giving tends to satisfy consumers' autonomy, competence, and relatedness needs. Research has uncovered certain moderators that include the following. First, gift giving increases shopping happiness of the giver especially when it facilitates close relationships, when the giver can see or imagine who the gift is making a difference in someone else's life, and when the gift is freely given (Ahuvia, 2015; Belk & Coon, 1993; Giesler, 2006).

Second, gift giving enhances shopping happiness for the giver, especially when the gifts are more experiential than material in nature. This is because experiential gifts induce higher levels of positive feelings than material gifts (Chan & Mogilner, 2017). Chan and Mogilner (2017) conducted an experiment to examine the effect of gift type (material gift vs. experiential gift) on intensity of positive affect and relationship strength. In the experiment, all gift givers were instructed to give a gift that their friend would consume without them and within the next week, to spend as close to the $15 as possible on the gift (experiential gift such as movie tickets or pass to a barre class vs. material gifts such as T-shirt or a poster). The results indicate that compared to material gifts, experiential gifts produce stronger positive emotions and greater improvements in relationship strength between the giver and the receiver (Chan & Mogilner, 2017). Thus, it can be said that gift giving enhances shopping happiness for the giver, especially when the gifts are more experiential than material in nature.

Third, consumer happiness can be increased when consumers give gifts on meaningful and special occasions (e.g., religious events, weddings, and deaths). These events tend to be more memorable than occasions that are less special and meaningful (Chun & Hiang, 2016).

Pro-social Spending

Prosocial spending (i.e., spending time and money for others) is associated with increased consumer happiness (Mogilner & Norton, 2016). Pro-social spending results in a perception of doing good for others, which in turn increases consumers' general happiness and purchase happiness (Schellong et al., 2019). Other-focused activities enhance happiness more than self-focused activities (Sääksjärvi et al., 2017), and spending money on others promotes happiness more than spending money on oneself (Dunn et al., 2008). The relationship between pro-social spending and consumer happiness appears to be universal and significant regardless of income (Dunn et al., 2014) and source of money (i.e., wage vs. windfall) (Geenen et al., 2014).

Spending time and money on others (prosocial spending) is associated with increased consumer happiness for the following reasons. First, prosocial spending contributes to consumer happiness because prosocial spending builds a sense of social connection with the beneficiary, satisfying relatedness needs. The positive relationship between prosocial spending and happiness is high when there is a strong tie between the pro-social spender and the recipients (Aknin et al., 2011).

Second, prosocial spending contributes to consumer happiness because prosocial spending makes a big impact on others, satisfying competence-related needs (Aknin et al., 2011; Hui & Kogan, 2018), That is, giving more money to charity leads to increased happiness when consumers give to causes that explained how these funds are used to make a difference in the life of a recipients (Aknin et al. 2013a, b). Thus, charity organizations need to provide donors with information on how these funds are used to make a difference in the lives of recipients.

Third, prosocial spending contributes to consumer happiness when consumers' prosocial spending is done out of their own volition, thus satisfying autonomy-related needs (Aknin et al., 2011; Weinstein & Ryan, 2010). That is, prosocial spending jacks up happiness when consumers' prosocial spending is done freely and confluent with their values. For example, research found that a positive relationship between prosocial spending and consumer happiness becomes more evident when the spending fits with consumers' self-transcendence values (i.e., concern for others). Conversely, pro-social spending does not increase happiness for those whose values do not emphasize concern for others (Hill & Howell, 2014). Research found that the effect of pro-social spending on consumer happiness is high when pro-social spending is directed to those with strong social ties (Aknin et al. 2013a, b) and that the effect of pro-social spending on consumer happiness is higher for women than for men (Hui et al., 2020) and those consumers with low materialism (Dittmar et al., 2014).

In summary, prosocial spending contributes to consumer happiness (Curry et al., 2018; Hui et al., 2020). Spending time and money on others (prosocial spending) is associated with increased consumer happiness because prosocial spending satisfies one or more psychological needs (relatedness, competency, and autonomy) (Aknin et al., 2011; Dunn et al., 2014; Weinstein & Ryan, 2010).

Frugal Spending

Frugal spending (spending less on material things) can increase consumption happiness. Frugal consumers would spend less and experience more shopping happiness using a variety of shopping strategies such as eliminating distressing debts, stretching positive shopping experiences through appreciation and savoring, recycling positive shopping experiences via variety and reminiscing, renting instead of buying, and resolutely focusing on intrinsic goals over extrinsic one (Chancellor & Lyubomirsky, 2011). Frugal consumers are less likely to engage in impulsive purchasing; they are less likely to be materialistic. Frugal consumers seek non-material satisfaction and are opposed to excessive consumption and material possessions. Examples of frugal spending include a voluntary simplicity lifestyle (Etzioni, 1998), an anti-consumption lifestyle (Lee et al., 2011), and a low ownership lifestyle (Ozanne & Ballantine, 2010).

First, consumers with a *voluntary simplicity* lifestyle seek non-materialistic satisfaction. They sustainably pursue a simple life and seek to pursue experiences that are nonmaterialistic (Etzioni, 1998). Voluntary simplicity as a lifestyle is a deliberate initiative that involves establishing a distance from the material world and possessions. In other words, consumers adopting a voluntary simplicity lifestyle pursue non-materialistic meanings in their consumption habits through a simpler and stress-free lifestyle (Elgin, 2010; Iyer & Muncy, 2009), thereby enhancing consumer happiness.

Second, consumers with *anti-consumption values* also seek non-material satisfaction by expressing concerns related to excessive consumption. Anti-consumerism is a consumer value that advocates stopping excessive consumption and returning to a green and simple consumption mode. Anti-consumption, an internally oriented value, can actively promote consumer happiness (Lee et al., 2011).

Third, consumers with a low ownership lifestyle pursue a life without many material possessions. They seek renting, leasing, and borrowing of material things instead of direct ownership. These consumers can reduce the number of products that they own without having to sacrifice the benefits that these products confer (Ozanne & Ballantine, 2010). As such, low-ownership consumers exert control over their spending, save more, and have a low marginal propensity to spend, all of which contribute to consumer happiness.

Frugal consumers are likely to have enhanced consumer happiness because they seek intrinsic goals that fit with their lifestyle. They do not seek extrinsic goals with materialistic value. They engage in rewarding and meaningful activities and seek satisfaction from intrinsic goals (Chancellor & Lyubomirsky, 2014) that serve to increase consumer happiness.

Justifiable Spending

Shopping happiness is high when consumers can justify the purchase of indulgent products. Consumers often engage in indulgent purchases (e.g., luxury products), unethical purchases, and impulsive purchases to increase feelings of pleasure and positive emotions (Haws & Poynor, 2008; Pozharliev et al., 2015; Silvera et al., 2008). Spending on indulgent and hedonic products for pleasure is harder to justify than spending on utilitarian products (Okada, 2005).

Consumers are happier when they have a justifiable reason to buy the products. Typical purchase justifications include self-reward experience (De Witt Huberts et al., 2014), special events to celebrate (Petersen et al., 2018), and altruistic purchase for others (Khan & Dhar, 2006). Without *due justification* for their purchases, consumers are likely to experience feelings of regret (Okada, 2005; Rosenzweig & Gilovich, 2012; Verplanken & Herabadi, 2001) or feelings of guilt (Nassani et al., 2013), which in turn act to deflate their self-esteem and shopping happiness.

Consumers' *justifiable spending* prevents decreases in consumption happiness for the following reasons. First, consumers' justifiable spending reduces a sense of guilt concerning hedonic consumption. Hedonic consumption evokes a sense of guilt, providing the consumer with a reason to mitigate the guilty feelings through indulgent spending (Okada, 2005; Xu & Schwarz, 2009).

Second, consumers' justifiable spending reduces a sense of regret in impulsive purchases. Impulsive purchases can evoke feelings of regret, and having a reason for impulsive spending reduces consumer regret after the purchase. Research has demonstrated that other-benefit justifications (e.g., gifts for others, contribution to society) are more effective to justify the impulsive purchase of a product than self-benefit justifications (e.g., own celebration, self-reward) (Moes et al., 2022).

Third, consumers' justifiable spending fits well with consumers' self-control tendencies, which contributes to positive self-concept and consumer happiness. Self-control is a personality trait defined as the ability to monitor one's behavior against specific standards and change or interrupt undesired behavioral tendencies (Baumeister, 2002). High self-control consumers are likely to feel happy when they have justifiable reasons to buy indulgent products (Petersen et al., 2018).

In summary, consumer's justifiable spending protects consumers from possible negative feelings (e.g., guilt, regret) in relation to indulgent and hedonic shopping.

Summary and Conclusion

Table 13.1 summarizes much of the chapter discussion related to factors influencing shopping happiness. As such, marketing strategies that organizations should adopt based on this research could be as follows:

- Increase shopping value by increasing the utilitarian and hedonic values of the shopping experience.
- Encourage shoppers to be more engaged in shopping by providing incentives to increase the frequency of shopping, but only up to an optimal level.
- Create strategies to increase harmonious shopping passion, not obsessive passion.
- Encourage shoppers to purchase hedonic products in conjunction with utilitarian products.
- Encourage shoppers to purchase sustainable products from organizations that have a reputation for being ethical.
- Encourage shoppers to purchase products that fit their personalities and values.
- Encourage shoppers to increase their purchases of experiential products.
- Encourage shoppers to increase their purchases of memorable products.
- Encourage shoppers to increase their purchases of time-saving products.

Table 13.1 Factors affecting happiness in a shopping context

Dimension	Impact on shopping happiness	Details
Shopping value	An increase in utilitarian shopping value contributes to shopping happiness.	Shopping happiness is greatly influenced by hedonic values rather than by utilitarian values in shopping.
	An increase in hedonic shopping value contributes to shopping happiness.	
Shopping engagement	Engagement in shopping activities contributes to shopping happiness.	The frequency of shopping engagement has a greater effect on shopping happiness than intensity or diversity. Excessive shopping participation deteriorates shopping satisfaction and shopping happiness.
Shopping passion	Shopping happiness is higher when consumers engage in shopping activities with harmonious passion.	The effect of shopping engagement on shopping illbeing (regret, rumination) is high when consumers have an obsessive shopping passion.
Products to shop	Shopping happiness is higher when consumers purchase hedonic products than when they purchase functional products.	Consumers experience strong positive affect from hedonic experiential products (e.g., delight and excitement) while consumers experience weak positive affect from functional products.
	Shopping happiness is higher when consumers purchase sustainable and ethical products.	The purchase of sustainable products increases positive emotions and reduces negative emotions
	Shopping happiness is high when consumers buy products that match their personality and values.	Green product shopping is positively associated with eudaimonic happiness for consumers with environmentally friendly self-identity.
	Shopping happiness is higher when consumers purchase experiential products than when consumers purchase material products for possession.	Experiences elicit greater in-the-moment happiness.
	Consumer happiness is high by purchasing memorable goods.	Memorable goods effectively make memories of good experiences and reduce consumers' recall bias.
	Consumers are happier when they spend on time-saving services.	Consumers with a preference for time over money are significantly happier than consumers with a preference for money over time.

References

Aaker, J. L., Rudd, M., & Mogilner, C. (2011). If money does not make you happy, consider time. *Journal of Consumer Psychology, 21*(2), 126–130.

Ahuvia, A. C. (2015). Nothing matters more to people than people: Brand meaning and social relationships. In *Brand meaning management* (Vol. 12, pp. 121–149). Emerald Group Publishing Limited.

Aknin, L. B., Sandstrom, G. M., Dunn, E. W., & Norton, M. I. (2011). It's the recipient that counts: Spending money on strong social ties leads to greater happiness than spending on weak social ties. *PLoS One, 6*(2), e17018.

Aknin, L. B., Dunn, E. W., Whillans, A. V., Grant, A. M., & Norton, M. I. (2013a). Making a difference matters: Impact unlocks the emotional benefits of prosocial spending. *Journal of Economic Behavior & Organization, 88*, 90–95.

Aknin, L. B., Barrington-Leigh, C. P., Dunn, E. W., Helliwell, J. F., Burns, J., Biswas-Diener, R., et al. (2013b). Prosocial spending and well-being: Cross-cultural evidence for a psychological universal. *Journal of Personality and Social Psychology, 104*(4), 635–652.

Arnold, M. J., & Reynolds, K. E. (2003). Hedonic shopping motivations. *Journal of Retailing, 79*(2), 77–95.

Babin, B. J., & Attaway, J. S. (2000). Atmospheric affect as a tool for creating value and gaining share of customer. *Journal of Business Research, 49*(2), 91–99.

Babin, B. J., Darden, W. R., & Griffin, M. (1994). Work and/or fun: Measuring hedonic and utilitarian shopping value. *Journal of Consumer Research, 20*(4), 644–656.

Baumeister, R. F. (2002). Yielding to temptation: Self-control failure, impulsive purchasing, and consumer behavior. *Journal of Consumer Research, 28*(4), 670–676.

Beaton, A. A., Funk, D. C., Ridinger, L., & Jordan, J. (2011). Sport involvement: A conceptual and empirical analysis. *Sport Management Review, 14*(2), 126–140.

Belk, R. W., & Coon, G. S. (1993). Gift giving as agapic love: An alternative to the exchange paradigm based on dating experiences. *Journal of Consumer Research, 20*(3), 393–417.

Berezan, O., Krishen, A. S., Agarwal, S., & Kachroo, P. (2018). The pursuit of virtual happiness: Exploring the social media experience across generations. *Journal of Business Research, 89*, 455–461.

Brown, K. W., & Kasser, T. (2005). Are psychological and ecological well-being compatible? The role of values, mindfulness, and lifestyle. *Social Indicators Research, 74*(2), 349–368.

Chan, C., & Mogilner, C. (2017). Experiential gifts foster stronger social relationships than material gifts. *Journal of Consumer Research, 43*(6), 913–931.

Chancellor, J., & Lyubomirsky, S. (2011). Happiness and thrift: When (spending) less is (hedonically) more. *Journal of Consumer Psychology, 21*(2), 131–138.

Chancellor, J., & Lyubomirsky, S. (2014). Money for happiness: The hedonic benefits of thrift. In M. Tatzel (Ed.), *Consumption and well-being in the material world*. Springer.

Chaouali, W., Lunardo, R., Ben Yahia, I., Cyr, D., & Triki, A. (2020). Design aesthetics as drivers of value in mobile banking: Does customer happiness matter? *International Journal of Bank Marketing, 38*(1), 219–241.

Chitturi, R., Raghunathan, R., & Mahajan, V. (2008). Delight by design: The role of hedonic versus utilitarian benefits. *Journal of Marketing, 72*(3), 48–63.

Chiu, Y. P., Lo, S. K., Hsieh, A. Y., & Hwang, Y. (2019). Exploring why people spend more time shopping online than in offline stores. *Computers in Human Behavior, 95*, 24–30.

Chun, H. H., & Hiang, Y. W. (2016). Free drink or free mug? Managing service experience with experiential vs. material complimentary gifts. *Service Science, 8*(2), 184–202.

Curran, T., Hill, A. P., Appleton, P. R., Vallerand, R. J., & Standage, M. (2015). The psychology of passion: A meta-analytical review of a decade of research on intrapersonal outcomes. *Motivation and Emotion, 39*(5), 631–655.

Curry, O. S., Rowland, L. A., Van Lissa, C. J., Zlotowitz, S., McAlaney, J., & Whitehouse, H. (2018). Happy to help? A systematic review and meta-analysis of the effects of performing acts of kindness on the well-being of the actor. *Journal of Experimental Social Psychology, 76*(May), 320–329.

Dabholkar, P. A., & Bagozzi, R. P. (2002). An attitudinal model of technology-based self-service: Moderating effects of consumer traits and situational factors. *Journal of the Academy of Marketing Science, 30*(3), 184–201.

De Witt Huberts, J., Evers, C., & de Ridder, D. (2014). Thinking before sinning: Reasoning processes in hedonic consumption. *Frontiers in Psychology, 5*(November), 1268.

De Young, R. (2000). New ways to promote pro-environmental behavior: Expanding and evaluating motives for environmentally responsible behavior. *Journal of Social Issues, 56*(3), 509–526.

DeLeire, T., & Kalil, A. (2010). Does consumption buy happiness? Evidence from the United States. *International Review of Economics, 57*(June), 163–176.

Dennis, C., Alamanos, E., Papagiannidis, S., & Bourlakis, M. (2016). Does social exclusion influence multiple channel use? The interconnections with community, happiness, and well-being. *Journal of Business Research, 69*(3), 1061–1070.

Desmeules, R. (2002). The impact of variety on consumer happiness: Marketing and the tyranny of freedom. *Academy of Marketing Science Review, 12*(1), 1–18.

Dhar, R., & Wertenbroch, K. (2000). Consumer choice between hedonic and utilitarian goods. *Journal of Marketing Research, 37*(1), 60–71.

Dias, R. S., Sharma, E., & Fitzsimons, G. J. (2022). Spending and happiness: The role of perceived financial constraints. *Journal of Consumer Research, 49*(3), 373–388.

Diener, E., Sandvik, E., & Pavot, W. (2009). Happiness is the frequency, not the intensity, of positive versus negative affect. In *Assessing well-being: The collected works of Ed Diener* (pp. 213–231). Springer Netherlands.

Dittmar, H., Bond, R., Hurst, M., & Kasser, T. (2014). The relationship between materialism and personal well-being: A meta-analysis. *Journal of Personality and Social Psychology, 107*(5), 879–924.

Duan, J., & Dholakia, R. R. (2017). Posting purchases on social media increases happiness: The mediating roles of purchases' impact on self and interpersonal relationships. *Journal of Consumer Marketing, 34*(5), 404–413.

Dunn, E. W., Aknin, L. B., & Norton, M. I. (2008). Spending money on others promotes happiness. *Science, 319*(5870), 1687–1688.

Dunn, E. W., Aknin, L. B., & Norton, M. I. (2014). Prosocial spending and happiness: Using money to benefit others pays off. *Current Directions in Psychological Science, 23*(1), 41–47.

Ekici, A., Sirgy, M. J., Lee, D. J., Yu, G. B., & Bosnjak, M. (2018). The effects of shopping well-being and shopping ill-being on consumer life satisfaction. *Applied Research in Quality of Life, 13*(2), 333–353.

El Hedhli, K., Chebat, J. C., & Sirgy, M. J. (2013). Shopping well-being at the mall: Construct, antecedents, and consequences. *Journal of Business Research, 66*(7), 856–863.

El Hedhli, K., Zourrig, H., & Chebat, J. C. (2016). Shopping well-being: Is it just a matter of pleasure or doing the task? The role of shopper's gender and self-congruity. *Journal of Retailing and Consumer Services, 31*, 1–13.

Elgin, D. (2010). *Voluntary simplicity* (2nd revised ed.). Harper.

Etzioni, A. (1998). Comments on Amitai Etzioni: Voluntary simplicity: Characterization, select psychological implications, and societal consequences-Reply. *Journal of Economic Psychology, 19*(5), 651–652.

Fiore, A. M., Jin, H. J., & Kim, J. (2005). For fun and profit: Hedonic value from image interactivity and responses toward an online store. *Psychology & Marketing, 22*(8), 669–694.

Ganglmair-Wooliscroft, A., & Lawson, R. (2011). Subjective well-being of different consumer lifestyle segments. *Journal of Macromarketing, 31*(2), 172–183.

Ganglmair-Wooliscroft, A., & Wooliscroft, B. (2019). Well-being and everyday ethical consumption. *Journal of Happiness Studies, 20*(1), 141–163.

Geenen, N. Y., Hohelüchter, M., Langholf, V., & Walther, E. (2014). The beneficial effects of prosocial spending on happiness: Work hard, make money, and spend it on others? *The Journal of Positive Psychology, 9*(3), 204–208.

Giebelhausen, M., Chun, H. H., Cronin, J. J., Jr., & Hult, G. T. M. (2016). Adjusting the warm-glow thermostat: How incentivizing participation in voluntary green programs moderates their impact on service satisfaction. *Journal of Marketing, 80*(4), 56–71.

Giesler, M. (2006). Consumer gift systems. *Journal of Consumer Research, 33*(2), 283–290.

Gilovich, T., & Gallo, I. (2020). Consumers' pursuit of material and experiential purchases: A review. *Consumer Psychology Review, 3*(1), 20–33.
Gilovich, T., Kumar, A., & Jampol, L. (2015). A wonderful life: Experiential consumption and the pursuit of happiness. *Journal of Consumer Psychology, 25*(1), 152–165.
Goodman, J. K., Malkoc, S. A., & Stephenson, B. L. (2016). Celebrate or commemorate? A material purchase advantage when honoring special life events. *Journal of the Association for Consumer Research, 1*(4), 497–508.
Guevarra, D. A., & Howell, R. T. (2015). To have in order to do: Exploring the effects of consuming experiential products on well-being. *Journal of Consumer Psychology, 25*(1), 28–41.
Guiry, M., Mägi, A. W., & Lutz, R. J. (2006). Defining and measuring recreational shopper identity. *Journal of the Academy of Marketing Science, 34*(1), 74–83.
Haws, K. L., & Poynor, C. (2008). Seize the day! Encouraging indulgence for the hyperopic consumer. *Journal of Consumer Research, 35*(4), 680–691.
Hershfield, H. E., Mogilner, C., & Barnea, U. (2016). People who choose time over money are happier. *Social Psychological and Personality Science, 7*(7), 697–706.
Hill, G., & Howell, R. T. (2014). Moderators and mediators of pro-social spending and well-being: The influence of values and psychological need satisfaction. *Personality and Individual Differences, 69*, 69–74.
Hirschman, E. C., & Holbrook, M. B. (1982). Hedonic consumption: Emerging concepts, methods and propositions. *Journal of Marketing, 46*(3), 92–101.
Horváth, C., & Adıgüzel, F. (2018). Shopping enjoyment to the extreme: Hedonic shopping motivations and compulsive buying in developed and emerging markets. *Journal of Business Research, 86*, 300–310.
Howell, R. T., & Hill, G. (2009). The mediators of experiential purchases: Determining the impact of psychological needs satisfaction and social comparison. *The Journal of Positive Psychology, 4*(6), 511–522.
Hu, Y., & Min, H. K. (2022). Enjoyment or indulgence: What draws the line in hedonic food consumption? *International Journal of Hospitality Management, 104*, 103228.
Hui, B. P., & Kogan, A. (2018). Daily ups and downs: An event-sampling study of the mediated moderation of prosocial engagement on well-being. *Social Psychological and Personality Science, 9*(6), 675–688.
Hui, B. P., Ng, J. C., Berzaghi, E., Cunningham-Amos, L. A., & Kogan, A. (2020). Rewards of kindness? A meta-analysis of the link between prosociality and well-being. *Psychological Bulletin, 146*(12), 1084–1116.
Iyengar, S. S., & Lepper, M. R. (2000). When choice is demotivating: Can one desire too much of a good thing? *Journal of Personality and Social Psychology, 79*(6), 995–1006.
Iyer, R., & Muncy, J. A. (2009). Purpose and object of anti-consumption. *Journal of Business Research, 62*(2), 160–168.
Khan, U., & Dhar, R. (2006). Licensing effect in consumer choice. *Journal of Marketing Research, 43*(2), 259–266.
Klein, L. R. (1998). Evaluating the potential of interactive media through a new lens: Search versus experience goods. *Journal of Business Research, 41*(3), 195–203.
Kumar, A., & Gilovich, T. (2016). To do or to have, now or later? The preferred consumption profiles of material and experiential purchases. *Journal of Consumer Psychology, 26*(2), 169–178.
Kumar, A., Killingsworth, M. A., & Gilovich, T. (2020). Spending on doing promotes more moment-to-moment happiness than spending on having. *Journal of Experimental Social Psychology, 88*(May), 103971.
Lambert, N. M., Gwinn, A. M., Baumeister, R. F., Strachman, A., Washburn, I. J., Gable, S. L., & Fincham, F. D. (2013). A boost of positive affect: The perks of sharing positive experiences. *Journal of Social and Personal Relationships, 30*(1), 24–43.
Lee, M., Roux, D., Cherrier, H., & Cova, B. (2011). Anti-consumption and consumer resistance: Concepts, concerns, conflicts and convergence. *European Journal of Marketing, 45*(11/12), 1680–1687.

Lee, D. J., Yu, G. B., Sirgy, M. J., Ekici, A., Gurel-Atay, E., & Bahn, K. D. (2014). Shopping well-being and ill-being: Toward an integrated model. In F. Russo & E. Drucia (Eds.), *Handbook of research on retailer-consumer relationship development* (pp. 27–44). IGI Global.

Liu, W., & Aaker, J. (2008). The happiness of giving: The time-ask effect. *Journal of Consumer Research, 35*(3), 543–557.

Mageau, G. A., Vallerand, R. J., Charest, J., Salvy, S. J., Lacaille, N., Bouffard, T., & Koestner, R. (2009). On the development of harmonious and obsessive passion: The role of autonomy support, activity specialization, and identification with the activity. *Journal of Personality, 77*(3), 601–646.

Markus, H. R., & Schwartz, B. (2010). Does choice mean freedom and well-being? *Journal of Consumer Research, 37*(2), 344–355.

Matz, S. C., Gladstone, J. J., & Stillwell, D. (2016). Money buys happiness when spending fits our personality. *Psychological Science, 27*(5), 715–725.

Moes, A., Fransen, M., Verhagen, T., & Fennis, B. (2022). A good reason to buy: Justification drives the effect of advertising frames on impulsive socially responsible buying. *Psychology & Marketing, 39*(12), 2260–2272.

Mogilner, C. (2010). The pursuit of happiness: Time, money, and social connection. *Psychological Science, 21*(9), 1348–1354.

Mogilner, C., & Norton, M. I. (2016). Time, money, and happiness. *Current Opinion in Psychology, 10*(August), 12–16.

Mogilner, C., Aaker, J., & Kamvar, S. D. (2012). How happiness affects choice. *Journal of Consumer Research, 39*(2), 429–443.

Nassani, A. M., Khader, J. A., & Ali, I. (2013). Consumer environmental activism, sustainable consumption behavior and satisfaction with life. *Life Science Journal, 10*(2), 1000–1006.

Netemeyer, R. G., Warmath, D., Fernandes, D., & Lynch, J. G., Jr. (2018). How am I doing? Perceived financial well-being, its potential antecedents, and its relation to overall well-being. *Journal of Consumer Research, 45*(1), 68–89.

Nicolao, L., Irwin, J. R., & Goodman, J. K. (2009). Happiness for sale: Do experiential purchases make consumers happier than material purchases? *Journal of Consumer Research, 36*(2), 188–198.

Okada, E. M. (2005). Justification effects on consumer choice of hedonic and utilitarian goods. *Journal of Marketing Research, 42*(1), 43–53.

Onwezen, M. C., Antonides, G., & Bartels, J. (2013). The Norm Activation Model: An exploration of the functions of anticipated pride and guilt in pro-environmental behavior. *Journal of Economic Psychology, 39*, 141–153.

Ozanne, L. K., & Ballantine, P. W. (2010). Sharing as a form of anti-consumption? An examination of toy library users. *Journal of Consumer Behaviour, 9*(6), 485–498.

Pappas, I. O., Kourouthanassis, P. E., Giannakos, M. N., & Chrissikopoulos, V. (2014). Shiny happy people buying: The role of emotions on personalized e-shopping. *Electronic Markets, 24*(3), 193–206.

Petersen, F. E., Dretsch, H. J., & Loureiro, Y. K. (2018). Who needs a reason to indulge? Happiness following reason-based indulgent consumption. *International Journal of Research in Marketing, 35*(1), 170–184.

Pozharliev, R., Verbeke, W. J., Van Strien, J. W., & Bagozzi, R. P. (2015). Merely being with you increases my attention to luxury products: Using EEG to understand consumers' emotional experience with luxury branded products. *Journal of Marketing Research, 52*(4), 546–558.

Prelec, D., & Loewenstein, G. (1991). Decision making over time and under uncertainty: A common approach. *Management Science, 37*(7), 770–786.

Ramanathan, S., & Williams, P. (2007). Immediate and delayed emotional consequences of indulgence: The moderating influence of personality type on mixed emotions. *Journal of Consumer Research, 34*(2), 212–223.

Ramos-Hidalgo, E., Diaz-Carrion, R., & Rodriguez-Rad, C. (2022). Does sustainable consumption make consumers happy? *International Journal of Market Research, 64*(2), 227–248.

Reis, H. T., Smith, S. M., Carmichael, C. L., Caprariello, P. A., Tsai, F. F., Rodrigues, A., & Maniaci, M. R. (2010). Are you happy for me? How sharing positive events with others provides personal and interpersonal benefits. *Journal of Personality and Social Psychology, 99*(2), 311–329.

Roets, A., Schwartz, B., & Guan, Y. (2012). The tyranny of choice: A cross-cultural investigation of maximizing-satisficing effects on well-being. *Judgment and Decision Making, 7*(6), 689–704.

Rosenzweig, E., & Gilovich, T. (2012). Buyer's remorse or missed opportunity? Differential regrets for material and experiential purchases. *Journal of Personality and Social Psychology, 102*(2), 215–223.

Rowe, Z. O., Wilson, H. N., Dimitriu, R., Charnley, F. J., & Lastrucci, G. (2019). Pride in my past: Influencing sustainable choices through behavioral recall. *Psychology & Marketing, 36*(4), 276–286.

Sääksjärvi, M., Hellén, K., & Desmet, P. (2017). The "you and I" of happiness: Investigating the long-term impact of self-and other-focused happiness-enhancing activities. *Psychology & Marketing, 34*(6), 623–630.

Schellong, M., Kraiczy, N. D., Malär, L., & Hack, A. (2019). Family firm brands, perceptions of doing good, and consumer happiness. *Entrepreneurship Theory and Practice, 43*(5), 921–946.

Schmitt, B., Brakus, J. J., & Zarantonello, L. (2015). From experiential psychology to consumer experience. *Journal of Consumer Psychology, 25*(1), 166–171.

Schröder, M. J., & McEachern, M. G. (2004). Consumer value conflicts surrounding ethical food purchase decisions: A focus on animal welfare. *International Journal of Consumer Studies, 28*(2), 168–177.

Schulz, P., Schulte, J., Raube, S., Disouky, H., & Kandler, C. (2018). The role of leisure interest and engagement for subjective well-being. *Journal of Happiness Studies, 19*(4), 1135–1150.

Schwartz, B. (2004). *The paradox of choice: Why more is less*. Harper Collins.

Seguin-Levesque, C., Lalibertea, M. L. N., Pelletier, L. G., Blanchard, C., & Vallerand, R. J. (2003). Harmonious and obsessive passion for the Internet: Their associations with the Couple's relationship. *Journal of Applied Social Psychology, 33*(1), 197–221.

Sevilla, J., Lu, J., & Kahn, B. E. (2019). Variety seeking, satiation, and maximizing enjoyment over time. *Journal of Consumer Psychology, 29*(1), 89–103.

Sheth, J. N., Newman, B. I., & Gross, B. L. (1991). Why we buy what we buy: A theory of consumption values. *Journal of Business Research, 22*(2), 159–170.

Silvera, D. H., Lavack, A. M., & Kropp, F. (2008). Impulse buying: The role of affect, social influence, and subjective wellbeing. *Journal of Consumer Marketing, 25*(1), 23–33.

Sirgy, M. J., Lee, D. J., Grace, B. Y., Gurel-Atay, E., Tidwell, J., & Ekici, A. (2016). Self-expressiveness in shopping. *Journal of Retailing and Consumer Services, 30*, 292–299.

Sirgy, M. J., Lee, D. J., & Yu, G. B. (2020). Shopping-life balance: Towards a unifying framework. *Applied Research in Quality of Life, 15*(1), 17–34.

Stenseng, F. (2008). The two faces of leisure activity engagement: Harmonious and obsessive passion in relation to intrapersonal conflict and life domain outcomes. *Leisure Sciences, 30*(5), 465–481.

Sun, M., & Trudel, R. (2017). The effect of recycling versus trashing on consumption: Theory and experimental evidence. *Journal of Marketing Research, 54*(2), 293–305.

Tay, L., Batz, C., Parrigon, S., & Kuykendall, L. (2017). Debt and subjective well-being: The other side of the income-happiness coin. *Journal of Happiness Studies, 18*(3), 903–937.

Tezer, A., & Bodur, H. O. (2020). The green consumption effect: How using green products improves consumption experience. *Journal of Consumer Research, 47*(1), 25–39.

Thaler, R. H., & Shefrin, H. M. (1981). An economic theory of self-control. *Journal of Political Economy, 89*(2), 392–406.

Tully, S., & Meyvis, T. (2017). Forgetting to remember our experiences: People overestimate how much they will retrospect personal events. *Journal of Personality and Social Psychology, 113*(6), 878–891.

Tully, S. M., Hershfield, H. E., & Meyvis, T. (2015). Seeking lasting enjoyment with limited money: Financial constraints increase preference for material goods over experiences. *Journal of Consumer Research, 42*(1), 59–75.

Vallerand, R. J. (2015). *The psychology of passion: A dualistic model. Series in positive psychology*. Oxford University Press.

Vallerand, R. J., Blanchard, C., Mageau, G. A., Koestner, R., Ratelle, C., Léonard, M., et al. (2003). Les passions de l'ame: On obsessive and harmonious passion. *Journal of Personality and Social Psychology, 85*(4), 756–767.

Van Boven, L., & Gilovich, T. (2003). To do or to have? That is the question. *Journal of Personality and Social Psychology, 85*(6), 1193–1202.

Van der Werff, E., Steg, L., & Keizer, K. (2014). Follow the signal: When past pro-environmental actions signal who you are. *Journal of Environmental Psychology, 40*(December), 273–282.

Veenhoven, R., Chiperi, F., Kang, X., & Burger, M. (2021). Happiness and consumption: A research synthesis using an online finding archive. *SAGE Open, 11*(1), 2158244020986239.

Verplanken, B., & Herabadi, A. (2001). Individual differences in impulse buying tendency: Feeling and no thinking. *European Journal of Personality, 15*(Suppl. 1), S71–S83.

Vieira, V., Santini, F. O., & Araujo, C. F. (2018). A meta-analytic review of hedonic and utilitarian shopping values. *Journal of Consumer Marketing, 35*(4), 426–437.

Weinstein, N., & Ryan, R. M. (2010). When helping helps: Autonomous motivation for prosocial behavior and its influence on well-being for the helper and recipient. *Journal of Personality and Social Psychology, 98*(2), 222–244.

Whillans, A. V., Weidman, A. C., & Dunn, E. W. (2016). Valuing time over money is associated with greater happiness. *Social Psychological and Personality Science, 7*(3), 213–222.

Whillans, A. V., Dunn, E. W., Smeets, P., Bekkers, R., & Norton, M. I. (2017). Buying time promotes happiness. *Proceedings of the National Academy of Sciences, 114*(32), 8523–8527.

White, K., Habib, R., & Hardisty, D. J. (2019). How to SHIFT consumer behaviors to be more sustainable: A literature review and guiding framework. *Journal of Marketing, 83*(3), 22–49.

Xu, J., & Schwarz, N. (2009). Do we really need a reason to indulge? *Journal of Marketing Research, 46*(1), 25–36.

Zheng, H., & Ma, W. (2021). Click it and buy happiness: Does online shopping improve subjective well-being of rural residents in China? *Applied Economics, 53*(36), 4192–4206.

Zhong, J. Y., & Mitchell, V. W. (2010). A mechanism model of the effect of hedonic product consumption on well-being. *Journal of Consumer Psychology, 20*(2), 152–162.

Zulauf, K., & Wagner, R. (2022). Online shopping therapy: If you want to be happy, shop around. *Journal of International Consumer Marketing, 34*(3), 332–345.

Chapter 14
Happiness in Relation to Material Possessions

Don't ever be ashamed of loving the strange things that make your weird little heart happy.

Elizabeth Gilbert; (https://www.countryliving.com/life/g4815/happy-life-quotes/?utm_source=google&utm_medium=cpc&utm_campaign=mgu_ga_clv_md_pmx_hybd_mix_us_18709966696&gad_source=1&gclid=EAIaIQobChMI2f61-qqEiAMVlE5HAR19uQsZEAAYASAAEgIeGPD_BwE)

What Is Happiness in Relation to Material Possessions?

The basic premise here is that consumers' possession of products contributes to happiness. Consumption wellbeing during the possession stage is material happiness. Specifically, happiness concerning material possessions refers to consumers' happiness resulting from satisfying material possessions (Andrews & Withey, 1976; Nakano et al., 1995; Sirgy et al., 1998; Smits & Steendijk, 2015).

If consumers' goal is to gain ownership of an object that is tangible and stays in one's possession (e.g., electronics, clothing, and jewelry), then it is a material purchase (Carter & Gilovich, 2012; Thomas & Millar, 2013). Material products are tangible and less unique (Nicolao et al., 2009), so it is easy for consumers to compare alternatives (Carter & Gilovich, 2010). Material purchases are rarely shared with others and are less socially engaging (Howell & Hill, 2009; Van Boven, 2005). As material products are quite similar and do not have much social value, consumers experience high levels of hedonic adaptation for their material products (Nicolao et al., 2009). Hedonic adaption refers to attenuation of affective reactions resulting from ongoing and repetitive ownership and usage of a particular product (e.g., Sheldon & Lyubomirsky, 2012; Wang et al., 2009; Yang et al., 2017). For example, one may experience strong positive emotions after buying a new automobile, but experiences of positive affect from the new car will become less frequent and less intense as consumers quickly adapt to the positive event.

D.-J. Lee, M. J. Sirgy, *Happiness in the Marketplace*, Social Indicators Research Series 64, https://doi.org/10.1007/978-3-032-04443-3_14

Popular material purchases typically allow for repeated usage over time. Material (vs. experiential) purchases, therefore, may allow for more frequent momentary happiness over time, even if experiential purchases provide more intense momentary happiness during specific instances in which they are enjoyed (Weidman & Dunn, 2016). To examine consumers' momentary happiness while consuming material vs. experiential purchases, two experiments were conducted by Weidman and Dunn (2016). In the first study, participants were randomly assigned to spend C$20 on a material versus experiential purchase and reported their momentary happiness regarding these purchases over 2 weeks using daily diary methodologies. In the second study, participants were randomly assigned to report a material versus experiential gift they received at Christmas and reported their momentary happiness over 2 weeks using experience sampling methodologies. Results suggest that material purchases provide more *frequent* momentary happiness over time (e.g., the number of times the consumer experiences happiness from the product), whereas experiential purchases provide more *intense* momentary happiness on individual occasions (e.g., the average degree of happiness the consumer experiences across occasions). Material purchases provide consumers with more *frequent* momentary happiness because material products allow for repeated and frequent usage over time.

Brand happiness is an example of happiness from material possessions. Although there is extensive research on emotional responses to brands (Bagozzi et al., 1999; Laros & Steenkamp, 2005; Richins, 1997), limited attention has been given to the brands' impact specifically on consumer happiness (Bettingen & Luedicke, 2009). Consumers make their purchases to enhance their happiness (Williams, 2014). Consumers' positive experiences with material products and brands make them feel happy about their brands (Bettingen & Luedicke, 2009), which in turn serve to enhance the image of these brands, their value, and loyalty (Mishra et al., 2014). Companies that focus on enhancing customers' happiness are likely to benefit from an enhanced corporate image, goodwill, and are more likely to prosper in the long run (Lee & Sirgy, 2004). We further explain the psychology behind material possessions and brand happiness in the sections below.

Material Possessions

Again, the central tenet is that consumers' possession of material products contributes to happiness concerning material possessions. This type of happiness refers to consumers' happiness resulting from satisfying material possessions. Satisfying possessions contribute to happiness for the following reasons. First, possession of material products provides consumers with a sense of fulfillment of physical and psychological needs as well as fulfillment of material aspirations. Material possession of utilitarian products provides consumers with satisfaction of functional needs. The fulfillment of physical and psychological needs from utilitarian products is especially important for consumers with low income (Howell & Howell, 2008). Research has shown that consumer life satisfaction is high when material products (e.g., automobile) serve to meet consumers' various developmental needs–safety, economic, family, social, esteem, actualization, knowledge, and aesthetics needs (Sirgy et al., 2006).

Second, satisfying material possessions serve to heighten a positive self-concept. Possessions of products can serve to signal, either to the self or to others, success, competence, or mastery in specific domains of life (Belk, 1988; Mandel et al., 2017; Rucker & Galinsky, 2012). Both *symbolic self-completion* and *self-enhancement* theories confirm that material objects are often used to help symbolically support an identity that combines potentially conflicting aspects of self, such as tensions between actual self and ideal self, ultimately enhancing or completing self-concept (Ahuvia, 2005; Wicklund & Gollwitzer, 2013). For example, when consumers have a strong belief about their self-view (e.g., I am an exciting person), they are motivated to buy symbolic products (e.g., brands with exciting personalities) that reinforce their original self-view (Gao et al., 2009).

In addition, possession of symbolic products can provide a means for individuals to cope with self-threats (Gao et al., 2009; Rucker et al., 2012). When consumers temporarily lose their self-confidence, they become motivated to choose possessions that help boost and regain their self-confidence (Gao et al., 2009). For example, when consumers' self-view (e.g., I am an intelligent person) is temporarily cast in doubt, they become motivated to choose symbolic products (e.g., pen, sophisticated books) that help recover their original self-view. Consumption of these symbolic products can help restore a momentarily shaken self-view by providing direct evidence about certain aspects of one's identity (e.g., intelligence) (Gao et al., 2009). In summary, satisfying possession of products contributes to material happiness because it maintains and enhances positive self-concept.

Third, satisfying material possessions serve to provide consumers with various benefits: functional benefits (e.g., high quality and good price), social benefits (e.g., enhancement of social concept), and emotional benefits (e.g., brand attachment) (Sweeney & Soutar, 2001). Empirical studies found that consumer happiness from the use of material products is positively associated with the degree to which the material product (e.g., mobile phone) provides various benefits (Sirgy et al., 2008). Research also found that consumer happiness from a material product is associated with the degree to which the material product (e.g., musical instruments and sports equipment) provides consumers with new life experiences that are related to positive self-concept and social satisfaction (Guevarra & Howell, 2015). In summary, material happiness is high when the use of material products provides consumers with many benefits.

Brand Happiness

Brand happiness is the consumers' greatest emotional fulfillment, a moment-based experience of pleasant high and low arousal emotions, induced at different brand contact points (Schnebelen & Bruhn, 2018). In other words, brand happiness is a positive emotional state that is subjective and time-limited, resulting from various possession experiences with a brand.

Satisfying ownership of a brand can contribute to brand happiness for the following reasons. First, consumers can experience a pleasant surprise or delight from interacting with a brand (Arnold et al., 2005). For example, consumers experience pleasure, fun, and enjoyment from their hedonic brands (Babin et al., 1994). Hedonic brands are brands that are primarily consumed for sensory gratification and emotional reasons (e.g., fun and enjoyment) (Hirschman & Holbrook, 1982; Holbrook & Hirschman, 1982), as well as emotional arousal (Mano & Oliver, 1993). Consequently, consumers' frequent experience of positive affect arising from the possession of a brand contributes to material happiness.

Second, consumers can experience a positive self-concept through the ownership of a symbolic brand. Satisfying ownership of a symbolic brand can provide consumers with self-enhancing experiences that include feelings of looking unique and trendy (Mansoor & Paul, 2022). Meeting the need for uniqueness leads consumers to feel happy (Koydemir et al., 2014). Satisfying ownership of a symbolic brand helps consumers visualize the best possible self and helps to approach their ideal self, which in turn contributes to material happiness (cf. Sheldon & Lyubomirsky, 2006).

Research has shown that ownership of "masstige brands" (i.e., brands with mass prestige) is positively associated with consumer happiness (Kumar et al., 2021). Exclusive luxury brands have extremely high prices and are unattainable for middle-income consumers. Masstige brands are premium brands accessible to the mass market (Paul, 2019). These brands are premium brands with an image of high product quality and mass prestige. Examples of measurement items of masstige brand image include "I would buy this brand because of its mass prestige," "I believe this brand is known for its high quality," and "Nothing is more exciting than this brand." Owning masstige brands provides consumers with self-enhancing experiences and feelings of excitement, thereby enhancing material happiness.

Enhancing Happiness in Relation to Material Possessions

The research suggests at least two ways to enhance happiness concerning material possessions, namely, what to own and how to own.

What to Own

Evidence points to several types of products that can contribute significantly to happiness concerning material possessions. These include conspicuous brands, experiential products, commemorative products, and anthropomorphized products.

Conspicuous Brands

Ownership of *conspicuous brands* contributes to material happiness. Veblen (1899) coined the term "conspicuous consumption" to describe extravagant spending on products intended chiefly to display wealth and thus signal status. Conspicuous consumption is characterized by a display of wealth using opulent leisure activities and luxury expenditures on goods and services (Trigg, 2001). Usually, many luxury brands rely on consumers' conspicuous consumption tendencies to consume highly visible goods to display their wealth and gain social status, even though not all luxury brands are as conspicuous as in the case of luxury private consumption (Kumar et al., 2022).

As such, *conspicuous consumption theory* posits that possession of conspicuous brands increases material happiness (De Leire & Kalil, 2010; Perez-Truglia, 2013). This may be due to the following reasons. First, ownership of conspicuous brands helps consumers approach ideal goals (i.e., their desired identity) (Arnould & Thompson, 2005), which in turn increases consumer pride that emanates from the sense of achievement (Kumar et al., 2022). Consumption of conspicuous products is perceived positively by others and could lead to happiness by generating a sense of accomplishment and pride. Evidence suggests that conspicuous consumption and feeling pride are positively correlated (Kumar et al., 2022).

Second, ownership of conspicuous brands provides consumers with consumption happiness because symbolic brands lead consumers to psychologically connect with the brand (Nobre & Simões, 2019) and provide consumers with self-pleasing experiences from the brands (Mansoor & Paul, 2022). Ownership of conspicuous brands induces a positive mood, diminishes a negative mood, and thus increases consumer happiness (Hudders & Pandelaere, 2012). The results of meta-analyses with 59 independent studies and 97 unique effect sizes indicate that conspicuous consumption is positively associated with happiness (Kumar et al., 2022).

Third, ownership of conspicuous brands serves consumers by enhancing their self-esteem. Conspicuous brands are used as a conduit for impression management (Escalas & Bettman, 2005). Ownership of conspicuous brands serves to satisfy the need for uniqueness (Koydemir et al., 2014), resulting in increases in self-esteem (Rindfleisch et al., 2009). In addition, conspicuous products serve to satisfy the need for affiliation; that is, consumers who use conspicuous products feel more connected with their aspirational groups, resulting in increases in self-esteem (Chaudhuri et al., 2011). The results of a survey of university students found that conspicuous consumption was positively associated with the Rosenberg Self-Esteem scores (Chaudhuri et al., 2011). The results of meta-analyses also indicate that conspicuous consumption is positively associated with perception of elaborated status (Kumar et al., 2022).

Despite the noted positive wellbeing effect of conspicuous brand ownership, it should be noted that overreliance on conspicuous brands may lead to negative responses from others (Chen et al., 2021). Consumers who use conspicuous brands in an attention-getting manner are often perceived as doing so for ulterior motives (e.g., to manage impressions or gain social approval). These "showing off" behaviors can be viewed as inappropriate and may ultimately reflect poorly on the brand itself (Ferraro et al., 2013). The results of a survey of consumers with purchase experience of luxury brands (n=398) indicate that low-key conspicuous behaviors have a positive influence on perceived self-image and perceived interpersonal relationships, both of which in turn have a significant influence on consumption happiness (Chen et al., 2021). Evidence also suggests that a responsible luxury brand that adopts an inconspicuous branding strategy triggers more favorable CSR (corporate social responsibility) beliefs than one with a conspicuous branding strategy (Janssen et al., 2017).

Additionally, research found that the effect of ownership of prestige brands on consumer happiness is stronger for young consumers, female consumers, and consumers with high self-discrepancy. Young consumers are likely to have limited experience and resources and thus are more likely to use conspicuous consumption to satisfy their self-enhancement needs (Spreitzer et al., 1997; Kumar et al., 2022). Female consumers show their status through the conspicuous consumption of clothing and apparel more than their male counterparts (O'cass, 2004; Kumar et al., 2022). Consumers with high self-discrepancies have a strong motive to pursue the goal of achieving an ideal self (Yu et al., 2016).

Experiential Products

Ownership of *experiential products* contributes to material happiness. The distinction between material and experiential is not always clear-cut, as some products are both undeniably a material good and something that serves as a vehicle for experience (Gilovich et al., 2015). Experiential products are meaningful mixed goods and experiences (e.g., swimming pools and musical instruments). That is, experiential products fall between material items and life experiences (Guevarra & Howell, 2015) and have both material quality and experiential quality (Weingarten et al., 2023).

To examine the relationship between material and experiential qualities of experiential products and material happiness, Weingarten et al. (2023) conducted an experiment in which participants recalled recent purchases they made that increased their happiness and reported their consumption happiness with each purchase. The consumption happiness is measured using measures adapted from Nicolao et al. (2009), "When you think about this purchase, how happy does it make you?" (1 = not happy, 4 = moderately happy, 7 = very happy) and "How much does this purchase contribute to your happiness in life?" (1 = not at all, 4 = moderately, 7 = very Much). Participants responded to questions about the *experiential qualities* of each product they purchased. "To what extent is each listing below an experiential purchase (one involving an intention to acquire a life experience—an event or series of events that you personally encounter or live through)? (1 = not at all, 7 = very much). Participants also responded to questions on the *material qualities* of each product they purchased. "To what extent is each listing below a material purchase (one involving an intention to acquire a material possession—a tangible object that you obtain and keep in your possession)? (1 = not at all, 7 = very much). The study results indicate that recalled consumption happiness is positively associated with experiential qualities of the product and with material quality of the product. In other words, experiential and material qualities of products can positively and additively contribute to recalled consumption happiness (Weingarten et al., 2023). The results are in line with Guevarra and Howell's (2015) study, which underscored the notion that experiential products contribute to consumption happiness just as much as life experiences do (Guevarra & Howell, 2015).

Commemorative Products

Ownership of *commemorative products* serves to increase material happiness too. Consumers often honor celebratory events with the purchase of commemorative products to make a stronger connection to the past special events. Ownership of *commemorative products* serves to increase material happiness for the following reasons. First, commemorative products are strongly connected to positive emotions experienced at the time of the event. Commemorative products allow consumers to be transported back to their positive emotions experienced at the time of the event (Goodman et al., 2016). In an experiment to examine the effects of commemorative products vs. experience on recalled happiness (Goodman et al., 2016), married participants were randomly assigned to either the commemorative product condition (i.e., ring) or experience condition (i.e., reception). In the commemorative product condition, participants were asked whether they had received a ring on their wedding day and, if they had, to describe their ring. In the experiential condition, respondents were asked whether they held a reception on their wedding day and, if they had, to describe their reception. Then, participants responded to questions on connections to the emotions felt at the time of the wedding. The measurement items for emotional connection include (1) "When you think about your wedding ring/reception, how much are you reminded of the feeling of love you felt at the time of your ceremony?" (1 = very little; 7 = a lot); (2) "How vividly do you remember the feeling of love you felt?" (1 = not at all vivid; 7 = extremely vivid); (3) "How well do you remember the feeling of being in love?" (1 = not well at all; 7 = extremely well). The results indicate that commemorative products are more strongly connected to the memorable event than experiential ones as the time since the event gets longer. Over time, commemorative products help consumers better connect to their emotions felt at the time of a special event (Goodman et al., 2016).

Second, commemorative products provide consumers with more frequent momentary happiness over time (Weidman & Dunn, 2016). Participants were randomly assigned to report on a material gift versus an experiential gift they received at Christmas. Participants reported their momentary happiness over 2 weeks of experience sampling. Specifically, participants were sent 3–5 text messages per day for two weeks. Participants responded to the text question: "How much is your gift contributing to your happiness in life right now?" (0 = none; 5 = very much). Frequency of momentary happiness was defined as the number of occasions during which participants reported deriving at least some happiness from using their gift (i.e., scores from 1–5). The study results indicate that over 2 weeks, material gifts provide more frequent momentary happiness over time than experiential gifts (Weidman & Dunn, 2016).

Commemorative products are material products that help remember experiences, and ownership of the commemorative products serves to increase the remembered utility of happy experiences (e.g., Goodman et al., 2016; Nicolao et al., 2009) and facilitates frequent memory of happy experiences (Weidman & Dunn, 2016). Thus, ownership of material products that help consumers remember happy experiences is likely to enhance ownership happiness.

The effect of commemorative products on consumption happiness is high when the commemorative products have sentimental value. Sentimental value refers to non-feature-related utility derived from positive associations with significant others or from the associations with special events or times in one's life (Fletcher, 2009; Givi & Galak, 2017; Yang & Galak, 2015). For example, consumers buy memorabilia and souvenirs to remember a major occasion (e.g., souvenirs from a vacation), to document an accomplishment (e.g., graduation rings), or to signal a close relationship with someone (e.g., gifts for a special person). Thus, products with sentimental value are emotionally laden and are associated with some positive aspects of one's life (Givi & Galak, 2017; Yang & Galak, 2015). Furthermore, Consumption happiness from highly sentimental products does not decrease much over time (Yang & Galak, 2015).

Anthropomorphized Products

Consumers' ownership of *anthropomorphized products* (e.g., products imbued with human-like characteristics) increases material happiness. Past research shows that consumers often anthropomorphize various non-human entities such as brands (e.g., play with Oreo cookies) (Puzakova et al., 2013); abstract concepts (e.g., Mother Nature); and consumer goods (e.g., giving a human name to one's car) (Epley et al., 2008). One key characteristic of anthropomorphized products is that although they are not real humans, consumers tend to interact with them as if they were (Aggarwal & McGill, 2007; Epley et al., 2008; Puzakova et al., 2013). Owning anthropomorphized products (e.g., products imbued with human-like characteristics) provides consumers with a feeling of social interaction with the product.

Consumers' ownership of anthropomorphized products increases material happiness because such ownership enhances consumers' feeling that they engage in social interactions with the anthropomorphized products. Interacting with anthropomorphized products provides consumers with the feeling of social interaction and reduces feelings of social exclusion (Epley et al., 2008). That is, ownership of anthropomorphized products provides consumers with the feeling that they have a company. It has been found that consumer happiness is higher when a product is consumed with others or involves social interactions (Caprariello & Reis, 2013).

For example, Lee et al. (2022) conducted a study to compare consumption happiness derived from various past purchases that participants recalled as experiential, material, or anthropomorphized material product (e.g., product with humanlike characteristics or anthropomorphic cues in its design). Participants in each product condition responded to measurement items tapping on the level of happiness induced by this product (i.e., "When you think about this product, how happy does it make you?" 1 = not at all,7 = very much) and also responded to the measurement items tapping on perceived consumption sociality (e.g., "To what extent does the product make you feel…"; 1 = extremely solitary, 7 = extremely social; "I feel like I have company because of this product";1 = not at all, 7 = very much) (Caprariello & Reis, 2013). The results indicate that anthropomorphized material purchases provided significantly greater happiness than material purchases and as much happiness as experiential purchases. The results also indicate that anthropomorphizing material purchases enhanced the perceived sociality of material purchases, which in turn boosted material happiness (Lee et al., 2022). Thus, it can be said that consumers' ownership of *anthropomorphized products* (e.g., products imbued with humanlike characteristics) increases material happiness because anthropomorphized products provide consumers with the feeling of social interaction and reduce feelings of social exclusion.

How to Own

How to own is the other approach to enhancing happiness concerning material possessions. The research points to several principles: brand engagement, psychological ownership of products, brand love, low-key conspicuous ownership behavior, social sharing, and materialism.

Brand Engagement

Consumers' *brand engagement* refers to consumers' resource investment in their brand interactions (Kumar et al., 2019). As such, consumers' brand engagement enhances consumers' happiness concerning material possessions.

Consumers engage in various activities such as sharing brand purchases on social media (Duan & Dholakia, 2017), creating word of mouth, and participating in brand communities (Hook et al., 2018). Consumers' active and passive engagement with a brand serves to enhance consumers' material happiness with the brand (Niedermeier et al., 2019). This occurs for the following reasons. First, those consumers who invest their resources (time, energy, and money) derive hedonic, self-esteem-enhancing, and social benefits from such relationships (Gummerus et al., 2012; Kuo & Feng, 2013), which in turn increase material happiness (Aureliano-Silva et al., 2018).

Second, those consumers with brand engagement tend to gain emotional support when they feel insecure. From the perspective of the theory of attachment (Bowlby, 1969; Cortina, 2013), brands may serve as figures of emotional support and influence emotional wellbeing when consumers feel insecure. In other words, there is a positive relationship between brand attachment and emotional wellbeing (Aureliano-Silva et al., 2018).

There is empirical evidence suggesting that consumers with a high level of brand engagement consider the brand as strongly connected to their own identity (Sprott et al., 2009). They invest their resources (time, energy, and money) in the relationship with the brand. And they experience increased positive affect and self-esteem from the brand relationship (Aureliano-Silva et al., 2018). In sum, consumers' high level of engagement with a brand serves to enhance their material happiness.

Psychological Ownership of Products

Consumers' *psychological ownership of products* enhances material happiness. Psychological ownership is the state in which individuals feel as though the target of ownership (material or nonmaterial) or a piece of it is theirs (Pierce et al., 2001). In other words, psychological ownership refers to an individual's feelings of ownership toward a material or immaterial object that can arise even in the absence of legal ownership (Pierce et al., 2003). The measure of psychological ownership with a product carries the following measurement items: "I feel like this is my product," "I feel a personal ownership of the product," and "I feel like I own this product (1 = strongly disagree; 7 = strongly agree) (Peck et al., 2013).

What are the antecedents of consumer psychological ownership? Three routes give rise to feelings of ownership: (1) exerting control over the target product, (2) investing oneself in the target product, and (3) intimately knowing the target product (Pierce et al., 2003). Each route can independently result in feelings of ownership (Pierce et al., 2003). First, consumers develop feelings about psychological ownership of a product by *exerting control over the product*. Consumers experience heightened perceptions of control through their ability to use and touch the product (Peck et al., 2013). The more consumers exert control over the target products, the higher their feelings of ownership. For example, a study was conducted to evaluate the effect of the touch of the product on psychological ownership of the product. In the study, actual products (e.g., Mug cup) were displayed in front of participants, and participants were instructed to touch (vs. no touch) the products. Then, participants in each condition responded to the measures of psychological ownership and valuation of the product. The results indicate that consumers' touch of the product increased consumers' psychological ownership and valuation of the product (Peck & Shu, 2009). In addition to actual touch, studies found that consumer's imaginary ownership (e.g., imagining to take the product home, thinking of the place to keep the product, and thinking of the things to do with the product) or imaginary haptic (e.g., imagining to touch the product) can also increase consumer's perception of physical control on the product and feeling of ownership of the product (Peck & Shu, 2009; Peck et al., 2013).

Second, consumers develop psychological ownership by *investing their time, energy, and effort in the product.* Consumers invest themselves in a target product by customizing it (Moreau et al., 2011) or by frequently interacting with the product (Spears & Yazdanparast, 2014). By personally investing in the product and consumers become closely connected to these products, resulting in a sense of psychological ownership. For example, consumers may have feelings of psychological ownership with a book they borrowed from others or the library when they spend a lot of time and effort reading the book, even though they do not have legal ownership of the book. The results of a study on the relationship between psychological ownership and material happiness indicate that psychological ownership of a book significantly increases happiness related to the ownership of the book (Li & Atkinson, 2020).

What are the consequences of a consumer's psychological ownership? We believe that consumers' psychological ownership of products increases anticipated material happiness because psychological ownership of a product serves to induce positive feelings toward the product while consumers meet psychological needs. Specifically, consumers with feelings of psychological ownership of a product are likely to experience strong positive feelings about the product because they have intimate knowledge about the product and have invested their time and efforts. Research has shown that consumers who feel a strong sense of psychological ownership of a product exhibit high customer satisfaction, increased purchase intention, and greater willingness to pay (Asatryan & Oh, 2008; Danckwerts & Kenning, 2019; Peck & Shu, 2009). Consequently, consumers' psychological ownership of products enhances material happiness. Research also indicates that consumers' psychological ownership of a product before actual consumption provides consumers with satisfaction of basic psychological needs, which in turn results in high levels of anticipated material happiness (Li & Atkinson, 2020).

Brand Love

Consumers' *brand love* positively influences consumers' material happiness. Brand love is conceptualized as a higher-order construct composed of passion, self-brand connection, positive emotional connection, anticipated separation distress if the brand were to go away, long-term commitment, positive attitude, and confidence (Batra et al., 2012). Specifically, consumers who are in love with a brand are likely to have a strong desire to use the brand, express their identity through the brand, become emotionally attached to the brand, anticipate distress without the brand, expect to extensively use the brand, have positive attitude and confidence toward the brand (Batra et al., 2012). In short, brand love refers to a degree of passionate emotional attachment a satisfied consumer has for a particular trade name (Carroll & Ahuvia, 2006). Brand love was found to be positively associated with brand loyalty and positive word-of-mouth communications (Batra et al., 2012).

While brand love induces a great deal of positive feelings towards the brand (Langner et al., 2015), consumers also experience a positive self-image through brand love. They can also feel a sense of belonging and engage in positive social interactions through the brand community. Why? First, consumers high on brand love are likely to incorporate the brand into their self-concepts (Escalas & Bettman, 2003) and identity with the brand (Stokburger-Sauer et al., 2012). Due to the strong self-brand connection with their loved brand, consumers are likely to experience increased positive self-concept—when they experience satisfaction from the brand they love. In other words, satisfaction of self-related needs serves to collectively generate a more positive self-concept that, in turn, contributes to material happiness from their brand (Bruhn & Schnebelen, 2017). Second, consumers with brand love are emotionally attached to the brand (Thomson et al., 2005) and are likely to actively engage in social interactions with other brand users through the brand community (Lastovicka & Fernandez, 2005; Rosenbaum et al., 2007). Active engagement in brand community allows consumers with brand love to experience social satisfaction (e.g., pleasure from social interactions with other brand users) that contributes to material happiness from their possession of the loved brand.

In summary, being involved with activities related to a specific brand that one loves is positively associated with wellbeing. That is, consumers' brand love positively influences consumers' feelings of happiness related directly to the possession of the brand.

Low-Key Conspicuous Ownership Behavior

Research related to *low-key conspicuous ownership* positively indicates that such ownership may influence consumers' material happiness. This may occur by enhancing a positive self-image and fostering positive social relationships. That is, consumers who engage in behaviors related to low-key conspicuous ownership show off their material possessions in an implicit, acceptable, and non-offensive way (e.g., small logo, implicit online posting of possessions). Those who engage in low-key conspicuous ownership tend to present a positive self-image and avoid a possible negative response from others (Chen et al., 2021). The positive self-image and good social relationships result from low-key conspicuous ownership contributes to material happiness.

The effect of low-key conspicuous ownership behavior on material happiness tends to be high for those consumers with a low need for status. Need for status refers to a tendency to purchase goods and services for the status or social prestige value that they confer on their owners (Eastman et al., 1999). Consumers with low need for status are likely to prefer a low-key conspicuous brand (e.g., a brand with a discreet and small logo) to an explicitly prominent brand (e.g., a brand with an explicit and large logo) (Han et al., 2010). In addition, consumers who engage in low-key conspicuous ownership behaviors are likely to have low materialism.

Social Sharing

Sharing one's material possessions with others tends to enhance material happiness. This effect may be explained as follows. First, sharing allows consumers to savor their positive experiences related to their material possessions, which in turn induces positive affect (Lyubomirsky et al., 2006) and facilitates positive social interactions and satisfaction with social life (Schnebelen & Bruhn, 2018). As such, one can easily argue that the experience of pleasure and positive feelings related to sharing one's material possessions contributes to material happiness.

Second, sharing one's material possessions can lead to an increase in the intensity of the positive emotions that are associated with these possessions (Langston, 1994; Gable et al., 2004). The evidence also suggests that social sharing is associated with prolonging both positive and negative emotions related to material possessions (Verduyn et al., 2011). As such, increased intensity and duration of positive affect related to material possessions serve to enhance material happiness.

Third, sharing information about one's owned products can help consumers build a self-image of being generous and compassionate (Karahanna et al., 2015). As such, sharing is likely to lead to positive feedback from others, which in turn, may lead to material happiness.

Materialism

Much research has documented the study finding of the negative relationship between *materialism* and happiness concerning material possessions (Dittmar et al., 2014; Sirgy, 1998). Richins (2004) conceptualized materialism in terms of three dimensions: (1) the centrality dimension (i.e., as placing possessions and money at the center of one's life; (2) the happiness dimension (i.e., believing that money brings happiness; and (3) the success dimension (i.e., judging one's own and others' success based on income and possessions). Kasser (2003) defined materialism as a tendency to prioritize extrinsic goals (e.g., money, fame, and physical attractiveness) over intrinsic goals (e.g., strong positive social relationships, growing as a person, and contributing to one's community).

Despite increases in consumer materialism over the past decades, particularly among young adults (Mazahir et al., 2016), research has uncovered a negative relationship between consumer materialism and material happiness (Dittmar et al., 2014; Kasser & Ahuvia, 2002; Sirgy, 1998; Sirgy et al., 1998). This finding can be explained as follows. First, materialistic consumers are likely to place an emphasis solely on material possessions and thus are likely to undermine satisfaction in other life domains such as financial life, family life, social life, etc. (Sirgy et al., 2021). For example, materialistic consumers are likely to experience lower levels of satisfaction in social life. Positive and close social relationships play an important role in creating a happy life. Yet, materialistic consumers often neglect their close social relationships (Pieters, 2013; Wallendorf & Arnould, 1988). Materialistic consumers generally do not share their material possessions with others (Belk, 1985; Richins

& Dawson, 1992), and materialistic values tend to oppose values such as being helpful and loyal, gaining true friendship and mature love, and having close, committed relationships. Materialistic consumers tend to act competitively in social interactions, which works against them in achieving satisfaction in social life and is less oriented toward relational goods (Ahuvia, 2015; Kasser, 2003; Kasser & Ahuvia, 2002).

Second, materialistic consumers are less likely to savor positive experiences with material possessions. Much of the pleasure in consumption comes from the pleasant anticipation of a purchase. Yet, materialistic consumers tend to do just the opposite and are particularly prone to impulse purchasing (Podoshen & Andrzejewski, 2012). Materialistic consumers focus on material possessions and make social comparisons (Sirgy et al., 2012); as such, they fail to fully immerse themselves in positive marketplace experiences (Zhang et al., 2014).

Third, materialistic consumers are likely to experience lower levels of financial wellbeing because they tend to overspend (Dittmar et al., 2014). Also, materialistic consumers are less likely to save and tend to borrow money for luxury goods, much more than their non-materialistic counterparts (Watson, 2003).

Fourth, materialistic consumers tend to invoke ideal expectations in making judgements about their standard of living and make upward social comparisons, paving the way to negative self-evaluations in their material life (Sirgy, 1998). Materialistic consumers are likely to have unrealistically high expectations in evaluating their standard of living, resulting in dissatisfaction with their standard of living and low present life satisfaction (Sirgy, 1998; Sirgy et al., 1998, 2013). They frequently engage in social comparisons (Sirgy et al., 2012), resulting in lower satisfaction with their standard of living (Yu et al., 2020). These negative self-evaluations tend to take a toll on material happiness and overall happiness too.

To fully understand the nature of the relationship between materialism and consumer happiness, one should first understand consumer motivation concerning materialism. That is, consumers have different reasons why they regard money and material possessions as very important compared to other resources. Gurel-Atay et al. (2021) identified three underlying motives underlying consumer materialism—why they regard money and material possessions to be very important. These motives include the *distinctiveness* (e.g. "I put high emphasis on material possession because material possessions are key to my unique identity"), *social recognition* (e.g., "I put high emphasis on material possessions because material possessions signal my success and status to others"), and *happiness* (e.g., "I put high emphasis on material possessions because I believe material possessions will make my life happy"). In their cross-cultural studies across six countries, Gurel-Atay and colleagues found that consumer materialism and life satisfaction are negatively related, but this negative relationship is mediated mostly by the happiness motive, not by the other two motives (distinctiveness and social recognition).

While it is generally accepted that materialism has a negative influence on consumer happiness (Dittmar et al., 2014; Kasser & Ahuvia, 2002), it should be noted that not all motives related to materialism are bad (Sirgy et al., 2013). In other words, the effect of materialism on consumer happiness depends on the materialism motive evoked in each context. First, materialism driven by the distinctiveness motive is positively associated with material happiness. This is because materialism driven by this motive induces consumers to achieve a higher standard of living (Sirgy et al., 2013). In other words, materialism driven by the distinctiveness motive leads consumers to work hard to purchase luxury fashion products, which in turn contributes positively to happiness (Hudders & Pandelaere, 2012).

Second, materialism driven by the social recognition motive is positively associated with material happiness. Through a large-scale representative survey of 7599 German adults, Sirgy et al. (2021) found that materialism driven by social recognition and success contributes to increases in present and future life satisfaction. This may be due to the possibility that this situation helps boost economic motivation and higher expectations related to their standard of living.

Third, materialism driven by the happiness motive is negatively associated with material happiness. Materialistic consumers driven by the happiness motive are likely to have unrealistically high expectations in evaluating their standard of living, resulting in dissatisfaction with their standard of living and present life satisfaction (Sirgy, 1998; Sirgy et al., 1998, 2013). They engage in frequent social comparisons (Sirgy et al., 2012). Specifically, the positive association between income and standard of living is negatively moderated by happiness materialism (Yu et al., 2020). In addition, consumers driven by the happiness motive are likely to place much emphasis on material possessions, and doing so is likely to undermine satisfaction in other life domains such as financial life, family life, social life, etc. (Sirgy et al., 2021). Because consumers high on happiness materialism have unrealistically high expectations, they refrain from becoming fully engaged in other life domains. This effect has a negative influence on life satisfaction.

In summary, materialism has a negative influence on consumer happiness (Dittmar et al., 2014; Kasser & Ahuvia, 2002), but it is important to understand which motive drives materialism for a particular consumer in a particular situation (Sirgy et al., 2013).

Summary and Conclusion

Tables 14.1 and 14.2 summarize much of the discussion related to strategies that consumers and organizations use to enhance happiness concerning material possessions. Specifically, Table 14.1 focuses on strategies to enhance happiness by addressing the question of "what to own." In contrast, Table 14.2 focuses on strategies designed to enhance happiness by addressing the question "how to own."

Table 14.1 Enhancing happiness in relation to material possessions: what to own

Dimension	Impact on happiness	Details
Products to own	Ownership of conspicuous brands (e.g., symbolic brand, luxury brand, and masstige brands) contributes to happiness.	Ownership of conspicuous brands helps consumers to accomplish their desired identity. Ownership of conspicuous brands provides consumers with positive self-esteem.
	Ownership of experiential products contributes to happiness.	Both experiential and material qualities of products contribute to material happiness.
	Ownership of commemorative products increases happiness.	Commemorative products allow consumers to be transported back to their positive emotions experienced at the time of the event.
	Ownership of anthropomorphized products (e.g., products imbued with human-like characteristics) increases happiness.	When material goods are anthropomorphized, consumers gain enhanced feelings of consumption sociality.

Table 14.2 Enhancing happiness in relation to material possessions: how to own

Dimension	Impact on happiness	Details
Brand engagement	Consumers' active and passive engagement with a brand enhances consumers' happiness with the brand.	Brand engagement derives hedonic, self-esteem-enhancing, and social benefits from brand relationships.
	Consumers' psychological ownership of products enhances happiness.	Consumers with psychological ownership of a product are likely to experience a strong positive affect and anticipated happiness from the product.
Brand love	Consumers' brand love positively affects consumers' feelings about happiness from the possession of the brand.	Consumers experience positive affect and positive self-image through brand love.
Low-key conspicuous ownership	Behaviors related to low-key conspicuous ownership positively influence consumers' happiness.	Behaviors related to low-key conspicuous ownership result in a positive self-image and improved social relationships.
Social sharing	Social sharing of material possessions serves to increase happiness.	Social sharing of material possessions allows consumers to savor their positive feelings, thus generating high levels of positive affect.
Materialism	Materialism is negatively associated with happiness.	Materialistic consumers are likely to experience low satisfaction in social life and are less likely to savor their positive experiences with others.

References

Aggarwal, P., & McGill, A. L. (2007). Is that car smiling at me? Schema congruity as a basis for evaluating anthropomorphized products. *Journal of Consumer Research, 34*(4), 468–479.

Ahuvia, A. C. (2005). Beyond the extended self: Loved objects and consumers' identity narratives. *Journal of Consumer Research, 32*(1), 171–184.

Ahuvia, A. C. (2015). Nothing matters more to people than people: Brand meaning and social relationships. In D. J. MacInnis & C. W. Park (Eds.), *Brand meaning management* (Vol. 12, pp. 121–149). Emerald Group Publishing Limited.

Andrews, F. M., & Withey, S. B. (1976). *Social indicators of well-being: Americans' perceptions of life quality*. Plenum Press.

Arnold, M. J., Reynolds, K. E., Ponder, N., & Lueg, J. E. (2005). Customer delight in a retail context: Investigating delightful and terrible shopping experiences. *Journal of Business Research, 58*(8), 1132–1145.

Arnould, E. J., & Thompson, C. J. (2005). Consumer culture theory (CCT): Twenty years of research. *Journal of Consumer Research, 31*(4), 868–882.

Asatryan, V. S., & Oh, H. (2008). Psychological ownership theory: An exploratory application in the restaurant industry. *Journal of Hospitality & Tourism Research, 32*(3), 363–386.

Aureliano-Silva, L., Strehlau, S., & Strehlau, V. (2018). The relationship between brand attachment and consumers' emotional well-being. *Journal of Relationship Marketing, 17*(1), 1–16.

Babin, B. J., Darden, W. R., & Griffin, M. (1994). Work and/or fun: Measuring hedonic and utilitarian shopping value. *Journal of Consumer Research, 20*(4), 644–656.

Bagozzi, R. P., Gopinath, M., & Nyer, P. U. (1999). The role of emotions in marketing. *Journal of the Academy of Marketing Science, 27*(2), 184–206.

Batra, R., Ahuvia, A., & Bagozzi, R. P. (2012). Brand love. *Journal of Marketing, 76*(2), 1–16.

Belk, R. W. (1985). Materialism: Trait aspects of living in the material world. *Journal of Consumer Research, 12*(3), 265–280.

Belk, R. W. (1988). Possessions and the extended self. *Journal of Consumer Research, 15*(2), 139–168.

Bettingen, J.-F., & Luedicke, M. K. (2009). Can brands make us happy? A research framework for the study of brands and their effects on happiness. *Advances in Consumer Research, 36*(1), 308–315.

Bowlby, J. (1969). *Attachment* (Vol. 1). Basic Books.

Bruhn, M., & Schnebelen, S. (2017). Integrated marketing communication–from an instrumental to a customer-centric perspective. *European Journal of Marketing, 51*(3), 464–489.

Caprariello, P. A., & Reis, H. T. (2013). To do, to have, or to share? Valuing experiences over material possessions depends on the involvement of others. *Journal of Personality and Social Psychology, 104*(2), 199–215.

Carroll, B. A., & Ahuvia, A. C. (2006). Some antecedents and outcomes of brand love. *Marketing Letters, 17*, 79–89.

Carter, T. J., & Gilovich, T. (2010). The relative relativity of material and experiential purchases. *Journal of Personality and Social Psychology, 98*(1), 146–159.

Carter, T. J., & Gilovich, T. (2012). I am what I do, not what I have: The differential centrality of experiential and material purchases to the self. *Journal of Personality and Social Psychology, 102*(6), 1304–1317.

Chaudhuri, H. R., Mazumdar, S., & Ghoshal, A. (2011). Conspicuous consumption orientation: Conceptualisation, scale development and validation. *Journal of Consumer Behaviour, 10*(4), 216–224.

Chen, M., Zhang, J., Xie, Z., & Niu, J. (2021). Online low-key conspicuous behavior of fashion luxury goods: The antecedents and its impact on consumer happiness. *Journal of Consumer Behaviour, 20*(1), 148–159.

Cortina, M. (2013). The use of attachment theory in the clinical dialogue with patients. *Psychodynamic Psychiatry, 41*(3), 397–417.

Danckwerts, S., & Kenning, P. (2019). "It's MY Service, it's MY Music": The role of psychological ownership in music streaming consumption. *Psychology & Marketing, 36*(9), 803–816.
De Leire, T., & Kalil, A. (2010). Does consumption buy happiness? Evidence from the United States. *International Review of Economics, 57*, 163–176.
Dittmar, H., Bond, R., Hurst, M., & Kasser, T. (2014). The relationship between materialism and personal well-being: A meta-analysis. *Journal of Personality and Social Psychology, 107*(5), 879–924.
Duan, J., & Dholakia, R. R. (2017). Posting purchases on social media increases happiness: The mediating roles of purchases' impact on self and interpersonal relationships. *Journal of Consumer Marketing, 34*(5), 404–413.
Eastman, J. K., Goldsmith, R. E., & Flynn, L. R. (1999). Status consumption in consumer behavior: Scale development and validation. *Journal of Marketing Theory and Practice, 7*(3), 41–52.
Epley, N., Waytz, A., Akalis, S., & Cacioppo, J. T. (2008). When we need a human: Motivational determinants of anthropomorphism. *Social Cognition, 26*(2), 143–155.
Escalas, J. E., & Bettman, J. R. (2003). You are what they eat: The influence of reference groups on consumers' connections to brands. *Journal of Consumer Psychology, 13*(3), 339–348.
Escalas, J. E., & Bettman, J. R. (2005). Self-construal, reference groups, and brand meaning. *Journal of Consumer Research, 32*(3), 378–389.
Ferraro, R., Kirmani, A., & Matherly, T. (2013). Look at me! Look at me! Conspicuous brand usage, self-brand connection, and dilution. *Journal of Marketing Research, 50*(4), 477–488.
Fletcher, G. (2009). Sentimental value. *The Journal of Value Inquiry, 43*(1), 55–65.
Gable, S. L., Reis, H. T., Impett, E. A., & Asher, E. R. (2004). What do you do when things go right? The intrapersonal and interpersonal benefits of sharing positive events. *Journal of Personality and Social Psychology, 87*(2), 228–245.
Gao, L., Wheeler, S. C., & Shiv, B. (2009). The "shaken self": Product choices as a means of restoring self-view confidence. *Journal of Consumer Research, 36*(1), 29–38.
Gilovich, T., Kumar, A., & Jampol, L. (2015). A wonderful life: Experiential consumption and the pursuit of happiness. *Journal of Consumer Psychology, 25*(1), 152–165.
Givi, J., & Galak, J. (2017). Sentimental value and gift giving: Givers' fears of getting it wrong prevents them from getting it right. *Journal of Consumer Psychology, 27*(4), 473–479.
Goodman, J. K., Malkoc, S. A., & Stephenson, B. L. (2016). Celebrate or commemorate? A material purchase advantage when honoring special life events. *Journal of the Association for Consumer Research, 1*(4), 497–508.
Guevarra, D. A., & Howell, R. T. (2015). To have in order to do: Exploring the effects of consuming experiential products on well-being. *Journal of Consumer Psychology, 25*(1), 28–41.
Gummerus, J., Liljander, V., Weman, E., & Pihlström, M. (2012). Customer engagement in a Facebook brand community. *Management Research Review, 35*(9), 857–877.
Gurel-Atay, E., Sirgy, M. J., Webb, D., Ekici, A., Lee, D. J., & Kahle, L. R. (2021). What motivates people to be materialistic? Developing a measure of materialism motives. *Journal of Consumer Behaviour, 20*(3), 590–606.
Han, Y. J., Nunes, J. C., & Drèze, X. (2010). Signaling status with luxury goods: The role of brand prominence. *Journal of Marketing, 74*(4), 15–30.
Hirschman, E. C., & Holbrook, M. B. (1982). Hedonic consumption: Emerging concepts, methods and propositions. *Journal of Marketing, 46*(3), 92–101.
Holbrook, M. B., & Hirschman, E. C. (1982). The experiential aspects of consumption: Consumer fantasies, feelings, and fun. *Journal of Consumer Research, 9*(2), 132–140.
Hook, M., Baxter, S., & Kulczynski, A. (2018). Antecedents and consequences of participation in brand communities: A literature review. *Journal of Brand Management, 25*, 277–292.
Howell, R. T., & Hill, G. (2009). The mediators of experiential purchases: Determining the impact of psychological needs satisfaction and social comparison. *The Journal of Positive Psychology, 4*(6), 511–522.
Howell, R. T., & Howell, C. J. (2008). The relation of economic status to subjective well-being in developing countries: A meta-analysis. *Psychological Bulletin, 134*(4), 536–560.

Hudders, L., & Pandelaere, M. (2012). The silver lining of materialism: The impact of luxury consumption on subjective well-being. *Journal of Happiness Studies, 13*(3), 411–437.

Janssen, C., Vanhamme, J., & Leblanc, S. (2017). Should luxury brands say it out loud? Brand conspicuousness and consumer perceptions of responsible luxury. *Journal of Business Research, 77*, 167–174.

Karahanna, E., Xu, S. X., & Zhang, N. (2015). Psychological ownership motivation and use of social media. *Journal of Marketing Theory and Practice, 23*(2), 185–207.

Kasser, T. (2003). *The high price of materialism*. MIT Press.

Kasser, T., & Ahuvia, A. (2002). Materialistic values and well-being in business students. *European Journal of Social Psychology, 32*(1), 137–146.

Koydemir, S., Şimşek, Ö. F., & Demir, M. (2014). Pathways from personality to happiness: Sense of uniqueness as a mediator. *Journal of Humanistic Psychology, 54*(3), 314–335.

Kumar, V., Rajan, B., Gupta, S., & Pozza, I. D. (2019). Customer engagement in service. *Journal of the Academy of Marketing Science, 47*, 138–160.

Kumar, A., Paul, J., & Starčević, S. (2021). Do brands make consumers happy? —A masstige theory perspective. *Journal of Retailing and Consumer Services, 58*, 102318.

Kumar, B., Bagozzi, R. P., Manrai, A. K., & Manrai, L. A. (2022). Conspicuous consumption: A meta-analytic review of its antecedents, consequences, and moderators. *Journal of Retailing, 98*(3), 471–485.

Kuo, Y. F., & Feng, L. H. (2013). Relationships among community interaction characteristics, perceived benefits, community commitment, and oppositional brand loyalty in online brand communities. *International journal of information management, 33*(6), 948–962.

Langner, T., Schmidt, J., & Fischer, A. (2015). Is it really love? A comparative investigation of the emotional nature of brand and interpersonal love. *Psychology & Marketing, 32*(6), 624–634.

Langston, C. A. (1994). Capitalizing on and coping with daily-life events: Expressive responses to positive events. *Journal of Personality and SocialPpsychology, 67*(6), 1112–1125.

Laros, F. J., & Steenkamp, J. B. E. (2005). Emotions in consumer behavior: A hierarchical approach. *Journal of Business Research, 58*(10), 1437–1445.

Lastovicka, J. L., & Fernandez, K. V. (2005). Three paths to disposition: The movement of meaningful possessions to strangers. *Journal of Consumer Research, 31*(4), 813–823.

Lee, D. J., & Sirgy, M. J. (2004). Quality-of-life (QOL) marketing: Proposed antecedents and consequences. *Journal of Macromarketing, 24*(1), 44–58.

Lee, J. C., Kim, S., & Wang, P. X. (2022). Anthropomorphizing makes material goods as happiness-inducing as experiences. *Marketing Letters, 33*(1), 61–73.

Li, D., & Atkinson, L. (2020). The role of psychological ownership in consumer happiness. *Journal of Consumer Marketing, 37*(6), 629–638.

Lyubomirsky, S., Sousa, L., & Dickerhoof, R. (2006). The costs and benefits of writing, talking, and thinking about life's triumphs and defeats. *Journal of Personality and Social Psychology, 90*(4), 692–708.

Mandel, N., Rucker, D. D., Levav, J., & Galinsky, A. D. (2017). The compensatory consumer behavior model: How self-discrepancies drive consumer behavior. *Journal of Consumer Psychology, 27*(1), 133–146.

Mano, H., & Oliver, R. L. (1993). Assessing the dimensionality and structure of the consumption experience: Evaluation, feeling, and satisfaction. *Journal of Consumer Research, 20*(3), 451–466.

Mansoor, M., & Paul, J. (2022). Mass prestige, brand happiness and brand evangelism among consumers. *Journal of Business Research, 144*, 484–496.

Mazahir, S., Masood, A., & Musarrat, R. (2016). Increased materialistic trends among youth. *Journal of Educational, Health and Community Psychology, 5*(3), 56–77.

Mishra, A., Dash, S. B., & Cyr, D. (2014). Linking user experience and consumer-based brand equity: The moderating role of consumer expertise and lifestyle. *Journal of Product & Brand Management, 23*(4/5), 333–348.

Moreau, C. P., Bonney, L., & Herd, K. B. (2011). It's the thought (and the effort) that counts: How customizing for others differs from customizing for oneself. *Journal of Marketing, 75*(5), 120–133.

Nakano, N., MacDonald, M., & Douthitt, R. (1995). Toward consumer well-being: Consumer socialization effects of work experience. In M. J. Sirgy & A. C. Samli (Eds.), *New dimensions of marketing/quality-of life research* (pp. 151–175). Quorum Books.

Nicolao, L., Irwin, J. R., & Goodman, J. K. (2009). Happiness for sale: Do experiential purchases make consumers happier than material purchases? *Journal of Consumer Research, 36*(2), 188–198.

Niedermeier, A., Albrecht, L., & Jahn, B. (2019). "Happy together": Effects of brand community engagement on customer happiness. *Journal of Relationship Marketing, 18*(1), 54–76.

Nobre, H., & Simões, C. (2019). NewLux Brand Relationship Scale: Capturing the scope of mass-consumed luxury brand relationships. *Journal of Business Research, 102*, 328–338.

O'cass, A. (2004). Fashion clothing consumption: Antecedents and consequences of fashion clothing involvement. *European Journal of Marketing, 38*(7), 869–882.

Paul, J. (2019). Masstige model and measure for brand management. *European Management Journal, 37*(3), 299–312.

Peck, J., & Shu, S. B. (2009). The effect of mere touch on perceived ownership. *Journal of Consumer Research, 36*(3), 434–447.

Peck, J., Barger, V. A., & Webb, A. (2013). In search of a surrogate for touch: The effect of haptic imagery on perceived ownership. *Journal of Consumer Psychology, 23*(2), 189–196.

Perez-Truglia, R. (2013). A test of the conspicuous–consumption model using subjective well-being data. *The Journal of Socio-economics, 45*, 146–154.

Pierce, J. L., Kostova, T., & Dirks, K. T. (2001). Toward a theory of psychological ownership in organizations. *Academy of Management Review, 26*(2), 298–310.

Pierce, J. L., Kostova, T., & Dirks, K. T. (2003). The state of psychological ownership: Integrating and extending a century of research. *Review of General Psychology, 7*(1), 84–107.

Pieters, R. (2013). Bidirectional dynamics of materialism and loneliness: Not just a vicious cycle. *Journal of Consumer Research, 40*(4), 615–631.

Podoshen, J. S., & Andrzejewski, S. A. (2012). An examination of the relationships between materialism, conspicuous consumption, impulse buying, and brand loyalty. *Journal of Marketing Theory and Practice, 20*(3), 319–334.

Puzakova, M., Kwak, H., & Rocereto, J. F. (2013). When humanizing brands goes wrong: The detrimental effect of brand anthropomorphization amid product wrongdoings. *Journal of Marketing, 77*(3), 81–100.

Richins, M. L. (1997). Measuring emotions in the consumption experience. *Journal of Consumer Research, 24*(2), 127–146.

Richins, M. L. (2004). The material values scale: Measurement properties and development of a short form. *Journal of Consumer Research, 31*(1), 209–219.

Richins, M. L., & Dawson, S. (1992). A consumer values orientation for materialism and its measurement: Scale development and validation. *Journal of Consumer Research, 19*(3), 303–316.

Rindfleisch, A., Burroughs, J. E., & Wong, N. (2009). The safety of objects: Materialism, existential insecurity, and brand connection. *Journal of Consumer Research, 36*(1), 1–16.

Rosenbaum, M. S., Ward, J., Walker, B. A., & Ostrom, A. (2007). A cup of coffee with a dash of love: An investigation of commercial social support and third place attachment. *Journal of Service Research, 10*(1), 43–59.

Rucker, D., & Galinsky, A. D. (2012). Compensatory consumption. In A. Ruvio & R. Belk (Eds.), *The Routledge companion to identity and consumption* (pp. 207–215). Routledge.

Rucker, D. D., Galinsky, A. D., & Dubois, D. (2012). Power and consumer behavior: How power shapes who and what consumers value. *Journal of Consumer Psychology, 22*(3), 352–368.

Schnebelen, S., & Bruhn, M. (2018). An appraisal framework of the determinants and consequences of brand happiness. *Psychology & Marketing, 35*(2), 101–119.

Sheldon, K. M., & Lyubomirsky, S. (2006). How to increase and sustain positive emotion: The effects of expressing gratitude and visualizing best possible selves. *The Journal of Positive Psychology, 1*(2), 73–82.
Sheldon, K. M., & Lyubomirsky, S. (2012). The challenge of staying happier: Testing the hedonic adaptation prevention model. *Personality and Social Psychology Bulletin, 38*(5), 670–680.
Sirgy, M. J. (1998). Materialism and quality of life. *Social Indicators Research, 43*(3), 227–260.
Sirgy, M. J., Lee, D. J., Larsen, V., & Wright, N. D. (1998). Satisfaction with material possessions and general well-being: The role of materialism. *Journal of Consumer Satisfaction, Dissatisfaction and Complaining Behavior, 11*, 103–118.
Sirgy, M. J., Lee, D. J., & Kressmann, F. (2006). A need-based measure of consumer wellbeing (CWB) in relation to personal transportation: Nomological validation. *Social Indicators Research, 79*(2), 337–367.
Sirgy, M. J., Lee, D. J., Kamra, K., & Tidwell, J. (2008). What determines the perceived quality-of-life impact of mobile phones? A model based on the consumption life cycle. *Applied Research in Quality of Life, 3*(4), 251–268.
Sirgy, M. J., Gurel-Atay, E., Webb, D., Cicic, M., Husic, M., Ekici, A., Herrmann, A., Hegazy, I., & Johar, J. S. (2012). Linking advertising, materialism, and life satisfaction. *Social Indicators Research, 107*(1), 79–101.
Sirgy, M. J., Gurel-Atay, E., Webb, D., Cicic, M., Husic-Mehmedovic, M., Ekici, A., Herrmann, A., Hegazy, I. L., & D-J. & Johar, J. S. (2013). Is materialism all that bad? Effects on satisfaction with material life, life satisfaction, and economic motivation. *Social Indicators Research, 110*(1), 349–366.
Sirgy, M. J., Yu, G. B., Lee, D. J., Joshanloo, M., Bosnjak, M., Jiao, J., Ekici, A., Gurel-Atay, E., & Grzeskowiak, S. (2021). The dual model of materialism: Success versus happiness materialism on present and future life satisfaction. *Applied Research in Quality of Life, 16*(1), 201–220.
Smits, J., & Steendijk, R. (2015). The international wealth index (IWI). *Social Indicators Research, 122*(1), 65–85.
Spears, N., & Yazdanparast, A. (2014). Revealing obstacles to the consumer imagination. *Journal of Consumer Psychology, 24*(3), 363–372.
Spreitzer, G. M., Kizilos, M. A., & Nason, S. W. (1997). A dimensional analysis of the relationship between psychological empowerment and effectiveness, satisfaction, and strain. *Journal of Management, 23*(5), 679–704.
Sprott, D., Czellar, S., & Spangenberg, E. (2009). The importance of a general measure of brand engagement on market behavior: Development and validation of a scale. *Journal of Marketing Research, 46*(1), 92–104.
Stokburger-Sauer, N., Ratneshwar, S., & Sen, S. (2012). Drivers of consumer–brand identification. *International Journal of Research in Marketing, 29*(4), 406–418.
Sweeney, J. C., & Soutar, G. N. (2001). Consumer perceived value: The development of a multiple item scale. *Journal of Retailing, 77*(2), 203–220.
Thomas, R., & Millar, M. (2013). The effects of material and experiential discretionary purchases on consumer happiness: Moderators and mediators. *The Journal of Psychology, 147*(4), 345–356.
Thomson, M., MacInnis, D. J., & Park, C. W. (2005). The ties that bind: Measuring the strength of consumers' emotional attachments to brands. *Journal of Consumer Psychology, 15*(1), 77–91.
Trigg, A. B. (2001). Veblen, Bourdieu, and conspicuous consumption. *Journal of Economic Issues, 35*(1), 99–115.
Van Boven, L. (2005). Experientialism, materialism, and the pursuit of happiness. *Review of General Psychology, 9*(2), 132–142.
Veblen, T. (1899). *The theory of the Leisure class: An economic study of institutions*. Random House.
Verduyn, P., Van Mechelen, I., & Tuerlinckx, F. (2011). The relation between event processing and the duration of emotional experience. *Emotion, 11*(1), 20–28.

Wallendorf, M., & Arnould, E. J. (1988). "My favorite things": A cross-cultural inquiry into object attachment, possessiveness, and social linkage. *Journal of Consumer Research, 14*(4), 531–547.

Wang, J., Novemsky, N., & Dhar, R. (2009). Anticipating adaptation to products. *Journal of Consumer Research, 36*(2), 149–159.

Watson, J. J. (2003). The relationship of materialism to spending tendencies, saving, and debt. *Journal of Economic Psychology, 24*(6), 723–739.

Weidman, A. C., & Dunn, E. W. (2016). The unsung benefits of material things: Material purchases provide more frequent momentary happiness than experiential purchases. *Social Psychological and Personality Science, 7*(4), 390–399.

Weingarten, E., Duke, K., Liu, W., Hamilton, R. W., Amir, O., Appel, G., et al. (2023). What makes people happy? Decoupling the experiential-material continuum. *Journal of Consumer Psychology, 33*(1), 97–106.

Wicklund, R. A., & Gollwitzer, P. M. (2013). *Symbolic self-completion*. Routledge.

Williams, P. (2014). Emotions and consumer behavior. *Journal of Consumer Research, 40*(5), viii-xi.

Yang, Y., & Galak, J. (2015). Sentimental value and its influence on hedonic adaptation. *Journal of Personality and Social Psychology, 109*(5), 767–790.

Yang, Y., Gu, Y., & Galak, J. (2017). When it could have been worse, it gets better: How favorable uncertainty resolution slows hedonic adaptation. *Journal of Consumer Research, 43*(5), 747–768.

Yu, Y., Jing, F., Su, C. T., Zhou, N., & Nguyen, B. (2016). Impact of material vs. experiential purchase types on happiness: The moderating role of self-discrepancy. *Journal of Consumer Behaviour, 15*(6), 571–579.

Yu, G. B., Lee, D. J., Sirgy, M. J., & Bosnjak, M. (2020). Household income, satisfaction with standard of living, and subjective well-being. The moderating role of happiness materialism. *Journal of Happiness Studies, 21*(8), 2851–2872.

Zhang, J. W., Howell, R. T., Caprariello, P. A., & Guevarra, D. A. (2014). Damned if they do, damned if they don't: Material buyers are not happier from material or experiential consumption. *Journal of Research in Personality, 50*, 71–83.

Chapter 15
Happiness in Relation to Marketplace Experiences

> *Top 15 Things Money Can't Buy: Time. Happiness. Inner Peace. Integrity. Love. Character. Manners. Health. Respect. Morals. Trust. Patience. Class. Common sense. Dignity*
>
> *—Roy T. Bennett, The Light in the Heart (https://www.xavier.edu/jesuitresource/online-resources/quote-archive1/happiness-quotes)*

What Is Happiness in Relation to Marketplace Experiences?

Consumption happiness in relation to marketplace experiences is the focus of this chapter. This form of happiness refers to consumption happiness from experiential consumption. Experiential consumption refers to purchases made with the primary intention of acquiring intangible life experiences (Carter & Gilovich, 2010; Howell & Hill, 2009; Thomas & Millar, 2013; Van Boven & Gilovich, 2003). If the purpose of a purchase is to obtain life experience (e.g., vacation, eating out, visiting theme parks), then it can be defined as an experiential purchase (Carter & Gilovich, 2012; Thomas & Millar, 2013). Experiences are intangible and unique (Nicolao et al., 2009), so it is hard for consumers to compare alternatives (Carter & Gilovich, 2010). Experiential purchases are usually shared with others and are more socially engaging (Howell & Hill, 2009; Van Boven, 2005). As experiences are unique and have social value, experiences are less subject to hedonic adaptation (Nicolao et al., 2009).

Many consumers' daily lives are spent co-creating service offerings and interacting with service providers, and such consumer experiences are likely to significantly affect consumption, consumer, and overall happiness. In contexts such as health care, education, and financial services, consumer experiences with the services significantly influence various forms of personal wellbeing (Anderson et al., 2013).

D.-J. Lee, M. J. Sirgy, *Happiness in the Marketplace*, Social Indicators Research Series 64, https://doi.org/10.1007/978-3-032-04443-3_15

Experiential happiness comes from purchases made with the primary intention of acquiring intangible life experiences (Van Boven & Gilovich, 2003). And of course, satisfaction with marketplace experiences contributes to consumption happiness (and consumer happiness and overall happiness) more prominently than satisfaction with material possessions. This relationship can be explained as follows. First, experiences are more self-defining than material possessions (Carter & Gilovich, 2012). Gilovich et al. (2015, p. 156) stress that "we are the sum total of our experiences. We are not the sum total of our possessions; however important they might be to us. As experiences are closely related to the self-concept, satisfaction of experiential satisfaction contributes to an enhanced self-image."

Second, experiences are unique (Carter & Gilovich, 2010) and thus are harder to compare against foregone alternatives (Rosenzweig & Gilovich, 2012). Satisfaction of experiences provides consumers with satisfaction of unique needs, which in turn enhances the self-concept, resulting in experiential happiness. In addition, the non-comparative nature of experiences reduces consumers' alternative and social comparisons—negative affect (e.g., regret and dissonance) usually results from comparisons of consumer goods.

Third, experiences are less prone to hedonic adaptation (Nicolao et al., 2009). Consumers actively participate in the experience process, and the experiences consumers engage in are not the same each time consumers engage in them. Thus, consumers are less likely to experience satiation or hedonic adaptation.

Fourth, experiences are socially connected. While consumers actively participate in the marketplace experience, they also engage in social interactions with others (Caprariello & Reis, 2013). Experiences have higher conversational value in social interactions, contributing to happiness (Bastos & Brucks, 2017). The marketplace fosters opportunities to cultivate social interactions, which may contribute to satisfaction with social life. In other words, spending time with others and social interactions contribute to experiential happiness (Chancellor & Lyubomirsky, 2011).

Fifth, experiences are closely related to the satisfaction of autonomy and competency needs. Experiences often involve learning skills such as mastering a new instrument or learning a foreign language (Chancellor & Lyubomirsky, 2011). Thus, experiences have a strong relationship with satisfaction of autonomy need and competency needs, which in turn play a significant role in experiential happiness (Weingarten & Goodman, 2021).

The Principle of Experiential Advantage

The *principle of experiential advantage* states that experiential consumption leads to greater happiness than material consumption. Compared to material possessions, experiential consumption has a stronger effect on satisfaction of psychological needs (i.e., autonomy, competency, and relatedness need), which in turn contribute more to overall happiness (Caprariello & Reis, 2013; Gilovich et al., 2015; Howell & Hill, 2009; Weingarten & Goodman, 2021).

How does experiential advantage work? First, compared to material possessions, experiences fulfill the *need for autonomy* (Howell & Hill, 2009; Thomas & Millar, 2013). Experience choice reveals more about the person's consumption choices and autonomy.

Second, compared to material possessions, experiences are more *self-defining* and reveal more about a consumer's identity (Carter & Gilovich, 2012). Experiences form a bigger part of a person's identity (Gilovich et al., 2015). As experiences tend to be more closely associated with oneself than possessions (Carter & Gilovich, 2012), satisfying experiences yield high-level positive self-evaluations.

Third, compared to material possessions, experiences provide more happiness through satisfaction of the fundamental *need for relatedness* (Howell & Hill, 2009). Experiences are more enjoyable to bring up in conversations and are perceived to have higher social value in conversations (Bastos & Brucks, 2017; Caprariello & Reis, 2013). In sum, research suggests that experiences foster social connection and social relations more readily and effectively than material goods (Gilovich & Gallo, 2020; Gilovich et al., 2015).

Fourth, compared to material possessions, experiences are evaluated more on their terms and *evoke fewer social comparisons* than material purchases (Gilovich & Gallo, 2020; Gilovich et al., 2015). As such, satisfaction with experiences is less subject to hedonic adaptation (Nicolao et al., 2009) or alternative comparisons (Rosenzweig & Gilovich, 2012).

It should be noted that the *experiential advantage is low* under the following conditions. First, the experiential advantage is low for negative experiences. In the case of purchases evaluated as positive, experiences led to more happiness than material possessions. For purchases that turn bad, experiences did not show an advantage over material goods (Nicolao et al., 2009).

Second, experiential advantage is *low for solitary experiences*. Caprariello and Reis (2013) have shown that spending money on experiences shared with other consumers causes more happiness than spending money on either solitary activities or material purchases. That is, solitary experiences exhibit no experiential advantage (Weingarten & Goodman, 2021).

Third, experiential advantage is low when consumers derive equivalent levels of happiness from each material or experiential product they have. That is, experiential advantage is low when consumers gain equivalent levels of happiness from sharing an experience with an object (Bastos, 2020).

Fourth, experiential advantage is high when short-term experiential happiness is measured, while experiential advantage is low when long-term experiential happiness is measured. Specifically, research found that the experiential advantage holds for short-term happiness, but data did not support the superiority of the experiential advantage for long-term happiness (Sääksjärvi et al., 2016).

In summary, the experiential advantage is low for negative experiences, for solitary experiences, for experiences with a similar level of utilitarian benefits, and long-term consumer happiness (Weingarten & Goodman, 2021). See Table 15.1 for a summary of this discussion.

Table 15.1 Material purchase vs. experiential purchase

	Material purchase	Experiential purchase
Purpose of purchase	To obtain ownership of a tangible object (e.g., electronics, clothing, and jewelry)	To obtain life experience (e.g., vacation, eating out, visiting theme parks)
Alternative comparisons	Easy to compare	Hard to compare Unique
Tangibility	Tangible	Intangible
Social sharing	Low	High
Hedonic adaptation	High	Low

Enhancing Happiness in Relation to Marketplace Experiences

Research has uncovered two approaches to enhancing happiness concerning marketplace experiences, namely what to experience and how to experience. We will discuss these approaches in some detail in the sections below.

What to Experience

Consumer experiences refer to an event or series of events that consumers personally encounter or live through, such as a trip or movie watching, while material things refer to tangible objects that the consumer obtains and keeps in his/her possession (Van Boven & Gilovich, 2003). What type of consumption experiences effectively contributes to consumer happiness? We believe that consumer happiness is effectively enhanced through the experience of hedonic experiences, freedom from (recovery) experiences, ordinary and extraordinary experiences, and freedom to (eudaimonic) experiences, flow experiences, and self-expressive experiences.

Hedonic Experiences

Hedonic experiences are experiences for sensory pleasure and social affiliation. Hedonic experiences provide variety of pleasurable experiences including (1) sensory (or physical) pleasure that is chiefly borne of the pleasant sensations induced during the experience, (2) social pleasure derived from one's interactions with others (or lack thereof, as in the pleasure of solitude), (3) emotional pleasure borne of feelings, ideas, or mental images, and (4) intellectual pleasure from appreciating the complexities and subtleties of things around the consumer (Dubé & Le Bel, 2003).

Hedonic experiences contribute to momentary pleasures and consumer happiness. Pleasurable experiences that are based on more senses are likely to be more effective and memorable compared to pleasurable experiences that are based on fewer senses (Pine & Gilmore, 2011). Research found that the effect of hedonic experiences on consumer happiness is high for those consumers with independent self-construal and consumers with an individualistic culture. Consumers with independent self-construal tend to be promotion-focused[1] and are likely to obtain much happiness from hedonic experiences (Lee et al., 2000). Consumers in an individualistic society actively seek positive emotional experiences (Kitayama et al., 2000). They are motivated to maximize leisure and minimize pain (Uchida et al., 2004).

Freedom from Experiences (as in Relation to Recovery)

Freedom from (recovery) experience is experience involving escape from the structure and confines of everyday affect and cognition (Cova et al., 2018). One example of freedom from (recovery) experiences is the recovery experience in travel. Recovery refers to the process through which consumers alleviate the detrimental effects of work and personal stressors through restorative experiences (Sonnentag & Fritz, 2007; Sonnentag & Natter, 2004). Consumers seek psychological detachment and relaxation in freedom from (recovery) experiences. Psychological detachment refers to the individual's sense of being away from the work situation (e.g., not thinking about work during off time) and is the process of refraining from job-related activities and thoughts (Etzion et al., 1998). Relaxation is a state of low activation and increased positive affect that results from activities such as muscle relaxation, taking a walk, or listening to music (Sonnentag & Fritz, 2007). Psychological detachment and relaxation are two recovery experiences that have positive effects on positive emotions (Sonnentag & Fritz, 2007). Freedom from (recovery) experiences is usually related to low positive emotional arousal (calm) and is more likely to foster hedonic, pleasure-based happiness (Gaston-Breton et al., 2020).

Recovery experience contributes to happiness concerning marketplace experiences because the recovery experience allows for previously depleted resources to be replenished and have feelings of control and mastery over their time and activities (Hobfoll, 1998; Stone et al., 1995). Recovery experience contributes to experiential happiness because psychological detachment reduces negative affect and stress (Iwasaki & Mannell, 2000), and relaxation experience will provide consumers with low arousal positive emotion (e.g., calm) (Gaston-Breton et al., 2020).

The effect of engagement in recovery experiences on consumption happiness is higher for those consumers under severe stress and threat. When individuals are under severe threat, consumers will seek "freedom from" anxiety and worries. Recovery experiences for the burnt-out consumers will have a positive influence on consumer life satisfaction (Chen et al., 2016). For example, taking a leisure trip

---

[1] A promotion-focused mindset emphasizes achieving positive outcomes, pursuing goals, and seeking advancement, focusing on the potential gains and rewards of success.

provides consumers with opportunities for a recovery experience including relaxation, pleasure, and detachment from stress.

The effect of engagement in recovery experiences on consumption happiness is likely to be greater for older consumers who have present-focused and view happiness in terms of calm experiences (Mogilner et al., 2012).

Extraordinary Experiences

Happiness in relation to marketplace experiences is strongly associated with *extraordinary experiences*. Extraordinary experiences as uncommon, infrequent experiences that go beyond the realm of everyday life (Bhattacharjee & Mogilner, 2014).

Extraordinary experiences are triggered by immersion in unusual events (Arnould & Price, 1993; Schmitt & Zarantonello, 2013). They are usually highly memorable and meaningful (Duerden et al., 2018; Schmitt & Zarantonello, 2013) and are associated with personal growth, the renewal of self, and adventure (Arnould & Price, 1993). And they result in intense emotions of excitement and pleasure (McIntyre & Roggenbuck, 1998).

The effect of engagement in extraordinary experiences on consumption happiness is higher for the young. Young consumers generally derive more happiness from extraordinary experiences than from ordinary experiences because the memories of extraordinary and meaningful life events exert a stronger impact on their self-definition and wellbeing (Bhattacharjee & Mogilner, 2014). Young consumers define happiness in terms of excitement, enthusiasm, and high states of arousal (Mogilner et al., 2011; Scheibe et al., 2013); they also view extraordinary experiences as self-defining experiences (e.g., experiences closely related to self-concept) (Bhattacharjee & Mogilner, 2014).

This implies that risk-taking may be viewed as an experience that fosters high hedonic benefits and intense emotions of happiness (Ayadi et al., 2017). Given that extraordinary experiences provide young consumers with intensive positive affect, personal growth, and memorable experiences, extraordinary experiences are likely to have a strong association with experiential happiness.

Ordinary Experiences

Experiential happiness is strongly associated with *ordinary experiences*. Ordinary experiences are experiences that are common, frequent, and within the realm of everyday life (Bhattacharjee & Mogilner, 2014; Schmitt & Zarantonello, 2013). Examples of ordinary experiences highlighted by study participants include daily walking, watching movies, drinking coffee, riding bike, having fun conversations, taking a shower, and others. Examples of extraordinary experiences include going to a concert, taking a vacation to a tropical island, getting married, buying a new car, travelling to a foreign country, and others (Bhattacharjee & Mogilner, 2014).

Research has documented the study finding that engagement in ordinary experiences leads to consumer happiness, and this effect is stronger for older consumers and those who savor such experiences. Savoring refers to the capacity to attend to, appreciate, and enhance the positive experiences in their lives (Bryant & Veroff, 2017). In other words, consumers can enhance experiential happiness by directing attention to their positive experiences, appreciating these experiences, and elaborating or enhancing the experience of these positive moments in their lives. In other words, savoring ordinary everyday experiences contributes to lasting happiness, especially for older consumers. Old consumers define experiential happiness in terms of calm, peacefulness, and low states of arousal (Mogilner et al., 2011; Scheibe et al., 2013), and ordinary experiences provide consumers with low-arousal positive affect (e.g., calm).

In sum, experiential happiness is strongly associated with ordinary experiences, especially for older consumers.

Eudaimonic Experiences

Eudaimonic experiences are experiences related to mastery, meaning, and autonomy needs (Ryan & Deci, 2001). They are also experiences where consumers engage in activities willingly, out of their own volition and choice. Such experiences are also about pursuing personal goals related to need fulfillment, long-term importance, positive affect, and meaningfulness.

Evidence suggests that engagement in eudaimonic experiences results in enhanced consumer happiness. How does this come about? First, engagement in eudaimonic experiences provides consumers with satisfaction of the need for mastery (e.g., overcoming challenge, knowledge development, and skill progression) (Newman et al., 2014). Examples of these activities could include intellectually stimulating tasks (e.g., playing chess or learning a foreign language) and physical challenges (e.g., training for a marathon) (Mojza et al., 2010). Mastery in leisure activities nevertheless promotes subjective wellbeing by providing individuals a sense of accomplishment, feelings of competency and self-efficacy, which in turn helps create a positive mood, all of which contribute to overall wellbeing (Iwasaki, 2007; Newman et al., 2014).

Second, engagement in eudaimonic experiences may be self-expressive (i.e., activities that are compatible with their values and daimon or the true self). When consumers engage in self-expressive activities, they gain something important or valuable in life, which contributes to eudaimonic wellbeing (Waterman et al., 2008).

Freedom to Experience (as in Relation to Eudaimonia)

Freedom to experience eudaimonia refers to one form of eudaimonic experience involving freedom to explore and enact the ideal self (Gaston-Breton et al., 2020). In other words, freedom to experience means the opportunity for consumers to explore, decide, and enact who they are or want to become. Freedom to experience also means that consumers make a significant effort to master special skills and knowledge that result in feelings of accomplishment, personal development, and a sense of belonging. The experience can be meaningful and fulfilling as consumers try to find their true selves. As such, this freedom is more frequently associated with high positive emotional arousal (excitement) and is more likely to foster eudaimonic, meaning-based happiness.

Engagement of freedom to experiences provides consumers with satisfaction of autonomy needs (e.g., engagement out of volition), mastery needs (e.g., overcoming challenge, knowledge development, and skill progression) and meaning needs (e.g., engaging in experiences that are compatible with consumer's values and true self, or daimon) (Ryan & Deci, 2001; Newman et al., 2014). Meeting these needs prompts experiences of positive affect, vitality, and a deep inner sense of wellbeing.

Research has shown that the effect of engagement in "freedom to experience" on consumption happiness is greater for those *consumers without much stress or threat*. When consumers are not under stress or threat, they are more likely to be able to be free to choose, thus engage in exciting and extraordinary experiences. In addition, research has also shown that the effect of this type of freedom on consumption happiness is greater for the young consumers who have a future focus and view happiness in terms of exciting experiences (Mogilner et al., 2012). In contrast, the more mature consumers tend not to have a future focus; as such, they are less likely to experience happiness from high-arousal arousal exciting events.

Flow Experiences

Flow experiences refer to an intrinsically rewarding state that results from intense engagement with daily activities (Csikzentmihaly, 1990). For example, engagement in sports offers opportunities to experience flow by posing both mental and physical challenges (Jackson & Csikszentmihalyi, 1999). Sports commonly involve highly structured, goal-directed, and rule-bound activities, competition with oneself and/or others, and require a high level of commitment (Swann, 2016). These activities also demand either vigorous physical exertion or the use of relatively complex physical skills, which are often performed in the presence of spectators. Indeed, elements of physical injury risk, exposure to the weather conditions, and interactions with teammates, coaches, opponents, and referees can all be present in sporting activities. Importantly, these factors present a variety of both mental and physical challenges, meaning that sporting activities are particularly well suited to experiencing flow states (Jackson & Csikszentmihalyi, 1999; Swann, 2016).

Consumers can also experience flow experiences during their shopping or leisure experiences. During flow experiences, consumers experience intense involvement, deep concentration, lack of self-consciousness, and loss of a sense of time. Focused involvement banishes not only unrelated thoughts but also potentially distracting feelings about the activity itself, such that consumers recognize the activity as enjoyable only at some point after its completion (Csikszentmihalyi, 2002; Decloe et al., 2009; Havitz & Mannell, 2005; Cheng & Lu, 2015).

What are the antecedents of flow experiences? Flow experiences result from matching a high level of challenges with a high level of skills (Csikzentmihaly, 1990; Csikszentmihalyi, 2002). Flow experience involves a balance of challenge and skill, and enjoyment. That is, flow experiences are rewarding experiences in an optimally challenging task. Yet, mismatching challenges and skills results in lower wellbeing. Consider a shopping activity such as the purchase of an automobile. If the consumer does not know much about automobiles and what constitutes good quality and value, this consumer is likely to be overwhelmed, which may result in feelings of low flow. Similarly, if the consumer is an expert on automobiles and is very familiar with what makes a good quality car and expected prices, that consumer is not likely to experience feelings of flow either. However, if the consumer knows enough about automobiles but is neither a novice nor an expert, s/he may experience flow. The consumer may feel challenged, and as such, s/he may experience intense involvement, deep concentration, lack of self-consciousness, and loss of a sense of time when shopping for an automobile.

What are the consequences of flow experiences? Flow experiences result in a sense of fulfilment, satisfaction with the event, and enhanced self-esteem (Csikzentmihaly, 1990; Csikszentmihalyi, 2002; Wells, 1988). Flow experiences result in enhanced hedonic and eudaimonic wellbeing (Csikzentmihaly, 1990; Peterson et al., 2005). In addition, flow experiences can protect individuals from stress and improve wellbeing (Csikzentmihaly, 1990). As such, engagement in flow experiences in the marketplace contributes to consumer happiness. Empirical evidence suggests that flow experiences result in a sense of fulfillment, enhanced satisfaction with the event, hedonic enjoyment, and eudaimonic self-growth (Asakawa, 2004; Chen et al., 2010; Peterson et al., 2005).

Self-Expressive Activities

Of course, engaging in *self-expressive activities* leads to feelings of self-expressiveness. Self-expressive activities are activities that are strongly representative of who the person is or would like to become. Self-expressiveness refers to the degree to which the participants perceive that the activity represents and is consistent with their self-concept and is most likely to be acknowledged publicly (Sharma et al., 2022). Feelings of self-expressiveness refer to feelings that the consumption experiences are in harmony with the true self (daimon) and one's intrinsic values--feelings of fulfillment from engaging meaningful activities towards personal growth and self-actualization (Deci & Ryan, 2008; Waterman, 1990; Waterman et al., 2008). In other words, feelings of self-expressiveness reflect feelings from realizing one's full personal potential and progressing toward achieving one's true nature.

What are the antecedents to feelings of self-expressiveness? First, consumers experience feelings of self-expressiveness when they engage in activities that are important to the self-concept, moderately challenging, require substantial effort, and have a high potential for self-actualization (Bosnjak et al., 2016; Waterman et al., 2008). In other words, consumers experience feelings of self-expressiveness when they engage in self-defining activities. Second, consumers experience feelings of self-expressiveness when they engage in activities in which they have intrinsic value (Waterman, 1990). Third, consumers experience feelings of self-expressiveness when there is a high level of self-congruity with the activity. That is, consumers experience feelings of self-expressiveness when the market-related activity serves to reduce the gap between actual and ideal self (Sharma et al., 2022).

What are the consequences of feelings of self-expression from an activity? First, feelings of self-expression from an activity have a positive impact on the attitude toward the market-related activity and its corresponding behavioral intention (Thorbjørnsen et al., 2007). Second, the feeling of self-expressiveness is positively related to positive affect and eudaimonic wellbeing. Research has uncovered the study finding that feelings of self-expressiveness are positively associated with improved health, positive affect, satisfaction of basic psychological needs, and meaning and vitality in their lives (Ryan et al., 2008; Waterman et al., 2008).

How to Experience

In this section, we will discuss several strategies designed to enhance consumption happiness by focusing on the process (i.e., how to experience). These strategies are savoring, anticipated savoring, savoring positive experiences in the present moment, reminiscence experiences, sharing positive events with others, engagement in diverse experiences, and arrangement and choice of hedonic experiences.

Savoring

Savoring refers to the capacity to attend to, appreciate, and enhance the positive experiences in their lives (Bryant & Veroff, 2017). Savoring is not positive emotion per se, but rather a meta-cognitive process involving an awareness of good feelings while they are unfolding (Bryant & Veroff, 2017).

Consumers involved in experiential consumption typically go through three phases of experience with a consumer good or service: (1) anticipated experiential consumption, which includes searching, planning for future purchases, daydreaming, budgeting, fantasizing; (2) momentary consumption experiences, which involve sensory experiences, satiation, satisfaction/dissatisfaction, arousal/flow, and transformation; and (3) remembered consumption which is related to reliving past experiences (Weidman & Dunn, 2016). In other words, consumers can increase their positive affect from their experiences by anticipating savoring of positive experiences, by savoring the positive experiences in the moment, and by remembering and sharing past positive experiences.

In sum, savoring processes encompass different time orientations. Besides savoring the present moment as it unfolds, one can also savor positive experiences from the past (reminiscence) or future (anticipation). Savoring the moment, reminiscence, and anticipation all serve to generate or regulate positive feelings in the present (Bryant & Veroff, 2017; Smith & Bryant, 2017).

Anticipated Savoring

Consumers can experience a heightened level of positive affect through *anticipated savoring,* such as an upcoming vacation (Nawijn, 2011) or anticipating an experiential purchase (Kumar et al., 2014). In other words, anticipated savoring refers to savoring of an upcoming experience as a cognitive process involving awareness of current pleasure from a target-specific, future consumption experience (Chun et al., 2017).

Why does this occur? First, consumers can experience intense positive affect from waiting, perhaps because of *uncertainty*. Uncertainty may lead consumers to have more frequent positive thoughts about future positive experiences (Kurtz et al., 2007). Empirical research has shown that thinking about future events triggers stronger emotions than thinking about the same events in the past (Van Boven & Ashworth, 2007; Caruso et al., 2008). As the time for pleasurable experiences gets closer, the intensity of positive feelings gets stronger (Bryant & Veroff, 2017).

Second, research has also shown that anticipated savoring may positively influence ongoing enjoyment and remembered enjoyment (Chun et al., 2017). To empirically examine the effects of savoring an upcoming event on remembered enjoyment of the event, consider the following study by Chun et al. (2017). Seven days before the spring break, participants in the savoring condition were asked to "write about your thoughts and feelings regarding how much you'll enjoy your upcoming spring break. Turn your attention to the good feelings you have now about enjoying your break." On the day after spring break ended, participants in both conditions responded to the questions on the extent to which participants liked spring break (1 = "disliked it very much," and 9 = "liked it very much") and the extent to which spring break was fun, enjoyable, and good (1 = "not at all," and 9 = "a great deal"). The results of this study indicate that participants in the savoring spring break condition remembered the experience as more enjoyable than did those participants who simply thought about activities during the spring break.

Furthermore, to empirically examine the effect of savoring upcoming events on ongoing enjoyment, the same authors conducted another study (Chun et al., 2017). Participants in the savoring condition watched a movie trailer (e.g., Toy Story). Then, they watched the actual movie clip and responded to questions on their ongoing enjoyment while they were watching the clip. The results indicate that participants in the savoring condition reported greater enjoyment while watching the movie compared with those in the control condition. Overall, the study results indicate that anticipated savoring positive influence on ongoing enjoyment and remembered enjoyment.

Additionally, there is empirical evidence suggesting that consumers derive more positive affect from *waiting for positive experiences than from waiting for material possessions* (Kumar et al., 2014; Kumar & Gilovich, 2016). Thus, anticipated savoring related to future experiences tends to increase positive affect, which in turn increases experiential happiness.

Savoring Positive Experiences in the Present Moment

Consumers can jack up their positive affect through *savoring positive experiences in the present moment*. Savoring the present moment refers to deliberately directing attention to the present pleasant experience (Nelis et al., 2011). Examples of savoring of the present moment include absorption (e.g., relax and exists only in the present; try not to think, but rather to get immersed in the present moment), sensory perceptual sharpening (e.g., focus on the sensations of a pleasant experience; identify pleasure by focusing on certain stimuli in the situation, and block out others) (Bryant & Veroff, 2017; Wood et al., 2003), and mindfulness of the present moment (e.g., being attentive to and aware of what is taking place in the present) (Brown & Ryan, 2003). As such, savoring of the moment increases intensity and duration of the positive affect that is experienced (Bryant, 2003).

Consumers can engage in the following savoring behaviors to heighten the positive effect of positive experiences. First, consumers can fully absorb themselves and sharpen their sensory perceptions on the present positive experience. That is, consumers can relax and get immersed in the moment and focus on the sensations of a pleasant experience. For example, the mindfulness of a tourist influences the tourist's appreciation and understanding of a site. One technique of savoring the present moment is mindful photography, in which people focus on capturing images that reflect what is beautiful or meaningful about a particular target object or setting (Kurtz & Lyubomirsky, 2013). Photo-taking can also naturally promote mindful attention to visual aspects of experiences of the moment and allow greater savoring of the moment itself by promoting mindful attention to the positive aspects of the experience (Diehl & Zauberman, 2022).

Second, consumers can express their positive emotions through behaviors such as laughing, jumping up and down, or making verbal sounds of appreciation (Bryant & Veroff, 2017; Quoidbach et al., 2010; Wood et al., 2003). Behavioral display of emotions plays a causal role in the subjective expression of emotions (Quoidbach et al., 2010).

Third, consumers can slow down the speed of experience "at the moment" to savor the positive experiences. Savoring positive experiences means consciously focusing on the pleasure they are experiencing to heighten and prolong it (Bryant & Veroff, 2017). In addition, consumers can segregate pleasurable experiences to savor the positive experiences.

To conclude, consumers' savoring of positive events increases happiness in relation to marketplace experiences (Quoidbach et al., 2010; Bryant et al., 2005; Jose et al., 2012). Savoring positive experiences serves to increase happiness, decrease depression, and heighten overall satisfaction with life (Smith & Hollinger-Smith, 2015). Additionally, savoring positive experiences increases the duration, frequency, and intensity of positive emotions (Fredrickson, 2001; Livingstone & Srivastava, 2012; Tugade & Fredrickson, 2007). Cultivation of positive emotions helps to build lasting resources that, in turn, enhance consumers' judgment of life satisfaction, increase the likelihood of experiencing future positive emotions, and foster resilience to negative emotions (Fredrickson & Branigan, 2005). Furthermore, the experience of savoring positive emotions facilitates social communications about positive experiences (such as social storytelling), which in turn amplifies positive affect (Gable et al., 2018).

Reminiscence Experiences

Consumers can have increased positive affect through remembering the positive experiences (Bryant et al., 2005). Reminiscence is the act of remembering long-past positive experiences. They look back and rekindle positive feelings associated with past experiences (Bryant et al., 2005). Research has documented the way consumers purposefully try to remember positive events by writing about their experiences in diaries or keeping their journals, taking pictures, and buying commemorative goods (Bryant & Veroff, 2017; Wood et al., 2003).

Specifically, photo-taking serves to enhance memory of positive experiences (Barasch et al., 2017; Diehl & Zauberman, 2022; Diehl et al., 2016). Having photographs enables consumers to remember positive experiences. Evidence points to the notion that people who take photographs during an experience recognize more of what they saw but less of what they heard (Barasch et al., 2017). However, there is a caveat. While photo-taking act can facilitate social sharing of experiences and boost satisfaction with the experience (Gilovich et al., 2015), photo taking with intention of posting on social media may increase self-presentation concerns and reduce positive affect of experiences especially for those consumers with low self-esteem (Barasch et al., 2018).

Second, collecting commemorative goods provides consumers with a tangible biography by associating the objects with positive experiences. In other words, commemorative goods provide consumers opportunities to savor the positive emotions associated with the events (Goodman et al., 2016; Quoidbach et al., 2015).

Overall, research indicates that consumers' conscientious efforts to remember the positive experiences of consumption events are positively associated with consumers' experiential happiness (Bryant et al., 2005; Lyubomirsky et al., 2006; MacLeod & Conway, 2005; Quoidbach et al., 2009).

Sharing Positive Events with Others

Consumers' sharing of positive events can enhance happiness concerning marketplace experiences. This may occur because sharing positive experiences provides consumers with satisfaction of relatedness need, enhanced self-esteem, and increased positive emotions related to the actual events.

Specifically, social sharing of experiences serves to *increase the quantity and quality of social relationships*, which in turn increases experiential happiness and overall wellbeing. Research suggests that consumers tend to frequently recount stories about their positive consumption experiences (more so than their material acquisitions) because positive experiences have more conversational value than material objects (Bastos & Brucks, 2017; Kumar & Gilovich, 2015). Sharing an experience with others contributes significantly to positive social interactions, reduces loneliness, and helps meet consumers' relatedness needs (Valkenburg et al., 2006). As such, social sharing of positive experiences is beneficial for consumers' experiential happiness (Bastos, 2020).

Second, social sharing of experiences serves to *enhance a positive self-image*, which in turn contributes to consumers' overall wellbeing (Langston, 1994). For example, consumers share their positive experiences by publicizing their experiences on social media. Posting one's positive experiences on social media serves to enhance self-esteem, especially when others reciprocate by sharing their own experiences (Raghunathan & Corfman, 2006; Burrow & Rainone, 2017).

Third, sharing positive experiences *induces positive emotions related to the positive experiences*. Sharing a positive event with others requires retelling the event, which creates an opportunity for reliving and re-experiencing the event (Gable et al., 2004). Evidence suggests that social sharing is associated with more time thinking about the positive events, which in turn increases the intensity and duration of the positive emotions (Hovasapian & Levine, 2018; Verduyn et al., 2011). As a result, sharing positive experiences with others is associated with increased positive affect and overall wellbeing, above and beyond the impact of the positive event itself (Gable et al., 2004). Research also suggests that consumers who receive enthusiastic support for their shared experiences report more positive emotions than consumers who did not receive enthusiastic support (Lambert et al., 2013). As such, social sharing of positive events serves the storyteller to experience greater positive affect and personal wellbeing (Gable et al., 2004, 2006). Consider the example of going on a cruise to an exotic destination and coming home and sharing the story with friends and family (Kim & Fesenmaier, 2017).

Engagement in Diverse Experiences

Consumers can have increased positive affect through *diverse consumption experiences*. There is empirical evidence suggesting that variety plays a significant role in contributing to overall happiness (Lyubomirsky et al., 2005; Mogilner et al., 2008). Diverse experiences can produce a positive effect on consumption happiness due to the following factors. First, diverse consumption experiences contribute to consumption happiness because consumers can choose consumption experiences that fit well with their physical and psychological makeup (Etkin & Mogilner, 2016). Having choices may improve the quality of consumers' lives as they help them select the exact consumption experiences they wish. As such, engagement in diverse consumption experiences may provide consumers with opportunities for satisfaction of their full spectrum of developmental needs, which in turn contribute significantly to their wellbeing (see discussion of need theory in Diener & Lucas, 2000).

The *needs theory of happiness* rests on the assumption that there are universal human needs and that individuals will experience feelings of happiness to the extent that these needs are met (Diener & Lucas, 2000). According to the needs theory, an individual's life satisfaction is high when people experience fulfilment of various needs, ranging from health and safety needs to belongingness and self-actualization needs (Maslow, 1954) or when they experience satisfaction in various life domains (Campbell et al., 1976). While satisfaction of various needs is important in the makeup of overall life satisfaction, there are individual differences dealing with the importance of specific needs and the resources required to fulfil these needs. For example, life satisfaction of people in an individualistic culture is strongly associated with self-esteem and self-consistency (Diener & Diener, 1995; Diener & Lucas, 2000; Suh, 2002). Some people need a lot of social contact to feel satisfied with life overall, while others need very little social contact.

Consumer's experiential happiness is high when consumers engage in various experiences. This is because various experiences provide consumers with opportunities to satisfy the full spectrum of human development needs (Sirgy & Lee, 2018; Sirgy, 2021, 2022). There is a satisfaction limit from a single experience, and engagement in a single experience does not provide consumers with satisfaction of various needs. In addition, engagement in various experiences provides consumers with opportunities for satisfaction of unique needs that are important for them (Sirgy & Lee, 2018). A variety of experiences enhances experiential happiness because consumers can choose experiences that fit well with their physical and psychological conditions (Etkin & Mogilner, 2016). Through a survey of 501 leisure sports participants (n = 501), Lee et al. (2024) found that diverse leisure engagement has a positive predictive effect on leisure wellbeing.

Second, engagement in *diverse consumption experiences results in a decrease in the rate of satiation and hedonic adaptation* (Redden, 2008). As such, experiencing diversity may contribute to positive outcomes in the lives of consumers by *alleviating boredom*. Furthermore, evidence suggests that diversity of consumption experiences can lead to increased social interactions and satisfaction in social life (Lee et al., 2018). Those consumers who focus on only one activity may experience hedonic adaptation. Engaging in the same leisure activities is likely to result in hedonic adaptation (e.g., Kuykendall et al., 2015; Newman et al., 2014).

Research clearly shows that the variety of activities engaged in during the vacation was positively associated with leisure satisfaction and psychological wellbeing (Wei & Milman, 2002). Thus, consumers need to engage in a variety of experiences for experiential happiness.

Arrangement and Choice of Hedonic Experiences

Consumers can increase consumption happiness from hedonic experiences by improving the arrangement of and choices of hedonic experiences without increasing the objective levels of external resources. Here are a few examples. First, consumption happiness can be increased by segregating positive experiences to reduce diminishing sensitivity to positive events. Thaler (1985) suggested that individuals choose to combine or separate multiple events in ways that make themselves happiest. Individuals are happier when they experience two positive events instead of one large positive event (e.g., winning a \$50 lottery and a \$30 lottery generates greater happiness than winning an \$80 lottery). When consumers experience one large positive event (e.g., a 4-h musical concert), they are likely to quickly adapt to the positive event and experience diminishing sensitivity to the positive event. In contrast, when they experience multiple positive events (e.g., two separate 2-h concerts), they maintain the original reference point (original expectation), allowing them to gain increased positive affect from each of the individual positive experiences. In sum, consumers can experience increased hedonic happiness by segregating positive events.

Second. consumption happiness from hedonic experiences can be increased by progressively increasing the quality of the experience, compared to experiences that are stable or declining in quality (Loewenstein & Prelec, 1993; Ross & Simonson, 1991). This is because consumption happiness is sensitive to changes in positive experiences. In an experiment by Loewenstein and Prelec (1993), participants were first asked to express their restaurant preferences, and most respondents expressed their preference for a French restaurant over a Greek restaurant. Then, participants were given the option of having two dinners in different sequence patterns: Greek and then French versus French and then Greek. Most participants preferred to defer the French dinner. This result indicates that when the choice sequence context is highlighted (e.g., having both dinners in sequence), consumers prefer an option that provides improved satisfaction over time. In another study, Ross and Simonson (1991) presented subjects with a series of hypothetical choices between sequences that ended with a loss (e.g., win \$85, then lose \$15) or a gain (lose \$15, then win \$85). Subjects overwhelmingly preferred sequences that ended with a gain. In sum, when consumers experience a series of events, they tend to experience the greatest consumption happiness when they experience progressively increasing quality. This is because progressively increasing experience quality reduces hedonic adaptation.

Third, consumption happiness can be increased by waiting for positive experiences before the actual occurrence (Kahneman, 1999). Specifically, consumers' anticipated happiness can be increased by allowing sufficient time to pass before experiencing the actual event and savoring the experience when it occurs. Loewenstein (1987) showed that anticipation of consumption has its benefits. He construed savoring as the positive utility derived from the anticipation of future consumption. In his well-known study, the author found that participants were willing to pay more to kiss their favorite celebrity three days in the future than to experience the kiss immediately, an indication that people get pleasure from anticipation. Yet, it should be noted that this degree of savoring is greater when consumers wait for experiences than when they wait for material possessions. To illustrate this point, Kumar et al. (2014) conducted a study in which participants were assigned to think about upcoming experiential purchase (e.g., ski pass, concert) or material purchase (e.g., clothing, laptops) after which they responded to their state of mind while waiting for their purchase. The participants reported that the anticipation of an experience was more pleasant and exciting than the anticipation of a material possession. This is because consumers are likely to savor the upcoming experiences by deriving positive utility from the anticipation of future experiences. In contrast, waiting for a material purchase is often fraught with more impatience. In sum, one can argue that anticipated happiness can be increased by allowing sufficient time to pass before experiencing the actual positive event (e.g., a reservation for the positive event).

Fourth, consumption happiness can be increased by introducing interruptions into the course of consumption (Nelson et al., 2009). In other words, consumers can reset the original reference point and reduce hedonic adaptation to the experiences by having interruptions. In a study by Nelson et al. (2009), participants were asked to watch an episode of a television show (e.g., Taxi). Approximately half the participants watched the program as is, whereas the remaining participants watched a version with the commercials removed. Then participants responded to the question on the degree to which they enjoyed the show and their willingness to spend money for a DVD compiling a season of the program. The results indicate that participants enjoy the television show more when commercial interruptions are included than when they have been removed. This is because commercials disrupt adaptation and help to maintain an overall high level of enjoyment. Consumers often adapt to the experience of watching television such that each successive minute is slightly less enjoyable than the previous one. Advertisements, although independently aversive, disrupt this adaptation process and can therefore make the overall experience more enjoyable. In sum, consumers can experience greater happiness by accepting interruptions (e.g., intermission time between the shows) during the experience to help reduce hedonic adaptation.

Fifth, consumption can be increased by reducing the overestimation of hedonic experience at the time of purchase. This can be done by doing a single evaluation of the product and by considering situational factors during the actual consumption. Consider the study conducted by Hsee and Zhang (2004). Suppose that a person is considering buying a house between two alternatives for the same price: a 3,000 square-foot house that is within walking distance to work and a 4000 square-foot house with an hour's driving distance to work. At the acquisition stage, consumers tend to rely on joint evaluations of the two alternatives (e.g., comparative evaluations based on quantitative differences: 3000 square feet vs. 4000 square feet). At this stage, consumers tend to rely on comparative evaluation of a quantitative attribute (e.g., house size) because this attribute is easy to compare. Specifically, consumers think living in a 4000 square-foot house should provide far more experiential happiness than living in a 3000 square-foot house. However, after consumers move into a house, they quickly adapt to the new space. In other words, consumers overpredict the utility difference between the two houses by making joint evaluations at the time of purchase (cf. Hsee & Hastie, 2006). At the stage of use, however, consumers tend to rely on a single evaluation of the house they chose. As such, their experiential happiness related to the house is largely influenced by qualitative experiential attributes (e.g., convenience, traffic conditions). Based on these study findings, we recommend that consumers should focus more on experiential attributes during actual use rather than on comparative evaluations of quantitative attributes.

Summary and Conclusion

Much has been said about happiness in relation to marketplace experiences. We made the distinction between happiness related to experiences of a marketplace event and experiences related to a marketplace good—the principle of experiential advantage. We then discussed strategies related to "what to experience" that can enhance experiential happiness: hedonic experiences, freedom from experience (as in relation to recovery), extraordinary experiences, ordinary experiences, eudaimonic experiences, freedom to experience as concerning eudaimonia, flow experiences, and self-expressive activities.

Much of this discussion is captured in Table 15.2. We then turned our attention to "how-to experience" strategies that can enhance happiness as savoring happiness, anticipated savoring, savoring positive experiences in the present moment, reminiscence experiences, sharing of positive events with others, engagement in diverse experiences, and arrangement and choice of hedonic experiences. Much of this discussion is captured in Table 15.3.

Table 15.2 Enhancing happiness: what to experience in the marketplace

Dimension	Impact on happiness in relation to marketplace experiences.	Details
Extraordinary experiences	Experiential happiness is strongly associated with extraordinary experiences.	Extraordinary experiences provide consumers with intensive positive affect, personal growth, and memorable experiences, especially for the young.
Ordinary experiences	Experiential happiness is strongly associated with ordinary experiences.	Savoring ordinary everyday experiences has been shown to enhance experiential happiness, especially for the old consumers.
Freedom to experience (eudaimonic)	Experiential happiness is strongly associated with the freedom to have (eudaimonic) experiences.	Freedom to experience (eudaimonic) can be meaningful and fulfilling to those consumers who try to express their true self.
Flow experience	Experiential happiness is strongly associated with flow experience.	Flow experiences result in a sense of fulfilment, satisfaction with the event, and enhanced self-esteem.
Self-expressive activities	Experiential happiness is strongly associated with self-expressive activities.	Feelings of self-expressiveness are positively associated with improved health, positive affect, satisfaction of basic psychological needs, and meaning and vitality in their lives.

Table 15.3 Enhancing happiness: how to experience in the marketplace

Dimension	Impact on experiential happiness.	Details
Savoring	Experiential happiness is strongly associated with savoring experiences.	Consumers can have increased positive affect from their experiences by anticipating savoring of positive experiences, savoring the positive experiences in the moment, and remembering/ sharing past positive experiences.
Sharing positive events with others	Experiential happiness is strongly associated with sharing positive events with others.	Social sharing of experiences positively influences the quantity/quality of social relationships, positive self-image, and positive affect.
Engagement in diverse experiences	Experiential happiness is strongly associated with engagement in diverse experiences.	Engagement in diverse consumption experiences will provide participants with many opportunities for satisfaction with the full spectrum of developmental needs and opportunities for self-development. Engagement in diverse experiences will reduce satiation and hedonic adaptation.
Hedonic experience	Experiential happiness is strongly associated with the arrangement of hedonic experiences.	Experiential happiness can be increased by segregating positive experiences, by having progressively increasing quality of experiences, by introducing interruptions into the course of consumption.

References

Anderson, L., Ostrom, A. L., Corus, C., Fisk, R. P., Gallan, A. S., Giraldo, M., et al. (2013). Transformative service research: An agenda for the future. *Journal of Business Research, 66*(8), 1203–1210.

Arnould, E. J., & Price, L. L. (1993). River magic: Extraordinary experience and the extended service encounter. *Journal of Consumer Research, 20*(1), 24–45.

Asakawa, K. (2004). Flow experience and autotelic personality in Japanese college students: How do they experience challenges in daily life? *Journal of Happiness Studies, 5*(2), 123–154.

Ayadi, N., Paraschiv, C., & Vernette, E. (2017). Increasing consumer well-being: Risk as potential driver of happiness. *Applied Economics, 49*(43), 4321–4335.

Barasch, A., Diehl, K., Silverman, J., & Zauberman, G. (2017). Photographic memory: The effects of volitional photo taking on memory for visual and auditory aspects of an experience. *Psychological Science, 28*(8), 1056–1066.

Barasch, A., Zauberman, G., & Diehl, K. (2018). How the intention to share can undermine enjoyment: Photo-taking goals and evaluation of experiences. *Journal of Consumer Research, 44*(6), 1220–1237.

Bastos, W. (2020). Consumers gain equivalent levels of happiness from sharing about an experience and an object. *European Journal of Marketing, 54*(1), 49–78.

Bastos, W., & Brucks, M. (2017). How and why conversational value leads to happiness for experiential and material purchases. *Journal of Consumer Research, 44*(3), 598–612.

Bhattacharjee, A., & Mogilner, C. (2014). Happiness from ordinary and extraordinary experiences. *Journal of Consumer Research, 41*(1), 1–17.

Bosnjak, M., Brown, C. A., Lee, D. J., Yu, G. B., & Sirgy, M. J. (2016). Self-expressiveness in sport tourism: Determinants and consequences. *Journal of Travel Research, 55*(1), 125–134.

Brown, K. W., & Ryan, R. M. (2003). The benefits of being present: Mindfulness and its role in psychological well-being. *Journal of Personality and Social Psychology, 84*(4), 822–848.
Bryant, F. (2003). Savoring Beliefs Inventory (SBI): A scale for measuring beliefs about savouring. *Journal of Mental Health, 12*(2), 175–196.
Bryant, F. B., & Veroff, J. (2017). *Savoring: A new model of positive experience*. Psychology Press.
Bryant, F. B., Smart, C. M., & King, S. P. (2005). Using the past to enhance the present: Boosting happiness through positive reminiscence. *Journal of Happiness Studies, 6*(3), 227–260.
Burrow, A. L., & Rainone, N. (2017). How many likes did I get? Purpose moderates links between positive social media feedback and self-esteem. *Journal of Experimental Social Psychology, 69*, 232–236.
Campbell, A., Converse, P. E., & Rodgers, W. L. (1976). *The quality of American life: Perceptions, evaluations, and satisfactions*. Russell Sage.
Caprariello, P. A., & Reis, H. T. (2013). To do, to have, or to share? Valuing experiences over material possessions depends on the involvement of others. *Journal of Personality and Social Psychology, 104*(2), 199–215.
Carter, T. J., & Gilovich, T. (2010). The relative relativity of material and experiential purchases. *Journal of Personality and Social Psychology, 98*(1), 146–159.
Carter, T. J., & Gilovich, T. (2012). I am what I do, not what I have: The differential centrality of experiential and material purchases to the self. *Journal of Personality and Social Psychology, 102*(6), 1304–1317.
Caruso, E. M., Gilbert, D. T., & Wilson, T. D. (2008). A wrinkle in time: Asymmetric valuation of past and future events. *Psychological Science, 19*(8), 796–801.
Chancellor, J., & Lyubomirsky, S. (2011). Happiness and thrift: When (spending) less is (hedonically) more. *Journal of Consumer Psychology, 21*(2), 131–138.
Chen, L. H., Ye, Y. C., Chen, M. Y., & Tung, I. W. (2010). Alegría! Flow in leisure and life satisfaction: The mediating role of event satisfaction using data from an acrobatics show. *Social Indicators Research, 99*(2), 301–313.
Chen, C. C., Petrick, J. F., & Shahvali, M. (2016). Tourism experiences as a stress reliever: Examining the effects of tourism recovery experiences on life satisfaction. *Journal of Travel Research, 55*(2), 150–160.
Cheng, T. M., & Lu, C. C. (2015). The causal relationships among recreational involvement, flow experience, and well-being for surfing activities. *Asia Pacific Journal of Tourism Research, 20*(Suppl. 1), 1486–1504.
Chun, H. H., Diehl, K., & MacInnis, D. J. (2017). Savoring an upcoming experience affects ongoing and remembered consumption enjoyment. *Journal of Marketing, 81*(3), 96–110.
Cova, B., Carù, A., & Cayla, J. (2018). Re-conceptualizing escape in consumer research. *Qualitative Market Research, 21*(4), 445–464.
Csikszentmihalyi, M. (2002). *Flow: The classic work on how to achieve happiness*. Random House.
Csikszentmihalyi, M. (1990). *Flow: The psychology of optimal experience*. New York: Harper & Row.
Deci, E. L., & Ryan, R. M. (2008). Self-determination theory: A macrotheory of human motivation, development, and health. *Canadian Psychology/Psychologie Canadienne, 49*(3), 182–185.
Decloe, M. D., Kaczynski, A. T., & Havitz, M. E. (2009). Social participation, flow and situational involvement in recreational physical activity. *Journal of Leisure Research, 41*(1), 73–91.
Diehl, K., & Zauberman, G. (2022). Capturing life or missing it: How mindful photo-taking can affect experiences. *Current Opinion in Psychology, 46*, 101334.
Diehl, K., Zauberman, G., & Barasch, A. (2016). How taking photos increases enjoyment of experiences. *Journal of Personality and Social Psychology, 111*(2), 119–140.
Diener, E., & Diener, M. (1995). Cross-cultural correlates of life satisfaction and self-esteem. *Journal of Personality and Social Psychology, 68*(4), 653–663.
Diener, E., & Lucas, R. E. (2000). Explaining differences in societal levels of happiness: Relative standards, need fulfillment, culture, and evaluation theory. *Journal of Happiness Studies, 1*(1), 41–78.

Dubé, L., & Le Bel, J. (2003). The content and structure of laypeople's concept of pleasure. *Cognition and Emotion, 17*(2), 263–295.

Duerden, M. D., Lundberg, N. R., Ward, P., Taniguchi, S. T., Hill, B., Widmer, M. A., & Zabriskie, R. (2018). From ordinary to extraordinary: A framework of experience types. *Journal of Leisure Research, 49*(3–5), 196–216.

Etkin, J., & Mogilner, C. (2016). Does variety among activities increase happiness? *Journal of Consumer Research, 43*(2), 210–229.

Etzion, D., Eden, D., & Lapidot, Y. (1998). Relief from job stressors and burnout: Reserve service as a respite. *Journal of Applied Psychology, 83*(4), 577–585.

Fredrickson, B. L. (2001). The role of positive emotions in positive psychology: The broaden-and-build theory of positive emotions. *American Psychologist, 56*(3), 218–226.

Fredrickson, B. L., & Branigan, C. (2005). Positive emotions broaden the scope of attention and thought-action repertoires. *Cognition & Emotion, 19*(3), 313–332.

Gable, S. L., Reis, H. T., Impett, E. A., & Asher, E. R. (2004). What do you do when things go right? The intrapersonal and interpersonal benefits of sharing positive events. *Journal of Personality and Social Psychology, 87*(2), 228–245.

Gable, S. L., Gonzaga, G. C., & Strachman, A. (2006). Will you be there for me when things go right? Supportive responses to positive event disclosures. *Journal of Personality and Social Psychology, 91*(5), 904–917.

Gable, S. L., Reis, H. T., Impett, E. A., & Asher, E. R. (2018). What do you do when things go right? The intrapersonal and interpersonal benefits of sharing positive events. In *Relationships, well-being and behaviour* (pp. 144–182). Routledge.

Gaston-Breton, C., Sørensen, E. B., & Thomsen, T. U. (2020). "I want to break free!" How experiences of freedom foster consumer happiness. *Journal of Business Research, 121*, 22–32.

Gilovich, T., & Gallo, I. (2020). Consumers' pursuit of material and experiential purchases: A review. *Consumer Psychology Review, 3*(1), 20–33.

Gilovich, T., Kumar, A., & Jampol, L. (2015). A wonderful life: Experiential consumption and the pursuit of happiness. *Journal of Consumer Psychology, 25*(1), 152–165.

Goodman, J. K., Malkoc, S. A., & Stephenson, B. L. (2016). Celebrate or commemorate? A material purchase advantage when honoring special life events. *Journal of the Association for Consumer Research, 1*(4), 497–508.

Havitz, M. E., & Mannell, R. C. (2005). Enduring involvement, situational involvement, and flow in leisure and non-leisure activities. *Journal of Leisure Research, 37*(2), 152–177.

Hobfoll, S. E. (1998). *Stress, culture, and community: The psychology and physiology of stress*. Plenum Press.

Hovasapian, A., & Levine, L. J. (2018). Keeping the magic alive: Social sharing of positive life experiences sustains happiness. *Cognition and Emotion, 32*(8), 1559–1570.

Howell, R. T., & Hill, G. (2009). The mediators of experiential purchases: Determining the impact of psychological needs satisfaction and social comparison. *The Journal of Positive Psychology, 4*(6), 511–522.

Hsee, C. K., & Hastie, R. (2006). Decision and experience: Why don't we choose what makes us happy? *Trends in Cognitive Sciences, 10*(1), 31–37.

Hsee, C. K., & Zhang, J. (2004). Distinction bias: Misprediction and mischoice due to joint evaluation. *Journal of Personality and Social Psychology, 86*(5), 680–695.

Iwasaki, Y. (2007). Leisure and quality of life in an international and multicultural context: What are major pathways linking leisure to quality of life? *Social Indicators Research, 82*, 233–264.

Iwasaki, Y., & Mannell, R. C. (2000). Hierarchical dimensions of leisure stress coping. *Leisure Sciences, 22*(3), 163–181.

Jackson, S., & Csikszentmihalyi, M. (1999). *Flow in sports: The keys to optimal experiences and performances*. Human Kinetics.

Jose, P. E., Lim, B. T., & Bryant, F. B. (2012). Does savoring increase happiness? A daily diary study. *The Journal of Positive Psychology, 7*(3), 176–187.

Kahneman, D. (1999). Objective happiness. In D. Kahneman, E. Diener, & N. Schwarz (Eds.), *Well-being The foundations of hedonic psychology* (pp. 3–25). Russell Sage Foundation.
Kim, J., & Fesenmaier, D. R. (2017). Sharing tourism experiences: The post trip experience. *Journal of Travel Research, 56*(1), 28–40.
Kitayama, S., Markus, H. R., & Kurokawa, M. (2000). Culture, emotion, and well-being: Good feelings in Japan and the United States. *Cognition & Emotion, 14*(1), 93–124.
Kumar, A., & Gilovich, T. (2015). Some "thing" to talk about? Differential story utility from experiential and material purchases. *Personality and Social Psychology Bulletin, 41*(10), 1320–1331.
Kumar, A., & Gilovich, T. (2016). To do or to have, now or later? The preferred consumption profiles of material and experiential purchases. *Journal of Consumer Psychology, 26*(2), 169–178.
Kumar, A., Killingsworth, M. A., & Gilovich, T. (2014). Waiting for merlot: Anticipatory consumption of experiential and material purchases. *Psychological Science, 25*(10), 1924–1931.
Kurtz, J. L., & Lyubomirsky, S. (2013). Happiness promotion: Using mindful photography to increase positive emotion and appreciation. In J. J. Froh & A. C. Parks (Eds.), *Activities for teaching positive psychology: A guide for instructors* (pp. 133–136). American Psychological Association.
Kurtz, J. L., Wilson, T. D., & Gilbert, D. T. (2007). Quantity versus uncertainty: When winning one prize is better than winning two. *Journal of Experimental Social Psychology, 43*(6), 979–985.
Kuykendall, L., Tay, L., & Ng, V. (2015). Leisure engagement and subjective wellbeing: A meta-analysis. *Psychological Bulletin, 141*(2), 364–403.
Lambert, N. M., Gwinn, A. M., Baumeister, R. F., Strachman, A., Washburn, I. J., Gable, S. L., & Fincham, F. D. (2013). A boost of positive affect: The perks of sharing positive experiences. *Journal of Social and Personal Relationships, 30*(1), 24–43.
Langston, C. A. (1994). Capitalizing on and coping with daily-life events: Expressive responses to positive events. *Journal of Personality and Social Psychology, 67*(6), 1112–1125.
Lee, A. Y., Aaker, J. L., & Gardner, W. L. (2000). The pleasures and pains of distinct self-construals: The role of interdependence in regulatory focus. *Journal of Personality and Social Psychology, 78*(6), 1122–1134.
Lee, S., Koffer, R. E., Sprague, B. N., Charles, S. T., Ram, N., & Almeida, D. M. (2018). Activity diversity and its associations with psychological well-being across adulthood. *The Journals of Gerontology: Series B, 73*(6), 985–995.
Lee, D. J., Yu, G. B., & Sirgy, M. J. (2024). The dual effects of passion on leisure wellbeing: Toward a theory of engagement in diverse leisure activities. *Applied Research in Quality of Life, 19*(1), 155–177.
Livingstone, K. M., & Srivastava, S. (2012). Up-regulating positive emotions in everyday life: Strategies, individual differences, and associations with positive emotion and well-being. *Journal of Research in Personality, 46*(5), 504–516.
Loewenstein, G. F. (1987). Anticipation and the valuation of delayed consumption. *The Economic Journal, 97*(387), 666–684.
Loewenstein, G. F., & Prelec, D. (1993). Preferences for sequences of outcomes. *Psychological Review, 100*(1), 91–108.
Lyubomirsky, S., Sheldon, K. M., & Schkade, D. (2005). Pursuing happiness: The architecture of sustainable change. *Review of General Psychology, 9*(2), 111–131.
Lyubomirsky, S., Sousa, L., & Dickerhoof, R. (2006). The costs and benefits of writing, talking, and thinking about life's triumphs and defeats. *Journal of Personality and Social Psychology, 90*(4), 692–708.
MacLeod, A. K., & Conway, C. (2005). Well-being and the anticipation of future positive experiences: The role of income, social networks, and planning ability. *Cognition & Emotion, 19*(3), 357–374.
Maslow, A. H. (1954). *Motivation and personality*. Harper and Row.
McIntyre, N., & Roggenbuck, J. W. (1998). Nature/person transactions during an outdoor adventure experience: A multi-phasic analysis. *Journal of Leisure Research, 30*(4), 401–422.

Mogilner, C., Rudnick, T., & Iyengar, S. S. (2008). The mere categorization effect: How the presence of categories increases choosers' perceptions of assortment variety and outcome satisfaction. *Journal of Consumer Research, 35*(2), 202–215.
Mogilner, C., Kamvar, S. D., & Aaker, J. (2011). The shifting meaning of happiness. *Social Psychological and Personality Science, 2*(4), 395–402.
Mogilner, C., Aaker, J., & Kamvar, S. D. (2012). How happiness affects choice. *Journal of Consumer Research, 39*(2), 429–443.
Mojza, E. J., Lorenz, C., Sonnentag, S., & Binnewies, C. (2010). Daily recovery experiences: The role of volunteer work during leisure time. *Journal of Occupational Health Psychology, 15*(1), 60–74.
Nawijn, J. (2011). Determinants of daily happiness on vacation. *Journal of Travel research, 50*(5), 559–566.
Nelis, D., Kotsou, I., Quoidbach, J., Hansenne, M., Weytens, F., Dupuis, P., & Mikolajczak, M. (2011). Increasing emotional competence improves psychological and physical well-being, social relationships, and employability. *Emotion, 11*(2), 354–366.
Nelson, L. D., Meyvis, T., & Galak, J. (2009). Enhancing the television-viewing experience through commercial interruptions. *Journal of Consumer Research, 36*(2), 160–172.
Newman, D. B., Tay, L., & Diener, E. (2014). Leisure and subjective well-being: A model of psychological mechanisms as mediating factors. *Journal of Happiness Studies, 15*(3), 555–578.
Nicolao, L., Irwin, J. R., & Goodman, J. K. (2009). Happiness for sale: Do experiential purchases make consumers happier than material purchases? *Journal of Consumer Research, 36*(2), 188–198.
Peterson, C., Park, N., & Seligman, M. E. (2005). Orientations to happiness and life satisfaction: The full life versus the empty life. *Journal of Happiness Studies, 6*(1), 25–41.
Pine, B. J., & Gilmore, J. H. (2011). *The experience economy*. Harvard Business Press.
Quoidbach, J., Wood, A. M., & Hansenne, M. (2009). Back to the future: The effect of daily practice of mental time travel into the future on happiness and anxiety. *The Journal of Positive Psychology, 4*(5), 349–355.
Quoidbach, J., Berry, E. V., Hansenne, M., & Mikolajczak, M. (2010). Positive emotion regulation and well-being: Comparing the impact of eight savoring and dampening strategies. *Personality and Individual Differences, 49*(5), 368–373.
Quoidbach, J., Mikolajczak, M., & Gross, J. J. (2015). Positive interventions: An emotion regulation perspective. *Psychological Bulletin, 141*(3), 655–693.
Raghunathan, R., & Corfman, K. (2006). Is happiness shared doubled and sadness shared halved? Social influence on enjoyment of hedonic experiences. *Journal of Marketing Research, 43*(3), 386–394.
Redden, J. P. (2008). Reducing satiation: The role of categorization level. *Journal of Consumer Research, 34*(5), 624–634.
Rosenzweig, E., & Gilovich, T. (2012). Buyer's remorse or missed opportunity? Differential regrets for material and experiential purchases. *Journal of Personality and Social Psychology, 102*(2), 215–223.
Ross, W. T., & Simonson, I. (1991). Evaluations of pairs of experiences: A preference for happy endings. *Journal of Behavioral Decision Making, 4*(4), 273–282.
Ryan, R. M., & Deci, E. L. (2001). On happiness and human potentials: A review of research on hedonic and eudaimonic well-being. *Annual Review of Psychology, 52*(1), 141–166.
Ryan, R. M., Huta, V., & Deci, E. L. (2008). Living well: A self-determination theory perspective on eudaimonia. *Journal of Happiness Studies, 9*(1), 139–170.
Sääksjärvi, M., Hellén, K., & Desmet, P. (2016). The effects of the experience recommendation on short-and long-term happiness. *Marketing Letters, 27*(4), 675–686.
Scheibe, S., English, T., Tsai, J. L., & Carstensen, L. L. (2013). Striving to feel good: Ideal affect, actual affect, and their correspondence across adulthood. *Psychology and Aging, 28*(1), 160–171.

Schmitt, B., & Zarantonello, L. (2013). Consumer experience and experiential marketing: A critical review. In N. K. Malhotra (Ed.), *Review of marketing research* (Vol. 10, pp. 25–61). Emerald Group Publishing Limited.

Sharma, T. G., Hamari, J., Kesharwani, A., & Tak, P. (2022). Understanding continuance intention to play online games: Roles of self-expressiveness, self-congruity, self-efficacy, and perceived risk. *Behaviour & Information Technology, 41*(2), 348–364.

Sirgy, M. J. (2021). *The psychology of quality of life: Wellbeing and positive mental health* (3rd ed.). Springer Nature Switzerland.

Sirgy, M. J. (2022). *The balanced life: Using strategies from behavioral science to enhance wellbeing*. Cambridge University Press.

Sirgy, M. J., & Lee, D. J. (2018). The psychology of life balance. In E. Diener, S. Oishi, & L. Tay (Eds.), *Handbook of well-being*. DEF Publishers.

Smith, J. L., & Bryant, F. B. (2017). Savoring and well-being: Mapping the cognitive-emotional terrain of the happy mind. In *The happy mind: Cognitive contributions to well-being* (pp. 139–156). Springer.

Smith, J. L., & Hollinger-Smith, L. (2015). Savoring, resilience, and psychological well-being in older adults. *Aging & Mental Health, 19*(3), 192–200.

Sonnentag, S., & Fritz, C. (2007). The Recovery Experience Questionnaire: Development and validation of a measure for assessing recuperation and unwinding from work. *Journal of Occupational Health Psychology, 12*(3), 204–221.

Sonnentag, S., & Natter, E. (2004). Flight attendants' daily recovery from work: Is there no place like home? *International Journal of Stress Management, 11*(4), 366–391.

Stone, A. A., Kennedy-Moore, E., & Neale, J. M. (1995). Association between daily coping and end-of-day mood. *Health Psychology, 14*(4), 341–349.

Suh, E. M. (2002). Culture, identity consistency, and subjective well-being. *Journal of Personality and Social Psychology, 83*(6), 1378–1391.

Swann, C. (2016). Flow in sport. In L. Harmat, F. O. Andersen, F. Ullen, J. Wright, & G. Sadlo (Eds.), *Flow experience: Empirical research and applications* (pp. 51–64). Springer International Publishing.

Thaler, R. (1985). Mental accounting and consumer choice. *Marketing Science, 4*(3), 199–214.

Thomas, R., & Millar, M. (2013). The effects of material and experiential discretionary purchases on consumer happiness: Moderators and mediators. *The Journal of Psychology, 147*(4), 345–356.

Thorbjørnsen, H., Pedersen, P. E., & Nysveen, H. (2007). "This is who I am": Identity expressiveness and the theory of planned behavior. *Psychology & Marketing, 24*(9), 763–785.

Tugade, M. M., & Fredrickson, B. L. (2007). Regulation of positive emotions: Emotion regulation strategies that promote resilience. *Journal of Happiness Studies, 8*(3), 311–333.

Uchida, Y., Norasakkunkit, V., & Kitayama, S. (2004). Cultural constructions of happiness: Theory and empirical evidence. *Journal of Happiness Studies, 5*(3), 223–239.

Valkenburg, P. M., Peter, J., & Schouten, A. P. (2006). Friend networking sites and their relationship to adolescents' well-being and social self-esteem. *CyberPsychology & Behavior, 9*(5), 584–590.

Van Boven, L. (2005). Experientialism, materialism, and the pursuit of happiness. *Review of General Psychology, 9*(2), 132–142.

Van Boven, L., & Ashworth, L. (2007). Looking forward, looking back: Anticipation is more evocative than retrospection. *Journal of Experimental Psychology: General, 136*(2), 289–300.

Van Boven, L., & Gilovich, T. (2003). To do or to have? That is the question. *Journal of Personality and Social Psychology, 85*(6), 1193–1202.

Verduyn, P., Van Mechelen, I., & Tuerlinckx, F. (2011). The relation between event processing and the duration of emotional experience. *Emotion, 11*(1), 20–28.

Waterman, A. S. (1990). Personal expressiveness: Philosophical and psychological foundations. *The Journal of Mind and Behavior, 11*(1), 47–73.

Waterman, A. S., Schwartz, S. J., & Conti, R. (2008). The implications of two conceptions of happiness (hedonic enjoyment and eudaimonia) for the understanding of intrinsic motivation. *Journal of Happiness Studies, 9*(1), 41–79.

Wei, S., & Milman, A. (2002). The impact of participation in activities while on vacation on seniors' psychological wellbeing: A path model application. *Journal of Hospitality & Tourism Research, 26*(2), 175–185.

Weidman, A. C., & Dunn, E. W. (2016). The unsung benefits of material things: Material purchases provide more frequent momentary happiness than experiential purchases. *Social Psychological and Personality Science, 7*(4), 390–399.

Weingarten, E., & Goodman, J. K. (2021). Re-examining the experiential advantage in consumption: A meta-analysis and review. *Journal of Consumer Research, 47*(6), 855–877.

Wells, A. J. (1988). Self-esteem and optimal experience. In M. Csikszentmihalyi & I. Csikszentmihalyi (Eds.), *Optimal experience: Psychological studies of flow in consciousness* (pp. 327–341). Cambridge University Press.

Wood, J. V., Heimpel, S. A., & Michela, J. L. (2003). Savoring versus dampening: Self-esteem differences in regulating positive affect. *Journal of Personality and Social Psychology, 85*(3), 566–580.

Index

D.-J. Lee, M. J. Sirgy, *Happiness in the Marketplace*, Social Indicators Research Series 64, https://doi.org/10.1007/978-3-032-04443-3

Q

R

S

T

GPSR Compliance

The European Union's (EU) General Product Safety Regulation (GPSR) is a set of rules that requires consumer products to be safe and our obligations to ensure this.

If you have any concerns about our products, you can contact us on ProductSafety@springernature.com

In case Publisher is established outside the EU, the EU authorized representative is:

Springer Nature Customer Service Center GmbH
Europaplatz 3
69115 Heidelberg, Germany

Batch number: 09118687

Printed by Printforce, the Netherlands